T0395059

# Like a Child Would Do

# Like a Child Would Do

## An Interdisciplinary Approach to Childlikeness in Past and Current Societies

Editors

Mathieu ALEMANY OLIVER, PhD

Russell W. BELK, PhD

Universitas Press
Montreal

# Universitas Press
Montreal

www.universitaspress.com

Published in May 2023

Library and Archives Canada Cataloguing in Publication

Title: Like a child would do : an interdisciplinary approach to childlikeness in past and current
  societies / editors, Mathieu Alemany Oliver, PhD, Russell W. Belk, PhD.
Names: Alemany Oliver, Mathieu, editor. | Belk, Russell W., editor.
Description: Published in paperback in 2021. | Includes bibliographical references and index.
Identifiers: Canadiana 20230219543 | ISBN 9781988963624 (hardcover)
Subjects: LCSH: Children in popular culture. | LCSH: Childishness—Social aspects. | LCSH: Consumer
  behavior.
Classification: LCC HQ767.9 .L57 2023 | DDC 305.23—dc23

# CONTENTS

# Introductory Chapter
## Childlikeness in Adults
### Mathieu Alemany Oliver and Russell W. Belk

All it takes is imagination and an anthropomorphic suspension of disbelief. Recently, our conversations with toys have been depicted in films about toys and their owners. Disney's film franchise *Toy Story* (episodes 1 to 4) uses the vantage point of enlivened toys to depict the intimate role of fantasy play with toys in the development of "Andy" from ages 6 to 17. The films are nostalgic depictions of childhood, and it was reported that *Toy Story 3* brought more than a third of adult viewers to tears (Bierly, 2010). The non-human characters at the heart of the story are either branded toys from a supposedly simpler past, like Mr. Potato Head and Slinky Dog, or invented toy characters like Woody the cowboy and Buzz Lightyear the astronaut (Kemper, 2015). Disney merchandised both characters and used them as theme park attractions (Lanier, Fowler, & Rader, 2014). The toy characters in the film serve as a critique of the commodification that has made them "mere toys" among a countless array of identical branded objects that line the shelves of "Al's Toy Barn." The big-box toy store is run by an unscrupulous owner who sees toys only as sources of profit. However, the films champion an alternative to the mere toy/commodity status: The toys are to be lovingly played with in an interactive play mode. The play mode in which Andy verbally interacts with his toys has been called imaginative anthropomorphism (Lanier, Rader, & Fowler, 2013), ventriloquism (Brown, 1998), or dialogical play (Henricks, 2018). It involves the deepest level of engagement with these anthropomorphized characters and is seen as a way to work through childhood dilemmas via fantasy role play. These objects not only become extensions of the self (Belk, 1988) but are also often enlivened by imagination.

As Stewart (1984) reminds us, dolls and dollhouses were originally the playthings of affluent adult women. In the mid-19th century, dolls started to be modeled on pre-adolescent children whose sexuality was erased (Hall, 1897). This all changed in 1959 and 1961 with Mattel's popular Barbie and Ken, which were sexualized young adult dolls. They did not make an appearance in *Toy Story 1* when Andy was young, but Barbies play a part in the subsequent three sequels as Andy and his sister Molly grow up. The biggest lesson of the *Toy Story* series is that toys must be put aside for the child to become an adult. As Rilke (1913-1914/2018) explains of such intimate toys:

> But [by the end of childhood] we soon realized we could not
> make it into a thing or a person, and in such moments it became
> a stranger to us, and we could no longer recognize all the
> confidences we had heaped over it and into it.

We will see, however, that the assessment that toy play ends with childhood is incorrect.

The "adult" of another series of enlivened toy films, *The Lego Movie* franchise, is President (or sometimes "Lord") Business—a real estate tycoon boss and builder. These films criticize the conformity of the capitalist system (Goggin, 2017; Hunter, 2018). The adventures in the first film, which also brings in Warner Brothers properties like Batman and Wonder Woman, is described in one review as offering a "bountifully inventive and digressive story that mimics a child's playtime adventure inspired by whatever may have tumbled out of the toy bin" (Filipi, 2014, p. 5). Like *Toy Story*, *The Lego Movie* relies on nostalgic themes that appeal to adults, even as it offers a critique of the "consumer-capitalist myth" of which it, Warner Brothers, and Lego are an integral part (Varul, 2018). Filipi (2014) calls it a two-hour commercial for Lego and Warner Brothers toys. The Lego Group subsequently brought out Lego packages to reproduce the buildings and objects shown in the films. The films were shot in pseudo-stop-motion fashion to imitate the amateur Lego films that can be found on YouTube. As the adult voices of the characters in these films reveal, the amateur filmmakers to whom homage is being paid are adults. They are part of an avid group of Lego followers who proudly call themselves AFoL or Adult Fans of Lego (Garlen, 2014; Muñiz, Antorini, & Schau, 2013).

Together, these two toy film series and their adult fans provide a glimpse of the central thesis that underlies this chapter's conceptual introduction to childlikeness. They offer a demonstration that contemporary consumption is driven in large part by adult play. This is not merely the compartmentalized playful consumption of music, art, television, and holidays that Holbrook and Hirschman (1982) insightfully highlighted. Nor is it the playful contemporary imaginative hedonism that Campbell (1987) posited as underlying the consumer revolution of late 18th and early 19th-century England. Instead, it is a pervasive ethos that underlies and motivates most discretionary consumption in contemporary affluent societies. In a nutshell, adult play is why conventional approaches associating play with childhood are bound to fail. Facts and economic logic will fail to satisfy consumers who are expecting to be entertained and engaged in play.

The thesis that contemporary consumers are engaged in play is beautifully illustrated by the series of Apple computer advertisements best remembered as "I'm a Mac" and "I'm a PC" (Livingstone, 2011). The characters, their dress, and their attitudes were designed to represent Apple (Mac) as playful, easy-going, creative, confident, and cool, while the PC was shown as "feelingless, formal, frustrated, and fun-deprived" (Livingstone, 2011, p. 211). In the North American version of the ads, Justin Long plays the Mac and John Hodgman plays the PC (different actors were used in the British and Japanese versions). Hodgman has close-cropped hair and glasses and appears in business suits of brown, green, or tan, while Long wears jeans and an untucked shirt or unzipped hoodie with blues, blacks, and grays as his wardrobe colors. The ads implicitly ask, "Which one are you?" For the contemporary technology consumer, the answer is self-evident: The image of the playful Mac closely represents their ideal. Added to the implicit image advantage of the Apple user, the humorous dialogue makes it clear the Mac is easier to use, less prone to problems, and altogether more fun.

### Smartphones are Toys

Cain (2019) notes that while our smartphones are tools that can be empowering, save time, and make us more capable, they are used predominately as playthings. Their multipurpose nature is part of what allows us to mistakenly characterize them as work tools. But:

> We don't play with tape measures, envelopes, maps, dictionaries, or calculators. We don't go to staple something and wind up watching a movie review. We don't play with our keys or debit cards when we're waiting for a bus—but we do play with our telephones, because they are now 90% toy. (paras. 19-20)

In fact, Cain (2019) calls the smartphone "the most compelling toy ever created." The pseudonymous blog describes how, even when pulling their phone out for business use like scheduling a meeting or looking up a fact, the writer can't help tapping on Instagram or a sports feed or whatever other icon catches their attention. Part of this results from the addictive nature of the device and its affordances. Part is driven by the fear of missing out (FOMO). And a large part is due to adults rediscovering the fun of play.

Similarly, one industry executive observes that "[v]irtual assistants allow people to play again" (Knudson, 2018, p. 12). Not only are our phones and digital assistants and their affordance a focus of adult play, but so are our laptops, tablets, smartwatches, smart speakers, action cameras, televisions, video game consoles, sports equipment, clothing, makeup, furniture, vehicles, boats, and other accoutrements of contemporary life that go with being an affluent individual in a consumer society. It is true not only that childhood play with miniature "play" versions of these things was a rehearsal for "adult" life but also that engaging with adult versions of these things is still a mode of play. Upscale real estate advertising and television "home improvement" channels offer a form of imaginative play in the form of "property porn" (Boland, 2019; Garber, 2000; Lord, 2020; Verdier, 2016). Instagram, Twitter, Facebook, WhatsApp, and WeChat offer food images and words that constitute "food porn" (Kozinets, Patterson, & Ashman, 2017; Romm, 2015). Similar feeds for photos and discussion by adult collectors of childhood objects offer a form of "toy porn" (Bryant, Bielby, & Harrington, 2014; Heljakka & Harviainen, 2019), with the pornographic tag indicating the addictive and exciting character of these depictions. The addict, photographer, and collector alibis involve what Stebbins (1980) calls serious leisure: a passionate pursuit that turns a ludic interest in something into a more socially acceptable work-like activity. Another legitimizing alibi is the investor motif that argues, "Someday these things will be worth a fortune" (Belk, 2001; Hillis & Petit, 2006; Koppelman & Franks, 2008). Nevertheless, Scott Eberle, vice president for play studies at the Strong National Museum of Play in New York State, asks:

> Do we stop playing with toys? Or is it that we change the toys we play with?. . . How about rocket engines, circuit boards, and radiotelescopes? Our attitude toward play changes toward the instrumental, and our toys get more specialized and complex . . . The play in collecting doesn't come from the object sitting on the shelf, but in the pursuit of it, the bargaining for it, the mastery of the subject, and the suspense before a completion that never quite happens. (Watkins, 2016, paras. 4, 13)

In addition to the ubiquitous adult play with "adult" objects and the legitimization of collector or serious leisure guises, there is also a segment of adults, both male and female, who need no alibi and unabashedly love to pursue, purchase, and play with action figures, dolls, and other "children's toys" (Dahlen, 2013; Loftus, 2017; Jailer, 1975; Silverstein, 2006). More than 65 percent of American adults admit to playing games. Sixty percent of these game-playing adults play them on their smartphones and 50 percent on computers or game consoles; 46 percent of them are women (Russ, 2010). Fifty percent of British adults still have a stuffed bear from childhood. And a Travelodge survey suggests that one in four business travelers carries a stuffed animal with them on their travels (Travelodge UK, 2010). Moreover, 10 percent of adult men and 15 percent of adult women still share their intimate secrets with a stuffed animal (McQueeney, 2012).

Along with the ubiquity of adult and child play involving toys, there has often been an accompanying desire to speak to these toys. Children have long created imaginative dialogues with their playthings. This is part of what Kuznets (1994) calls the private world of childhood. Recent breakthroughs in artificial intelligence–supported voice recognition and speech synthesis have also allowed considerable advances to be made in the conversational ability of toys. AI capabilities potentially allow for a sense of conversation with these toys. Some applications even allow the toys to recognize emotions like sadness, boredom, happiness, and anger in the voices of the child users and to respond accordingly (Yacoub et al., 2003). The ideal is to create a responsive voice-interactive toy that is also fun and appealing to the child or, as one paper put it, "Barbie with Brains" (Ravishankar et al., 2020). With adults, the focus of voice-interactive devices need not be limited to objects that present themselves as toys: The bland and functional appearance of in-home digital devices using Alexa (Amazon), Siri (Apple), Google Nest, and Cortana (Microsoft) provides an alibi that these are digital helpers rather than playful or seductive toys. These personified feminine digital assistants are routinely personified and treated as friends (Purington et al., 2017). A recent survey of 1,000 people revealed that 26 percent of respondents admitted to having had a sexual fantasy about their digital assistant (Pesce, 2017). As the devices get better at reading our emotions and responding to them, the degree of intimacy we have with these devices is likely to increase (Bland, 2018).

### On the Concept of Childlikeness

Because play has been considered in relation to children for so long, we could not introduce this book without highlighting the degree to which adults can be playful too, especially when it comes to consumption. As Alemany Oliver (2015) notes, childlikeness is a critical engine of consumer society:

> If childlikeness is so critical in consumer society, it is because marketing is an illusion . . . it offers paradise on earth through possessions, but also gives consumers the possibility of constructing their own paradise through the manipulation of symbols and narratives. In this context, play, imagination, and magical thinking, which are traditionally envisioned as childlike elements, become the conditions of existence of marketing, but also the conditions of consumers' acceptance of their finite existence. (p. 287)

While play has long been envisioned as the possibility to better accept and re-enchant reality (Winnicott, 1971), marketing plays a role in re-enchanting reality through playfulness. But even though playfulness is at the heart of childlikeness, it is only one visible aspect of it, which indicates a socially constructed and permeable boundary between childhood and adulthood, as well as different norms and values for each of these two concepts. This boundary is scientifically supported by developmental psychology and biology, but in these same disciplines we also find evidence that humans today are in part childlike versions of their ancestors. We are a neotenous species. Moreover, even though childhood, adulthood, and childlikeness may be biological facts, culture provides the means for these concepts to be understood and made meaningful in our lives.

Grammatically, childlikeness means the state or quality of being childlike. It uses the adjective childlike, which signifies like a child would do. Childlikeness and childishness are also synonymous. While the two terms have taken on different shades of meaning in their everyday usage, with childishness having a more pejorative connotation, we purposively do not differentiate between the two terms in this book as the different connotations have to be separated from what a child would do. By using childlikeness and childishness interchangeably, we do not make them exist through converse relations. They exist as one, and they only reveal the multiplicity of what a child would do. Whether some elements of this multiplicity are perceived as pejorative or ameliorative belongs to another multiplicity—that of social judgment and control. In other words, it is not the one (childlikeness) or the other (childishness), but one (multiplicity) with another among others: what a child would do with another more geographically and timely bounded multiplicity (e.g., social judgments) among other multiplicities (e.g., social control, the logics of the market, etc.), which decides about the meaning and content of what a child would do, but not about the very idea that childhood and adulthood were never born to ignore each other.

Adult childlikeness is familiar to everyone, regardless of whether it is because we were once implored to "grow up!" when we were overly emotional or because we have observed adults engaging in playful activities that we normally think of as children's games. On the one hand, social norms prevent us from behaving like children; on the other hand, we appreciate the childlike spirit of the artist. In addition, brands invite us to consume and play in a childlike way, and pop psychology magazines encourage us to feed our inner child. What does all this tell us about childlikeness and our cultures? In another context, research has highlighted the many challenges facing adulthood and the need to redefine this period of life. For example, psychologist Jeffrey Arnett (2000) has proposed creating a new stage of life between adolescence and adulthood that he calls the "emerging adult." At the same time, a rising number of young adults say they do not want to become adults. But then, what can they become in societies that have told us that we, as biological adults, must become "good" adults by performing different rituals and adopting specific norms and values?

At the time of this writing, we are witnessing demonstrations by children and adolescents against the poor capacity of adults to deal with the problem of climate change. At the same time, presidents whose behavior has been repeatedly described as "childish" have been elected to lead great nations but have found themselves unable to manage crises when the game ended badly. Members of Parliament are regularly caught playing on their cell phones while debating bills. Such behavior can be denounced and shared, but as is often the case on social media and in the myriad data that floods us, we move on and forget. It is one more form of entertainment in a society fed by great expectations, as envisioned by Boorstin (1962). Like in a DeLillo novel, the adult consumer copes with the situation as long as the consumer society produces the opium that holds this same adult consumer in the market, where true and false have given rise to a buffer zone, an intermediate space in which the frustrations of some and the desires of others find a happy outcome—a market that wants to be playful, imaginative, and conducive to an individual or collective escape as if to forget the somewhat darker political, health, and social realities of this world. There is a website called *Pokémon Go Death Tracker* that lists adults who died or got injured from catching Pokémon characters in augmented reality. We learn from this website that the Pokémon Go game has triggered a shooting, heart attacks, fatal car accidents, and falls from cliffs. In the same vein, playing during work hours has led some companies to post notes to remind employees that they are not getting paid to chase fictional video game characters (Szczesny, 2016).

From the very first lines of his book, Barber (2007) warns us that consumer capitalism is driven by an infantilist ethos that undermines our democracies. For his part, Bernardini (2014) contrasts the infantilization of adults with the "standard conception of maturity" in a series of binaries that include seeking instantaneous pleasure vs. long-term happiness; dependence vs. independence; rights vs. obligations; narcissism vs. sociability; impermanence vs. stability; individuality vs. community; and insecurity vs. self-confidence. Infantilism among adults is not a recent development, however. Aldridge (1970) noted that his generation had been unable to reinvent an adult life that youth could happily enter, which helped explain the reluctance of young people to leave childhood and adolescence. Nearly 30 years later, Calcutt (1998) became concerned about the importance of childlikeness in pop culture, which celebrates a model of self that is vulnerable and childlike and focused largely on the present in a society becoming obsessed with long-term security. He writes:

> A new political order has emerged in which the victim is supreme, and adults are treated more like children. Meanwhile, many adults are more likely to think of themselves as victims, or to identify with the motif of the authentic, innocent child. The result is a convergence between on the one hand the spontaneous development of a cultural personality which is victimized and childlike, and on the other hand the remoulding of the individual's relationship to the state in in accordance with his supposed immaturity. (Calcutt, 1998, p. 233)

According to him, the counterculture movement of the 1950s and 1960s, as well as current pop culture, has allowed the creation of a language of victimization that forms part of the erosion of adulthood and the pervasiveness of childlikeness.

But childlikeness is not (only) a symbol of societal failure or a possible chapter in a dystopian novel. Many societies have considered childlikeness a source of creativity, daring, or adaptation. Just as it can take the form of blinders to make us forget the finiteness of existence by promising us the illusion of eternal youth, it can simultaneously keep us alive, help us resist the aging and stiffening of our thinking, and aid us in welcoming rather than resisting change. Steeped in William Blake's and William Wordsworth's romantic poetry, childlikeness is still associated with purity, perfection, or innocence. The idealized child is this being full of life who does not yet understand that they will one day wish to return to what they are living now: a carefree existence where everything ends well. While some speak of our societies as societies of risk (Beck, 1986; Giddens, 1991), there is a great temptation to idealize the world of the child still hermetically isolated from the risk generated by an uncertain future—and sometimes to withdraw into this hermetic world. In other places and at other times, childlikeness has also been idealized. For instance, in the China of the 16th and 17th centuries, writings of the Ming dynasty put forward a desire to rediscover the innocence of childhood by developing spontaneity, sincerity, and emotion (Weightman, 2006).

As we can see here, childlikeness is understood depending on what we are willing to understand about childhood and adulthood, but also according to what we wish to be or become. Childlikeness is like a door left open between the possibility of distorting reality—making it malleable, safe, and subject to our desires—and the imposition of a constraining and disenchanted reality that we cannot reject. Childlikeness can also be comprehended from the perspective of existentialist philosophy. We invest our desires, our fears, and our doubts in childlikeness: both a desire for freedom and a fear of having too much freedom, doubts about our models of society that dictate a conception of Man dominated by the modern adult figure, among other possible conceptions without ever knowing if these would be better. Childlikeness reflects human souls; the best as well as the worst. It also reflects a will to live intensely, to do more than live, as Maffesoli (2003) points out:

> The close union of death and life . . . takes on a concrete form in musical production, in its excessive forms, in film creation, where cruelty is omnipresent, without forgetting, of course, daily life, which is marked by the fascination of those who, in all fields— from the rock singer to the bloody mobster, via the princess who makes her name in the newspapers—will push the rationale of "living more" to the limit. (p. 95)

This desire to do more than just live, which we find in childlikeness and Maffesoli (2007) calls the eternal child, is perhaps what pushes Bauman's modern figure of the "pilgrim" to proliferate and become four postmodern or liquid figures: the tourist, the player, the stroller, and the vagabond (Bauman, 1996). These four figures describe a society always in search of motion, novelty, simulation, and opportunities—a kind of eternal youth in which one could always start from scratch and live several lives in one.

Finally, childlikeness allows us to capture other related conceptualizations such as those related to adulthood and childhood, as well as their positions in society, with all the underlying ideologies that these conceptualizations contain. There is something Deleuzian about childlikeness as it bears witness to a becoming-child of the adult, a becoming that liberates desire and nourishes itself with it. Speaking not of the becoming-child but the becoming-animal of Man, Deleuze and Guattari (2003) write:

> Becomings-animal are basically of another power, since their reality resides not in an animal one imitates or to which one corresponds, but in themselves, in that which suddenly sweeps

us up and makes us become—a proximity, an indiscernibility that
extracts a shared element from the animal far more effectively
than domestication, utilization, or imitation could. (p. 279)

The becoming-child follows the same logic as the becoming-animal: Its reality does
not inhere in the child that one would imitate or the child that one has been. It is a
proximity that extracts something irremediably human. In another context, where the
dominant figure of our society would not be that of a serious, responsible, and rational
adult, the becoming-child would also extract something irremediably and legitimately
adult. This becoming-child, like any Deleuzian becoming, introduces the subversive
multiplicity, creativity, and energy necessary to challenge the dominant construction
of the reflective, serious, and responsible adult. This dominant construction results
from disciplinary discursive processes that have been aggregated and repeated over
time, mostly attempting to reject childlikeness in the fringe areas of the construction—
those same areas capable of both consolidating the dominant status of the adult when
they are kept under control and destabilizing it when they get out of control.

## A Zero Mile Marker and Multiple Directions

The book starts by taking a step back and putting the concept down to better define it
and, above all, to understand it in its entirety. This book indicates a single zero-mile
marker but for multiple directions. It was conceived at the outset as an interdisciplinary
work with the idea that childlikeness would be better described by having a thousand
people take a thousand paths rather than a thousand people taking the same path. Some
of these paths will eventually converge; others will not. But they will all have a zero
point, a more or less temporary reference point from which it will be possible to start
again or to stop and discuss (e.g., the existence and the very position of this zero-
mile marker, or possible directions). Without a zero-mile marker for the concept of
childlikeness, it continues to be anything we want it to be, which means it does not
exist in a scientific sense.

Before presenting the several chapters or paths that the reader is about to
take, it is important to agree on the zero-mile marker by proposing a common definition
for these chapters. In this book, we define childlikeness as the tendency of an adult to
think, feel, and act like a child would do. Because thoughts, emotions, and actions are
the result of interactions between the natural and social worlds, childlikeness is both
an evolutionary consequence of being human and a time- and place-dependent cultural
consequence of our individual and collective efforts to give meaning and order to the
world.

Three objectives were set for this book. First, to envision. By revising
childlikeness and considering it as a concept in its own right, readers should come to
realize that what we consider as taken for granted can be understood in a new way.
Second, to explicate. By offering different perspectives from different disciplines,
readers should come to see some of the richness and complexity of the concept, as
well as aspects that are shared over time and space. Finally, to relate. The different
perspectives should inspire and help readers establish their own relationships between
childlikeness and the concepts with which they are used to working.

The first chapter of this book, "Humans as a Neotenous Species," begins with
a radically different approach than the other chapters by focusing on human evolution.
David Bjorklund explains how the adult human beings of today are in part the children
of the past. Not because every adult was once a child but because every human being
has retained some of the juvenile traits of their distant ancestors. In other words, from
a biological but also a psychological point of view, all adults have an innate childlike
part in them as a result of neoteny. And it is partly thanks to this childlike part that
we have been able to develop such great cognitive abilities and develop lasting social

relationships. As Bjorklund reminds us, humans are considered a neotenous species. Neoteny (literally "to stretch youth;" Kollmann, 1885) is a slower developmental process than that experienced by the same species' ancestors and causes the retention of juvenile traits in its descendants. In human beings, Bjorklund shows that these juvenile—and, therefore, childlike—traits include the baby schema, neural, cognitive, and behavioral plasticity; playfulness; and unrealistic optimism. Interestingly, play and the baby schema are two important tools that marketers use to interact with consumers. While the presence of play is obvious in marketing, Brown (2010, p. 219) also observes the baby schema and says that anthropomorphic brand characters "get younger, more cherubic, more cuddly, more childlike, more and more cute with the passing years." The pervasiveness of cuteness in popular and consumer culture is further evidence of people's sensitivity to the presence of juvenile physical traits.

The second chapter, "The Inner Child in Jungian Analytic Frameworks," deals with childlikeness from a Jungian psychoanalytic perspective. Juliet Rohde-Brown focuses on the inner child and shows how it continues to occupy an important place not only in people's lives but also in the collective unconscious. The concept of the inner child, which is very popular in pop psychology magazines, can even be found in the advertisements of major brands such as Mercedes, Evian, and McDonald's. It is important to note that the inner child can be understood as a set of fragments of our childhood that would continue to influence our behavior into adulthood (Missildine, 1963) or as an archetypal figure of the child—the Divine Child, who represents "the preconscious, childhood aspect of the collective psyche" (Jung 1959, p. 161). Situated between psychoanalytic theories and her personal experiences as a therapist, Rohde-Brown shows how the Jungian approach makes the inner child and its acceptance a sign of the person's maturity and not a more or less conscious desire to remain the child that one has been. On the contrary, the inner child allows adults to engage in a process of individuation. She also highlights how the symbolic child (i.e., the Divine Child archetype) is found in dreams, films, and literature and how it sometimes cohabits with the empirical child we once were.

Next comes "The Trickster Figure in Literature and Consumer Society Narratives: Potentialities and Liminality," a chapter based on another archetypal figure often associated with childlikeness: the Trickster. However, the two authors, Mathieu Alemany Oliver and Lorna Wilkinson, present this figure not from a psychoanalytical point of view but from a literary and cultural one. The figure of the Trickster can be found in many mythological and folkloric stories of all ages and cultures. It is also found in the theater, particularly on the Shakespearean stage, for example in the guise of Sir John Falstaff and Sir Toby Belch, Feste, Touchstone, *King Lear*'s Fool, Edmund, Richard III, Prospero, and *Measure for Measure*'s Duke. Finally, the figure of the Trickster is found in more contemporary narratives, including those produced within consumer society—by consumers themselves, brands, and institutions. Alemany Oliver and Wilkinson show that these different figures of the Trickster are united around the concept of potentiality. These Tricksters reflect a will for change, notably by resisting social norms and constructions, overthrowing the established order, and claiming a right to freedom. They are the product of previous Trickster characters but also of the questioning, anxieties, and worldviews of a generation and of the authors of the story themselves.

We made this point earlier and believe the previous chapters bear it out: Childlikeness is understood through what we want to understand about childhood and adulthood but also about what we want to be or become. Childlikeness, therefore, is given meaning in part because of how we view it in relation to a particular time and place. If Alemany Oliver and Wilkinson are interested both in Shakespeare's work and in contemporary consumer society, the place does not change: It is the West. With Frances Weightman and her chapter entitled "Childlike Minds and Childish Men: Dilemmas of Classical Chinese Fiction," we embark on a journey to 17th-century China and more precisely to classical Chinese fiction. Weightman highlights that the concept of childlikeness also comes up against two different conceptions of the child in Chinese traditional thought. Indeed, the child is both a symbol of purity and of incompleteness bringing little to society. While Chinese literature of the time idealized childlikeness (especially in the writings of Li Zhi, who seeks spontaneity and authenticity), the success of childlikeness among late Ming dynasty writers distorts and caricatures the primary conception of childlikeness. By focusing on male characters from Pu Songling's *Liaozhai*, Weightman shows how their childlike naïveté makes them unable to deal with the practical aspects of life, such as sex or finances.

"Because science," says Belk (1986, p. 24), "is a simplified abstraction to explain an action, and art is an embellished elaboration of an experience, we can often rely on art to provide the more complete and multidimensional multisensory perspective to help us understand rather than simply explain." In Edwige Comoy Fusaro's chapter on "Childlikeness and Art," she focuses on the experience of childlikeness in contemporary art. In particular, she shows how artists, from the second half of the 19th century onward, tried to understand and express the child's point of view while simultaneously seeking out a sense of freedom and purity. While the 20th-century art world already emphasized self-taught artists and childlike practices and aesthetics, the 1990s and street art really made childlikeness a core concept in the artistic process. It did this, according to Comoy Fusaro, by inviting artists to play with the rules and transgress the codes while searching for another form of authenticity, but also by involving the beholder-consumer-user of art in playfulness. Another interesting point to note in Comoy Fusaro's chapter is that street art in part brings childlikeness into public and ordinary spaces, while adult play has often remained in the private sphere.

By focusing on the child within consumer society, at work, in court, or in psychiatric institutions, the subsequent chapters show that childlikeness goes beyond innate characteristics found in the human being (neoteny) or a personal and/ or artistic approach to become integrated into institutional logics and mechanisms. Where myths highlight the existence and role of childlikeness within a culture, the next chapters underline the use of childlikeness and how its consequences in societies have extracted childlikeness from the inner world of individuals, as well as from the collective unconscious, to make it an instrument of emancipation, productivity, and control. Thus, childlikeness is not only thought of individually or collectively through art or psychology to offer new perspectives to the being but used as the wheel of an institutional gear that responds to the population's individual needs (e.g., to secure, entertain, or emancipate) or the needs of the institutions themselves (e.g., the need to maintain order and to be profitable to continue existing as legitimate and dominant institutions).

In the sixth chapter, "Consumer Childlikeness," Mathieu Alemany Oliver and Russell W. Belk elaborate on consumer childlikeness based on the concept of mentality as developed by the Annales school in history. They suggest that consumer childlikeness is a particular (although not fixed) mentality reflected through individual assumptions about nature, self, and society. In particular, childlikeness is reflected in consumer society through the idealization of nature as opposed to civilization, the association of the authentic self with the newborn and what we have already been, and the development of polymorphously perverse relationships. While this hedonistic mentality influences consumer and marketing practices, it is important to stress that marketing partly provides the conditions of its (profitable) existence as well.

Childlikeness is very present in the consumer culture of adults. If brands for adults play on certain aspects of childlikeness to appeal to some consumers, the consumer trend toward regressive consumption is best represented by brands that have traditionally targeted children but are now focusing on adult consumer segments. This is the case, for example, with toy brands, as Katriina Heljakka shows us in "From Playborers and Kidults to Toy Players: Adults who Play for Leisure, Work and

Pleasure." Her chapter examines playfulness and adult toy players. She explains that the toy industry these days is seriously interested in adult consumers but still reduces them, wrongly, to a homogeneous group of kidults when there are, in fact, several types of adult toy players. She also describes how childlikeness, through mercantilist processes of toyification and gamification, as well as an overlap of production and playful consumption, has penetrated the world of work and given rise to playborers (i.e., player-laborers).

In a perfect world, this alliance of play and work would seem to be a gift to humanity. Whereas work can constrain, playbor liberates. But if concepts such as gamification at work or playbor continue to develop, it is not out of pure philanthropy. The inclusion of childlikeness at work through performative and joyful narratives of an authentic self does not come without control, coercion, or restrictions. As Fleming and Sturdy (2010) write, "the combination of 'fun,' 'play' and displays of authenticity . . . is not freedom from control, as numerous management commentators and advocates claim, but managerially prescribed freedom around control." The inclusion of childlikeness in the economic system is made legitimate and enviable only because it does not condemn but supports an economic model by making consumers even more emotional and workers even more productive. The inclusion of childlikeness in the economic system is, in a way, the encounter between the natural aspiration of adults to play, on the one hand, and nudge theory, on the other hand, which, like an adult toward a child, knows that it is often better to suggest indirectly than to oblige. In this context, it is difficult to end the book without mentioning possible links between childlikeness and its use by disciplinary institutions (Foucault, 1975). Although Simon Gottschalk does not link his piece to this Foucaldian concept, Yoad Eliaz directly refers to it, and their work in the last two chapters shows how childlikeness can contribute to the practice of a disciplinary power that subordinates Man to the injunctions, expectations, and needs of society, while we have seen in the previous chapters that childlikeness helps adults pull back from society's expectations.

In the chapter entitled "Click to Disable: Infantilization in Terminal Interactions and/at Work," Simon Gottschalk discusses the infantilizing process that results from our interactions with computer terminals. In his view, interactions between people are highly mediated by new computer technologies (laptops, PCs, tablets, smartphones, GPS devices, etc.) that end up infantilizing the users of these terminals. Apart from the purposively childlike interfaces of software and applications, it is our relationship and subordination to the terminal and the modalities of its use that ultimately make us dependent, cognitively inhibited, and under permanent surveillance, despite feeling an illusory omnipotence. Gottschalk describes it as "the most sophisticated system of social control ever invented," not least because it asks us to stop thinking.

We end this book with "Childishness as Social Control," in which Yoad Eliaz argues that the concept of childlikeness is a tool for control that disciplines the population. Through an analysis of the use of the terms childlike and childish in legal proceedings and as used to describe certain elderly or mentally disabled people, Eliaz suggests that the labeling of a person as childlike or childish plays a role in shaping the person who, as a result, comes to see themself becoming a constructed, restricted, and disciplined object kept under control. As in the previous chapter, we find here the face of a child to whom we can say and do anything—a child who is malleable at will, no longer an actor of the re-enchantment of the world but a potential victim of its disenchantment.

We now ask the readers to enter this in-between world of childlikeness and form their own understanding of the concept. We would like to thank all the formidable authors of this book for their contributions and their patience. We also thank the reviewers for the constructive suggestions they made to the authors and especially our publisher, Universitas Press—Cristina, for the degree of freedom they gave us.

## References

Aldridge, J. W. (1970). *In the country of the young*. HarperCollins.

Alemany Oliver, M. (2015). *A realist(ic) interpretivist approach to childlikeness in consumer research: Neoteny, play, reality, and the reterritorializing adulthood* [Doctoral dissertation, Aix-Marseille Université, IAE Aix]. AMU Campus Library.

Arnett, J. J. (2000). Emerging adulthood. *American Psychologist, 55*(May), 469-480.

Barber, B. R. (2007). *Consumed: How markets corrupt children, infantilize adults, and swallow citizens whole*. Norton.

Bauman, Z. (1996). From pilgrim to tourist—Or a short history of identity. In S. Hall & P. du Gay (Eds.), *Questions of Cultural Identity* (pp.18-36). Sage.

Beck, U. (1986/1992). *Risk society: Towards a new modernity*. Sage.

Belk, R. W. (1986). Art versus science as ways of generating knowledge about materialism. In D. Brinberg & R. J. Lutz (Eds), *Perspectives on methodology in consumer research* (pp. 3-36). Springer.

Belk, R. W. (1988). Possessions and the extended self. *Journal of Consumer Research, 15*(2), 139-168.

Belk, R. W. (2000). May the farce be with you: On Las Vegas and consumer infantilization. *Consumption, Markets, & Culture, 4*(2), 101-123.

Belk, R. W. (2001). *Collecting in a consumer society*. Routledge.

Belk, R. W., Weijo, H., & Kozinets, R. V. (2021). Enchantment and perpetual desire: Theorizing disenchanted enchantment and technology adoption. *Marketing Theory, 21*(1), 25-52.

Bernardini, J. (2014). The Infantilization of the postmodern adult and the figure of the kidult. *Postmodern Openings, 5*(2), 29-55.

Bierly, M. (2010, June 21). 'Toy Story 3' poll: Did you cry? *Entertainment Weekly*. https://ew.com/article/2010/06/21/toy-story-3-poll-did-you-cry/

Bland, B. (2018, January 5). *Alexa, hug me: Exploring human-machine emotional relations*. Medium.https://medium.com/@ben.bland/alexa-hug-me-exploring-human-machine-emotional-relations-1f0f6e04e1db.

Boland, J. (2019, February 23). John Boland on TV: Property-porn Addicts Get a Double Fix on RTÉ. *Irish Independent*. https://www.independent.ie/entertainment/television/tv-reviews/john-boland-on-tv-property-porn-addicts-get-a-double-fix-on-rte-37840692.html

Boorstin, D. J. (1962/1992). *The image: A guide to pseudo-events in America*. Vintage.

Brown, B. (1998). How to do things with things (A Toy Story). *Critical Inquiry, 24*(Summer), 935-964.

Brown, S. (2010). Where the wild brands are: Some thoughts on anthropomorphic marketing. *The Marketing Review, 10*(August), 209-224.

Bryant, K., Bielby, D., & Harrington, C. L. (2014). Populating the universe: Toy collecting and adult lives. In L. Duits, K. Zwan, & S. Rijnders (Eds.), *The Ashgate research companion to fan cultures* (pp.23-34). Ashgate.

Cain, D. (2019, May 22). *Smartphones Are Toys First, Tools Second*. Raptitude.com. raptitude.com/2019/05/smartphones-are-toys-first-tools-second/

Calcutt, A. (1998). *Arrested development: Pop culture and the erosion of adulthood*. Cassell.

Campbell, C. (1987/2008). *The Romantic ethic and the spirit of modern consumerism - extended edition*. Palgrave Macmillan.

Dahlen, C. (2013, October 22). *Opinion: The Pleasures of Being an adult and Playing with Toys*. Polygon. https://www.polygon.com/2013/10/22/4862422/opinion-the-pleasure-of-being-an-adult-and-playing-with-toys.

Deleuze, G., & Guattari, F. (1980/2003). *A Thousand Plateaus*. Continuum.

Filipi, D. (2014). The Lego movie. *Film Comment, 50*(5), 75.

Fleming, P., & Sturdy, A. (2010). 'Being yourself' in the electronic sweatshop: New forms of normative control. *Human Relations, 64*(2), 177-200.

Foucault, M. (1975/1995). *Discipline and Punish: The Birth of the Prison*. Random House.

Garber, M. (2000). *Sex and real estate: Why we love houses*. Anchor Books.

Garlen, J. (2014). Block party: A look at adult fans of LEGO. In K. Barton & J. Lampley (Eds.), *Fan CULTure: Essays on participatory fandom in the 21st century* (pp. 119-130). McFarland Publishing.

Giddens, A. (1991). *Modernity and self identity: Self and society in the Late Modern Age*. Polity Press.

Goggin, J. (2017). 'Everything is awesome:' The LEGO movie and the affective politics of security. *Finance and Society, 3*(2), 143-158.

Hall, S. (1897). *A study of dolls*. E. L. Kellogg and Co.

Heljakka, K. & Harvianen, T. (2019). From display and dioramas to doll dramas: Adult world building and world playing with toys. *American Journal of Play, 11*(3), 351-378.

Henricks, T. (2018). Theme and variation: Arranging play's forms, functions, and 'colors.' *American Journal of Play, 10*(2), 133-167.

Hillis, K. & Petit, M. (Eds.) (2006). *Everyday eBay: Culture, collecting, and desire*. Routledge.

Holbrook, M. & Hirschman, E. (1982). The experiential aspects of consumption: Consumer fantasies, feelings, and fun. *Journal of Consumer Research, 9*(2), 132-140.

Hunter, M. (2018). Bric[k]olage: Adaptation as play in the Lego movie (2014). *Adaptation, 11*(3), 273-281.

Jailer, M. (1975, December 14). An adult's fancy often turns to childhood toys. *The New York Times.* https://www.nytimes.com/1975/12/14/archives/an-adults-fancy-often-turns-to-childhood-toys-a-costly-hobby-adult.html.

Jung, C. G. (1959/1980). *The archetypes and the collective unconscious*. Princeton University.

Kemper, T. (2015). *Toy Story: A critical reading*. The British Film Institute and Bloomsbury Publishing.

Knudson, J. (2018). Improving conversational virtual assistants with natural language processing. *Speech Technology, 23*(4), 10-14.

Kollmann, J. (1885). Das ueberwintern von Europaischen frosch- und tritonlarven und die umwandlung des Mexikanischen Axolotl. *Verhandlungen der Naturforschenden Gesellschaft in Basel, 7*, 387-398.

Koppelman, S. & Franks, A. (Eds.) (2008). *Collecting and the Internet: Essays on the pursuit of old passions through new technologies*. McFarland & Company Publishers.

Kozinets, R. V., Patterson, A., & Ashman, R. (2016). Networks of desire: How technology increases our passion to consume. *Journal of Consumer Research, 43*(5), 659-682.

Kuznets, L. (1994). *When toys come alive: Narratives of animation, metamorphous and development*. Yale University Press.

Lanier, C. Jr., Fowler III, A., & Rader, C. S. (2014). 'What are you looking at ya hockey puck?!:' Anthropomorphizing brand relationships in the Toy Story trilogy. In S. Brown & S. Ponsonby-McCabe (Eds.), *Brand mascots: And other marketing animals* (pp. 35-54). Routledge.

Lanier, C. Jr., Rader, C. S., & Fowler III, A. (2013). Anthropomorphism, marketing relationships, and consumption worth in the Toy Story trilogy. *Journal of Marketing Management, 29*(1-2), 26-47.

Livingstone, R. (2011). Better at life stuff: Consumption, identity, and class in Apple's 'Get a Mac' Campaign. *Journal of Communication Inquiry, 35*(3), 210-234.

Loftus, J. (2017, April 7). Who's buying superhero toys? (Spoiler alert: not children). Inverse. https://www.inverse.com/article/29841-superhero-toys-market-adult-collectors.

Lord, A. (2020, June 2). 'If looks could sell:' Netflix series selling sunset shows property porn that will make you drool. *The Independent.* https://www.independent.co.uk/arts-entertainment/tv/features/netflix-selling-sunset-property-porn-hills-a9543931.html

Maffesoli, M. (2000/2003). *L'instant éternel: Le retour du tragique dans les sociétés postmodernes*. La Table Ronde.

Maffesoli, M. (2007). *Le réenchantement du monde*. La Table Ronde.

McQueeney, K. (2012, February 22). Bear necessities: 35 per cent of British adults 'still take a teddy to bed with them,' stuffed toys help grown-ups de-stress and relax, research suggests. *DailyMail - Mail Online.* https://www.dailymail.co.uk/news/article-2104641/Travelodge-survey-reveals-35-cent-British-adults-teddy-bed-them.html.

Missildine, W. H. (1963). *Your inner child of the past.* Simon & Schuster.

Muñiz, A. Jr., Antorini, Y., & Schau, H. J. (2013). The brick treatment: Religiosity among the adult fans of lego. In R. W. Belk & R. Llamas (Eds.), *Routledge companion to digital consumption* (pp. 308-316). Routledge.

Pesce, N. (2017, April 6). *A quarter of us want to have sex with Alexa.* Marketwatch. https://www.marketwatch.com/story/a-quarter-of-us-want-to-have-sex-with-alexa-2017-04-06-148821.

Purington, A., Taft, J., Sannon, S., Bazarova, N., & Taylor, S. (2017). 'Alexa is my new BFF:' Social roles, user satisfaction, and personification of the Amazon Echo. *CHI EA '17: Proceedings of the 2017 CHI Conference on Human Factors in Computer Systems,* 2853-2859.

Ravishankar, H., Jasmine, J., Bhat, K., & Keerthana, L. G. (2020). Barbie with brains: An interactive robot. *International Journal of Advanced Research in Computer Science, 11*(3), 59-62.

Rilke, R. M. (1913-1914/2018, May 25). The unfortunate fate of childhood dolls. *The Paris Review.* https://www.theparisreview.org/blog/2018/05/25/the-unfortunate-fate-of-childhood-dolls/.

Romm, C. (2015, April 20). What 'food porn' does to the brain: What's the psychological appeal of looking at food that can't be tasted? *The Atlantic.* https://www.theatlantic.com/health/archive/2015/04/what-food-porn-does-to-the-brain/390849/.

Russ, H. (2010, May 9). U.S. adults are Spending big on video games, playing mostly on smartphones. *The Guardian.* https://www.theguardian.pe.ca/news/world/us-adults-are-spending-big-on-video-games-playing-mostly-on-smartphones-309738/.

Silverstein, J. (2006, January 6). Action figures for adults who won't grow up. *ABC News.* https://abcnews.go.com/Business/story?id=346227&page=1.

Stebbins, R. (1980). Serious leisure: A conceptual statement. *Pacific Sociological Review, 25*(April), 251-272.

Stewart, S. (1984). *On longing: Narratives of the miniature, the gigantic, the souvenir, the collection.* Johns Hopkins University Press.

Szczesny, M. (2016, July 15). Gaming at work: Pokémon Go or Pokémon no? *Hartford Business Journal.* http://www.hartfordbusiness.com/article/20160715/NEWS01/160719945/gaming-at-work-pok%C3%A9mon-go-or-pok%C3%A9mon-no

Travelodge UK. (2010, August 16). Over a third of British adults still sleep with a teddy bear [Press release]. https://www.travelodge.co.uk/press-centre/press-releases/over-third-british-adults-still-sleep-teddy-bear.

Varul, M. (2018). The cultural tragedy of production and the expropriation of the brickolariat: The Lego movie as consumer-capitalist myth. *European Journal of Cultural Studies, 21*(6), 724-743.

Verdier, H. (2016, March 2). Satisfaction guaranteed—Why property porn is better than porn. *The Guardian.* https://www.theguardian.com/tv-and-radio/2016/mar/02/satisfaction-guaranteed-why-property-porn-is-better-than-porn

Watkins, D. (2016, November 21). *Why we stop playing: The science behind moving from playing with toys to collecting them.* SyFy Wire. https://www.syfy.com/syfywire/why-we-stop-playing-science-behind-moving-playing-toys-collecting-them.

Weightman, F. (2006). Ideals of childlikeness in late imperial China. *Ming Qing Yanjiu, 14*(1), 178-218.

Winnicott, D. W. (1971/1982). *Playing and Reality.* Routledge.

Yacoub, S., Simske, S., Lin, X., & Burns, J. (2003). Recognition of emotions in interactive voice response systems. In *Proceedings of the 8th European Conference on speech communication and technology* (pp. 729-732). ISCA Archives.

# Chapter I.
## Humans as a Neotenous Species
David F. Bjorklund

We are a young species in many ways. From an evolutionary perspective, anatomically modern *Homo sapiens* first walked the earth a mere 300 thousand years ago, although we evolved from a line of increasingly human-like apes in Africa, last sharing a common ancestor with contemporary chimpanzees (*Pan troglodytes*) and bonobos (*Pan paniscus*) 5 to 7 million years ago. This too is not that a great time span, given the relatively slow pace of most evolutionary change and the vast cognitive and social differences that were needed to transform a tree-dwelling ape living in small social groups to one who created language, science, art, and civilization.

Our species may have been quick to evolve, but we are slow to develop, staying immature longer than any other mammal. Within primates, the closer a species' common ancestor is with *Homo sapiens*, the longer before they reach sexual maturity: in lemurs approximately 2 years, in macaques approximately 4 years, in chimpanzees approximately 8 years, and in humans about 15 years (Poirier & Smith, 1974). The estimate of 15 years for humans is itself quite liberal, as age of first birth for women in hunter-gatherer societies is usually in the late teens or early 20s (see Rozzi, 2018). Humans also display physical and behavioral features that, compared to modern apes and presumably our *hominin* ancestors (the group consisting of modern humans, extinct human species, and all our immediate forebearers), are immature in nature. Look at the faces of an infant chimpanzee and an infant human and you can't miss the similarity. Chimpanzee faces, however, develop, with jaws jutting out and brow ridges emerging over their eyes. Humans, in contrast, show less-drastic facial change with age, retaining many of the characteristics of infant primates (Gould, 1977; Montagu, 1989). Humans also display some behavioral and cognitive features typical of young primates. Perhaps most notable is play, something seen in the young (but rarely the adults) in all social primates, but that continues throughout life, in varying degrees, in *Homo sapiens*. And perhaps less obvious but more important is the ability to learn and modify our actions and thinking as a result of experience (Bjorklund, 2020). All primates show substantial brain *plasticity* (the ability to change) early in life, which is reduced as animals age. The same trend occurs in humans, but our kind retains a high degree of neural, cognitive, and behavioral plasticity, more typical of young animals, throughout life, which is, I think it's fair to say, responsible for our species' planetary hegemony.

There are many other examples of human childlikeness, often attributed to economic and cultural factors. People in developed nations can afford to stay "young at heart" and to delay true adult responsibilities ("adulting" is the new catch word), sometimes decades beyond when our ancestors had to grow up. But humans are by nature a youthful species, and, to a significant extent, we evolved to be the species we are by retaining many juvenile features that our ancestors grew out of. This is referred to as *neoteny*, which is the retention of infantile or juvenile traits into later development, or slowing some aspects of development in comparison to our ancestors. Although it is clearly inappropriate to think of humans evolving solely by retaining into adulthood juvenile features of our ancestors (we clearly have evolved larger brains, for example, than our ape progenitors), many theorists, dating back at least to the early decades of the 20th century, have proposed that humans are primarily a neotenous species. Consider, for example, this quote from Dutch Professor of human anatomy Louis Bolk (1926):

> There is no mammal that grows as slowly as man, and not one in
> which the full development is attained at such a long interval after

> birth... What is the essential in Man as an organism? The obvious
> answer is: The slow progress of his life's course. (p. 470)

Or consider the opinion of anthropologist Ashley Montagu (1989), some 60 years later:

> [E]volution has consisted of a shedding of the adult traits of our
> ancestral forms, and an increasing retention and development of
> the juvenile traits of those forms... [W]e are designed to fulfill the
> bountiful promise of the child; to grow and develop as children,
> rather than into the kind of adults we have been taught to believe
> we ought to become. . . In other words, the spirit of the child is, in
> the profoundest sense, the spirit of humanity, an adaptive trait of
> the greatest biological value. (pp. 61, 94, 95)

Bolk and Montagu may be accused of exaggerating and romanticizing the childlike nature of *Homo sapiens*, but more contemporary research has demonstrated that aspects of youthfulness are indeed part of our evolved biology, affecting brain development, our ability to cooperate with conspecifics, as well as many features of our psychology.

In this chapter, I first examine the phenomenon of neoteny as a type of *heterochrony*, genetic-based differences in developmental timing, and how it can affect the evolution of a species. Specifically, I examine humans' retention of prenatal-brain growth rates well into the second year of life that allowed for brain expansion and, along with an extended childhood, the time and cognitive abilities to master the complexities of human social life. I next look at research showing that human domestication of animals, such as dogs and cattle, produces retention of both juvenile physical and behavior characteristics; I then provide evidence that humans domesticated themselves through neoteny (the *self-domestication hypothesis*), retaining lower levels of reactive aggression that permitted greater cooperation among group members. This is followed by a look at a number of features of immaturity that are maintained, to varying degrees, into adulthood and have benefits both for the children and the adults who display them. These include: *kindchenschema*, or *baby schema*, or, more colloquially, *babyness;* neural, cognitive, and behavioral plasticity; playfulness; and unrealistic optimism. I conclude arguing that our species' unique psychology is, to a large extent, attributable to the retention of aspects of youthful, some may say immature, characteristics into adulthood. We clearly become smarter and more in control of our actions as we age, which is necessary if we are to accomplish the many tasks of adulthood. Yet, to a significant degree, much of what humans have achieved has been because of a childlike approach toward life.

## Developmental Timing and Human Evolution

I previously defined heterochrony as genetic-based differences in developmental timing. Different parts of an organism can develop and change independent of other parts (the concept of *modularity* in evolutionary developmental biology, or Evo Devo; Carroll, 2005; Raff, 1996), such that the development of one component of an organism can be accelerated or delayed (relative to the development of our ancestors) compared to other components, with these changes being subject to *natural selection*—Darwin's seminal idea that features of an organism associated with survival and reproduction will be maintained, or selected for, in a species. Differences in the timing of a trait can happen via changes in *regulatory genes*, genes that determine when in development sets of protein-manufacturing (structural) genes will be activated and the rates at which different parts of an organism develop. Mutations need not occur in structural genes for major differences to occur, but can happen in regulatory genes. For example, recent research comparing the DNA of chimpanzees and humans shows that some of the greatest genetic differences between the two species are in regulatory genes that affect the development of the brain (e.g., Arbiza et al., 2013; Prabhakar et al., 2006; McClean et al., 2011).

## Neoteny and Brain Development

Heterochrony seems to have been a frequently-used mechanism to bring about evolutionary change, and aspects of many species show signs of both heterochronic acceleration and retardation.[1] Although humans experienced both acceleration and retardation of development relative to our ancestors, many human features are clearly neotenic in nature, as Bolk and Montagu observed, whereas other important features are not so obviously so. For example, the angle the skull connects to the backbone is similar in humans and quadrupedal animals such as dogs during the fetal period. In dogs, the angle changes over prenatal development so that a dog is looking forward when standing on all fours. In contrast, this angle changes less in humans over the prenatal period so that a person is looking forward when standing on two legs (Montagu, 1989). In other words, the evolution of bipedality, an important and early adaptation in hominin evolution, was due in part to retarding development that typically occurs in other four-limbed mammals.

Perhaps the neotenic adaptations that had the most profound effect on human evolution are related to brain development. Human brains have obviously developed beyond the brains of our ancestors in size. In that sense, our large brain is not neotenic at all. There has been much speculation about the pressures that led to increased human brain size and cognitive abilities. For example, the *social brain hypothesis* proposes that enhanced human intelligence (and thus a larger brain) was needed to deal with humans' increasingly complicated social world (e.g., Alexander, 1989; Dunbar, 2003). Associated with increased brain size and social complexity was an extended developmental period, providing children the time required to learn the complexities of their social group (e.g., Bjorklund & Bering, 2003; Bjorklund, Cormier, & Rosenberg, 2005). Evidence of this comes from a study of social primates (including hunter-gatherer humans) that reported a relation between brain size, size of the social group, and length of the juvenile period: the three were strongly intercorrelated so that animals with larger brains tended to live in larger social groups and have longer juvenile periods (Joffe, 1997).

The pressure to increase brain size in ancient humans ran into a serious obstacle, however. If human prenatal development followed the typical great-ape schedule, birth would occur once the fetus' brain was between about 40% and 45% of its eventual adult weight (DeSilva, 2016; Trevathan & Rosenberg, 2016). This would result in a neonate's head being too large to fit through a bipedal woman's birth canal, the so-called *obstetrical dilemma* (Washburn, 1960). (Upright-stance evolved before increased brain size in hominin evolution.) The solution to this conundrum was for human infants to be born early relative to their primate cousins, when their brains were about 28% of their eventual adult weight (DeSilva, 2016). However, early birth was associated with a *retention of the rapid prenatal rate of brain growth*, so that

[1] Technical note: Following McKinney and McNamara (1991), there are three types of heterochronic retardation: (1) *progenesis*, or earlier onset of some aspect of development; (2) *neoteny*, or reduced rate of development; and (3) *post-displacement*, or delayed onset of development. For ease of reading, I do not differentiate between these three types of retardation here, often using the term neoteny to refer to retardation of development in general. McKinney and McNamara also identified three forms of heterochronic acceleration: (1) *hypermorphosis*, or delayed offset of development; (2) *acceleration*, or increased rate of development; and (3) *pre-displacement*, or earlier onset of growth (from Bjorklund, 2007, p. 44).

much brain development that would have occurred prenatally in a dark, protective womb had ancestral women followed the great-ape schedule (and remained pregnant for perhaps another year) was now done postnatally.

There are many consequences to human babies' large heads and early birth. One is obstetrical complications, necessitating women in most hunter-gatherer cultures to give birth with the assistance of other women. Death in childbirth, for both the mother and infant, was a real possibility for most of human history and prehistory.

Young infants were also highly dependent on their parents (particularly their mothers) for longer than other primates, and this prolonged dependency made it difficult for mothers to raise a child without assistance, as is typically the case in other great apes. One form of help came from fathers. Although human fathers spend little time in childcare in most cultures, they are among the 5% of mammal males that contribute something to their offspring, as well as to the support of their mates. This bonding between fathers, their mates, and their offspring may have evolved due to the needs of women trying to care for both themselves and a highly dependent infant. Relatedly, in all human cultures, mothers of young children are supported by a cadre of mostly female kin and friends who help rear a child. Unlike most other primate mothers, human mothers are not reluctant to share their infants with other females. This phenomenon of multiple caretakers for young children led Sarah Hrdy (1999) to propose that humans are *cooperative breeders*, with multiple people within a social group aiding in the rearing of the young.

Another consequence of premature birth that may have contributed importantly to *Homo sapiens'* unique intellect is the effect on brain development by experiencing a three-dimensional world of objects, people, sounds, and relationships while the brain is still immature and rapidly developing. Chimpanzee brains, for example, are proportionally larger, relatively to their eventual adult size, than human infants' brains when they first have to deal with eating, the force of gravity, and interacting with other members of their species. Human infants' brains start dealing with aspects of the physical and social world while they are still immature. A number of scientists have proposed that this extended gestation into postnatal life (called, among other things, *extrauterine spring, exterior gestation,* and *the fourth trimester*) had (and continues to have) a profound impact on social-cognitive development (e.g., Portmann, 1990; Montagu, 1989; Konner, 2010; Trevathan & Rosenberg, 2016). Portmann (1990) went as far as proposing that human's early birth and extended prenatal-rate of brain development was responsible for our species' unique cognitive and social abilities. He asks us to imagine

the developing human spending the important maturation period of its first year in the dark, moist, uniform warmth of its mother's womb. . . It will gradually become clear that world-open behavior of the mature form is directly related to early contact with the richness of the world, an opportunity available only to humans. (p. 93)

### Inventing New Stages of Development

*Homo sapiens'* early birth and the retention of prenatal brain-growth rates transformed infancy in many ways, relative to other primates, setting the stage for a cognitive revolution of sorts. Yet a modified infancy alone was not enough for young humans to master the social and technological (i.e., tool use) complexities that characterize all human cultures. An extended pre-reproductive period was also required, which, as mentioned previously, reflects the extreme of a general primate pattern (Poirier & Smith, 1974). However, ancient humans not only delayed becoming adults relative to their ancestors, but evolved new stages of development along the way. All mammals go through three stages of development: infancy, lasting from birth to weaning; the juvenile period (called middle childhood in humans by psychologists and educators), extending from weaning to sexual maturity; and adulthood. Animals during the juvenile period are relatively independent from their mothers, obtain their own food, and, in social mammals, often interact and play with other juveniles. Anthropologist Barry Bogin (1999, 2001, 2006) proposed that *Homo sapiens* evolved two new stages of development, both necessary for attaining the abilities that differentiate the species from other apes: *childhood* and *adolescence*.

### Childhood

Childhood is the period from about 2 or 3 years (post-infancy) to about 6 or 7 years of age. Children are typically weaned by this time but, unlike juveniles, are still almost completely dependent on their parents for survival. They have baby teeth, requiring that their food be specially prepared for them, and they lack the strength, dexterity, and cognitive abilities to successfully fend for themselves, even marginally. In modern culture we typically refer to children during this stage as preschoolers, and the Swiss psychologist Jean Piaget (1983) described the thinking of children during this time as *preoperational*. Children possess language and their thinking is based on the use of symbols, a substantial improvement from the earlier *sensorimotor stage* of infancy; however, their thinking is generally intuitive rather than logical (or operational). For example, in the classic Piagetian *conservation of mass task*, children are shown two equal balls of clay, which they attest to indeed have the same amount of clay in them. As children watch, an experimenter rolls out one ball into a sausage, then asks the children if the amount of clay is still the same in the two clumps. Whereas older (juvenile-aged) children almost always say the amount of clay in unchanged (to prove it, they may say you could just transform the sausage back into a ball), preschool children typically say the amounts now differ. They will say there is now more in the ball than in the sausage because the ball is fatter (or more in the sausage than in the ball because the sausage is longer), even though they admit that the quantity was the same initially. They cannot ignore the appearance of a difference between the ball and the sausage, despite the logical necessity of the quantity being the same. Although over the years the field of cognitive development has questioned many of Piaget's assumptions, his description of young children's thinking captures well the general cognitive limitations of preschoolers.

The invention of childhood may have been necessary not just to provide more time to develop, but also for the acquisition of some of the social-cognitive features that differentiate humans from our simian relatives and our hominin ancestors. Nielsen (2012, 2018) notes that it is during childhood that children acquire the social-learning abilities that set our species apart from the great apes. For example, although chimpanzees are impressive social learners, their primary form of social learning is *emulation*, understanding the goal of a model but achieving that goal using whatever means seems most effective. For example, an ape watching another ape jumping on a log to expose ants that are then eaten, may later approach the same or a different log but, instead of jumping on the log, roll it to achieve the same outcome (tasty ants for a meal). In contrast, human children, beginning around 3 years of age, are most likely to imitate the exact actions of a model, even if some of those actions are irrelevant (e.g., Gellén & Buttelmann, 2019; Lyons et al., 2007; see Hoehl et al., 2019; Whiten, 2019 for reviews). This latter phenomenon, termed *overimitation*, continues to be displayed by older children, is found cross-culturally, and even in adults (e.g., McGuigan, Makinson, & Whiten, 2011; Hewlett, Berl, & Roulette, 2016), but has not been observed in any of the great apes (see Clay & Tennie, 2018; Nielsen, 2012). Overimitation, although initially appearing inefficient (Why engage in superfluous actions when a task can be achieved by ignoring some unnecessary behaviors of a model?), serves to acquire important technological skills (adults surely know what they're doing when they use tools), as well as important social norms and ritualistic behaviors (this is what "we" do, what is normative for members of "our" group). According to Nielsen (2018, p. 266), "Children show they are prepared socially and cognitively to adopt the ritualized behaviors of those around them in many ways . . ., the most compelling of which is overimitation" (see also Legare & Nielsen, 2015; Watson-Jones & Legare, 2016). Consistent with this argument, preschoolers are more likely to imitate meaningless actions made by in-group than by out-group members (Gruber et al., 2019).

A second important social-cognitive acquisition of childhood is *counterfactual reasoning*, representing objects and people in a form other than what they really are, and taking an "as-if" stance (e.g., Cemore & Herwig, 2005; Lillard et al., 2013). This is most clearly seen in pretend (or fantasy) play, which is first observed in early childhood. For example, a child playing "school" pretends to be "the teacher" while other children are "the students," and they must stick with their roles throughout the play bout. According to Nielsen (2012),

> by pretending children thus develop a capacity to generate and reason with novel suppositions and imaginary scenarios, and in so doing may get to practice the creative process that underpins innovation in adulthood. (p. 176)

Counterfactual thinking is also important in more advanced forms of social learning, such as teaching. According to Tomasello, Kruger, and Ratner (1993),

> To learn from an instructor culturally—to understand the instruction from something resembling the instructor's point of view—requires that children be able to understand a mental perspective that differs from their own, and then to relate that point of view to their own in an explicit fashion. (p. 500)

Mithen (1996) similarly speculated that *Homo sapiens'* slow brain growth and extended childhood period was necessary to produce what he called *cognitive fluidity*. Mithen argued that the human mind-brain consists of different modules, each specialized in certain types of cognitive processing, along with a general intelligence, necessary to coordinate communication among these modules and to produce the cognitive architecture of modern humans. This is consistent with Geary's (1995, 2005) proposal that humans possess separable domains of mind, including those dealing with folk psychology (understanding the self and social world), folk biology (understanding the natural world), and folk physics (understanding the physical world, including tool invention and use), as well as a domain-general central executive. Mithen claimed that an extended childhood was needed to develop communication among these systems. In support of this, Mithen points to evidence that Neanderthals, modern humans' now-extinct cousins, showed only minimal signs of cognitive fluidity and attained adulthood much faster than ancient or contemporary *Homo sapiens*. Without an extended childhood, Mithen proposed, the modern human brain could not develop.

### Adolescence

Adolescence, the time between the juvenile period and adulthood, is characterized by a rapid growth spurt, changes in brain organization, and low fertility in females. This is often described as a time when young people develop their adult identity and practice aspects of adult behavior before actually having "real" responsibilities of adulthood. Adolescents typically show heightened levels of sensation seeking and risk-taking, which provides them with new skills and experiences and may facilitate their separation from their parents and independence as young adults. Recent research has documented brain changes during adolescence, which reflect something different than a gradual change from the juvenile period to adulthood (see e.g., Dennis et al., 2013; Giedd, 2015; Giedd et al., 1999; Luna et al., 2001). For example, while myelination of neurons (fostering faster transmission of nervous signals) increases during adolescence, amount of gray matter decreases, reflecting pruning of neuronal cell bodies. Changes are also seen in the distribution of neurotransmitters, such as dopamine and serotonin, both in the frontal cortex and the limbic system. Furthermore, maturation of the prefrontal lobes, involved in higher-order cognition, is slower than areas of the limbic system, the latter associated with processing emotions, causing what some researchers refer to as a mismatch in maturation (Giedd, 2015; Mills et al., 2014).

Based on fossil and dental evidence, Bogin argues that the stage of childhood was first seen in hominin evolution about 2 million years ago, in *Homo habilis*, increasing in length through *Homo erectus* to modern *Homo sapiens*. Adolescence, Bogin proposed, is unique to humans. Although modern chimpanzees and bonobos apparently also have a post-menarche period of low fertility (see Bogin, 1999), no other species shows the rapid growth spurt and brain reorganization observed in humans.

Human's slow march to adulthood, a neotenous feature in itself, is accompanied by what many psychologists and educators have described as extended periods of immature cognition –*childhood*, in comparison to the juvenile period, and *adolescence,* in comparison to adulthood. The thinking of children and adolescents should not necessarily be viewed as handicaps, however, but rather as adaptive responses to the demands of growing up in increasingly complex social and technological cultures. Natural selection favored youth who could acquire over time the skills of one's particular society, and to do this required using immaturity in a modified infancy and in new stages of childhood and adolescence.

## Humans as a Self-Domesticated Species

Humans are not the only neotenous species on the planet. For example, the salamander axolotl, also known as the Mexican walking fish, has a larval stage as a water-living tadpole, eventually transforming into a sexually mature, air-breathing salamander. But under some environmental conditions, the animal will attain sexual maturity while still a tadpole (see Gould, 1977). This is an excellent example of neoteny, with the reproductive system maturing independently of the still-juvenile body form.

Most domestic animals can also be considered neotenous. Domesticated dogs, cattle, goats, and sheep all evolved from wild forms and were tamed by humans by selectively breeding human-tolerant animals with other human-tolerant animals. Domesticated animals' greater tameness reflects the retention of juvenile (less-wild) behavior into adulthood. Domesticated animals' greater tameness is often accompanied by a more juvenile appearance. Dogs, for example, retain a more puppy-like look than wolves.

The neotenous nature of domesticated animals was demonstrated nicely in studies by the Russian zoologist Dmitry Belyayev and his colleagues, whose goal was to selectively breed wild foxes (*Vulpes vulpes*) to make them dog-like pets. By breeding human-tolerant fox pups with other human-tolerant fox pups, over the course of 20 generations about 35 percent of the foxes showed puppy-like behavior; they were eager for human contact and acted much like dogs, licking and sniffing humans and whimpering to gain attention (Trutt, 1999). What was particularly interesting about these tamed foxes was that they retained many puppy-like *physical* characteristics, such as floppy ears, shortened heads, legs, tails, snouts, and upper jaws. This caused Lyudmila Trut, who took over the project after Belyayev's death, to write,

> The shifts in the timing of development brought about by selection of foxes for tameability have a neotenic-like tendency: the development of individual somatic [body] traits is decelerated, while sexual maturation is accelerated. (Trut, Oskina, & Kharlamova, 2009, p. 354).

The relevance of this work to our species is that a number of theorists have proposed that humans also display many features of domesticated animals: more infantile physical features compared to great apes and a greater "tameness" permitting smoother social interaction (e.g., Hare, 2017; Hood, 2014; Wrangham, 2018, 2019). Increasing neoteny in physical features can be seen in the fossil record in transitions from *australopithecines* to *Homo habilis* (Grove, 1989), and then continuing within the *Homo* line. For example, although adult females retain more infantile physical features than adult males, *Homo sapiens* male faces continued to become more neotenous (and thus more feminine), dating back as far as 315,000 years ago, with the process accelerating over more recent *Homo sapiens* evolution (Wrangham, 2019). Perhaps of greater significance was the behavioral changes that apparently accompanied the neotenous physical changes: Humans, like selectively bred domesticated animals and Belyayev's foxes, became "more tame," which had important implications for human social evolution.

Unlike dogs and cattle, however, humans were not tamed, or domesticated, by another species; rather, they domesticated themselves—we became a *self-domesticated species*. The pressure for enhanced tameness was related to the need to better cooperate with conspecifics. Following the social brain hypothesis discussed earlier, human evolution was driven in large part by the need to survive in increasingly complex social groups. Social living can be difficult, and this is especially true when animals display high levels of *reactive aggression*, aggression in response to a real or perceived threat: an individual is provoked to aggress. Chimpanzees also live in socially complex groups, but they have high levels of reactive aggression, making it difficult for groups of individuals to work together to achieve a common goal without near-constant conflict. Humans are in better control of their reactive aggression (i.e., they are more neotenous with respect to reactive aggression), and as a result they are able to cooperate more successfully with one another, a hallmark of *Homo sapiens* and perhaps the number-one reason for our species' planetary domination. Natural selection favored people (especially males) who could control their aggression and thus increase their cooperation with others and the attainment of important goals that an individual alone would not be able to accomplish.

Evidence that delayed (neotenous) development can result in reduced aggression comes from a selective-breeding study in which low-aggressive mice were bred with other low-aggressive mice over several generations. The researchers reported that later generations of low-aggressive mice did not show the typical age-related increases in aggression observed in the foundational generation but rather maintained lower-levels of aggression into adulthood (Cairns et al., 1990). Cairns and his colleagues attributed this change to neoteny, "the progressively longer persistence of 'immature' features in the ontogeny of descendent generations" (p. 59).

Humans did not give up all of their aggressive tendencies, however. In fact, according to Wrangham (2018, 2019), humans excel at *proactive,* or *instrumental, aggression,* which is premeditated. The importance of high levels of proactive aggression is that it sometimes had to be used against individuals within a group who were bullies or who broke social rules. Wrangham (2018, 2019) proposed the *execution hypothesis,* in which groups of males would kill those people who consistently violated group norms. There is an irony that increased proactive aggression was used to enforce the cooperative benefits of reduced reactive aggression, but this practice can be seen in traditional societies across the globe and in the legal systems within developed countries.

What is important to emphasize here is that the retention of a juvenile feature (reduced reactive aggression) likely played a critical role in human behavioral and social evolution. This neotenous characteristic was favored by natural selection because it permitted enhanced cooperation that led eventually to hypersociality. These neotenous behavioral changes over evolutionary time were accompanied by neotenous physical changes, similar to what was seen in Belyayev's foxes. Whether the physical features piggybacked onto the behavioral features or vice versa, or whether both the behavioral and physical changes were independently favored by natural selection, must remain speculative at this time.

## The Benefits of Immaturity

Perhaps the most ardent advocate of humans as a neotenous species in the latter part of the 20th century was anthropologist Ashley Montagu (1962, 1989). Montagu saw adult humans as possessing a host of childlike features. Montagu listed 27 "Basic Behavioral Needs" that appeared early in life and extended into adulthood that he regarded as neotenous. Although I have claimed elsewhere (Bjorklund, 2020) that Montagu may have missed the mark in classifying many of these features as neotenous (e.g., *love, friendship, need to work, need to organize, dance, song*; not all youthful or early-appearing characteristics are neotenous), on reflection I think that most of the these "needs" fall under three broad features that are indeed neotenous: (1) neural, cognitive, and behavioral plasticity; (2) playfulness; and (3) unrealistic optimism. In the following sections I look at each of these neotenous features, examine how they benefit children in dealing with their immediate environment and how they are extended into adulthood. Before looking at these three types of behavioral (or cognitive) neoteny, I first discuss perhaps the most studied and obvious sign of neoteny, human infants' immature physical (especially facial) features and their effect on the adults who care for them.

### Baby Schema

John Bowlby (1969), the father of attachment theory, recognized that infant-mother attachment had a strong survival function. All mammals are dependent on their mothers for care and nutrition during the infancy period, and human infants especially so because of their limited physical, social, and cognitive abilities. Babies can also be difficult. Their need for care often deprives parents of sleep, their cries can be irritating, and they can be difficult to soothe. To increase the chance that often-difficult babies will receive the care they need from their parents (mostly their mothers), infants possess a suite of features that elicit caregiving from adults, the most potent of these being immature facial features, or what the Nobel Prize-winning ethologist Konrad Lorenz (1943) called *kindschenschema*, or *baby schema*. Compared to adult faces, infant faces have fat cheeks, flat noses, rounded heads that are large relative to body size, and large eyes relative to head size. These are features that adults find endearing, which, Lorenz reasoned, increase the chance that adults will care for a helpless, highly dependent infant.

  Bowlby and Lorenz were generally correct in their hypothesis. Research over the past 70 years has consistently found that adults do indeed find infant faces cute and are more likely to devote care to such infants (or say they would) than to infants with less-cute (less baby-schema-like) faces (see Franklin & Volk, 2018; Kringelbach et al., 2016; and Lucion et al., 2017 for reviews). Infants with faces with greater degrees of baby schema are rated as cuter, more sociable, friendlier, easier to care for, and more helpless and powerless than less-baby-faced infants (e.g., Leibenluft et al., 2004; Senese et al., 2013; Sprengelmyer et al., 2009). Adults are more apt to make hypothetical adoption decisions for cuter than for less-cute infants (Volk, Lukjanczuk, & Quinsey, 2007); recommend less-severe punishment for more baby-faced 4-year-olds than for children with more mature faces (Zebrowitz, Kendall-Trackett, & Field, 1991); and premature infants, who display fewer of the baby-schema features, are more apt to be abused sometime during childhood than full-term infants (see Martin et al., 1974). The effects of the baby schema are found in both men and women, but, not surprisingly, they are stronger in women, who historically have had greater responsibility caring for infants (e.g., Cárdenas et al., 2013; Sprengelmeyer et al., 2009; Yamamoto et al., 2009). Viewing infant faces elicits strong responses to specific areas of the brain, particularly those associated with processing emotion (e.g., Glocker et al., 2009; Hahn & Perrett, 2014; Leibenluft et al., 2004).

The benefit of the baby schema to infants is obvious—it increases their chances of getting care from adults and thus of surviving. Are there any corresponding benefits for adults? On the one hand, keeping their children alive is in the parents' best inclusive-fitness interest as well as that of their offspring, so being responsive to infants' cues of need also benefits the parents. But on the other hand, infants' and parents' interests are not identical. Babies want all the investment from their parents they can get, but parents need to take into consideration not only the baby in front of them but also themselves and any children they currently have or may have in the future. In many hunter-gatherer cultures, parents may choose *not* to invest in an infant who would divert resources needed for siblings' or the mother's own survival, and being responsive to the baby schema could "trick" mothers to investing in an infant when it is not in her best inclusive-fitness interest to do so.

One aspect of the baby schema that may prevent mothers from providing unwarranted investment in a child is the fact that the effects of baby schema are most potent, not at birth when infants are most dependent on adults for survival, but between 3 and 6 months of age (Franklin & Volk, 2018; Franklin et al., 2018). This may have provided ancestral mothers time to evaluate the health of an infant and to make decisions about whether to invest in a newborn or not, especially when resources were limited; abandonment or infanticide was an option if an infant was not likely to survive. Women also show greater brain activation when viewing photos of their own infants than of other babies (e.g., Nitschke et al., 2004; see Rigo et al., 2019 for a review), which may not only increase the likelihood of women investing in their own infant, but prevent them from investing inappropriately in other genetically-unrelated babies.

The positive effects of baby schema extend only to 4 or 5 years of age, after which adults' judgments of likeability and attractiveness are similar to their judgments for adult faces (Luo, Li, & Lee, 2011). There is also evidence that brain activation differs as a function of the age of the person depicted in a photo, with activation being greatest for infants, least for adults, and at an intermediate level for prepubescent children (Proverbio et al., 2011). Yet, 5- and 6-year-old children are still highly dependent on adults, and there is evidence that adults are sensitive to other types of cues of immaturity in evaluating preschool-age children. One such cue is voices; children with more immature voices are rated as more likeable, cuter, friendlier, nicer, and helpless than children with more mature voices (Hernández Blasi et al., 2018). Another cue is expressions of cognitive immaturity. For example, adults judge hypothetical children displaying some forms of cognitive immaturity (e.g., "The sun's not out because it's mad") as displaying more positive characteristics (e.g., friendly, likeable) and fewer negative characteristics (e.g., sneaky, likely to lie, feel more irritated with) than same-age children expressing more mature cognition (e.g., "The sun's not out because a cloud is in front of it") (Bjorklund, Hernández Blasi, & Periss, 2010; Hernández Blasi, Bjorklund, & Ruiz Soler, 2015; Hernández Blasi & Bjorklund, 2018; Hernández Blasi, Bjorklund, & Ruiz Soler, 2017; Periss, Hernández Blasi, & Bjorklund, 2012). In these studies, both the maturity of the voices and maturity of cognition better predicted adults' positive and negative assessments of the children than did facial features. These findings indicate that as children age they use other forms of immaturity to cue adults to their need for caregiving. Language blossoms during the preschool years, and both its physical nature (maturity of children's voice) and content (expressions of immature cognition) are now better indications of children's developmental status than their physical appearance.

**Plasticity**

Perhaps the most important form of behavioral/cognitive neoteny for humans is *plasticity*, the ability to change. Neural, behavioral, and cognitive plasticity is greatest early in life for all primates but declines with age. Losing plasticity means reducing opportunities to acquire new skills, which, on the surface, seems like a bad thing. However, there are many abilities that, once acquired, we don't want to change (at least not much), and animals are better off dedicating neurons to these abilities at the expense of retaining plasticity. Think of the perceptual systems, which develop as a result of environmental stimulation (sights and sounds for vision and hearing, for example) impinging on sense organs and organizing portions of the brain. Once established, one does not want them to remain too flexible, lest they lose their specialized purpose. For a human-unique ability consider language. Children acquire language seemingly effortlessly. They are not taught it, but their brains are sufficiently flexible (plastic) to acquire any of the world's 6,000 or so languages merely through exposure to them. Acquiring a second language as an adult would be greatly facilitated if we retained the language-learning plasticity of early childhood. But doing so would jeopardize the proficiency we have with our first language. Given that our ancestors likely rarely encountered people who spoke a different language, it made good sense to dedicate neurons to one's mother tongue, even if that meant struggling with learning a second language later in life.

But animals do not lose all of their plasticity as they age. Any animal that depends on learning must have a brain that can make new synaptic connections to retain information about the local ecology and adjust its behavior to environmental contingencies. All primates and mammals retain some plasticity into later life, but none to the extent that humans do. Humans are able to change their thinking, behavior, and brains to a significant degree well into adulthood. This is afforded in part by the retention of prenatal brain growth rates into infancy (discussed earlier) and the protracted development of the brain into the third decade of life.

Young children's high levels of plasticity permit them to learn the ways of any of the thousands of human cultures. *Homo sapiens* is a cultural species. Although human cultures share much in common with one another, children must learn to navigate the particular physical and social worlds they are born into, using the technology (artifacts and tools) of their group. Given the diversity of human societies, children could not evolve a narrow set of innate behaviors that could be successfully activated to deal with any cultural circumstance. Rather, they evolved sets of psychological mechanisms (adaptations) that prepared them to make sense of life in a social group, but which are dependent on specific experience for their development (e.g., Bjorklund, 2015, 2020; Bjorklund & Ellis, 2014; Geary, 2005). This high degree of plasticity permits children to become functioning members of any of many diverse societies, from indulgent hunter-gatherer groups that place few demands on children, to developed countries that emphasize formal education, to traditional cultures that place infants on ant piles to facilitate walking (see Lancy, 2015).

Young children's substantial plasticity serves as some protection from brain insults or the adverse effects of a deleterious early environment. For example, recovery from brain damage early in life, especially to areas of the brain dealing with language, is greater for infants and young children than for older children and adults. According to Witelson (1987),

> there is a remarkable functional plasticity for language functions following brain damage in childhood in that the eventual cognitive level reached is often far beyond that observed in cases of adult brain damage, even those having extensive remedial education. These results attest to the operation of marked neural plasticity at least in the immature brain. (p. 676)

Similar patterns are observed for less-severe brain injuries such as concussions (see Yeats & Taylor, 2005).

Young children are also able to recover from the negative effects of early deprivation, as found for children who spend their early months in overcrowded, understaffed orphanages and who receive little in the way of intellectual and social stimulation. Infants show signs of social, emotional, and intellectual dysfunction after as little as three or four months in such institutions, and these psychological effects persist into adulthood if children continue to be raised in such stultifying conditions. However, because of children's extended period of brain growth, these effects can be reversed when children experience more positive rearing conditions (e.g., Beckett et al., 2006; Nelson et al., 2007; Rutter et al., 2007). Plasticity is not infinite, however, but declines into the second year of life, such that institutionalized children who are not moved to more supportive homes much before their second birthdays continue to display social, emotional, and cognitive deficits, with accompanying changes in brain structure and functioning (e.g., Tottenham et al., 2010), which may persist into adulthood (e.g., Bick et al., 2018; Merz et al., 2016; Nelson et al., 2007).

Although plasticity is reduced by children's second birthdays, it continues to be high in many parts of the brain. Consider how much new information and social and cognitive skills children acquire between the ages of about 2 and 5. They are learning language, as well as learning social conventions and how to use the tools of their culture. There is likely no time in development when individuals learn so much in so little time. Synaptic density in the prefrontal cortex increases steadily between birth and about 4 years of age, before declining as a result of synaptic pruning (Huttenlocher & Dabholkar, 1997); and metabolism of the brain increases sharply after the first year of life, peaking at about 150% percent of the adult rate from ages 4 to 5 years (Chugani, Phelps, & Mazziotta, 1987). Although neural plasticity declines as we age, it does not disappear, with older children and adults retaining higher levels of plasticity (and thus the ability to learn and change) than other adult mammals.

There is evidence than some of older humans' enhanced plasticity is due to individual neurons maintaining some neotenic features beyond the typical primate schedule. For example, the process of forming new synapses (connections between neurons, synaptogenesis) is largely responsible for cognitive and behavioral plasticity and is greatest early in life for all mammals. Synaptic activity and neuronal metabolism peak later in humans than in other primates, thus extending neural plasticity into adulthood (e.g., Goyal et al., 2014; Petanjek et al., 2011; Somel et al., 2009). This is reflected by research that identified genes in the cerebral cortexes of both chimpanzees and humans associated with synaptogenesis. The activity of these genes is greatest in chimpanzees shortly before their first birthdays, but does not peak in humans until about 5 years of age (Liu et al., 2012). In other research, gene expression in *adolescent* and *adult* humans associated with synaptogenesis in the cortex is similar to that observed in *juvenile* chimpanzees (Somel et al., 2009). In addition, *myelination*—the coating of axons with a fatty tissue resulting in faster nerve transmission with less electrical interference—is extended later in development in humans than in chimpanzees (Miller et al., 2012). According to Miller and his colleagues (2012, p. 16482), "activity-mediated myelin growth early in human life has the capacity to be shaped by postnatal environmental and social interactions to a greater degree than in other primates, including chimpanzees." As a result of these and related differences, humans retain a higher level of plasticity and the ability to change their thoughts and behaviors well into adulthood in comparison to the great apes. In their review of neuronal neoteny, Bufill, Agustí, and Blesa (2011) concluded that,

> human neurons belonging to particular association areas retain
> juvenile characteristic throughout adulthood, which suggests that
> a neuronal neoteny has occurred in *H. sapiens*, which allows the
> human brain to function, to a certain degree, like a juvenile brain

during adult life. . . Neuronal neoteny contributes to increasing information storage and processing capacity throughout life, which is why it was selected during primate evolution and, to a much greater extent, during the evolution of the genus *Homo*. (p. 735)

This brings us back to Montagu's long list of "basic needs," and I believe at least seven of them can be classified as being due to extending neural, cognitive, and behavioral plasticity into adulthood. For example, the need *to think soundly, to know, to learn,* and *to organize* (to make sense out of new experiences) is each associated with acquiring, storing, or making decisions about events in the outside world, and such processing requires a plastic (learning) brain to accomplish. Two other needs, *flexibility* and *resiliency,* are almost synonyms for plasticity, and the need *to wonder* implies an inquisitive mind that contemplates not just one's current knowledge but stretches the mind to what might be, and this, too, is clearly a reflection of plasticity. In short, many of *Homo sapiens'* intellectual attributes can trace their origins, at least in part, to the neotenous retention of plasticity into adulthood.

**Play**

Play is the quintessential activity of children. Children in all cultures play, barring weather extremes, malnutrition, or war. The very ubiquity of childhood play can cause people to overlook its importance, viewing it as a frivolous activity that children engage in until they have the cognitive and behavioral sophistication for more serious endeavors, such as work or formal education. In fact, the very definition of play implies its "purposelessness:" play is engaged in voluntarily with no other purpose other than its own activity. Moreover, it is not just human children who play, but so do all social mammals. Children and young animals do not play in order to acquire new skills, improve current ones, or to establish social relations. Rather, play is engaged in for its own sake and pleasure. Yet, all scholars who have studied play recognize that it indeed has important consequences for young animals. This is reflected by Karl Groos, an early scholar of play, who wrote, "animals cannot be said to play because they are young and frolicsome, *but rather they have a period of youth in order to play*" (Groos, 1898/1975, p. 75). Young animals may not play with the intention of learning anything useful, but they do learn in the process, acquiring skills that are useful for dealing with their immediate environment as well as future ones.

Play is a youthful feature of most mammals and is typically absent among adults, excepting occasional bouts initiated by juveniles. The exception is *Homo sapiens*, who extend play into adulthood. This is exemplified by historian Johan Huizinga (1950), who described humans as *Homo ludens*, or "playful man," writing, "Play is older than culture, has not been essentially changed by civilization, and has permeated from the beginning 'the great archetypal activities of human society'" (p. 1). Human adults do not play as much as children, for they indeed must devote time and effort to activities that directly affect their inclusive fitness (work, social relations, mating, rearing children). Yet, they maintain a higher level of play than seen in another other species.

Play has immediate benefits for children. *Locomotive play* involves running (and chasing), climbing, wrestling, and play fighting, each of which serves to foster physical development, coordination, learning about the local environment, enhancing spatial cognition, and, when performed with other children, learning about social interaction, including skills that might be useful in adulthood (see Bjorklund & Pellegrini, 2002 and Pellegrini & Smith, 1998 for reviews). For instance, some researchers have suggested that the play fighting of boys in hunter-gatherer societies is similar to adult fighting (Keeley, 1996). *Object play* involves manipulating and "playing with objects," and helps children learn the *affordances* of objects—the quality or property of an object that defines its possible uses, for example, a hammer is for hitting, a is cup for putting things into, a chair is for sitting (Lockman, 2000; Pellegrini, 2013). According to Peter Smith (1982, p. 151), object exploration and play help prepare children to use tools "over and above what could be learnt through observation, imitation, and goal-directed practice." The most studied type of play is *fantasy play*, discussed briefly earlier in this chapter. Fantasy, or pretend or make-believe play, involves taking an "as if" perspective, which requires *counterfactual reasoning*, representing objects and people in a form other than what they really are. This is seen in *sociodramatic play*, in which children engage in make-believe with other children, each taking a role in an imaginary situation and staying "in character," knowing that the roles they are engaging in are deviations from reality (e.g., Lillard et al., 2013).

Adults in traditional societies rarely do any direct teaching. In fact, when teaching does occur in hunter-gatherer cultures, children rather than adults are more apt to play the role of teacher (Lew-Levy et al., 2020). Rather, children learn the ways of their culture mainly through observation and play (Gray, 2016; Lancy, 2015). Much of children's activities in traditional cultures involves playing at adult tasks, such as hunting or cooking (e.g., Bock & Johnson, 2004). Although children in developed societies are explicitly taught by their parents and later by their teachers, play, especially social play, remains an important context for learning about the world. There is also evidence that engaging in fantasy play facilitates children's basic cognitive abilities, particularly *executive function*, processes involved in regulating one's attention and behavior and in planning and behaving flexibly. Executive function has three components: *working memory* (or *updating*), involved in storing and manipulating information; *inhibition*, withholding responses and resisting interference; and *shifting* (or *cognitive flexibility*), the ability to switch between different sets of rules or different tasks (e.g., Garon, Bryson, & Smith, 2008; McAuley & White, 2011). Several studies have reported positive relations between the amount of time children spend in free play and levels of executive function (e.g., Barker et al., 2014; Carlson, White, & Davis-Unger, 2014; Elias & Berk, 2002). Other research has reported social-emotional benefits for adults who engaged in high levels of free play as children: the amount of free play adults engaged in as children was positively associated with self-esteem, friendship, and general psychological and physical health, and these effects of childhood free play on adult outcomes were mediated by greater adaptivity (flexible goal adjustment) (Greve & Thomsen, 2016; Greve, Thomsen, & Dehio, 2014).

Play in childhood has demonstrable immediate benefits for children, and perhaps predicts aspects of later adult adjustment. But why should play itself be maintained into adulthood? Play has costs: children get hurt, and sometimes die, while playing, and the time adults spend playing could seemingly be better used acquiring/ maintaining resources, mates, or rearing children. Yet, adults do play, and, although the research on adult play is less extensive than on children's play, there are benefits to adults engaging in seemingly purposeless playful behavior.

I earlier provided a lean definition of play as a behavior engaged in voluntarily that has no immediate benefit. Such a sparse definition can be applied to nonhuman animals as well as to humans. But when we think of play in people, of any age, we also think that the activity is *fun*. For example, Van Vleet and Feeny (2015) state that the goal of play is "enjoyment and fun" and that play requires an "enthusiastic and in-the-moment approach." Other researchers have defined playfulness as "an internal predisposition characterized by creativity, curiosity, pleasure, sense of humor, and spontaneity" (Guitard, Ferland, & Dutil, 2005, p. 9). These are all qualities that most people also see in children's play, although we would be reluctant to attribute them to the play of nonhuman animals.

Given this broader definition of play, it is not surprising that playfulness in adults has been associated with greater levels of creativity, curiosity, sense of humor, pleasure, and spontaneity (see Guitard et al., 2015). Other research has looked at playfulness within close relationships and finds play (or a playful attitude) is associated with enhancing several aspects of relationship quality, including intimacy, trust, and communication (e.g., Betcher, 1981; Van Vleet & Feeny, 2015; Vanderbleek et al., 2011). Other research has shown that playfulness among college students was associated with better academic performance (grades and exams), although it was not associated with measures of psychometric intelligence (Proyer, 2011). In other research, Chick, Yarnal, and Purrington (2012) presented data consistent with the proposal that playfulness is used by men and women in selecting desirable mates, with women using a man's playfulness as a signal for nonaggressiveness and men using women's playfulness as a sign of youth and thus fecundity.

Using a human-centric definition of play, it is difficult *not* to see humans as a playful species—Huizinga's *Homo ludens*. Humans are not all play, but neither are we all work, and when we are all work, it does indeed make Jack a dull boy (and Jill a dull girl). Our broader definition of play captures, I believe, 13 of Montagu's neotenous "basic needs." Some of them reflect the "fun" associated with play, including *enthusiasm, sense of humor, joy, song, dance* (a type of locomotive play), and *laughter and tears* (or the laughter part, anyway); whereas others reflect the discovery and inquisitiveness that typifies play, including *open-mindedness, explorativeness, experimental-mindedness, curiosity, creativity*, and *imagination* (and of course, *playfulness* itself). Some of these youthful characteristics may overlap with extended plasticity (for example, *curiosity, imagination, experimental-mindedness*, and *open-mindedness*), and this should not be surprising. Some of the selective pressures that fostered extending play into adulthood are surely the same as those that fostered prolonged plasticity, and it is likely that the same neural tissues associated with greater plasticity are also associated with the "basic need" to play.

## Optimism

Children are the Pollyannas of the world, especially when they're thinking about themselves. Preschool and early-school-age children consistently believe they are smarter (e.g., Spinath & Spinath, 2005; Stipek, 1981), have better memories (e.g., Yussen & Levy, 1975), are more skilled at imitating models (Bjorklund, Gaultney, & Green, 1993), have greater physical abilities (Schneider, 1998), evaluate themselves as tougher, stronger, and of higher social status (e.g., Boulton & Smith, 1990), and know about how things work (Mills & Keil, 2004) than is actually the case. This could be attributed to poor cognition in general: perhaps young children just can't tell who is skilled at a task and who is not. This seems not to be the case, however. Young children are generally accurate in evaluating the skills and characteristics of other children; they reserve the overly optimistic evaluations for themselves (Stipek, 1981). Several studies have shown that young children who overestimate their cognitive abilities actually show higher levels of performance (or faster improvement on a task) than more accurate children (e.g., Bjorklund et al., 1993; Shin, Bjorklund, & Beck, 2007). Children become more accurate in their self-assessments by middle childhood (Stipek, 1984), at which time children who are better at assessing their abilities tend to show a cognitive advantage (see Schneider, 1985), a reversal of what is found for younger children.

One explanation for young children's unrealistic optimism stems from Bandura's (1997) theory of *self-efficacy*. People with high levels of self-efficacy perceive themselves to be in control of specific aspects of their lives and behave accordingly. Young children's overestimation of their abilities may cause them to persist at tasks where children more in touch with their abilities (actually inabilities) might quit. Young children are universal novices, and if they were aware of how poorly they were actually performing a task, their sense of self-efficacy could be damaged and they likely would not be so bold in trying new things, nor persisting at tasks they do attempt. Similarly, children believe that physical and psychological traits are more apt to improve rather than to decline over time and that people have a good deal of control in changing traits, what Lockhart and her colleagues called *protective optimism* (Lockhart, Chang, & Tyler, 2002; Lockhart, Goddu, & Keil, 2017). All of this is consistent with Seligmann's (1991) claim that young children's extreme optimism was selected in human evolution:

> The child carries the seed of the future, and nature's primary interest in children is that they reach puberty safely and produce the next generation of children. Nature has buffered our children not only physically—prepubescent children have the lowest death rate from all causes—but psychologically as well, by endowing them with hope, abundant and irrational. (p. 126)

As I mentioned, children's "abundant and irrational" optimism declines in middle childhood, when children become more in touch with their abilities and limitations. But optimism never totally disappears. Adult humans maintain an unrealistic appraisal of their own traits and abilities, albeit not quite to the extent that 4- and 5-year-old children do. Adults' overly rosy self-perceptions come in several forms. For example, *unrealistic optimism* is defined as "a favorable difference between the risk estimate a person makes for him- or herself and the risk estimate suggested by a relevant, objective standard" (Shepperd et al., 2013, p. 396). Dozens of studies demonstrate that unrealistic optimism is typical in adults for things such as the grades college students will get on an exam, their starting salaries after graduation, and how long it will take to complete a tax return, solve a puzzle, or perform other mundane tasks (e.g., Griffin & Buehler, 1999; Sheppard et al., 1996; see Shepperd et al., 2013 for a review).

Another robust phenomenon is the *better-than-average effect* (*BTAE*), in which adults perceive they have greater abilities than the average person. In a meta-analysis of 124 published studies with more than 950,000 participants, Zell and his colleagues (2020) reported a statistically strong effect of BTAE and that the effect varies little across cultures, race, or gender. The effect size (the strength of relation between two variables) was larger (.78) than most effect sizes in social-personality psychology (.43). The better-than-average effect did vary with age, however, with children (5 years) displaying stronger BTAE effects than young (20 years) and middle-age (45 years) adults. Furthermore, Zell and colleagues found that BTAE was positively correlated with self-esteem ($r = .34$) and overall life satisfaction ($r = .33$).

Other research has shown that optimistic people are generally happier and tend to cope more effectively with life's stressors than pessimistic people (e.g., Nes & Segerstrom, 2006; Snyder, 1994; Taylor et al., 2003). For example, in one study men who scored high on an optimism scale made faster recoveries from coronary artery bypass surgery than men scoring lower on the scale, even when the medical conditions that led to surgery were equivalent (Scheier et al., 1989). A likely explanation for this and related findings is that positive thinking causes people to devote their efforts to solving their problems, which in turn leads to positive results. In contrast, pessimists are relatively more likely to say, "It won't work out anyway, so why bother?"

Optimism was one of Montagu's neotenous "basic needs." In describing children's overly rosy view of the world, he wrote, "Children are natural optimists, for the future appears to them to be suffused with promises that will surely be fulfilled with growth. That is why children are so impatient to grow up" (1989, p. 158). Although adults learn to temper their overly optimistic views of themselves and the world, they never give it up completely, and those who retain more of this childish disposition seem to be happier and better psychologically adjusted than those less so inclined.

### Human Evolution by Neoteny

Since the 1930s with the advent of the Modern Synthesis (or neoDarwinism), there have been two pillars of evolutionary theory: genetics and natural selection. Evolution occurred as a result of changes in gene frequency with natural selection determining which combination of genes produced animals that were better suited to their local environments. There were also two main sources of evidence supporting evolutionary change: fossils and genes. Development, either as a possible contributor to evolutionary change or as a source of evidence for evolution, had no role. What happened over the course of an organism's lifetime played no part in its evolution, principally because experience could not change genes or their expression in the gametes. To suggest otherwise was to advocate for Lamarckism, the inheritance of acquired characteristics, a totally discredited position within mainstream biology.

This perspective began to change with the rise of the field of evolutionary developmental biology, or Evo Devo, in the latter decades of the 20th century (e.g., Carroll, 2005; Raff, 1996; West-Eberhard, 2003). Evo Devo examines how different developmental mechanisms affect phylogenetic change, giving development an important role to play in explaining the evolution of species. According to Carroll (2005),

> Evo Devo constitutes the third major act in a continuing evolutionary synthesis. Evo Devo has . . . provided a critical missing piece of the Modern Synthesis—embryology—and integrated it with molecular genetics and traditional elements such as paleontology. (p. 283)

As I've emphasized here, one important component of Evo-Devo is heterochrony, and one especially important type of heterochrony for human evolution was neoteny. Human evolution was a mosaic pattern of developmental changes relative to our ancestors, some reflecting accelerations and others retardations. But it was the slowing of developmental patterns and the retention of infantile (or fetal) rates of growth or functioning into adulthood that, to a large extent, define our species. We are the intelligent and highly cooperative species we are today—able to coordinate actions across large numbers of people we know only slightly or not at all—because we increased our brain size and neural plasticity through the retention of fetal and juvenile rates of growth, extended the length of time it took to reach adulthood, and reduced our levels of reactive aggression, each of which contributed to our species' increased sociality and technological prowess. In the process, aspects of cognition characteristic of childhood, such as play and an optimistic view of one's abilities, served an adaptive role for youth at a particular time in development (Bjorklund, 1997). Many of these same neotenic features persist into adulthood and contribute to the (mostly) effective functioning of the adult *Homo sapiens*. To revisit Montagu one last time, many of the traits that make for a successful adult are remnants of childhood functioning, making "the spirit of the child . . . an adaptive trait of the greatest biological value" (Montagu, 1989, p. 95).

## References

Alexander, R. D. (1989). Evolution of the human psyche. In P. Mellers & C. Stringer (Eds.), *The human revolution: Behavioural and biological perspectives on the origins of modern humans* (pp. 455-513). Princeton University Press.

Arbiza, L., Gronau, I., Aksoy, B. A., Hubisz, M. J., Gulko, B., Keinan, A., & Siepel, A. (2013). Genome-wide inference of natural selection on human transcription factor binding sites. *Nature Genetics, 45*, 723-729.

Bandura, A. (1997). *Self-efficacy: The exercise of control.* Freeman.

Barker, J. E., Semenov, A. D., Michaelson, L., Provan, L. S., Snyder, H. R., & Munakata, Y. (2014). Less-structured time in children's daily lives predicts self-directed executive functioning. *Frontiers in Psychology, 5*, 1-16.

Beckett, C, Maughan, B., Rutter, M., Castle, J., Colvert, E., Groothues, C, Kreppner, J., Stevens, S., O-Connor, T. G., & Sonuga-Barke, E. J. S. (2006). Do the effects of early severe deprivation on cognition persist into early adolescence? Findings from the English and Romanian Adoptee Study. *Child Development, 77*, 696-711.

Betcher, R. W. (1981). Intimate play and marital adaptation. *Psychiatry, 44*, 13-33.

Bick, J., Zeanah, C. H., Fox, N. A., & Nelson, C. A. (2018). Memory and executive function in 12-year-old children with a history of institutional rearing. *Child Development, 89*, 495-508.

Bjorklund, D. F. (1997). The role of immaturity in human development. *Psychological Bulletin, 122*, 153-169.

Bjorklund, D. F. (2007). *Why youth is not wasted on the young: Immaturity in human development.* Blackwell.

Bjorklund, D. F. (2015). Developing adaptations. *Developmental Review, 38,* 13-35.

Bjorklund, D. F. (2020). *How children invented humanity: The role of development in human evolution.* Oxford University Press.

Bjorklund, D. F., & Bering, J. M. (2003). Big brains, slow development, and social complexity: The developmental and evolutionary origins of social cognition. In M. Brüne, H. Ribbert, & W. Schiefenhövel (Eds.), *The social brain: Evolutionary aspects of development and pathology* (pp. 133-151). Wiley.

Bjorklund, D. F., Cormier, C., & Rosenberg, J. S. (2005). The evolution of theory of mind: Big brains, social complexity, and inhibition. In W. Schneider, R. Schumann-Hengsteler, & B. Sodian (Eds.), *Young children's cognitive development: Interrelationships among executive functioning, working memory, verbal ability and theory of mind* (pp. 147-174). Erlbaum.

Bjorklund, D. F., & Ellis, B. J. (2014). Children, childhood, and development in evolutionary perspective. *Developmental Review, 34,* 225-264.

Bjorklund, D. F., Gaultney, J. F., & Green, B. L. (1993). "I watch, therefore I can do": The development of meta-imitation over the preschool years and the advantage of optimism in one's imitative skills. In R. Pasnak & M. L. Howe (Eds.), *Emerging themes in cognitive development,* Vol. 1 (pp. 79-102). Springer-Verlag.

Bjorklund, D. F., Hernández Blasi, C., & Periss, V. (2010). Lorenz revisited: The adaptive nature of children's supernatural thinking. *Human Nature, 21*, 371-392.

Bjorklund, D. F., & Pellegrini, A. D. (2002). *The origins of human nature: Evolutionary developmental psychology.* American Psychological Association.

Bock, J., & Johnston, S. E. (2004). Play and subsistence ecology among the Okavango Delta Peoples of Botswana. *Human Nature, 15*, 63-81.

Bogin, B. (2001). *The growth of humanity.* Wiley-Liss.

Bogin, B. (1999). *Patterns of human growth* (2nd ed.). Cambridge University Press.

Bogin, B. (2006). Modern human life history: The evolution of human childhood and fertility. In K. Hawkes & R. R. Paine (Eds.), *The evolution of human life history* (pp. 197-230). Curry.

Bolk, L. (1926). On the problem of anthropogenesis. *Proc. Section Sciences Kon. Akad. Wetens. Amsterdam, 29*, 465-475.

Boulton, M. J., & Smith, P. K. (1990). Affective bias in children's perceptions of dominance relations. *Child Development, 61*, 221-229.

Bowlby, J. (1969). *Attachment and loss: Vol. 1: Attachment.* Hogarth.

Bufill, E., Agustí, J., & Blesa, R. (2011). Human neoteny revisited: The case of synaptic plasticity. *American Journal of Human Biology, 23,* 729-739.

Cairns, R. B., Gariepy, J-L., & Hood, K. E. (1990). Developmental microevolution and social behavior. *Psychological Review, 97,* 49-65.

Cárdenas, R. A., Harris, L. J., & Becker, M. W. (2013). Sex differences in visual attention toward infant faces. *Evolution and Human Behavior, 34,* 280–287.

Carlson, S. M., White, R. E., & Davis-Unger, A. C. (2014). Evidence for a relationship between executive function and pretense representation in preschool children. *Cognitive Development, 29,* 1-16.

Carroll S. B. (2005). *Endless forms most beautiful: The new science of Evo Devo.* Norton.

Cemore, J. J., & Herwig, J. E. (2005). Delay of gratification and make-believe play of preschoolers. *Journal of Research in Early Childhood Education, 19,* 251–266.

Chick, G., Yarnal, C., & Purrington, A. (2012). Play and mate preference: Testing the signal theory of adult playfulness. *American Journal of Play, 4,* 407-440.

Chugani, H. T., Phelps, M. E., & Mazziotta, J. C. (1987). Positron emission tomography study of human brain functional development. *Annals of Neurology, 22,* 487-497.

Clay, Z., & Tennie, C. (2018). Is overimitation a uniquely human Phenomenon? Insight from human children as compared to bonobos. *Child Development, 89,* 1535-1544.

Dennis, E. L., Jahanshad, N., McMahon, K. L., de Zubicaray, G. I., Martin, N. G., Hickie, I. B., Toga, A. W., Wright, M. J., & Thompson, P. M. (2013). Development of brain structural connectivity between ages 12 and 30: A 4-Tesladiffusion imaging study in 439 adolescents and adults. *NeuroImage, 64,* 671-684.

DeSilva, J. M. (2016). Brains, birth, bipedalism, and he mosaic evolution of the helpless infant. In W. R. Trevathan & K. R. Rosenberg (Eds.), *Costly and cute: Helpless infants and human evolution* (pp. 67-86). School for advanced Research Press.

Dunbar, R. I. M. (2003). The social brain: mind, language, and society in evolutionary perspective. *Annual Review of Anthropology, 32,* 163-181.

Elias, C. L., & Berk, L. E. (2002). Self-regulation in young children: Is there a role for executive function and pretense representation in preschool children. *Cognitive Development, 29,* 1-16.

Franklin, P., & Volk, A. A. (2018). A review of infants' and children's facial cues' influence on adults' perceptions and behaviors. *Evolutionary Behavioral Sciences, 12,* 296-321.

Franklin, P., Volk, A. A., & Wong, I. (2018). Are newborns' faces less appealing? *Evolution and Human Behavior, 39,* 269-276.

Garon, N., Bryson, S. E., & Smith, I. M. (2008). Executive function in preschoolers: A review using an integrative framework. *Psychological Bulletin, 134,* 31-60.

Geary, D. C. (1995). Reflections of evolution and culture in children's cognition: Implications for mathematical development and instruction. *American Psychologist, 50,* 24-37.

Geary, D. C. (2005). *The origin of mind: Evolution of brain, cognition, and general intelligence.* American Psychological Association.

Gellén, K., & Buttelmann, D. (2019). Rational imitation declines within the second year of life: Changes in the function of imitation. *Journal of Experimental Child Psychology, 185,* 148-163.

Giedd, J. N. (2015). Risky teen behavior is drive by an imbalance in brain development. *Scientific American, 312,* Issue 6, 33-37.

Giedd, J. N., Bluenthal, J., Jeffries, N. O., Castellanos, F. X., Lrj, H., Zijdenbos, A., PauAs, A., Evans, A. C, & Rapoport, J. L. (1999). Brain development during childhood and adolescence: A longitudinal MRI study. *Nature Neuroscience, 2,* 861-863.

Glocker, M. L., Langleben, D. D., Ruparel, K., Loughead, J. W., Valdez, J. N., Griffin, M.D., et al. (2009). Baby schema modulates the brain reward system in nulliparous women. *PNAS, 106,* 9115–9119.

Gould, S. J. (1977). *Ontogeny and phylogeny.* Harvard University Press.

Goyal, M. S., Hawrylycz, M., Millwre, J. A., Snyder, A. Z., & Raichle, M. E. (2014). Aerobic glycolysis in the human brain is associated with development and neotenous gene expression. *Cell Metabolism, 19,* 49-57.

Gray, P. (2016). Children's natural ways of educating themselves still works: Even for the three Rs. In D. C. Geary & D. B. Berch (Eds.). *Evolutionary perspectives on education and child development* (pp. 66-94). Springer.

Greve, W., & Thomsen, T. (2016). Evolutionary advantages of free play during childhood. *Evolutionary Psychology*, October-December, 1–9.

Greve, W., Thomsen, T., & Dehio, C. (2014). Does playing pay? The fitness-effect of free play during childhood. *Evolutionary Psychology, 12,* 434-447.

Griffin, D., & Buehler, R. (1999). Frequency, probability, and prediction: Easy solutions to cognitive illusions? *Cognitive Psychology, 38,* 48-78.

Groos, K. (1898/1975). *The play of animals.* Appleton.

Groves, C. P. (1989). *A theory of human and primate evolution.* Clarendon Press.

Gruber, T., Deschenaux, A., Frick, A., & Clément, F. (2019). Group membership influences more social identification than social learning or overimitation in children. *Child Development, 90,* 728-745.

Guitard, P., Ferland, F. & Dutil, É. (2005). Toward a better understanding of playfulness in adults. *OTJR: Occupation, Participation & Health, 25,* 9-22.

Hahn, A. C., & Perrett, D. I. (2014). Neural and behavioral responses to attractiveness in adult and infant faces. *Neuroscience and Behavioral Reviews, 46,* 591-603.

Hare, B. (2017). Survival of the friendliest: *Homo sapiens* evolved via selection for prosociality. *Annual Review Psychology, 68,* 155–186.

Hernández Blasi, C., & Bjorklund, D. F. (2003). Evolutionary developmental psychology: A new tool for better understanding human ontogeny. *Human Development, 46,* 259-281.

Hernández Blasi, C., & Bjorklund, D. F. (2018). Adolescents' sensitivity to children's supernatural thinking: A preparation for parenthood? *Psicothema, 30,* 201-206.

Hernández Blasi, C., Bjorklund, D. F., & Ruiz Soler, M. (2017). Children's supernatural thinking as a signaling behavior in early childhood, *British Journal of Psychology, 108,* 467–485.

Hernández Blasi, C., Bjorklund, D. F., Agut, S, Lozano, F., & Martínez, M. A. (July 2018). *Vocal cues as signaling behavior in early childhood.* 30th Annual Meeting of the Human Behavior and Evolution Society, Amsterdam, The Netherlands.

Hernández-Blasi, C., Bjorklund, D. F., & Ruiz Soler, M. (2015). Cognitive cues are more compelling than facial cues in determining adults' reactions towards young children. *Evolutionary Psychology, 13,* 511-530.

Hewlett, B. S., Berl, R. E. W., & Roulette, C. J. (2016). Teaching and overimitation among Aka hunter-gatherers. In H. Terashima, B. S. Hewlett (Eds.), *Social learning and innovation in contemporary hunter-gatherers, Replacement of Neanderthals by Modern Humans Series* (pp. 35-45). Springer.

Hoehl, S., Keupp, S., Schleihauf, H., McGuigan, N., Buttelmann, D., & Whiten, A. (2019). 'Overimitation:' A review and appraisal of a decade of research. *Developmental Review, 51,* 90-108.

Hood, B. (2014). *The domesticated brain.* Pelican.

Hrdy, S. B. (1999) *Mother nature: A history of mothers, infants and natural selection.* Pantheon.

Huizinga, J. (1950). *Homo ludens: A study of the play-element in culture.* Beacon Press.

Huttenlocher, P. R., & Dabholkar, A. S. (1997). Regional differences in synaptogenesis in human cerebral cortex. *Journal of Comparative Neurology, 387,* 167-178.

Joffe, T. H. (1997). Social pressures have selected for an extended juvenile period in primates. *Journal of Human Evolution, 32,* 593-605.

Keeley, L. H. (1996). *War before civilization: The myth of the peaceful savage.* Oxford University Press.

Konner, M. (2010). *The evolution of childhood: Relationships, emotions, mind.* Belknap Press.

Kringelbach, M. L., Stark, E. A., Alexander, C., Bornstein, M. H., & Stein, A. (2016). On cuteness: Unlocking the parental brain and beyond. *Trends in Cognitive Science, 20,* 545-558.

Lancy, D. (2015). *The anthropology of childhood* (2nd edition). Cambridge University Press.

Legare, C. H., & Nielsen, M. (2015). Imitation and innovation: The dual engines of cultural learning. *Trends in Cognitive Sciences, 19,* 688-699.

Leibenluft, E., Gobbini, M. I., Harrison, T., & Haxby, J. V. (2004). Mothers' neural activation in response to pictures of their children and other children. *Biological Psychiatry, 56,* 225–232.

Lew-Levy, S., Kissler, S. M., Boyette, A. H., Crittenden, A. N., Mabulla, I. A., & Hewlett, B. S. (2020). Who teaches children to forage? Exploring the primacy of child-to-child teaching among Hazda and BaYaka hunter-gatherers to Tanzania and Congo. *Evolution and Human Behavior, 41,* 12-22.

Lillard, A. S., Lerner, M. D., Hopkins, E. J., Dore, R. A., Smith, E. D., & Palmquist, C. M. (2013). The impact of pretend play on children's development: A review of the evidence. *Psychological Bulletin, 139,* 1-34.

Liu, X., Somel, M., Tang, L., Yan, Z., Jiang, X., Guo, S., Yuan, Y., He, L., Anna Oleksiak, A. Zhang, Y., Li, N., Hu, Y., Chen, W., Qiu, Z., Pääbo, S., & Khaitovich, P. (2012). Extension of cortical synaptic development distinguishes humans from chimpanzees and macaques. *Genome Research, 22,* 611-622.

Lockhart, K. L., Chang, B., & Tyler, S. (2002). Young children's belief about the stability of traits: Protective optimism. *Child Development, 73,* 1408–1430.

Lockhart, K. L., Goddu, M. K., & Keil, F. C. (2017). Overoptimism about future knowledge: Early arrogance? *Journal of Positive Psychology, 12,* 36-46.

Lockman, J. J. (2000). A perception-action perspective on tool use development. *Child Development, 71,* 137-144.

Lorenz, K. Z. (1943). Die angeboren Formen moglicher Erfahrung [The innate forms of possible experience]. *Zeitschrift fur Tierpsychologie, 5,* 233-409.

Lucion, M. K., Oliveira, V., Bizarro, L., Rahde Bischoff, Pelufo Silveria, P., & Kauer-Sant'Anna, M. (2017). Attentional bias toward infant faces—Review of the adaptive and clinical relevance. *International Journal of Psychology, 114,* 1-8.

Luna, B., Thulborn, K. R., Monoz, D. P., Merriam, E. P., Garver, K. E., Minshew, N. J., Keshavan, M. S., Genovese, C. R., Eddy, W. F., & Sweeney, J. A. (2001). Maturation of widely distributed brain function subserves cognitive development. *NeuroImage, 13,* 786-793.

Luo, L. Z., Li, H., & Lee, K. (2011). Are children's faces really more appealing than those of adults? Testing the baby schema hypothesis beyond infancy. *Journal of Experimental Child Psychology, 110,* 115–124.

Lyons, D. E., Young, A. G., & Keil, F. C. (2007). The hidden structure of overimitation. *PNAS, 104,* 19751-19756.

Martin, H., Breezley, P., Conway, E., & Kempe, H. (1974). The development of abused children: A review of the literature. *Advances in Pediatrics, 21,* 119-134.

McAuley, T., & White, D. A. (2011). A latent variables examination of processing speed, response inhibition, and working memory during typical development. *Journal of Experimental Child Psychology, 108,* 152-166.

McClean, C. Y., Reno, P. L., Pollen, A. A., Bassan, A. I., Capellini, T. D., Guenther, C., . . . Kingsley, D. M. (2011). Human-specific loss of regulatory DNA and the evolution of human-specific traits. *Nature, 471,* 216–219.

McGuigan, N., Makinson, J., & Whiten, A. (2011). From over-imitation to super-copying: Adults imitate causally irrelevant aspects of tool use with higher fidelity than young children. *British Journal of Psychology, 102,* 1–18.

McKinney, M. L., & McNamara, K. (1991). *Heterochrony: The evolution of ontogeny.* Plenum.

Merz, E. C., Harlé, K. M., Noble, K. G., & McCall, R. B. (2016). Executive function in previously institutionalized children. *Child Development Perspectives, 10,* 105-110.

Miller, D. J., Duka, T., Stimpson, C. D., Schapiro, S. J., Baze, W. B., McArthur, M. J., Fobbs, A. J., Sousa, A. M. M., Šestan, N., Wildman, D. E., Lipovich, L., Kuzawa, C. W., Hof, P. R., & Sherwood, C. C. (2012). Prolonged myelination in human neocortical evolution. *PNAS, 109,* 16480-16485.

Mills, C. M., & Keil, F. C. (2004). Knowing the limits of one's understanding: The development of an awareness of an illusion of explanatory depth. *Journal of Experimental Child Psychology, 87,* 1-32.

Mills, K. L., Goddings, A. L., Clasen, L. S., Giedd, J. N., & Blakemore, S. J. (2014). The developmental mismatch in structural brain maturation during adolescence. *Developmental Neuroscience, 36,* 147-160.

Mithen, S. (1996). *The prehistory of the mind: The cognitive origins of art, religion, and science.* Thames & Hudson.

Montagu, M. F. A. (1962). Time, morphology, and neoteny in the evolution of man. In M. F. A. Montagu (Ed.), *Culture and the evolution of man* (pp. 324-342). Oxford University Press.

Montagu, A. (1989). *Growing young* (2nd Ed.). Bergin & Garvey.

Nelson, C. A. Ill, Zeanah, C. H., Fox, N. A., Marshall, P. J., Smuke, A. T., & Guthrie, D. (2007). Cognitive recovery in socially deprived young children: The Bucharest Early Intervention Program. *Science, 318*, 1937-1940.

Nes, L. S., & Segerstrom, S. C. (2006). Dispositional optimism and coping: A meta-analytic review. *Personality and Social Psychology Review, 10*, 235–251.

Nielsen, M. (2012). Imitation, pretend play, and childhood: Essential elements in the evolution of human culture? *Journal of Comparative Psychology, 126*, 170-181.

Nielsen, M. (2018). The social glue of cumulative culture and ritual behavior. *Child Development Perspectives, 12*, 264-268.

Nitschke, J. B., Nelson, E. E., Rusch, B. D., Fox, A. S., Oakes, T. R., & Davidson, R. J. (2004). Orbitofrontal cortex tracks positive mood in mothers viewing pictures of their newborn infants. *Neuroimage, 21*,5 83–592.

Pellegrini, A. D. (2013). Object use in childhood: Development and possible functions. *Behaviour, 150*, 813–843.

Pellegrini, A. D., & Smith, P. K. (1998). Physical activity play: The nature and function of neglected aspect of play. *Child Development, 69*, 577-598.

Periss, V., Hernández Blasi, C., & Bjorklund, D. F. (2012). Cognitive "babyness": Developmental differences in the power of young children's supernatural thinking to influence positive and negative affect. *Developmental Psychology, 48*, 1203–1214.

Petanjek, Z., Judaš, M., Šimić, G., Roko Rašin, M., Uylings, H. B. M., Rakic, P., & Kostović, I. (2011). Extraordinary neoteny of synaptic spines in the human prefrontal cortex. *PNAS, 108*, 13281-13286.

Piaget, J. (1983). Piaget's theory. In P. Mussen (ed.), *Handbook of child psychology* (4th edition) (pp. 703-732). Vol. 1. Wiley.

Poirier, F. E., & Smith, E. O. (1974). Socializing functions of primate play. *American Zoologist, 14*, 275–287.

Portmann, A. (1990) *A zoologist looks a humankind.* (Judith Schaefer, Trans.). Columbia University Press. (Originally published in 1944)

Prabhakar, S., Noonan, J. P., Pääbo, S., & Rubin, E. M. (2006). Accelerated evolution of conserved noncoding sequences in humans. *Science, 314,* 786.

Proverbio, A. M., Riva, F., Zani, A., & Martin, E. (2011). Is it a baby? Perceived age affects brain processing of faces differently in women and men. *Journal of Cognitive Neuroscience, 23*, 3197–3208.

Proyer, R. (2011). A multidisciplinary perspective on adult play and playfulness. *International Journal of Play, 6*, 241-243.

Raff, R. A. (1996). *The shape of life: Genes, development, and the evolution of animal form.* Chicago, IL: University of Chicago Press.

Rigo, P., Kim, P., Esposito, G., Putnick, D. L., Venuti, P., & Bornstein, M. H. (2019). Specific maternal brain responses to their own child's face: An fMRI meta-analysis. *Developmental Review, 51*, 58-69.

Rozzi, F. V. (2018). Reproduction on the Baka pygmies and drop in their fertility with the arrival of alcohol. *PNAS, 115*, E6126-E134.

Rutter, M., Beckett, C. Castle, J., Colvert, E., Kreppner, J., Mehta, M., et al. (2007). Effects of profound early institutional deprivation: An overview of findings from a UK longitudinal study of Romanian adoptee. *European Journal of Developmental Psychology, 4*, 332-350.

Scheier, M. F., Matthews, K. A., Owens, J. F., Magovern, G. J., Lefebvre, R., Abbott, R. C., & Carver, C. S. (1989). Dispositional optimism and recovery from coronary artery bypass surgery: The beneficial effects of optimism on physical and psychological well-being. *Journal of Personality and Social Psychology, 57*, 1024–1040.

Schneider, W. (1985). Developmental trends in the metamemory-memory behavior relationship: An integrative review. In D. L. Forrest-Pressley, G. E. MacKinnon, & T. G. Waller (Eds.), *Cognition, metacognition, and human performance, Vol. 1* (pp. 57-109). Academic Press.

Schneider, W. (1998). Performance prediction in young children: Effects of skill, metacognition and wishful thinking. *Developmental Science, 1,* 291-197.

Seligman, M. E. P. (1991). *Learned optimism: How to change your mind and your life* (1st edition). Free Press.

Senese, V. P., De Falco, S., Bornstein, M. H., Caria, A., Buffolino, S., & Venutti. P. (2013). Human infant faces provoke implicit positive affective responses in parents and non-parents alike. *PLoS ONE, 8,* e80379.

Shepperd, J. A., Klein, W. M. P., Waters, E. A., & Weinstein, N. D. (2013). Taking stock of unrealistic optimism. *Perspectives on Psychological Science, 8,* 395-411.

Sheppard, J. A., Ouellette, J, A., & Fernandez, J. K. (1996). Abandoning unrealistic optimism: Performance estimates and the temporal proximity of self-relevant feedback. *Journal of Personality and Social Psychology, 70,* 844-855.

Shin, H.-E., Bjorklund, D. F., & Beck, E. F. (2007). The adaptive nature of children's overestimation in a strategic memory task. *Cognitive Development, 22,* 197-212.

Smith, P. K. (1982). Does play matter? Functional and evolutionary aspects of animal and human play. *Behavioral and Brain Sciences, 5,* 139-184.

Snyder, C. R. (1994). *The psychology of hope: You can get there from here.* Free Press.

Somel, M., Franz, H., Yan, Z., Lorenc, A., Guo, S., et al. (2009). Transcriptional neoteny in the human brain. *PNAS, 106,* 5743–5748.

Spinath, B., & Spinath, F. M. (2005). Development of self-perceived ability in elementary school: The role of parents' perceptions, teacher evaluations, and intelligence. *Cognitive Development, 20,* 190-204.

Sprengelmeyer, R., Perrett, D. I., Fagan, E. C., Cornwell, R. E., Lobmaier, J. S., Sprengelmeyer, A., et al. (2009). The cutest little baby face: A hormonal link to sensitivity to cuteness in infant faces. *Psychological Science, 20,* 149–154.

Stipek, D. (1981). Children's perceptions of their own and their classmates' ability. *Journal of Experimental Child Psychology, 73,* 404-410.

Stipek, D. (1984). Young children's performance expectations: Logical analysis or wishful thinking? In J. G. Nicholls (Ed.), *Advances in motivation and achievement: Vol. 3. The development of achievement motivation.* JAI.

Taylor, S. E., Lerner, J. S., Sherman, D. K., Sage, R. M., & McDowell, N. K. (2003). Are self-enhancing cognitions associated with healthy or unhealthy biological profiles? *Journal of Personality and Social Psychology, 85,* 605–615.

Tomasello, M., Kruger, A. C., & Ratner, H. H. (1993). Cultural learning. *Behavioral and Brain Sciences, 16,* 495-511.

Trevathan, W. R., & Rosenberg, K. R. (2016). Human evolution and the helpless infant. In W. R. Trevathan & K. R. Rosenberg (Eds.), *Costly and cute: Helpless infants and human evolution* (pp. 1-28). School for advanced Research Press.

Trut, L. (1999). Early canid domestication: The Farm-Fox Experiment. *American Scientist, 87*(2): 160.

Trut, L., Oskina, I., & Kharlamova, A. (2009) Animal evolution during domestication: The domesticated fox as a model. *BioEssays, 31,* 349-360.

Van Fleet, M., & Feeney, B. C. (2015). Play behavior and playfulness in adulthood. *Social Personality Psychology Compass, 9,* 630-643.

Vanderbleek, L., Robinson, E. H., Casado-Kehoe, M. & Young, M. E. (2011). The relationship between play and couple satisfaction and stability. *The Family Journal, 19,* 13-139.

Volk, A. A., Lukjanczuk, J. L., & Quinsey, V. L. (2007). Perceptions of child facial cues as a function of child age. *Evolutionary Psychology, 5,* 801–814.

Washburn, S. (1960). Tools and human evolution. *Scientific American, 203,* 3-15.

Watson-Jones, R. E., & Legare, C. H. (2016). The social functions of group rituals. *Current Directions in Psychological Science, 25,* 42-46.

West-Eberhard, M. J. (2003). *Developmental plasticity and evolution.* Oxford University Press.

Whiten, A. (2019). Conformity and over-imitation: An integrative review of variant forms of hyper-reliance on social learning. *Advances in the Study of Behavior, 51,* 31-75.

Witelson, S. F. (1987). Neurobiological aspects of language in children. *Child Development, 58,* 653-688.

Wrangham, R. W. (2018). Two types of aggression in human evolution. *PNAS, 115,* 245-253.

Wrangham, R. (2019). *Goodness paradox: The strange relationship between virtue and violence in human evolution.* Pantheon Books.

Yamamoto, R., Ariely, D., Chi, W., Langleben, D. D., & Elman, I. (2009). Gender differences in the motivational processing of babies are determined by their facial attractiveness. *PLoS ONE, 4.*

Yeats, K. O., & Taylor, G. H. (2005). Neurobehavioral outcomes of mild head injury in children and adolescents. *Pediatric Rehabilitation, 8,* 5-16.

Yussen, S., & Levy, V. (1975). Developmental changes in predicting one's own span of short-term memory. *Journal of Experimental Child Psychology, 19,* 502-508.

Zebrowitz, L.A., Kendall-Tackett, K., & Fafel, J. (1991). The impact of children's facial maturity on parental expectations and punishments. *Journal of Experimental Child Psychology, 52,* 221-238.

Zell, E., Strickhouser, J. E., Sedikides, C., & Alicke, M. D. (2020). The better-than-average effect in comparative self-evaluation: A comprehensive review and meta-analysis. *Psychological Bulletin, 146,* 118-149.

# Chapter II.
## The Inner Child in Jungian Analytic Frameworks
### Juliet Rohde-Brown

The main purpose of this chapter is to explore, from a Jungian/post-Jungian, or analytic, perspective, how the motif of the child follows individuals through time and how it benefits psychological health both to include and to transcend actual childhood experience (inner child) and thus expand into the lived experience of the symbolic or archetypal child motif (divine child). An abundance of literature, particularly from the traditional and contemporary schools of psychoanalysis, has been published on the emotional wounds of childhood and their implications for psychological development. Although first developed by Sigmund Freud, outbranches of psychoanalysis continue to expand to this day. Initially notable was the analytic approach developed by Carl Jung, which has been furthered in the current post-Jungian context. Both Freud and Jung promoted the idea of multiple aspects of the self that are experienced either consciously or outside of conscious awareness. These views have influenced a variety of psychological approaches, such that it has now become commonplace, even among lay people, to speak of "parts" or different "selves" within, including the child self or inner child (Mair, 1977; Schwartz, 1997). A major goal of psychotherapy is to become aware of and integrate these often unconscious, socially constructed aspects of the self.

Rather than providing an exhaustive overview of theories of personality and treatment approaches to inner child processes, even if limited to one overriding tradition such as psychoanalysis with its abundant theories and treatment approaches, this chapter presents a distinctly analytic exploration of the symbolic child or, in Jungian terms, the divine child or archetypal child within. Accepting the premise that unconscious emotional experiences related to the 'child within' play a major role in either harmful or generative attitudes toward self and others, I first set the theoretical frame by comparing and contrasting the two theorist/practitioners, Freud and Jung, who initiated the inquiry into unconscious processes in psychological development. The rationale for choosing the more transpersonal route of Jung and the post-Jungians' explorations of inner-child processes and manifestations is included. I then provide a brief introduction to popular approaches, developed mostly in the 1970s, of working with the concept of multiple selves in psychotherapy. These selves are distinguished by bringing voice to internalized affective outcomes of socially constructed and family-of-origin influences on the inner 'actual' child of one's past. While accepting that it is now common in psychotherapy to explore how these influences from childhood impact one's psychological state and behavior, I instead pivot into a consideration of imaginal/symbolic or "divine child" archetypal considerations. For readers not versed in psychological traditions or terminology, especially regarding Jungian or post-Jungian frameworks, some basic terms and concepts associated with the child motif are provided. I briefly explore the child in the contexts of culture and society before venturing further into Jungian conceptualizations of the child motif as a symbol beckoning for wholeness, as a theme of personality integration, and
within the dynamics of the therapeutic relationship. A discussion of current trends in understanding the field of consciousness furthers the notion that the divine child, as an emergent phenomenon, functions as a process rather than an objective or ontological fact, paralleling what is often referred to in Buddhism as 'beginner's mind' (Hogenson, 2004; Suzuki, 1973). The inner child continues to be a prevalent symbol in our individual lives and in the collective psyche. This chapter bridges several pieces of the analytic puzzle to expand an understanding about creative avenues in Jungian psychotherapy that embrace the elusive construct of the child within.

## Theoretical Frame

In the 20th century, the advent of Freudian psychoanalysis and subsequent branching modalities gave rise to consideration of the actual child's role and function within family and society, conceptualizations of life stages, and the psychological health of the child and its impact on adult development. Freud introduced ideas about psychosexual stages of personality development with a heavy emphasis on how early childhood experiences influence adult personality function. He seriously considered and processed images from his patient's dreams using a technique he termed *free association* (1922/1966). His psychological conceptualizations included the Oedipus myth and other myths, although his focus was predominantly confined to the personal unconscious and particular family-of-origin contexts, with implications for the way in which personality development and psychotherapeutic processes transpired. With Freud's (1915/1957) introduction of concepts such as transference and countertransference, reenactments of parent–child relationships could conceivably be recognized in the therapeutic encounter, expanding ways to analyze functionality based on early childhood relationships.

Augmenting Freud's research in psychoanalysis, a variety of 20th-century and contemporary theorists include assertions regarding stages of psychosocial and ego development in the structure of the personality and the capacity for social engagement across the lifespan (Erikson, 1950) and the impact of birth order placement on personality development (Adler, 1969). Social psychoanalytic perspectives on personality development (Fromm, 1941; Horney, 1950) were put forth as were object relations theories regarding early attachment and the resulting relational patterns in adulthood as well as self psychology (Ainsworth et al, 1978; Winnicott, 1960; Aron, 2006; Kohut, 1977). Later developments included conceptualizations of the "imaginal order" and the impact of language acquisition and ideals of selfhood on psychological development (Lacan, 1956/1968) as well as phenomenological and narrative approaches within psychoanalysis (Atwood & Stolorow, 1984). Studies in affect regulation and neurobiology spurred some interest in field theory as well (Schore, 1994; Katz, 2018). This review sets the historical and ideological context for distinguishing between Freud's and Jung's contributions to a framework within which to consider the concept of the inner child.

Freud proposed that the structure of the personality was comprised of the id, ego, and superego, often compared to the wild horse, the rider, and the one who takes the reins. The amount of energy confined to each of these components was thought to determine levels of chaos, containment, or rigidity in the personality, and an array of psychological defenses were proposed regarding how someone might attempt to subdue anxiety related to thwarted instinctual drives. The premise of much subsequent research is that disruptions in one's early life prevent the development of ego strength and emotional integration into mature and engaging adulthood and the capacity for intimacy, thereby keeping an individual or society at a childish or egoic center of gravity. Regression and repression were proposed to be two among many psychological defenses that, when excessive, would thwart healthy movement from childhood into adulthood, resulting in an individual becoming stuck at an emotional level equivalent to the place in childhood when development was obstructed or becoming vulnerable to regressive tendencies as a defense in emotionally stressful situations (Erikson, 1950; Freud, 1915/1957).

Jung did not disagree with some of these notions and, in fact, was inspired by many of Freud's concepts and therapeutic applications, which also nurtured Jung's burgeoning interest in mythology (Hogenson, 2004). However, Jung came to view Freud's model as reductionistic and narrowly centered on the causal and biological.

He was moved to describe libido as involving more than personal psychosexual stage confinements and broadening into teleological and deeper structural and functional collective phenomena (Corbett, 2018). This major area of disagreement resulted in Jung and Freud parting ways. As Jung ventured off into his expanded vision of psychological life, he proposed that causal definitions of emotional development based on the personal past of an individual were incomplete or, as some would say, paralyzed by "intrapsychic determinism" (Schneider, 2003, p. 150). He instead asserted that all humans share a collective unconscious in which the entire history of life is symbolically and intersubjectively present, namely in archetypal motifs that show up in dreams and complexes (Jung, 1951/1969a).

Jung, mentored by Eugen Bleuler at the Burghölzli Hospital in Zurich, the site of his initial psychiatric work, was drawn to both phenomenological and scientific inquiry. Bleuler assigned him projects such as assessing patients with the Word Association Test developed by psychologist Wilhelm Wundt (1912/2013). Jung added physiological measures to the test to augment the data he was gathering. In this test, people were given a word prompt and asked to say the first word that came to mind; their responses were timed. Jung's (1937/1973) data demonstrated some significant correlations; for instance, he found that mothers and daughters tended to respond to the prompt with the same word response and to do so almost instantaneously. During this time, Jung was also influenced by others, such as French psychologist Pierre Janet, who helped pioneer the concept of dissociation and advocated for the idea of "partial personalities" in the psyche (Hogenson, 2004).

While Jung was living among and working with psychotic patients at the Burghölzli Hospital, listening to these patients' communications began to deepen his perspective about the dynamic and patterned nature of the shared human psyche. A particular schizophrenic man repeatedly spoke about a sun god in the sky with a phallus facing north who caused the wind to blow. At first, Jung dismissed the man's words as simply psychotic disturbances, but he came to realize that, somehow, this patient's psyche was expressing exactly what devotees of the Mithras cult in ancient Rome had believed, suggesting a collective element not confined to current affairs or individual fantasy. It seemed to him highly unlikely that the patient would have had concrete access to the myth, having been confined to psychiatric institutions for much of his adult life, contemporaneously with the myth's initial translation. Jung increasingly trusted what emerged from the unconscious, and taking the images seriously, viewed this patient's visions as dynamic in their own right even if they were not directly connected to the individual's personal history.

Jung (1966) was influenced by philosophical traditions and even referred to his therapeutic style as phenomenological. Though he honored Freud for introducing the exploration and analysis of dreams and free association as the core foundation of psychotherapy, Jung stressed that rather than jumping from one image and association to another, patients should be encouraged to stay for some time with associations to a particular image for its own sake, for what it wished to communicate. He referred to his practice of inquiring into the image with questions and noting responses and associations as "amplification" in the process of "active imagination" (1954/1969, p. 205). Jung (1952/1968) asserted that a dream or even waking image or symbol was to be explored from all angles—personal, collective, mythological—and in relation to world cultures and spiritual traditions as well as linguistic and alchemical aspects. In addition, with his later interactions with the physicist Wolfgang Pauli, it appears that Jung was on the brink of finding more accurate language to describe his views (Atmanspacher & Fuchs, 2014). It follows that he would likely have advocated for the notion of emergent phenomenon discussed in current quantum physics and philosophical frameworks (Cambray, 2009; Hogenson, 2004). It is due to this intriguing parallel between Jungian and post-Jungian conceptualizations and the advent of emergence frameworks that I find the focus on inner child phenomena most compelling. Notably, both psychanalysis and Jungian/post-Jungian approaches to psychotherapy currently embrace field theory conceptualizations, where "it is the unconscious process and fantasies of the field that are the specific objects of interest in a therapeutic process, rather than those of the analysand understood as a separate individual" (Katz, 2018, p. 149).

Considering the notion of multiple selves within the personal unconscious related to one's past childhood offers an intriguing jumping-off point before moving into Jungian and post-Jungian concepts and the idea of the child within as an archetypal potential and aspect of the collective unconscious. Exploring the child within initially from the framework of multiples selves brings the image alive conceptually.

## Multiple Selves

Although I am focusing on Jungian conceptualizations related to the 'child within,' briefly pivoting into popular notions of the construct of multiple selves within other traditions offers a valuable basis for then making distinctions between adult experiences of the actual or "empirical" child of one's past and the subtle child experienced though liminal processes in an adult (Hancock, 2009, p. 129).

Eric Berne's theory of a multiplicity of selves has been a useful and popular approach to exploring the internalized child self. Borrowing from the Freudian concepts of id, ego, and superego, Berne linked them with child, adult, and parent aspects within ourselves, often in conflict with one another. His theory made an early impact on both professionals and lay people, largely because of his successful book, *Games People Play* (1969) and his transactional analysis approach. In modalities that bring to life a multiplicity of selves within a client, the therapist will often guide the client to speak, move, and interact from a particular self and then dialogue with other selves or parts. In group setting, depending on the approach used, participants may choose other individuals to enact a part of themselves such as the child or a family member. In each of these modalities, the idea is to facilitate full expression of all parts of the self within the therapeutic container, leading to amplifying and witnessing them, accepting and relating to them, and ultimately integrating them.

Berne was not alone in resonating with and proposing the concept of multiple selves. Psychologists Hal and Sidra Stone (1998), over decades, developed, practiced, and taught Voice Dialogue for relating with different parts of oneself. Similar processes in psychoanalysis involving sand play and sand tray (Kalff, 2020) and other projective techniques such as House-Tree-Person drawings (Buck, 1966) have been utilized in therapy to explore where and how the child self is experienced and where unresolved trauma or interpersonal wounding may have had an impact on a patient's emotional, relational, and perceptual field. Psychiatrist Roberto Assagioli's (2007) introduction of psychosynthesis in the 1970s and certainly the Gestalt empty chair approach (Polster & Polster, 1974) are other examples of bringing to life different parts of the self toward the goal of confronting, accepting, and integrating those aspects that may have been pushed away, internalized with shame, or projected onto others.

In applying these types of approaches in psychotherapy, however, the therapist must have the ability to attune to the readiness of an individual to be emotionally present to the profound vulnerability of the inner child self when it emerges, as it frequently carries deep interpersonal wounds from one's actual past. Miriam Dyak (1999), a trainer and facilitator of Voice Dialogue, emphasized that in bringing alive the various parts of oneself, it is crucial to consider that each has served a function and that some roles, such as the Protector, came into being due to feelings that may have been too overwhelming for the child to metabolize. If the therapist delves deeply too rapidly and without the solid ego strength to therapeutically hold the sense of helplessness and strong emotions that may emerge, they could actually harm someone. For this reason, trauma experts advise that therapists become finely attuned to and accepting of their own vulnerability and woundedness and only in the later phase of integrating their own various selves should they attempt to meet clients in that place (Dyak, 1999; Kalsched, 1996). Some therapists have used guided imagery as a gentle first step for clients to visit the image of themselves as a child, offering comfort and protection as a soft place to start a relationship with the wounded child self.

In weekend workshops that I have co-led, focusing on restorative justice in a men's correctional facility, we engaged "lifer" inmates in writing letters to their child selves. We were struck by the vulnerability that they showed as well as a kind of reparenting that could be initiated, thus engaging these dynamic aspects of themselves in new ways. Hearing the trauma stories that cut off access to their own child selves was extraordinarily moving. One man told how, as a child, he would bathe his infant brother in the kitchen sink and try to feed him with whatever he could find, as their mother was lost to addiction, and their father was absent. That experience and, later, entering a gang, encouraged by his mother, further split off his genuine feelings and stunted his ability to care for himself or acknowledge his harmful actions toward others. These inmates' stories often included profound marginalization within society from an early age and indicate important sociopolitical and sociocultural contexts with regard to feelings of safety as a child as well as accessing compassion for one's child self in adulthood. Creative avenues such as writing to one's younger self may be an entry into what may later deepen into expansions into the archetypal child motif and further integration, given the correct circumstances, such as a safe psychotherapeutic container.

With his introduction of the notion of "the community of self," clinical psychologist and psychotherapist Miller Mair (1977, p. 125) offered a coherent way of bridging personal construct theory (Kelly, 1955) with the notion of metaphor. Mair proposed that we enter a sort of healthy "make-believe" (p. 130) interaction with the "others" (p. 131) in our own personal community of selves and resolve difficulties through recognizing them and dialoguing with them. For instance, parts, or selves, that have been pushed away by shame or that are bitter and cruel may be better tolerated when other "friendly" parts can begin a relationship with them (p. 134). In the therapeutic model Mair proposed, communication is encouraged not only among the various selves but also between communities that are internalized, such as political organizations and so forth. He reached back toward Plato to support the notion of a community of selves and was likely inspired by similar imagery and ideas within Tibetan Buddhism, such as the Buddha families and Dakini deities, who are said to have both wisdom and obscured aspects amplified by elements of nature and acknowledged in meditative practices (Allione, 2018). Apparently actively involved in a Tibetan community for many years (Proctor, 2011), Mair (1977) emphasized how we are continuously constructing our realities in the process of becoming and indicated metaphor as a valuable avenue of exploration, yet he warned against becoming seduced, as it were, by thinking that we "really are communities of various kinds" (p. 149). Specifically, he said, "It is easy to reduce any metaphor to meaninglessness by pressing it too far or not far enough. It is very easy, too, to fall into the trap of reifying that which is metaphor" (p. 149).

Mair's (1977) caution is noteworthy; nevertheless, outside of psychotic literalization, taking seriously those parts of one's self as valid autonomous forces and engaging in the hard work of emotional integration is not to be ridiculed or dismissed, for oppressive, unwelcome, and unintegrated parts of ourselves can wreak havoc psychologically, socially, and even physically. Exploring parts of one's self each in their own right is crucial for psychological integration. For instance, the main principle of Richard Schwartz's (1997) Internal Family Systems (IFS) approach is that the family of characters in the psyche are not merely metaphorical but rather are real, living and feeling subtle beings within ourselves, and their voices must be taken seriously and respected. In this approach to psychotherapy, the therapist is thus advised to ask permission to speak to a particular "person" and begin a collaborative inquiry into needs, fears, and so forth, with further permission to invite other voices in for dialogue. Jungian analyst Donald Kalsched (1996) incorporates this object-relations kind of approach in his therapeutic work with trauma, expanding upon it with reference to archetypal defenses, mythological motifs, imaginal processes, and the transcendent function, terms which are discussed later in this chapter.

As one's initial encounter with the inner child develops and deepens, one may then begin to experience the essence of the child beyond its personal woundedness or confinements and discover the qualities of wholeness, divinity, and primordial universality of the child archetype identified by Jung (1951/1969b), which promote deep healing or, in other words, integration. I offer a statement by Jung (1951/1959), employing alchemical terms regarding the focused and finetuned work of integration:

> *Imaginatio* is the active evocation of (inner) images *secondum*
> *naturam*, an authentic feat of thought or ideation, which does not
> spin aimless and groundless fantasies "into the blue"—does not,
> that is to say, just play with its objects, but tries to grasp the inner
> facts and portray them in images true to their nature. This activity
> is an opus, a work. (p. 219)

It is with this respect for imagination that the significance of the archetypal child is explored in the next pages in terms of its contextuality and complexity that go beyond the personal, empirical child and into collective aspects as they intersect within the individual. First, some Jungian terms and concepts found in this chapter are defined.

## Main Jungian Terms and Concepts Relevant to the Child Within

In order to assist the reader who may not be familiar with psychological terms, especially those arising from Jungian theory, I offer the following definitions of the main concepts found in this chapter and indicate how they interrelate.

### Archetypes

In discussing archetypes, it takes a bit of a "leap of faith" to pause for a moment, away from dichotomies regarding "subjective imagination" and "objective reality," and suspend assumptions about known reality (Stenner & Zittoun, 2020, p. 241). The notion of the archetype suggests a nonlocal aspect, or what philosopher David Chalmers (1997) coined as the "hard problems" of consciousness (p. 9).

Jung (1951/1969a) distinguished archetypes from myths. Whereas myths have form and structure that can be traced back through time, archetypes are said to function as spontaneous and unconscious processes in the psyche. Archetypes emerge around a central image or motif. Among archetypal motifs identified by Jung is that of the shadow, comprised of aspects of oneself often experienced as unacceptable and aversive and thus avoided. The *Self* (capital intended) is another of Jung's proposed archetypes, representing the whole of the psyche, as distinct from the *self*, which is narrowed to one's personal history, ego, and identity. The mandala symbol often seen in Jungian images is commonly associated with the Self. One is said to be going through an individuation process by integrating opposing forces within and coming closer to a realization or awareness of that which was always present, the larger encompassing transpersonal Self. Other archetypes not elaborated here are the anima and animus, the hero, wise old man and woman, and so on. They interact with each other in a manner similar to that of the multiple representational or internalized selves proposed by Mair

(1977). Archetypes, however, are not defined as representational categories but rather have a subtle, emergent, and potential nature. I mention the shadow archetype because its integration into the whole of the personality may be cultivated or edged along by the divine child archetype, which Jung (1951/1969b) identified as a primordial force that serves to reconcile opposites within oneself.

I refer the reader to an excellent chapter on archetypes, written by Jungian analyst George Hogenson (2004). He teased out distinctions in the way Jung may have understood archetypes, reflecting on how Jung was influenced by Goethe's philosophical explanation of the intuitive, "dynamic," and "process" or "holistic" nature of archetypes, in contrast and dialogue with Richard Owen's focus on a "structural" and more literal or biological model (p. 44). Of note is that even today, as Jungian theorists review Jung's words and surmise that he was struggling to find a middle way between the form and non-form aspects of the archetype, no concrete definition of the archetype has been provided, as it seems impossible to lock down or reduce it into operational terms. Instead, some see the archetype functioning more as a potential or subtle process, illusive and elusive, outside of scientific realism, yet profoundly meaningful in semiotic ways (Hogenson, 2004).

Useful for an understanding of archetypes' relationship to the intersubjective field is the way in which Jungian analyst Joseph Cambray (2009), clinical psychologist Terry Marks-Tarlow (2008), and others offer the concept of Indra's Jeweled Net, a hologram-like symbol emerging from both Buddhist and Hindu philosophy and representing the interdependent nature of existence. Each jewel in the net is said to be reflective of the other jewels in a paradox of both containment and infinity. The symbol serves as a fractal metaphor for a wholeness that is *not* the sum of its parts, as each jewel is whole in itself, yet infinitely connected and dependent on all the other jewels. Indra's Net is an esoteric concept, like the archetype, a rich metaphor that enlivens symbolic and intersubjective understanding. The ability to recognize tension in archetypal motifs objectively and to live symbolically leads to what Cambray (2009) would refer to as a more developmentally complex center of gravity, with impacts even on a biological level. The psychological centers of gravity shift in the intersubjective field, especially during important and "liminal" times of change, and when "worlds collide, unravel, blur, or are ruptured" (Stenner & Sittoun, 2020, p. 241). Social structures are impacted by archetypal motifs on a collective level as well (Rowland, 2020).

With regard to the archetypal child, the phenomenological and transpersonal basis of Jungian-oriented psychology indicates that something resides deeper in the psyche than the experiences of and inner representations of the "real" child— something of a spiritual nature calling for the animation of authenticity, meaning, and "awe" (Wesley, 2019; Schneider, 2015, p. 73). For now, a discussion of the Jungian concept of complexes serves to inform an understanding of the archetype's role in psychological functioning, of which the child essence is a crucial part.

**Complexes**

In Jungian thought, psychological complexes are conceptualized as arising out of interpersonal wounding from childhood and the resulting emotional reactions and patterns that are triggered by reminders of those wounds, most often unconsciously (Stein, 1998). A metaphor often used to describe the relationship of archetypes to complexes is that of the nucleus of a cell. Imagine the center of the cell as holding the dynamic energy of a particular archetypal image. Surrounding that central nucleus, or archetype, are dendrites, a cluster of feelings made up of emotions and associations from one's empirical past (personal unconscious) connected to the central archetypal motif (collective unconscious), such that the central image and its accompanying emotions constitute a cluster referred to as a complex (Stein, 1998, p. 53). Emotions are thus attached, as it were, like glue to certain symbols or images that carry not only the anxieties and reactions to one's personal history but also the powerful energy of age-old subtle systems within the collective psychic field. When, for protective purposes, the psyche's defense is to split off feelings of vulnerability, anger, and grief attached to interpersonal wounds, the feelings become unconscious, and one may have a tendency to dissociate and attach to the powerful image of the central core (archetype) as an imaginal life saver. The danger here is depending too much on the imaginal world for solace. This attachment may move one into fantasy and delusion, which takes the place of authentic human intimacy and relationship as well as relationship to the self. In psychoanalytic terms, one must have a healthy ego in order to recognize, integrate, and benefit from the richness of the imaginal as opposed to being captive to it. An apt image offered by Kalshed (2013) is that of an Inuit mask with one eye open and the other eye closed, indicating the capacity to function in the everyday external world of interpersonal relationships, work, and play and also maintain a deep relationship with the inner, introverted, spiritual, imaginal world in a regulated, healthy way, where choice rather than domination or capture takes over.

Because archetypes have both a personal and a collective vitality and meaning, the power of a complex when it overtakes causes a kind of knee-jerk emotional and behavioral reaction rather than a paused, regulated, and mindful response. In Jungian terms, when the emotional reaction is triggered, it is said to be *constellating* a complex. One could, for instance, have feelings about a personal parent while simultaneously being influenced emotionally by a larger-than-life inner image of a God-like, all-powerful parent of mythological proportions. Both are said to exist in the psyche of a particular individual; however, the archetypal parent is shared among all members of the human species, and it carries the psychic weight of idealized beneficence, care, and protection as well as monstrous abuse, devourment, and power. In healthy functioning, these larger-than-life influences in the psyche are integrated, brought down to earth in functional, realistic relationship to one's life, and the archetypal symbol is not unconsciously projected onto others or crippling one with internal intensity. In a similar vein, attached to one's personal memories of the child who once was are emotions that one carries with this remnant of the inner child, while at the same time, every member of the human species carries the symbolic, archetypal, divine child that functions on implicit or intuitive levels within the psyche. To the extent that one's real child self was robbed of its full expression by, perhaps, a narcissistic, neglectful, or overcontrolling parent, one may experience triggers that evoke shame or feelings of inferiority or helplessness, resulting in compensatory behavior that may show up, but not be limited to grandiosity or impulsivity. An image of invincibility, wisdom, energy, beauty, charm, and innocence that one carries within can cause one to respond unconsciously to these emotional triggers by acting out in unbounded ways associated with childishness, which may include tantrum-like behavior or even unconsciously seductive behavior. Jungian analyst Marie-Louise von Franz (2000) and others have spoken, for instance, about the seductive behavior of the *puer aeternus* and *puella* ("eternal boy" and "girl") archetypes in relation to an adult who continues to function at the emotional level of burgeoning adolescence, not wanting to be confined by commitment or any kind of restriction on new experiences, romances, and adventures.

What is it that, with the aid of psychotherapy, moves integration along and facilitates the unraveling of the grasping nature of complexes, allowing the child within, with full and authentic feeling, to be freed and integrated as opposed to feeding the defended and false self? In Jungian terms, the transcendent function is conceptualized as the force that moves the integration of the personality toward wholeness (Jung, 1958/1969).

In his book, *Synchronicity: Nature and Psyche in an Integrated Universe*, Cambray (2009) reflected on the capacity for empathy and the construct of "symmetry breaking" (p. 62) in the intersubjective field. He astutely suggested that "learning to identify and engage with moments of complexity as they constellate would give increased flexibility to clinicians" (p. 109), as they would recognize where people push away from developmental shifts as "defenses against emergent processes" (p. 109). Discussing emergent processes in the context of what Jung referred to as the *psychoid realm*, Cambray offered a definition of *psychoid* that may correlate with the divine child's subtle essence: "the capacity or propensity for organization that emerged out of the hypothesized singularity (from which came the Big Bang), the origin point of our universe" (pp. 108–109). This concept is in line with Jung's (1951/1959) reference to the divine child archetype as "preconscious and . . . post-conscious" (p. 178) and "begotten . . . out of living Nature herself" (p. 170). Regarding archetypes, complexes, and transcendent or religious functions in the psyche, we are thus required to suspend assumptions around fixed notions of reality and enter a constructive position, trying on the notion of co-created worlds that function as symbolic and emergent phenomena within all systems. This venture invites the reader to play a bit with the unknown in the context of the essential nature of the child within.

With this initial understanding of Jungian concepts attached to archetypes and complexes, a brief explication of what it means to be a 'concrete' child is now offered, as well as a brief discussion of cultural and societal constructs of inner child phenomena.

## Being a Child

Social, anthropological, and psychological literature has discerned distinct shifts in the history of the Western World regarding the role and perception of the actual or 'real' child. There were times, for instance, when children labored alongside adults. Child kings and queens have made major decisions affecting entire societies. Child marriages took place in Western societies until recently and continue to occur in certain cultures around the globe. This practice implies the acceptance of a child on parallel terms to an adult and an expectation to behave in society accordingly. In our current Western constructs, many of these scenarios would be viewed as callous exploitation or abuse. Currently, the consensus is that children are to be protected, nurtured, and managed, and adolescence is conceived as a transitional phase, functioning as a time to prepare for adulthood. Notably, indigenous and religious communities throughout the various cultures of the world conduct ritualized rites of passage when a child is moving into adolescence, marking a distinction from childhood and a growing awareness of the nuances of the maturation process and responsibilities that accompany them.

Although anthropological and sociological contexts have provided much insight into how the cultures of the world have viewed children and development, in the 20th century, the advent of Freudian psychoanalysis and subsequent branching modalities gave rise to conceptualizations of life stages, with a focus on the psychological health of the child and its impact on adult development. Psychological theories focused largely on individual development within the family of origin, but in today's world, there is much greater emphasis on broader societal and multicultural contexts.

## Contextuality: The Child, Culture, and Society

It is crucial for therapists to cultivate awareness of and respect for the cultural and societal contexts of their clients. Kazuko Behrens (2004), a Japanese researcher now living in New York, has conducted extensive studies on early childhood attachment patterns and how they manifest in adults in psychoanalysis. In an intriguing paper, she distinguished behaviors resulting from insecure early attachment from those that are generally accepted as healthy. With a focus on childlike behavior, Behrens accented how cultural context is the first focus of exploration before turning to individualized appraisals, lest they be culturally biased. Exemplifying this approach, she discussed the concept of *amae*, a word whose root has to do with sweetness and the quality of acting like a sweet child. She described *amae* as a generally accepted way of acting in the Japanese culture, whereby, in certain situations, it is not perceived as inappropriate to act in a childlike manner in order to establish more closeness in relationships, to gain acceptance, or to ask for help, for instance. She noted, however, that when used excessively or in blatantly manipulative ways, this kind of behavior can cross the threshold of acceptance. It may also lead to misunderstandings in sexually ambiguous situations and accentuate hierarchical patterns in other contexts. In general, though, Japanese people's engagement in *amae* supports friendly social interaction.

Behrens's (2004) research alerts us to be aware of diversity, nuances, cultural distinctions and the danger of relying on Eurocentric biases and assumptions regarding attitudes about the value or devaluing of childlikeness in adults. We cannot speak of human development or the inner child construct in the 21st century and "lived" or "felt" experience without adopting a multicultural, transdisciplinary perspective.

Furthering cultural considerations, African American Jungian analyst and educator Fanny Brewster (2019) writes and speaks about the child motif in relation to slavery's legacy of child loss and the grief that continues to be held in the psyche and descendants' bodies generations later. Regarding "what the phantoms of enslaved mothers and their children present to us" (p. 91), Brewster asserted that this loss of the child, empirically and symbolically, is "a premise of archetypal grief. It becomes embodied because it is intergenerational and it is cultural" (p. 93).

Brewster (2019) reported that in the Beng tradition of West Africa, infants are believed to carry the souls of the ancestors and are thus treated as spiritual messengers, in a sense, of the experiences of those who have lived before. This belief indicates a "compatibility that addresses co-existence in death and life" (p. 95). In this way, a sense of a loss of liveliness may be conceived as current embodied trauma of the ancestral past. For instance, in a candid disclosure of her own experience as an African American woman, Brewster related, "It has taken many from each of my generational ancestral lineage to have those of us who live today, actually be alive today" (p. 83). She posited that these descendants' dreams thus combine the personal and archetypal in this relationship with the child within.

In a similar vein, Jungian analyst, storyteller, and curandera Clarissa Pinkola Estés (1992) spoke of the effects of trauma that leave one wishing for a new life and manifests in the psyche as the "spirit child" or "*la niña milagrosa*, a miracle child, who has the ability to hear the call, hear the far-off voice that says it is time to come back to oneself. The child is part of our medial nature" (p. 273). She discussed this mainly in the context of traumas that women have experienced in their lives and the loss of the feminine, feeling function in those who have become deadened to their own needs and feelings due to marginalization and oppression in families and larger social systems.

With all that is occurring in the world today, there is current focus on expanding the psychological context beyond the consulting room and into the sociopolitical realm (Brewster, 2019; Gherovici & Christian, 2019; Hoffman et al., 2015; Singer, 2008). Culture, ethnicity, gender, sexual orientation, systemic racism, and the effects of oppression and poverty versus power and privilege are now seriously included in conceptualizations about trauma and psychological health. This breadth of reference is also relevant as how the child within may be thwarted by marginalization and violence. Adversity in childhood may impact the capacity to trust or to feel safe. From the European social psychoanalytic perspective, physician and psychoanalyst

Wilhelm Reich (1933) and developmental psychologist and psychoanalyst Erik Erikson (1950) both wrote about the thwarting of the natural child's essence and vibrancy in the context of fascism. Psychoanalysts Erich Fromm (1941) and Karen Horney (1950) elaborated on social impacts on psychological development as well. Currently, Brewster (2019) along with clusters of psychoanalytic theorists and practitioners are bringing to the forefront a cultural and sociopolitical consciousness. In a chapter titled "Collective Trauma and Cultural Complexes," Jungian analysts Eli Weisstub and Esti Galili-Weisstub (2004) examined studies that gathered the dreams of children in places where there is political and/or religious unrest and violence. In addressing the material arising from these dreams, the authors found that cultural trauma has a substantial influence on the children's dreams. This finding indicates that a therapist should seek to discern whether a monstrous and attacking figure or element in a person's dream was an internalized parental figure from the client's particular abuse in childhood morphed into archetypal proportions or if it reflected cultural trauma and unrest, or both. An example of how cultural trauma enters the child's dream world was reported by Weisstub and Weisstub in regard to research they conducted with the Mehinaku, an Amazonian indigenous group, where "more than one-third of the dreamed assaults for both sexes were by Brazilian men," which was the case in waking life as well (p. 149). Indications of the child within gone awry in an adult's behavior, or what archetypal psychologist James Hillman (2007) referred to as the "monster" child (p. 99), appear in certain social contexts such as fascism. Harsh regimes, when trickling down into families intergenerationally, may rigidify the childhood emotional experience and counteract the development of healthy ego function, resulting in adults who function at immature and even sociopathic levels, much like the "non-ego of a child" (Roy, 2008, p. 70).

The child archetype follows us through time. Jung (1951/1969b) and others attribute this constancy largely to its being "a system functioning in the present whose purpose is to compensate or correct, in a meaningful manner, the inevitable one-sidedness and extravagance of the conscious mind" (p. 162). Many psychological approaches, for instance, are focused on rationality of thought, behavioral goals, and quantifiable behavioral outcomes rather than present-moment, phenomenological, imaginal, relational, feeling-toned, and somatic experience. Although day-to-day pragmatic functioning is obviously important, as a purpose for psychotherapy, it is incomplete in and of itself. Jungian and post-Jungian-oriented therapy, on the other hand, often inquires into the client's own, unique relationship to the archetype of the child within, in all of its paradoxical nature, holding that the rational and irrational are meant to be in relationship rather than in battle with each other, as are the personal and collective.

Sociopolitical and cultural contexts are paramount in understanding how both the personal inner child and divine child essence may be nurtured or thwarted. According to post-Jungian thought and in theories of complexity and emergence, just as nature has both destructive and productive elements, or opposite forces, so does the rest of living existence. It is how we relate to and what we do with these forces acting upon us and within us that makes the difference in psychological and societal health. Hillman (2007) referred to the "revolution of the child" in our world today as the emergence of that which has been "repressed" (p. 93), neglected, pushed away. He proposed that, rather than reinforce an egoic stance of attempting to parent the child within, both therapist and client must invite the child's "subjective misery" to be present and witnessed, as it is important to allow feelings of helplessness and to "bring the child back to abandonment" and grieve it before moving forward in psychotherapy. We may, then, instill a kind of remembrance and embodiment of the liveliness of the child through authentic feeling and "imaginative power" (p. 121). This is a never-ending process, not resulting in getting to some other place. We come to recognize this when we are abandoning the core of our aliveness, most usually through over-rationalization and rigid inner parenting. We cultivate awareness through psychotherapy and practices that condition us to face the child within directly and invite all its colors; as we do so, paradoxically, a certain lively containment may emerge as well.

## The Child Archetype as a Symbol of Wholeness

Jung (1951/1969b) viewed the child archetype as both a "preconscious and post-conscious" essence, meaning a blending of the "unconscious state of earliest childhood" and "anticipation by analogy of life after death" (p. 178). In his analysis, the archetype thus beckons us to "wholeness" or a "potential future" (p. 179), calling attention to aspects seeking recognition to facilitate advancements in the developmental and integrative process. The child motif shows up in dreams as an indication of how we may be functioning psychologically at any given time and where split-off aspects of psyche may be causing suffering. Jungian-oriented therapists who work with dreams have noticed that when adult clients come in with very difficult life transitions or challenges, the child will often manifest in their dreams as "abandoned" or "misunderstood" (Jung 1951/1969b, p. 180). These dreams are quite different than the dreams where the child clearly resembles their actual selves as children in their families-of-origin. There is an orphaned element in the experience of the numinous dream child, removing it from parentified forces and suggesting the emergence of a universal essence coming forth in the psyche to guide the person through a life transition. In these cases, nonhuman symbols also arise that amplify the child archetype, such as a golden egg or primal water, suggesting an essence that is more than human, sacred, and thus "divine" (Jung, 1951/1959, p. 36; Kerenyi, 1941/1949). Emphasizing the ambiguous and unpredictable qualities of symbols such as these and how they manifest in dreams in times of potential change, Jung (1951/1959) asserted that the divine child archetype has a "potential existence only" (p. 179) and thus lives in emergent and subtle processes.

Jungian analyst Deborah Wesley (2019) and others have echoed Jung's observation, contrasting the personal and particular dream images of recognizable childhood themes to child images that are "altogether strange and unknown" (p. 454). The personal childhood experiences appearing in dreams and the client's emotional responses are to be brought to conscious awareness and processed in psychotherapy; however, the numinosity of the archetypal child motif invites a deeply contemplative reflection and often inspires a sense of awe and possibility with its hints of major change in the works. Cambray and Jungian analyst Linda Carter (2006) captured this attitude regarding dream motifs and other archetypal phenomena by proclaiming that Jung's "synthetic approach . . . is not reducible to making the unconscious conscious." Rather, it involves finding "the means of engaging with unconscious processes that allow ongoing mutual influence (conscious and unconscious upon one another)" (p. 121). They posited that "at the edge of chaos and order," depth psychotherapy is conducted at "the locus for the origins of life itself" (p. 122).

If perceived as an essence, a quality that resists being locked down in rational terms, then one could say that the perennial child seeks to be known implicitly and may be urged along via the transcendent function, which is understood as an internal push toward wholeness, seeking to facilitate the unification of opposites (Jung, 1951/1959). This is not such an easy undertaking, as the archetype is both illusive and elusive, "a vessel which we can never empty and never fill" (Jung, 1951/1959, p. 179), yet this presence of the archetype and its beckoning forth toward transformation is also "intimately connected with the ego's object-relations and environmental provision" (Kalsched, 1996, p. 111). For this reason, it is helpful to have a skilled psychotherapist collaborate with the client in attending to the imagery that emerges from the psyche via dreams. Dreams are a valuable resource for starting the inquiry and deepening the question of one's relationship to the child within.

## Dream Imagery

### Experiencing Meaning in the Dream Imagery of the Archetypal Child

As mentioned above, clients often share primordial images of orphan birth as they are transitioning through difficult times. I offer an example of a dreamer who experienced being born from an egg in the depths of an ancient ocean. She expressed that she could feel the pressure at the top of her head with the gradual hatching of the egg and experienced shivering over her entire body as she was born in the depths of the ocean. As an amphibious and androgynous being, she was able to breathe underwater and discover other living beings welcoming her in a circle as she arrived at what she described as a rocky, white-sanded, shoreline. For me, this report of her dream imparts a visceral feeling of potentiality and unfolding as well as a sense of mystery. It also bears an uncanny resemblance to a myth from the Rig-Veda, accented in Greek mythology scholar, Karol Kerenyi's (1941/1949) chapter titled "The Primordial Child in Primordial Times." In waking life, this client had experienced the death of her domineering mother and a marriage within the past couple of years. She had begun to recognize and own a pattern of feeling terrified of making commitments as well as feelings of profound helplessness regarding her own autonomy. The latter was amplified by an actual Tyrolean traverse experience where she dangled helplessly and weak for long moments on a rope over a canyon without perceiving that she had the arm strength to get to the other side. This ropes course experience was a profoundly insightful moment for her, as she realized her pattern of wanting to be rescued like a small child would be. She translated this as not wanting to take responsibility for her choices or ownership of her power and capacities. The birth of the egg in the deep ancient ocean marked an emergence that she was no longer resisting, having cultivated the capacity to face her terror and helplessness and to be born in a different way.

Amplifying the witnessing of the birth of something new and out of the ordinary in the psyche, a Caucasian, middle-aged, female dreamer recounted this dream:

> *I am standing in a hut with dirt floor somewhere in an indigenous part of South America, like Peru or Guatemala. Several National Geographic-type researcher/photographers are standing with me in a semicircle. We watch in awe as a man, who looks somewhat feminine, too, like Jesus with shoulder-length golden-brown hair, is lying on the floor giving birth. He has a larger-than-life erect phallus, and just below his phallus is his open vulva and a healthy big baby is coming out. The man himself looks like he is amazed by the birthing, too, as he surrenders to the experience.*

In this dream, the dreamer is witness to the hermaphrodite (integration of opposites) birth of a new, healthy baby. A divine child essence is being witnessed, and the response of the dreamer in both the dream and waking state was one of awe and wonder along with a clear feeling of bodily invigoration, aliveness, and open-heartedness. At the time, the dreamer had been in therapy and paying attention to dreams for some time. She was in the painful process of coming to terms with having projected romantic fantasies on others in a kind of addiction to the numinous experience of infatuation. She had been feeling a sense of deadness, as she was in a phase of individuation where she could no longer project the numinous energy on another object of attraction. There was little libido remaining of that old pattern; however, she had not yet been able to recognize that her numinous attraction to union was actually a yearning to unite with an essential part of herself. The dream marked an important transitional time for her, as she was gaining back the vitality that she had sought in love objects and integrating this sense of aliveness, purpose, and interaction of opposites inside herself. This hermaphrodite birthing dream amplified an emergent process unfolding. The unusual and awe-inspiring image in the dream suggested that the divine child was coming back to serve her overall wholeness. The dream suggested that she was not resisting or defending against an emergent process within herself, that she was ready for bearing the pain of birthing a new chapter in her life and shifting some outlived patterns to further her personality integration, often referred to as the individuation process in Jungian therapy.

Having the dream and describing it is, however, not enough to foster the shift in the organization of her inner world. Many people have dreams such as these, particularly when they are going through transitional times such as getting a divorce, completing a dissertation, applying for a new job, moving, experiencing the onset of a serious medical diagnosis, losing a loved one, or facing an important interpersonal interaction. Simply reciting the dream content to the therapist or writing it down is only the beginning. Beyond that step, a valuable path is continuing engagement in the therapeutic relationship combined with facilitating growth or synthetization through somatically experiencing what is calling for attention and through active imagination, the practice of focused dialogue with unconscious aspects and images that manifest in fantasies, dreams, and creative means of expression through the arts (von Franz, 2016).

Von Franz (2016) described the process of active imagination as having a particular sequence that consists of emptying the busy-ness of the mind, allowing feelings and images to emerge, and making contact with and dialoguing with what has emerged (without flying off into free associating). Von Franz added that one must also take seriously the messages that are gathered from the active imagination process as well as commit to staying in relationship to these images on an ongoing basis, with curiosity, just as one would with a new friend. Even questions such as "Who are you? Who are we together?" may be asked. Other dream work practitioners such as Robert Bosnak (2009) invite the dreamer to enter the hypnogogic state and to speak in the present tense describing the feelings, sensations, and perceptual field from the point of view of different images within the dream in a process Bosnak refers to as "embodied imagination," bringing voice and even movement to experience. This is sometimes facilitated in group formats.

With these imaginal approaches, clients have the means to express feelings in the safety of the therapeutic relationship, where the therapist offers gentle challenging and attuned listening, mirroring, and responding and honoring what emerges in dreams, somatic experiences, and imagery. Cultural associations and mythic amplifications may take place as well. The safety of the therapeutic container is particularly important in the context of addressing interpersonal trauma that took place in childhood and the defenses that were built around keeping the inner child subdued and protected in the unconscious.

### The Role of the Dream in Confronting Childhood Trauma

Kalsched (1996, 2013) offers erudite descriptions of the processes by which early interpersonal injuries may cause a child to rely on dissociative avenues for self-care. He has demonstrated how these defense processes involve distinct imagery that serves the parallel purposes of attempting to protect the psyche of the child while also imprisoning one in one's inner world.

Kalsched (2013) described how, in some cases, childhood trauma can begin to crumble and split the personality, resulting in a "hellish pairing of infantilism with grandiosity—of dependent vulnerability on the one hand, and righteous, tyrannical rage (if the dependency is injured) on the other" (p. 110). Kalsched (1996) referred to the injury and splitting of the personality as a loss of "generative innocence" as one falls into a "malignant innocence" or "victim-perpetrator dynamic" (Bollas, as cited/quoted in Kalsched, 2013, p. 110). The way into shifting this split, along with following the narrative descriptions, is often through inquiring about what is occurring in the client's body, as the feelings braid into implicit memory systems and cannot be accessed through rational avenues. A therapist may ask the client, "What are you experiencing in your body right now as you tell me this? Where do you feel that in your body? Is there an image associated with this feeling?" The body is where the child we once were resides. The dreams and images that emerge will, with the compassionate and questioning presence of the therapist, blend the past with what is calling out for transformation and a different experience of embodiment, sometimes referred to as the child motif in "embodied subjectivity" (Jones, 2011, p. 91).

I often refer to the myth of Phaethon in attempting to describe the dysregulation and dissociation that occurs with interpersonal trauma when teaching students about the pervasiveness of disturbance across the body-mind-spirit system. There are a couple of versions of the myth, but the storyline goes as follows.

When Phaethon, who has not known his father, Helios (Sun God), first makes contact with him as he is emerging into young adulthood, he wishes to take the reins of Helios' sun chariot. Wanting to make up for all the lost years and please his son, Helios reluctantly agrees. Only a moment after taking the reins, Phaethon loses control of the horses and begins to fluctuate between shooting too far up into the sky and away from the sun, with the risk of freezing the earth, and dropping down so low as to potentially scorch the earth and cause it to burst into flames. When Zeus becomes aware of what is happening, he contemplates what must be done for the greater good, lest Phaethon destroy the entire planet and everyone on it with his inability to mediate the horses and chariot. He strikes Phaethon with lightning, causing him to fall to the depths of the river Eridanus, while the horses and chariot return to Helios' corral and seasoned management.

Phaeton's sisters witness his death and put him back together again to compassionately memorialize him. They then turn into poplar trees, the sap their tears, honoring the boy he once was, while being grateful for the renewed health of the world and what was learned along the way. His life, death, and memorial were held by the deep feeling and love of his sisters (Graves, 1960; Grimal, 1996). This myth exemplifies the painful experiences of feelings of abandonment, desires for connection, defenses against actually receiving authentic love, and reconciliation with self and others. It also provides a metaphor for dissociation, splitting off from consciousness, the capacity to feel for the injured and deadened child of the past, making way for a new child to emerge, a divine essence, a saving grace.

Through the work of active imagination and relational psychotherapy, the inner child may be released from its shackles, and the ego's relationship with unconscious processes may serve a human life rather than destroy it (Kalsched, 1996). In dreams, waking imagery, and embodiment, the entry of a new child symbolizes the capacity for a new patterning of the self (Hillman, 2007). An alchemical marriage between previously fragmented aspects of the self becomes possible, but it involves "breaking the symmetry of the precursor state" at various points along the way and opening to the unexpected (Cambray, 2009, p. 52). In a section of Jung's (2009) *The Red Book*, entitled "The Conception of the God," he wrote that the "melting together" of opposing parts of himself was like being "born as a child from my own human soul" (Cambray, 2009, p. 171).

At this point in one's individuation process, images relating to the inner child may well shift from neglect to nurture; for instance, a client of mine who dreamed of neglecting a human infant in the form of a fish skeleton left abandoned in the ice and snow began to have, through attuned psychotherapy, somatic inquiry, and active imagination, distinctly different imagery and affect in dreams. One dream, for example, had this client cradling and exchanging a loving gaze with a chubby, rosy-cheeked baby in a contained and warm vehicle. Down to earth, yet full of wonder, the image blended the magic of the numinous and human intimacy, care, and love. This does not mean that her process of synthesizing was complete. In a spiral-like pattern, the abandoned, ignored child can emerge again, but each time, if attended to with relational care, there is further integration. As Kalsched (1996) stated when reflecting on Jung's conceptualizations regarding the child motif,

> the child, then, is a boundary concept, stretching between the potential wholeness of the Self and its actualization in the ego's world of reality. It represents the eternal in time. It links up the real and imaginal worlds and holds the promise that the imperishable numinous world might find life in this world. (p. 203)

Authentic engagement with images such as the inner or divine child that emerge in dreams may open to accessing what Estés (1992) called the "river beneath the river" (p. 3), the place where the collective unconscious interconnects in a chthonic, rhizome-like manner with all of life in a reciprocal loop of supportive action. One may then have increased moments of being able to sit with uncertainty and even allow the presence of deep levels of terror and grief, along with equanimity and compassion. In addition to attending to dreams with active imagination, attuned psychotherapy can offer other creative avenues that deepen inquiry and insight into the child within.

## Creative Therapeutic Applied Perspectives on the Child Within

### Music

According to neuropsychiatrist Mauro Mancia (2006), greater complexity and change, such as that encountered in the treatment of childhood trauma, can be accommodated through the voice and attuned presence of the therapist on an implicit level. He proposed that this is a kind of "music" (p. 83) in the intersubjective field between therapist and patient. Music is more than a useful metaphor in this regard. Mancia spoke of melody in both the prosody of voice and the silence between sounds and gestures as well as in the beating of heart to heart and attunement of breath. Notably, as documented by those whose therapeutic work extends to individuals who have suffered strokes and other brain injuries, many of these patients, while regaining the capacity to speak, for instance, have shown more awake-ness in response to both the melodious prosody of a speech therapist's voice as well as to actual music (Ansdell, 1995, p. 141; Sacks, 2008).

In regard to music that may emerge in the dream state and in the subtle field of psychotherapy, Joel Kroeker (2019), who developed Jungian music psychotherapy, claimed, "When psyche sings, she sings exactly what she means" (p. 128). He invites people to express feelings through tones made with musical instruments, the voice, or the sharing of meaningful music. Comparing composers and analysts, Kroeker said, "Both live, at times, in a world of metaphor where the qualities of one realm are imaginally generalized over to another" (p. 23). Composer Peter Michael Hamel (1976), referring to "the esoteric world of sound," spoke of tones, rhythms, scales, and harmonies as analogous to "the inner man" (p. 130). Appling philosopher Martin Buber's "I–thou" concept, music therapist Gary Ansdell (1995) reflected on music therapy as a "space" that is "not just metaphor" but rather an actual "musical meeting, . . . [where] music acts like gravity pulling the layers into relationship" (p. 74). Some speak of the concept of "worlds" or "spheres of experience" in an "ever dynamic set of relational transactions" creating, through the arts, imagination, and literature, "liminal transformation" (Stenner & Zittoun, 2020, p. 243).

Cambray and Carter (2006) discussed the "co-constructed field or analytic third" in psychotherapy and emphasized engaging the liminal realm, which could be considered a rapport zone, and moving toward integration of emerging material via the therapeutic relationship (p. 123). Through an attuned psychotherapeutic relationship that opens to creative exploration, aspects of the child archetype, when integrated, may bring someone back to life, so to speak. Following other creative avenues in the therapeutic field and exploring responses to what arises in active engagement with, say, the objects chosen and placed in certain positions in a sand tray or the images in a client's painting are alternatives to simply relying on verbal avenues of inquiry and expression. These methods create an opening to implicit ways of knowing, to the waters of feeling, the golden egg of possibility, the mystery of death and rebirth, and the experience of beginning and end—in other words, to the realm of primordial archetypal child. Along with music, film and literature may amplify the fates of the inner child and the emergence of the divine child motif.

## Film and Literature

For an individual whose childhood story was dominated by interpersonal trauma, who is prone to a lack of trust in human relationships, and who uses dissociation as a means of defense, it is not good practice to confront the trauma immediately and directly. Instead, viewing a similar story and defense strategy and seeing a trusting relationship enacted in film as part of the healing of the abandoned child may be a nonthreatening, initial way to open the door toward integration. A therapist and client may explore aspects of a compelling film or story together, relating to various parallel aspects and ways of responding.

For instance, in the film *Precious* (Daniels, 2009), the teenaged protagonist, Precious, escapes into fantasy as a defense from overwhelming feelings due to chronic emotional abuse from her mother and continuous sexual abuse from her father. Robbed of the protected innocence of childhood, she dissociates and creates elaborate fantasy scenes of celebrity, adoration, and otherworldly power. She is barely functioning, meeting everyday life with a collapsed numbness. As Jungian analyst Lionel Corbett (2007) explained, "if the divine essence of the child is not mirrored, or worse, if the child's connected to that level is envied or hated, it may become submerged and difficult to access" (p. 110).

It is only and finally through a teacher from her school and another mentor's authentic care, compassionate challenging, and steady presence that Precious opens to another way of being in relationship with herself. The film amplifies her growth by her giving birth to a child and breaking the chain of abuse, while held by the care offered in these new and supportive human relationships. Through her relationship with mentors and their modeling, Precious is now symbolically re-parenting or re-*patterning* (Hillman, 2013) herself as she cares for her baby in a loving way. This infant in the film can be seen as a symbol of renewal, of a divine child archetype presenting itself. At this point, the historic or actual child from memory has been nurtured through addressing the hurts and realities of life in authentic relationships with mentors and the opportunity for caring for another.

My client's experience of watching this film was difficult for her, but enlightening. At first, she expressed a desire to turn away from it for fear of being retraumatized and was given the space to do so, if needed, but chose instead to engage with the film. She was deeply moved by how this created profound shifts, even if just momentarily, in her own relationship to the child she once was and the way she had shut her off from feeling. She referred back to the film on a number of occasions and began to understand how the trauma she had experienced was linked to a chain of repetitive traumas across generations in her family. This acknowledgment and her association with the character Precious, bolstered her burgeoning capacity for self-compassion and, as an extension, an expanded feeling of care for all those who came before her.

Likewise, the film, *Pan's Labyrinth* (del Toro, 2006) offers images of both a childhood lost and a divine child found and a quintessential representation of the individuation process taking form in the face of complex trauma on individual and collective levels. Readers are referred to a brief review of the film in *Psychological Perspectives* (Rohde-Brown, 2007) that amplifies the lost and found child motif from a Jungian perspective and references Kalsched's (1996) theory on trauma.

Another example of the use of film in my own practice involves a client who had experienced a great deal of emotional abuse and harsh judgment from both his father and mother due to their lack of understanding of his introverted and artistic temperament. Their rigid ideas of how he should present himself manifested in punitive parenting, namely aggressive ridicule alternating with dismissiveness. His dream images consistently demonstrated the theme of any display of emotions as out of control or devouring. He had an extraordinarily developed intellect and used this superior quality as a defense against feeling, only to have unexpected outbursts of rage and to pull back in therapy, distrusting any sense of closeness in the therapeutic relationship. Slowing down to be attuned to the moment and to trust occurred gradually. Sandplay and gentle somatic exploration were introduced, and subtle shifts began to take place as he was prompted to pay attention to what he was experiencing in his body and where he pulled back in feelings of intimacy and trust in the therapeutic relationship and in relationship with others. Initially, he had felt attacked by even gentle questions, reminded of his experience as a child and never feeling good enough, loved, or wanted.

A theme running through this client's dreams was attempting to travel on his own, but being burdened by carrying his father's heavy luggage. Likewise, his dreams often had female figures entrapping or turning on him in an attacking way as soon as he had soft feelings. At one point in the therapy, I had just seen the film *Whale Rider* (Caro, 2002), and something compelled me to mention the film to him. The film is a story of a Maori child who, because she is female, is dismissed in the lineage of Paikea (Whale Rider) as the next in line for leadership. Her twin brother, who was in line to be the new Chief, and mother had died in the process of childbirth. The story unfolds to show that she is truly a whale rider, but it is a painful path toward being acknowledged for her essence, her skill, her leadership/chiefdom qualities.

My client came back the next week and expressed that he had viewed the film and had unexpectedly burst out in uncontrollable sobs. He related that his tears flowed sporadically for that entire week and that he had never been that affected by a film in his entire life. His viewing of the film opened an avenue for sharing in a very intimate way about himself and moments of being available to feel compassion for himself. He was able to acknowledge how he felt seen by me and accepted for who he was. Hogenson (2004, p. 51) would describe a kind of "ontological change" taking place as the young girl in the film amplified my client's own child within and assisted in his "recovery of a lost sense of the sacred" in himself. The incorporation of film had entered the therapeutic field as an additional support in the work to come.

Aside from incorporating film in therapeutic contexts, introspection and emotional changes arise from poetic and other literary adjuncts to psychotherapy as well as nature-based contexts (Berry, 1982; Chalquist, 2007). Inviting engagement with children's literature is valuable for amplifying child motifs, often embedded in animal or natural themes, as portals to our true nature, a divine child essence which is neither imprisoned by the past nor worried about the future (Hancock, 2009; Marks-Tarlow, 2008; Rowland, 2012). Jungian scholar Susan Rowland (2012) claimed that when reading such stories as *The Secret Garden* (Burnett, 2019) or *The Lion, the Witch, and the Wardrobe* (Lewis, 1998), we are led by the child, or one could even say the symbolic or divine inner child in nature, into the nonhuman realm and thus a deeper understanding of our place in the universe. With the nonhuman realm in children's literature as portal, the abandoned child, lost to false performances to win the affections of parents or society, may thus be found again, at least for brief moments.

Throughout myth and fairy tale are depictions of the child archetype, often symbolized by nature figures or miniature images (Hancock, 2009). Estés (1990), in her compelling manner of storytelling, amplified the abandoned child motif in *Warming the Stone Child.* She spoke of the pain that lingers on into adulthood and the impact of storytelling on the reduction of suffering. Perhaps one of the other benefits of turning to literature and other creative forms of storytelling such as film is that, by immersing ourselves in the characters and their qualities, we are prompted to make associations with a multiplicity of characters within ourselves. This relates back to the section on multiple selves in this chapter. We may experience a glimpse of how certain self states within our own psyches exist in relationship to the child self, the inner child motif, or the fractal and perennial divine child core. Another way of relating to the unexpected, emergent, and liminal child within is through an understanding of what Buddhism calls *beginner's mind,* cultivated through age-old mindfulness meditative practices and embraced by current, mainstream, secular culture and within psychotherapeutic contexts (Chodron, 2018; Suzuki, 1973; Young-Eisendrath & Muramoto, 2002).

### Mindfulness in Psychology, the Field of Consciousness, and the Perennial Child

Buddhist nun, Pema Chodron (2018) related that practices such as meditation foster one's awareness such that one may, "in post-meditation, be a child of illusion," whereby one increasingly recognizes the illusory nature of existence (p. 21). In making connections between Jungian approaches to psychological integration and Buddhist concepts and practices, the late philosopher Henry Corbin (2014) observed,

> Jungian psychology places high value on fundamental Buddhist intuition, which our rational philosophy confronts as a paradox painful to the point of hallucination, or which our historical criticism considers and then relegates to the position of an imposing but strange and exotic curiosity. (p. 47)

This statement speaks about the slow movement within mainstream paradigms of embracing the value of intuition and the subtle field of awareness, the emergent context from which the divine child essence may be recognized. That is shifting a bit with the advent of quantum physics and field theory. In quantum physics terms, one could say that the perennial child, the *no-thing* is related to the Buddhist concept of *no-self (anatta)* or is "everywhere at once," full and empty at the same time (Levy, 2018, p. 89). Some within the psychoanalytic world have initiated discussions about Buddhist concepts' entrance into the Western zeitgeist and Jungian psychotherapy (Katsky, 2021; Spiegelman & Miyuki, 1985; Young-Eisendrath & Muramoto, 2002). With this blended perspective, the Buddhist concept of beginner's mind is childlike openness or emergence as opposed to egoic dominance.

In making distinctions about egoic tendencies' impact on psychological health, psychiatrist Mark Epstein (1995) blended psychoanalysis and Buddhist concepts and expounded on narcissism in our time as a hindrance to beginner's mind. He claimed that the deepest injury of pathological narcissistic organization is a lack of the capacity to grasp the concept and deep awareness of No-Self and impermanence. Epstein presented a comprehensive analysis of *Samsara*, the wheel of life and rebirth, and the psychological patterns, *samskaras* (or in analytic terms, complexes), that may entrap us along our human path. Egoic identification with the divine child archetype or specialness or other inflated states are examples of being in the web of a power complex, suggesting unhealthy characterological patterns. We see many variations of this pattern in our world today, particularly represented in political contexts where an identification with an archetype of power may overcome a person. On the other hand, sometimes, when one has been rigid and overcontrolled, for instance, it is necessary to take the opposite route and try on the qualities with which one would normally not identify. Psychotherapist John Wellwood (2000) provided an example of his client, Paul, whom Wellwood helped to try on the feeling and experience of being inflated or, one could say, childish, to compensate for Paul's stoic and rigid interpretation of Buddhist practice and ethics of behavior. Wellwood noted that Paul actually needed to wake up his own inner child's aliveness. As Hillman (2007) emphasized, it is important not only to acknowledge where the child within has been abandoned on the way to adulthood, but to also be able to give oneself over to an "abandonment **to** the child when the child returns" (p. 118). Wellwood's exercise with Paul would serve to open him to the possibility of a renewed sense of aliveness as well as to reduce any propensities for repressions to be acted out unconsciously or to continue to rigidly parent or police this part of himself.

The Tibetan Book of the Dead, which is also a Buddhist map for living mindfully, symbolically presents the ability to come to terms with one's own projections through meditative practices as it offers an image of mother and child uniting at the time of death (Guru Rimpoche & K. Lingpa, 2003). This is another powerful depiction of integration, with a divine child image opening the way for another cycle of rebirth while being held within by feelings of lovingkindness. Many psychotherapists have used the metaphor of a river or seedling growing into a tree by being cultivated (Estés, 1992; Jung, 1954/1967). Relevant to depictions of the nature of the divine inner child, the seed metaphor is quite similar to Tibetan Buddhist order Arya Maitreya's (2000) amplification of Buddha Nature as the "precious treasure . . . contained within (the ground beneath)," a "seed" out of which the "substance of a majestic tree will gradually come about" (p. 35).

Some parallels are suggested between what Buddhism terms "indivisible," Hillman's (2007, p. 122) idea of the "perennial child," Jung's (1941/1949, p. 8) notion of the child archetype as "primordial" and quantum physics concept of *no-thing* (Levy, 2018, p. 89). Thus, in terms of exploring the inner child in psychotherapy, while historical, family-of-origin, and multiple voices of internal selves (including the child self) are important, what Jungian and post-Jungian therapy offers is an expansion into acknowledging the child within as a divine seedling in the field of emergent, nonlinear, and nonlocal systems and potentiality. There is a tension between the child as form and memory of the past and the feeling in our biological bodies of that which is subtle, enlivening, and indefinable. such as that which presents itself as the divine child archetype in dreams. The archetype of the divine child is a beckoning to that which may be possible in the fractal/natural order of things, that which may serve a life rather than hinder it.

## Closing Thoughts

This chapter explored, from a Jungian/post-Jungian perspective, the archetypal child motif (divine child), which is distinguished by an emphasis on subtle, emergent processes including but also expanding beyond the empirical child and its inner representations within an adult's psyche. The divine inner child can be considered an ontological reality within the mosaic of subtle lived experience. Its intelligence defies reductive definitions and materialist validation yet continually calls us to authenticity. My purpose here was to amplify how persistent, powerful, and significant the archetype of the child is personally and collectively. The child motif crosses political, cultural, ideological, and historical boundaries and blends the personal and particular with the universal. In our lives today, the child continues to call, giving us another chance to live symbolically rather than concretely, to blend conscious and unconscious, to be authentically embodied.

> The muse is a little girl, impossibly polite.
> She arrives when you're talking
> or walking away from your car.
> She's barefoot, she stands
> next to you, mute; she taps your sleeve,
> not even on your skin, just touches the cloth
> of your plaid shirt, touches it twice
> with her index finger
> and you keep talking, or you don't.
> She will wait one minute. She is not hungry
> or unhappy or poor. She goes somewhere else
> unless you turn and look at her
> and write it down. Or maybe
> she's a horse you want to ride, she's a tall horse,
> she's heavy, as if she could bear armor.
> You can't catch her with apples.
> I don't know how you get on.
> I remember my cold fingers
> grasping the black mane.

(Marjorie Saiser, "The Muse Is a Little Girl")

# References

Adler, A. (1924/1969). *The practice and theory of individual psychology*. Littlefield, Adams & Co.

Ainsworth, M. D. S., Blehar, M. D., Waters, E., & Wall, S. (1978). *Patterns of attachment: A psychological study of the strange situation*. Erlbaum.

Allione, L. T. (2018). *Wisdom rising: Journey into the mandala of the empowered feminine*. Enliven.

Ansdell, G. (1995). *Music for life: Aspects of creative music therapy with adult clients*. Jessica Kingsley Publishers.

Aron, L. (2006). Analytic impasse and the third: Clinical implications of intersubjectivity theory. *International Journal of Psychoanalysis, 87*(2), 349–368.

Maitreya, A., Taye J. K. L., & Gyamtso, K. T. (2000). *Buddha nature: The Mahayana Uttaratantra Shastra with commentary*. Snow Lion Publications.

Assagioli, R. (2007). *Transpersonal development: The dimension beyond psychosynthesis*. Inner Way Productions.

Atmanspacher, H., & Fuchs, C. A. (2014). *The Jung–Pauli conjecture and its impact today*. Imprint Academic.

Atwood, G., & Stolorow, R. (1984). *Structures of subjectivity: Explorations in psychoanalytic phenomenology*. Analytic Press.

Behrens, K. Y. (2004). A multifaceted view of the concept of amae: Reconsidering the indigenous Japanese concept of relatedness. *Human Development, 47*(1), 1–27.

Berne, E. (1996). *Games people play: The basic handbook of transactional analysis*. Ballantine Books.

Berry, P. (1982). *Echo's subtle body: Contributions to an archetypal psychology*. Spring Publications.

Bosnak, R. (2009). The physician inside. In S. Aizenstat and R. Boznak (Eds.), *Imagination and medicine: The future of healing in an age of neuroscience* (pp. xv–xxiv). Spring Journal Books.

Brewster, F. (2019). *Archetypal grief: Slavery's legacy of intergenerational child loss*. Routledge.

Buck, J. N. (1966). *The house-tree-person technique: Revised manual*. Western Psychological Services.

Burnett, F. H. (2019). *The secret garden*. SeaWolf Press.

Cambray, J. (2009). *Synchronicity: Nature and psyche in an interconnected universe*. Texas A & M University Press.

Cambray, J., & Carter, L. (2006). Analytic methods revisited. In J. Cambray & L. Carter (Eds.), *Analytical psychology: Contemporary perspectives on Jungian analysis* (pp. 116–148). Routledge.

Caro, N. (Director, Writer). (2002). *Whale rider* [Film]. Newmarket Films.

Chalmers, D. (1997). *The conscious mind: In search of a fundamental theory*. Oxford University Press.

Chalquist, C. (2007). *Terrapsychology: Reengaging the soul in place*. Spring Journal Books.

Chodron, P. (2018). *Start where you are: A guide to compassionate living*. Shambhala.

Corbett, L. (2007). *Psyche and the sacred: Spirituality beyond religion*. Spring Journal Books.

Corbett, L. (2018). Jungian approaches to psychotherapy. In M. Charles (Ed.), *Introduction to contemporary psychoanalysis: Defining terms and building bridges* (pp. 33–62). Routledge.

Corbin, H. (2014). The Tibetan book of the dead (J. Cain, Trans.). In M. Cazenave (Ed.), *Jung, Buddhism, and the incarnation of Sophia: Unpublished writings from the philosopher of the soul* (pp. 47–66). Inner Traditions.

Daniels, L. (Producer, Director). (2009). *Precious* [Film]. Lee Daniels Entertainment.

del Toro, G. (Producer, Director). (2006). *Pan's labyrinth* [Film]. Telecinco Cinema/ Estudios Picasso.

Dyak, M. (1999). *The voice dialogue facilitator's handbook: Part 1. A step by step guide to working with the aware ego*. Life Energy Press.

Edinger, E. (1994). *Anatomy of the psyche: Alchemical symbolism in psychotherapy*. Open Court Publishing.

Epstein, M. (1995). *Thoughts without a thinker: Psychotherapy from a Buddhist perspective*. Basic Books.

Erikson, E. (1950). *Childhood and society*. W. W. Norton & Company.

Estés, C. P. (1990). *Warming the stone child: Myths and stories about abandonment and the unmother.* Sounds True.

Estés, C. P. (1992). *Women who run with the wolves: Myths and stories of the wild woman archetype.* Ballantine Books.

Freud, S. (1922/1966). *Introductory lectures on psychoanalysis.* W. W. Norton.

Freud, S. (1915/1957). *The standard edition of the complete works of Sigmund Freud* (Vol. 19, pp. 159–205). Hogarth Press.

Fromm, E. (1941). *Escape from freedom.* Farrar & Rinehart.

Gherovici, P., & Christian, C. (2019). *Psychanalysis in the barrios: Race, class, and the unconscious.* Routledge.

Graves, R. (1960). *The Greek myths. Volume One.* Penguin.

Grimal, P. (1996). *The dictionary of classical mythology.* Blackwell Publishers.

Guru Rimpoche, & Lingpa, K. (2003). *The Tibetan book of the dead: The great liberation through hearing in the bardo.* Shambhala.

Hamel, P. M. (1976). *Through music to the self.* Shambhala Publications.

Hancock, S. (2009). *The child that haunts us.* Routledge.

Hillman, J. (2007). *Mythic figures.* Spring Publications.

Hillman, J. (2013) *Archetypal psychology.* Spring Publications Books.

Hoffman, L., Cleare-Hoffman, H., & Jackson, T. (2015). Humanistic psychology and multiculturalism: History, current status, and advancements. In K. J. Schneider, J. F. Pierson, & J. F. T. Bugental (Eds.), *The handbook of humanistic psychology: Theory, research, and practice* (2$^{nd}$ ed., pp. 41–55). Sage.

Hogenson, G. B. (2004). Archetypes: Emergence and the psyche's deep structure. In J. Cambray & L. Carter (Eds.), *Analytical psychology: Contemporary perspectives in Jungian analysis* (pp. 32–55). Routledge.

Horney, K. (1950). *Neurosis and human growth: The struggle toward self-realization.* W. W. Norton and Company.

Jones, R. A. (2011). The 'child' motif in theorizing about embodied subjectivity. In R. A. Jones (Ed.), *Body, mind, and healing after Jung: A space of questions.* Routledge.

Jung, C. G. (1941/1949). The psychology of the child archetype. In C. G. Jung & C. Kerényi, *Essays on a science of mythology: The myth of the divine child and the mysteries of Eleusis* (R. F. C. Hull, Trans.) (pp. 70–100). Princeton University Press.

Jung, C. G. (1951/1959). *Aion: Researches into the phenomenology of the self* (R. F. C. Hull, Trans.). In H. Read, M. Fordham, G. Adler, & W. McGuire (Eds.), *The collected works of C. G. Jung* (Vol. 9ii). Princeton University Press.

Jung, C. G. (1954/1966). *Practice of psychotherapy* In H. Read, M. Fordham, G. Adler, & W. McGuire (Eds.), *The collected works of C. G. Jung* (Vol. 16). Princeton University Press.

Jung, C. G. (1954/1967). The philosophical tree (R. F. C. Hull, Trans.). In H. Read, M. Fordham, G. Adler, & W. McGuire (Eds.), *The collected works of C. G. Jung* (Vol. 13, pp. 251–350). Princeton University Press.

Jung. C. G. (1952/1968). *Psychology and alchemy* (R. F. C. Hull, Trans.). In H. Read, M. Fordham, G. Adler, & W. McGuire (Eds.), *The collected works of C. G. Jung* (Vol. 12, 2nd ed.). Princeton University Press.

Jung, C. G. (1951/1969a). *The archetypes and the collective unconscious* (R. F. C. Hull, Trans.). In H. Read, M. Fordham, G. Adler, & W. McGuire (Eds.), *The collected works of C. G. Jung* (Vol. 9i). Princeton University Press.

Jung, C. G. (1954/1969). On the nature of the psyche (R. F. C. Hull, Trans.). In H. Read, M. Fordham, G. Adler, & W. McGuire (Eds.), *The collected works of C. G. Jung* (Vol. 8, 2nd ed., pp. 159–234). Princeton University Press.

Jung, C. G. (1951/1969b). The psychology of the child archetype (R. F. C. Hull, Trans.). In H. Read, M. Fordham, G. Adler, & W. McGuire (Eds.), *The collected works of C. G. Jung* (Vol. 9i, 2$^{nd}$ ed., pp. 151–181). Princeton University Press.

Jung, C. G. (1958/1969). The transcendent function. In H. Read. M. Fordham, G. Adler, & W. McGuire (Eds.), *The collected works of C. G. Jung* (R. F. C. Hull, Trans.) (Vol. 8, 2nd ed., pp. 67–91). Princeton, NJ: Princeton University Press.

Jung, C. G. (1937/1973). On the psychological diagnosis of evidence: The evidence-experiment in the Näf trial (R. F. C. Hull, Trans.). In H. Read, M. Fordham, G. Adler, & W. McGuire (Eds.), *The collected works of C. G. Jung* (Vol. 2, pp. 605–613). Princeton University Press.

Jung, C. G. (2009). *The red book: A reader's edition*. W. W. Norton.

Kalff, D. (2020). *Sandplay: A psychotherapeutic approach to the psyche*. Analytical Psychology Press.

Kalsched, D. (1996). *The inner world of trauma: Archetypal defenses of the human spirit*. Routledge.

Kalsched, D. (2013). *Trauma and the soul: A psychospiritual approach to human development and its interruption*. Routledge.

Katsky, P. (2021). Enlightenment, individuation, and nonduality: Reflections on a dream. *Jung Journal, 15*(1), 104–128.

Katz, M. (2018). Psychoanalytic field theory. In M. Charles (Ed.), *Introduction to contemporary psychoanalysis: Defining terms and building bridges* (pp. 145–164.). Routledge.

Kelly, G. A. (1955). *The psychology of personal constructs* (Vol.1). Norton.

Kerényi, C. (1941/1949). The primordial child in primordial times. In C. G. Jung & C. Kerényi, *Essays on a science of mythology: The myth of the divine child and the mysteries of Eleusis* (pp. 25–69). Princeton University Press.

Kohut, H. (1977). *The restoration of the self*. International Universities Press.

Kroeker, J. (2019). *Jungian music psychotherapy: When psyche sings*. Routledge.

Lacan, J. (1956/1968). *The language of the self: The function of language in psychoanalysis*. Johns Hopkins University Press.

Levy, P. (2018). *The quantum revelation: A radical synthesis of science and spirituality*. Select Books.

Lewis, C. S. (1998). *The lion, the witch, and the wardrobe*. Collins.

Mair, J. M. M. (1977). The community of self. In D. Bannister (Ed.), *New perspectives in personal construct theory* (pp. 125–149). Academic Press.

Mancia, M. (2006). Implicit memory and early unrepressed unconscious: Their role in the therapeutic process (How the neurosciences can contribute to psychoanalysis, *The International Journal of Psychoanalysis, 87*(1), 83–103.

Marks-Tarlow, T. (2008). *Psyche's veil: Psychotherapy, fractals, and complexity*. Routledge.

Polster, E., & Polster, M. (1974). *Gestalt therapy integrated: Contours of theory and practice*. Vintage Books.

Proctor, H. (2011). Miller Mair: The caring radical. *Personal Construct Theory and Practice, 8*, 19–23.

Reich, W. (1933). *Character analysis: Principles and techniques for psychoanalysis in practice and training*. Orgone Institute Press.

Rohde-Brown, J. (2007). Pan's labyrinth [Review of the film *Pan's labyrinth*]. *Psychological Perspectives, 50*(1), 167–169.

Rowland, S. (2012). *The ecocritical psyche: Language, evolutionary complexity and Jung*. Routledge.

Roy, M. (2008). When a religious archetype becomes a cultural complex: Puritanism in America. In T. Singer & S. L. Kimbles (Eds.), *The cultural complex: Contemporary Jungian perspectives on psyche and society* (pp. 64–77). Routledge.

Sacks, O. (2008). *Musicophilia: Tales of music and the brain*. Vintage.

Schore, A. (1994). *Affect regulation and the origins of the self: The neurobiology of emotional development*. Lawrence Erlbaum.

Schneider, K. (2003). Existential-humanistic psychotherapies. In A. S. Gurman & S. B. Messer (Eds.), *Essential psychotherapies* (pp. 149–181). Guilford.

Schneider, K. (2015). Rediscovering awe: A new frontier in humanistic psychology, psychotherapy, and society. In K. J. Schneider, J. F. Pierson, & J. F. T. Bugental (Eds.), *The handbook of humanistic psychology: Theory, research, and practice* (pp. 73–82). Sage.

Schwartz, R. F. (1997). *Internal family systems therapy*. Guilford Press.

Singer, T. (2008). The cultural complex and archetypal defenses of the group spirit: Baby Zeus, Elian Gonzales, Constantine's sword, and other holy wars (with special attention to the "axis of evil"). In T. Singer & S. L. Kimbles (Eds.), *The cultural complex: Contemporary Jungian perspectives on psyche and society* (pp. 13–34). Routledge.

Spiegelman, M. J., & Miyuki, M. (1985). *Buddhism and Jungian psychology*. New Falcon Publications.

Stein, M. (1998). *Jung's map of the soul*. Open Court.

Stenner, P. & Zittoun, T. (2020). On taking a leap of faith: Art, imagination, and liminal experience. *Journal of Theoretical and Philosophical Psychology, 40*(4), 240–263.

Stone, H., & Stone, S. (1998). *Embracing our selves: The voice dialogue manual*. New World Library.

Suzuki, S. (1973). *Zen mind, beginner's mind*. Weatherhill.

von Franz, M.-L. (2000). *The problem of the puer aeternus*. Inner City Books.

von Franz, M.-L. (2016). Confrontation with the collective unconscious, *Psychological Perspectives: A Quarterly Journal of Jungian Thought, 59*, 295–318.

Weisstub, E., & Galili-Weisstub, E. (2004). Collective trauma and cultural complexes. In T. Singer & S. L. Kimbles (Eds.), *The cultural complex: Contemporary Jungian perspectives on psyche and society* (pp. 146–170). Routledge.

Wellwood, J. (2000, Spring). The psychology of awakening. *Tricycle: The Buddhist Review*. https://tricycle.org/magazine/psychology-awakening/

Wesley, D. (2019). The divine child. *Psychological Perspectives, 62*(4), 446–454.

Winnicott, D. W. (1960). *The maturational process and the facilitating environment: Studies in the theory of emotional development*. Karnac Books.

Woodman, M. (1998). *Sitting by the well: Bringing the feminine to consciousness through language, dreams, and metaphor*. Sounds True.

Wundt, W. M. (2013). *An introduction to psychology*. Muller Press.

Young-Eisendrath, P., & Muramoto, S. (2002). *Awakening and insight: Zen Buddhism and psychotherapy*. Routledge.

Chapter III.

# The Figure of the Trickster in Literature and Consumer Society Narratives: Liminality and Potentialities[2]

Mathieu Alemany Oliver and Lorna Wilkinson

For Campbell (1949), myths are neither true nor false but metaphors that reflect our societies' concerns. Myths also establish exemplary and prohibited models for behaviors (Eliade, 1963). In the context of this book, we can say that childlikeness is represented by two archetypal figures that are found in myths and correspond to both socially exemplary and prohibited behaviors: the figures of the Child and the Trickster.

The Child archetype originally appears in folklore, where it can take the form of a dwarf or an elf but also a hermaphrodite or simply a young boy. Mass media often portray the Child as a hero who succeeds in an adult world despite their youth. With many of Marvel's characters, for instance, the hero has often lost their parents in childhood, had to grow up too soon, and taken on responsibilities as an inexperienced and naive child. These heroes often receive divine help and develop a supernatural power to save the world, avenge relatives or friends, or complete their quest for identity. According to Jung (1959), the Child archetype represents potential, day, and light, all of which are synonymous with consciousness. It involves progress toward independence and serves as compensation for abandonment. It brings attention to the existence of a child/adult frontier and the need to become an adult, which means being responsible, conscious, and wise. Here, the Child represents exemplary childlikeness, which relies on the very modern conceptualization of childhood as a journey toward freedom, consciousness, responsibility, rationality, and, more generally, citizenship. The Child has to learn how to become a benefactor to society.

Unlike the Child, the Trickster often succeeds where others fail, sometimes thanks to their apparent stupidity or naivety. The Trickster is "a faithful reflection of an absolutely undifferentiated human consciousness, corresponding to a psyche that has hardly left the animal level" (Jung 1980, p. 260). They are said to be half-animal and half-divine. What makes the Trickster superior to humans in some ways and inferior in others is their cleverness, unreason, and unconsciousness (Hynes & Doty, 1993). The Trickster appears in different forms and with different names in various cultures: Hermes/Mercury and Dionysus/Bacchus/Liber in Greek and Roman mythologies, Loki in Norse mythology, Huitaca in the pre-Colombian Muisca mythology, Carancho in the Choco Indian mythology, the Coyote in the Winnebago Indian mythology, and the Hare and Eshu in the Yoruba mythology (morphing into Br'er Rabbit in the southern United States). Eshu is known as Elegua in Cuba and Legba in the West African Fon mythology and Haitian Voodoo. We also find the Trickster figure represented by the traits of Anansi the Spider in the Akan mythology that later spread to West Africa and the Caribbean, and Susanoo in Japanese mythology. This figure also appears outside of mythology: in movies, picaresque novels, carnivals, creation stories, magic rites of healing, and others. While the Child represents exemplary childlikeness, the Trickster gathers together all sorts of prohibited behaviors and better symbolizes exemplary childishness. Childishness is understood here as the partially pejorative version of childlikeness and, as illustrated by the Trickster figure, directly relates certain human behaviors to people's antisocial and animal side (Hyde, 2008).

[2] This chapter includes some parts that have been taken from both authors' unpublished doctoral dissertations and slightly modified for publication.

Hillman (1983) highlights the American tendency to oscillate between the order, tradition, and power represented by the Senex (the adult version of the Child) on the one hand, and the overthrow of traditions, transgression, and spiritual excesses as represented by the Trickster-puer on the other hand. Mythological narratives also reveal that the Child and the Trickster sometimes resemble each other. For example, the Trickster is often a hero-trickster, like the Hare in Winnebago culture (Kerényi, 1956). They may be a buffoon, but they are also a benefactor and considered the creator of the world and culture—not unlike the Child. Trickster figures are both the beginning and the end of the human cycle. They represent a period of change and childhood, as well as the childlike aspects of men and women (Blowsnake, 1956). They experiment with both male and female genders, while the Child is sometimes portrayed as a hermaphrodite. Finally, the Trickster archetype generally includes the figures of the Hero, Eros, the King's son, or the Messiah to form the puer or childlike archetype (Hillman 1991). Mythological archetypes make childlikeness and childishness two sides of the same coin; which is dominant depends on the zeitgeist of the time and place.

This chapter focuses on the Trickster figure in an attempt to connect its depiction in literature with some aspects of contemporary consumer society. This chapter also echoes several other chapters in the book as it presents the Trickster figure as a character full of desire and potentialities who lets their authentic self express (see chapter VI by Alemany Oliver & Belk), transgress, and play with the codes (see chapter V by Comoy Fusaro), often with a certain naivety that makes it difficult for them to integrate into society and causes them to be tricked as well (see chapter IV by Weightman). We begin with an introduction to the Trickster that covers the figure's roots and manifestations and details some relevant criticism of the subject. We then highlight how the Trickster is manifested in the figures of the buffoon, court jester, and magical servant on the Shakespearean stage, and how the characteristics of the mythological and Shakespearean Trickster are still very relevant to many contemporary narratives, in particular the ones found in consumer society.

### The Trickster Figure in Myth and Folktale

Those familiar with Perrault's fairy-tales will likely have encountered "Hop-o'-My-Thumb." This story, first published in 1697 and very likely based on pre-existing oral tales, centers on the eponymous hero, the youngest of seven brothers abandoned by their parents in the woods and forced to shelter in an ogre's house. Though allowing the brothers to sleep in his daughters' bedroom, the ogre secretly plans to kill them at night. Suspicious of his host, however, Hop-o'-My-Thumb swaps the sleeping daughters' crowns with the hats worn by him and his brothers, causing the ogre to kill his own daughters by mistake. The boy's cunning and brutal triumph over a stronger adversary places Hop-o'-My-Thumb within a category of characters that have long fascinated anthropologists, psychologists, and literary critics alike: the category of the Trickster (Paulme, 1976).

Narratives across a multitude of cultures have made use of such Tricksters. Usually outsiders to their milieus, these paradoxical figures regularly observe or manipulate those around them, offer shrewd insight, undermine authority, upend social structures, and act the fool. Despite apparently disparate sources and personalities, characters in various cultures have been deemed Tricksters because they share the trait of introducing subversive energy into their various fictional worlds and challenging existing systems—much as Hop-o'-My-Thumb's shrewdness challenges the authority of age and strength.

There has been some dispute over the origin of the word "Trickster" as used in connection with an archetype. Landay (1998, p. 2) tells us: "The term 'trickster' originates in Daniel Brinton's 1868 study of the contradictory figure of North American tales who is both fooler and fooled, heroic and base." Williams (2012, p. 7) similarly attributes the coinage of this word to Brinton's 1868 *The Myths of the New World*, as does Pelton (1980, pp. 6-7), who adds: "by the end of the nineteenth century, the term had become standard." In his seminal work on mythological Tricksters, however, Hyde (2008, p. 355, notes 7n) questions why Brinton is "commonly given credit" for the term, professing to be unable to find it in Brinton's book—which, upon investigation, does appear devoid of the word "trickster." Hyde (2008) suggests Franz Boas was the first to use the term in an anthropological context in 1898, thus apparently contradicting Pelton's (1980) assertion that, by that point, it was already in common use in scholarship. Hyde's theory seems the most plausible, as there do not appear to be any instances of the word in anthropology studies prior to Boas; nevertheless, the unclear origin of the term nicely reflects the Trickster's ambiguity.

Despite this abstruse origin, it is clear that the Trickster "field of research emerged only in the nineteenth century and developed exponentially in the post-war period" (Lipovetsky, 2011, p. 27). Scholars of anthropology from the 20th century onward have analyzed the Trickster as an archetype in ancient tales around the world, from Amerindian oral tales to Greek mythology. As Fox (1994, p. 299) observes, "to trace all of" the Trickster characters in folklore "would be a lifetime's task"— considering this, we will not attempt to present an index of every Trickster from traditional tales. It is important, however, to establish the traits and functions that define this figure. Greedy, selfish, and lustful, yet compelling heroes, Tricksters in myth have been seen to "personify all the traits of man raised to the highest degree" (Ricketts, 1966, p. 347): They embody the various flaws and talents that define humanity and continually express them in creative ways. Within their narratives, Tricksters are highly subversive presences, often using "impersonation, disguise, theft, and deceit to expose hypocrisy and inequality, to subvert existing social systems, and to widen their sphere of power" (Landay, 1998, p. 2). In myths and folktales, such subversion is found in small animals outwitting their more obviously advantaged adversaries through tricks or, occasionally, sheer luck—as seen, for instance, in Br'er Rabbit undermining Br'er Fox in Cherokee stories or the tortoise trouncing the hare in Aesop's fable.

As well as tricking others, the folkloric Trickster "may also be tricked himself" (Kononenko & Kukharenko, 2008, p. 14): Because of their arrogance and clowning, other creatures sometimes outwit them, and yet their insouciant resilience lets them return, unscathed, for another adventure. In this way, the Tricksters crucially obscure the boundary between authority and subservience. While they may initially appear to be the underdog, their tricks intimate a form of control that ultimately places them at the center of their narrative. Indeed, having a temporary spell in power is arguably a fundamental part of the Trickster continuum in folklore, which makes them at once hegemonic and subversive and establishes the Trickster, as Landay (1998, p. 11) suggests, as "a symbol of doubleness."

Their propensity for tricking and being tricked underscores the Trickster as "the embodiment of humor—all kinds of humor" (Ricketts, 1966, p. 347): The observer alternately laughs *with* and *at* them. Humor is key to the folkloric Trickster, and often, as Kononenko and Kukharenko (2008) have noted,

> deals with the most basic of things: the body and its functions, the physical world and its rules. A typical "trick" revolves around a creature's failure to understand a law of nature; the trickster leads the victim into this state of misunderstanding, undermining

> the victim's ability to make fundamental distinctions. . . . The animal trickster misleads at the most basic level, and the tricks are primitive and often centred on the body and bodily functions. (p. 9)

The Trickster twisting the natural world may be seen in the British folk story of the fox tricking the wolf into believing the moon's reflection to be a piece of cheese (Briggs, 1970), while their connections to grotesque body-tricks have been well documented in anthropology studies. For instance, Hyde (2008) recounts the Amerindian tale in which the Coyote throws his own eyeballs into a tree; Babcock-Abrahams (1975, p. 159) comments on Tricksters' involvement in "scatological and coprophagous episodes which may be creative, destructive, or simply amusing"; and Fox (1994, p. 300) speaks of "the scatological side of the Trickster, along with his gluttony and lust." A preoccupation with the unrepressed body is not limited to crafty animals of myth but also found in Trickster gods—Loki, for instance, is placing "himself in obscene or disgusting situations" (Davidson, 1979, p. 9)—and in the gluttonous buffoons of the early modern stage. Koepping (1985, p. 194) posits there to be "two forms of action and thought that seem to designate the trickster across all cultural variations, namely, his cunning form of intelligence and the grotesqueness of the body imagery used to indicate the inversion of order." These two traits seem incongruous and exemplify the Trickster's core nature as a conciliator of antitheses who fuses cerebral power with the corporeal, and intelligence with farce. Pelton (1980, p. 4) proposes that the mythological Trickster merges the "human" with the "sacred" to conceive the contradictoriness of humanity as they "encompas[s] both nobility and messiness—feces, lies, and even death." Thus, the Trickster suggests the capacity for apparent opposites to co-exist and cooperate in a manner that helps conceive new cultural possibilities.

Thus, the Tricksters of myths and folktales are emblems of liminality: never wholly one thing nor the other, always in-betweens. They are shape-shifters, and their identity is highly fluid (Lipovetsky, 2011). As Ricketts (1966, pp. 327-328) states, the Trickster combines "in one personage no less than two and sometimes three or more seemingly different and contrary roles" and incorporates "clownish, heroic, and sometimes even divine elements in one figure." In the 20th century, critics extensively discussed this mutability. Hyde (2008, p. 6) terms mythological Tricksters "lords of in-between," observing their ability to cross boundaries and even "move between heaven and earth, and between the living and the dead." Similarly, Lévi-Strauss (1955, p. 440) argues that the equivocality of North American folkloric Tricksters is expressed through their being "carrion-eating animals"—those who eat meat but do not themselves hunt, thus acting as "mediators" between herbivores and carnivores and, accordingly, between life and death. Makarius (1993, p. 84) also views the Trickster as a "mediator" due to their magical powers that, acquired by violating prohibitions, mean they "transcen[d] the human condition, without . . . attaining to the divine." Meanwhile, Babcock-Abrahams (1975) suggested that the Trickster's

> expression of ambiguity and paradox, of a confusion of all customary categories . . . epitomizes the paradox of the human condition and exploits the incongruity that we are all creatures of the earth and yet not wholly creatures of the earth in that we have need of clothing and spiritual ideals . . . Further, he embodies the fundamental contradiction of our existence: the contradiction between the individual and society, between freedom and constraint. (pp. 160-161)

Like Pelton (1980) and Ricketts (1966), Babcock-Abrahams (1975) highlights the Trickster's function to express paradoxes that are central to the human condition.

Crucially, the Trickster demonstrates the possibility of progress despite and even because of these paradoxes: As Ricketts (1966, p. 347) notes, while "continually being buffeted about," the Trickster nevertheless "has his fun and he always comes up laughing" and, thus, promises that man will triumph despite being "slow to learn from his mistakes."

Consequently, the Trickster acts as a vehicle for creation in many traditional oral narratives by exemplifying the resilience of humankind and indicating that the world contains infinite potential. Thus, Krupat (2005, p. 448) calls the Trickster of Native American oral tales "a boundary-breaker but also an important boundary-maker; a destroyer of order and an institutor of order." Likewise, Ricketts (1966) remarks how many myths attribute the creation of order to the Trickster's actions. The animal Trickster's body-tricks act as another form of creation, despite often being initially destructive of a seemingly natural system: Jung (1959) observes that these characters frequently change sex to bear children, sever certain parts of their bodies to pursue independent tasks, and make plants from other body parts. As Grilli (2007) aptly summarizes:

> The trickster undermines the stability, apparent comprehensibility, and structured pattern of the safely organized world because he belongs to the world of disorder. Yet, what he brings about is not, as a paradox, utter destruction: with a slip of the tongue, error or oversight on his part a new world comes into being. He is, to be precise, a creative figure, though he creates by means of subverting, of exposing contradictions, of throwing everything into question. (p. 67)

The figure of the mythological Trickster, then, is ultimately appealing because it suggests the possibility of finding a solution despite apparent setbacks and rethinking orders that initially seem immutable.

Thus far, we have focused on scholarship surrounding the Trickster gods and animals that pervade ancient tales dealing with the creation of the world. There are, however, also human Tricksters, who are found in the field of folk- and fairy-tales: traditionally oral narratives that overlap with myth but are generally less concerned with cultural genesis and more with instructing the reader or listener how to behave. It is possible to divide these human Tricksters into multiple categories: for instance, the subversive hero, who may be either cunning or lucky, and the altruistic helper. The subversive hero is the fairy-tale Trickster closest to the wily animals of folklore. He is the protagonist of the story, and, as the Trickster animal may be disadvantaged by his size, the subversive hero is frequently the youngest child who outdoes their older, stronger, or wiser siblings on a quest: As Ashliman (2008, p. 141) comments, in fairy-tales, "it is virtually always the youngest brother who emerges victorious." Kononenko and Kukharenko (2008) further expand on the human folk Trickster:

> Although the trickster may appear foolish or naïve, he gets the best of even the most clever of men. . . . The trickster triumphs by his seeming stupidity. . . . In this group of trickster tales, the hero is often an instrument of social justice, punishing the greedy and exacting revenge for the wrongs perpetrated upon the lowly and the meek. Whether he is truly stupid, accomplishing what he does by accident, or remarkably clever, exacting justice in a way that leaves him immune to punishment, is always open to question. (p. 9)

In this quotation, the authors touch on a key division in subversive heroes. Shrewd Tricksters are found in such characters as Hop-o'-My-Thumb or Molly Whuppie from the Scottish fairy-tale, a young daughter who saves herself and her sisters by outfoxing a giant. Meanwhile, serendipitous Tricksters, who are foolish rather than clever and succeed through luck, include Ivan the Fool, the youngest son, a recurring character in Russian fairy-tales, whose "luck suddenly turns and he becomes an extraordinarily successful person. His luck changes not because he is wiser, but because he is still doing the most idiotic things" (Sinyavsky, 2007, p. 38). Ivan's unexpected success stems from his foolishness, echoing the mythological Trickster's ultimate triumph despite setbacks. Another lucky Trickster is found in "The Story of the Youth Who Went Forth to Learn What Fear Was," a traditional German oral tale transcribed by the Brothers Grimm. In this story, the hero's naive lack of fear leads him inadvertently to win the hand of the princess. Such characters illustrate a common theme in the Trickster lineage: an undermining of conventional logic by instinct.

Fairy-tale heroes who do not rely on Trickster cunning or luck may instead succeed with the help of a magical or crafty creature, as seen, for instance, in the Grimms' "The Golden Goose." This brings us to the second type of fairy-tale Trickster: the altruistic helper, a mysterious figure who lingers on the margins of the story rather than taking the role of hero, and whom Propp identifies as the "donor" (2003, p. 39). Prominent examples include the fairy godmother in "Cinderella" and Faithful John, a servant in a European fairy-tale who engenders a romance between his master and a princess. Aarne and Thompson's (1961) classification of folktales includes "Supernatural Helpers" as Tale Types *500–559*, recognizing such beings as a crucial trope in folk- and fairy-tales. These shadowy aides are Tricksters in their catalytic and subversive presences and use intelligence or magic to help the hero overcome an authoritative adversary; they are also reflected in the crafty servants on the classical and early modern stages. This chapter will now turn to a closer examination of these creatures.

### The Trickster on the Shakespearean Stage

According to Koepping (1985, pp. 193-194), Trickster characters appear in "primitive mythology and in classical antiquity as well as in modern deritualized and more secular form as the fool and jester in the prankster tales of the time of the Reformation" and in "the dramas of Shakespeare." In traditional theatre, the Trickster characters vary, bringing subversive energy to the plays but expressing it through different personalities. As Fox (1994) explains, the more literary forms of narrative that have developed since oral tales "begin to make the characteristics of the Trickster more fragmented and to assign different aspects to different characters, rather than trying to bundle them all up in one contradictory, protean roustabout" (Fox, 1994, p. 300). In part, this seems to be the result of the characters' diverse sources of influence. Dynes (1993), for instance, observes that Tricksters on the Jacobean stage may have developed from "the *dolosus servus*, the crafty servant of Roman New Comedy, and the Vice of the English morality play" (1993, p. 366). Certainly, the tricky slave of Roman New Comedy is a Trickster figure: More altruistic than the Trickster of folklore, they are usually scheming to help the lovers who seek to be together. O'Bryhim (2001, p. 108) defines him as "a stock character in New Comedy who abuses the character who threatens to block the successful resolution of the play." The Vice of medieval morality plays presents a more demonic type of Trickster, who "attempts to lure the Everyman hero from the straight and narrow road of virtue onto the primrose path of dalliance and sin" and is "a conniving, comic hypocrite who delights in chicanery for its own sake and speaks directly to the audience" (Deats, 2010, p. 6). Critics have suggested that Shakespearean figures like Sir John Falstaff, Claudius, and Iago may be traced back to these Vice characters (Glasgow, 1995; Ribner, 1960), who permeate plays with duplicity and debauchery. Meanwhile, the commedia dell'arte, which developed in Italy from the 16th century onward, made use of tricky servants called "zanni." These figures were more selfish than the servants of New Comedy and typically took to mocking their masters. The zanni would later influence figures in the Victorian harlequinade (Harrison, 1998; McCormick, 2004; Storey, 1978) and the wicked puppet in the English Punch and Judy shows (Davis, 2003; Forti-Lewis, 1998).

Thus, a strong Trickster legacy is apparent in the theatre in numerous eras and cultures. For the sake of example, we will focus on the Trickster of the Shakespearean stage, as Shakespeare is a highly influential playwright who likely took inspiration from pre-existing sources—not merely from medieval morality plays and Roman New Comedy but also from folktales prevalent in England at the time. Burton (1988) suggests that Shakespeare's *The Winter's Tale* was based on structures and themes from English folktales, while Fox and Woolf (2002) demonstrate the importance of vernacular culture and oral tales in early modern Britain. Belsey (2007), similarly, has produced an extensive study of Shakespeare's indebtedness to folk- and fairy-tales, including Trickster tales such as "Child Rowland" and "Jack the Giant Killer," in which the unlikely boy-hero triumphs. Belsey (2007) posits that the shapes of Shakespeare's plays would have been familiar to early modern audiences due to their appropriation of folktales. Woodford (2004) comments on the elements of "The Goose Girl in the Well" that are implicit in *King Lear*, and Woodbridge (1993) argues that Shakespeare deliberately researched folktales to gather material for his work.

Assuming, then, that the playwright would have encountered Trickster characters in folklore, we can divide Shakespeare's own Tricksters into several groups. There are buffoons like Sir John Falstaff and Sir Toby Belch, court jesters such as Feste, Touchstone, and *King Lear*'s Fool, magical servants like Puck and Ariel, scheming villains including Iago, *King Lear*'s Edmund, and Richard III, and omniscient manipulators such as Prospero and *Measure for Measure*'s Duke. These characters are diverse (some are frivolous comedians, others thrive upon tragedy), yet all are subversive outsiders with access to unconventional forms of intelligence. We concentrate here on those who most closely resemble the comical, chaotic Tricksters of folk- and fairy-tale: the buffoon, court jester, and magical servant.

The buffoon, or clown, is perhaps the Shakespearean figure closest to the traditional Trickster of myth and folktale. Not as harmless as his name suggests, he is epitomized by the character of Sir John Falstaff: According to Bell (2011, p. 19), "Everything Shakespeare knew, loved, and distrusted about clowns goes into Falstaff." Like those folkloric animals, he is primarily a boundary-crosser: a trait immediately evident in his appearance in multiple plays and genres, namely the two histories of *Henry IV* and the comedy *The Merry Wives of Windsor*. His boundary-crossing is further evinced by his blurring of social status: Falstaff's knighthood and eloquence with language seem incongruous with his roguish behavior, which establishes him as a vessel for contradiction. Dynes (1993, p. 384) tells us that, at the end of a Jacobean play, "The trickster may be expelled or subsumed back into society." Drawing from Dynes's (1993) theory, it can be argued that Falstaff, at different points, puts up with both these treatments. At the end of *The Merry Wives of Windsor*, he is forgiven and welcomed to the feast (5.5.168–170). Meanwhile, in the final scene of *Henry IV, Part Two*, Falstaff visits Hal—now king—and expects to be rewarded by his old friend but is turned away with nothing, thus returning to his shady taverns and brothels (5.5.50–73). In this history play, Falstaff, like the Trickster of folklore, is fated to live on the margins of society, a space that facilitates his rebellious creativity.

Along with being an outsider in the realm of the play, Falstaff also plays with the fabric of the fiction itself by standing between the audience and the characters, threatening to break through the artificial and enter the real. Welsford (1968, p. xii) proposes that clownish characters act "as an intermediary between the stage and the auditorium," and Bell (2011, p. 38) describes how "Falstaff regularly soliloquizes or directly addresses the audience [and] plays to two audiences: the one within fiction and the one outside of the fiction." The buffoon, like all of Shakespeare's Tricksters, thus exemplifies a sense of doubleness as he exists within the narrative but also shows awareness of the world beyond the fourth wall; "simultaneously actor and role, spectator and spectacle, observer and observed" is a description Bell (2011, p. 28) uses in relation to the "motley fool" but may be applied to every type of Shakespearean Trickster. Chiming with the mythological Trickster's physical excesses, Falstaff is old, fat, and lecherous and has been associated with Bakhtin's concept of the "grotesque body" (Grover-Friedlander, 2005; Pfister, 2002). Also, like the animal Trickster, he both tricks and is tricked: for instance, in *Henry IV, Part One*, Falstaff deceives his friends at the Tavern by recounting how he and other friends were robbed by a hundred men just after committing their own robbery, not knowing that he was actually robbed by the friends he is recounting the story to (2.2.100–109). Bell (2011, p. 45) calls it "a game of trick the trickster." Likewise, the imbroglio of *The Merry Wives of Windsor* begins with Falstaff plotting to woo the wealthy Mistresses Page and Ford simultaneously, a scheme that backfires when both women repeatedly trick Falstaff. At the end of the play, Falstaff accepts the joke and begrudgingly tells the women: "Well, I am your theme. You have the start of me" (5.5.159–160). Like the animal Trickster of myth, he embodies different levels of comedy; we laugh at him and with him. Ricketts (1966) describes the mythological Trickster as one who "meets a human need directly, by enabling men to endure the burden of the failures of their lives in self-forgetful laughter. . . . They laugh at him until they are laughing at themselves. He endures their ridicule like a suffering saviour, and in the end he saves them, through their laughter" (Ricketts, 1966, pp. 347-348). Welsford (1968), in turn, ascribes a similarly cathartic function to the fool figure in culture and literature:

> if the fool is "he who gets slapped," the most successful fool is "he who is none the worse for his slapping," and this introduces a new and more interesting factor into the comic situation. The fool is now no longer a mere safety-valve for the suppressed instincts of the bully, he provides a subtler balm for the fears and wounds of those afflicted with the inferiority complex, the greater part of humanity . . . It is all very well to laugh at the buffeted simpleton; we too are subject to the blows of fate, and of people stronger and wiser than ourselves, in fact we are the silly Clown, the helpless Fool. (pp. 314-315)

Thus, much as the folkloric Trickster confirms that life is a game, rogues as might be found in Shakespeare convince us "that wasted affection, thwarted ambition, latent guilt are mere delusions to be laughed away" (Welsford, 1968, p. 318).

Closely related to the buffoon is the figure of the court jester. While the buffoon may be recognized as a "natural" fool, the court jester is often labeled an "artificial" fool because he dresses in motley and acts idiotically in order to entertain (e.g., Corrigan, 2016, p. 143; Ghose, 2008, p. 95; Halio, 1992, p. 7): He is "a sophisticated courtly performer" (Bell, 2011, p. 12). As with Trickster heroes of folktales, it is difficult to discern whether the court jester is truly foolish or just cleverly mimicking the natural fool. The latter seems more likely, as the main function of this character-type is to provide insightful commentary on the actions of the other characters that often underscores the characters' follies for the audience but uses self-consciously foolish statements to obscure his wisdom. His observations are prescient but typically ignored by the other characters. Consequently, the court jester in Shakespeare has been promulgated as the "wise fool" (e.g., Duthie, 2005, p. 73): an oxymoron that echoes the paradoxical folkloric Tricksters. The character may appear mad but ultimately reveals some truths to the audience, thus occupying a liminal space between audience and narrative—as Welsford (1968, p. 319) observes, "the fool knows the truth because he is a social outcast, and spectators see most of the game."

Certainly, few character-types have the Shakespearean court jester's capacity for insight and wit. Touchstone in *As You Like It* was the first of these to be gifted with the Trickster's eloquence, and Bell (2011) notes two of Touchstone's characteristics that seem pertinent to understanding the Trickster. Firstly, he tells us that Touchstone's puns epitomize fooling "by implying contradictory possibilities" (Bell, 2011, p. 22) and that, by uttering lines with multiple meanings, the jester "fragments our perspectives, confusing our conceptions of reality by introducing radically different, even diametrically opposed, perspectives" (Bell, 2011, p. 23). In this regard, the court fool is displaying a doubleness of vision typical of the Trickster while also echoing the creative power of the Trickster's language, which has been explored by Vizenor (1989). Secondly, Bell (2011, p. 25) highlights how Touchstone is "always plumping for physical pleasures and bodily needs, the first to say he is tired, hungry, or horny," which is analogous to the folkloric Trickster's carnal appetites—and the Shakespearean buffoon's physical grotesqueness.

The court jester embodies the spirit of carnival, which is almost metonymic with comedy. Bakhtin (1984) has crucially established carnival as a period that sees the inversion of normal social hierarchies, when a person's "behavior, gesture, and discourse are freed from the authority of all hierarchical positions (social estate, rank, age, property) defining them totally in noncarnival life, and thus from the vantage point of noncarnival life become eccentric and inappropriate" (Bakhtin, 1984, p. 123). In the early modern period, carnival existed as a means of purging unrest within the community: It was a transient period during which rebellion could be safely acted out and expunged, subsequently making it possible for the citizens to settle contentedly back into normal hierarchies (Bakhtin, 1984). This cycle of dissolution and restoration resonates with the disruptive Trickster figure. We have seen how the Trickster of myth and folklore acts subversively to heal mankind, create boundaries, and further the progression of culture; in a similar way, Shakespearean Tricksters, in particular the court jester, temporarily upend "normality" to ultimately reaffirm it.

Carnival connects with comedy, and the Trickster has established roots in humor; yet, the Trickster does not appear merely in Shakespeare's comedies but also brings their cycle of disruption and reconsolidation to the tragedies, along with some sharp insights. *King Lear*'s Fool, a court jester "like Touchstone and Feste, is an 'all-licensed' critic who sees and speaks the truth about the people around him" (Welsford, 1968, p. 254). Welsford (1968) suggests that, while Feste's and Touchstone's amusing insights simply heighten their charisma, Lear's Fool presents disquieting questions about the barriers between madness and sense. In this play, the Fool is twinned with Lear, establishing a parallel "between someone who was fearing for his own sanity and someone who professionally pretended to be crazy, between a near-fool and a would-be fool" (Törnqvist, 2015, p. 30). With his typical Trickster traits of subversion, artifice, and ambiguity, the court jester probes distinctions between performance and identity, thereby blurring boundaries of the self.

We now move from the court jester to the tricky servant, who may be the most recognizable of the early modern stage Tricksters and is not limited to Shakespeare. Like the benevolent court jester, the tricky servant may use their wiles to aid the hero's endeavors, as can be seen with characters like Moll Cutpurse in Dekker and Middleton's *The Roaring Girl*, Jonson's Brainworm in *Every Man in His Humour*, or Shakespeare's Puck and Ariel. Dynes (1993, p. 376-377) refers to a "preponderance of villainous or egocentric tricksters" on the Jacobean stage and notes that "the altruistic trickster, a much rarer figure, most often appears as a servant or attendant who contradicts the wishes of a master in order to effect the marriage of the master's son." Indeed, the tricky servant usually adopts a more selfish role—as seen with Jonson's Mosca in *Volpone*. Ultimately, Tricksters' natures throughout folklore, theatre, and prose fiction are almost always ambiguous: As figures of contradiction, they can act both altruistically and selfishly.

Bell (2011, p. 16) describes *A Midsummer Night's Dream*'s Puck as "Mercurial and protean, . . . a trickster and a shape-shifter." This crafty sprite, acting on his master's orders, is responsible for the hierarchical upheaval that takes place in the play; like the folkloric Trickster, he is not above making mistakes, and his act of applying the love potion to the eyes of Lysander rather than the intended Demetrius instigates the play's romantic entanglement (2.2.84). Yet, guided by Puck's chicanery, the turmoil is eventually resolved, and, in the manner customary of comedies, the play ends with a wedding. The Trickster's mischief, radiating the spirit of carnival, has caused tensions to be purged so that peace can return. Puck, like so many of Shakespeare's Tricksters, breaks the fourth wall and addresses the audience. The most obvious example is found in his epilogue speech: "If we shadows have offended,/ Think but this, and all is mended:/ That you have but slumbered here,/ While these visions did appear" (5.1.2275–2278). This saucy address not only allows Puck to step through the veil of fiction but also seemingly threatens to place the audience within the sphere of fiction, making them, like Bottom, the dreamers accountable for the action—or "visions"—of the play. Puck is suggesting that the spectators have been complicit in the narrative: that they, like Shakespeare himself, have helped weave the story. Indeed, the Trickster in Shakespearean theatre casts confusion over the boundaries between character, spectator, and author—through Puck's activity, we witness such roles fuse together as part of a wider communion between reality and imagination. This communion, as we suggest below, is also what supports the relevance of the Trickster in consumer society.

### A Figure of Consumer Society Narratives

The previous sections portrayed the Trickster as distanced from modern society, whether a "culture hero" engrained in ancient myth (Boas, 1898, p. 4) or a stock character employed by Renaissance playwrights. Hyde (2008) argues that the notion of a modern Trickster is problematic because the contemporary world lacks the necessary sacred context. Similarly, Storey (1996, p. 170) suggests that crafty servants in modern literature are but "reduced" versions of the Trickster figures found on the classical and early modern stage. Since the latter decades of the 20th century, however, criticism has also recognized the importance of Tricksters in contemporary narratives. Artemis (2010), for instance, explores the Trickster in Virginia Woolf's *Orlando*, and Becker (2010) discusses tricksterism in Franz Kafka's "A Hunger Artist." Sheehan (2013) proposes that Ralph Ellison's *Invisible Man* reimagines the traditional folk Trickster, Kononenko and Kukharenko (2008) herald the protagonist of Larry Charles's 2006 film *Borat* as a trickster rooted in mythology, and Landay (1998) investigates the rise of female Tricksters in modern American culture. There is also another type of contemporary narratives that significantly relies on the Trickster and that we develop here: the contemporary marketplace narratives, in which the mythological Trickster is today intercepted and (re-)interpreted by consumers, marketers, and mass media—like many archetypes (Hirschman, 2000; Thompson, 2004).

We suggest here that narratives about consumers, as well as the narratives that consumers develop, connect them, in some situations and in many respects, to the Trickster figure. Take, for instance, this excerpt from Ballinger (1989/2004) about the Trickster figure in Native American tales:

> It is usually not clear in the stories if Trickster believes that he can successfully imitate others, but it ultimately does not matter; in either case he is caught in the internecine warfare of self and social deception. Grasping at social status, Trickster attempts to draw upon resources he doesn't have and calls the attempt "power" when in fact it is nothing but warped and self-defeating self-aggrandizement. The magic acts of self-immolation by those he imitates are sign that they have lived beyond the Self in ways that serve the community. In Trickster's hands the tricks become self-mutilation. Driven by his appetites for the social status that individual power would give him, Trickster is doomed to defeat and frustration, even danger, because he fails to see two things: first, that true power doesn't come from self alone and certainly doesn't derive simply from boastful claims; and second that true power leads beyond oneself (evidenced in Bungling Host stories by the power holder's ability to provide for others). All in all, in spite of Trickster's violations of moral and social restraints (the crossing of boundaries that we mistakenly call marginality), he fails to cross the most important boundary to be crossed if there is to be community: the boundary of Self. (p. 78)

In many ways, what Ballinger writes about here unintentionally draws an interesting parallel with today's consumers and their identity issues, power relations, individualism, and social performance in consumer society. Another parallel is the power given to magical thinking and imagination. Because marketing is the art of offering what is never totally true nor totally false, the real and fantasy worlds blur into a magical intermediate space called the marketplace, where imagining and manipulating others and ourselves with signs and narratives is common practice. Marketing creates an intermediate space at the service of consumers' bulimia, pursuit of personal development, and happiness. By saying this, we make marketing a tricksterlike entity too, just as we consider consumers potential tricksters who fit the contemporary, neoliberal narratives of liquid life particularly well.

Cova and Cova (2012) identify three key consumer figures that have emerged from marketing discourses over the past 40 years: individualistic, hedonistic, and creative consumers. These three key figures, we believe, not only represent consumer figures that fit the ideology of the marketplace but also highlight the relevance of the Trickster figure among other consumer figures because they reveal both the creative consumer who is following the pleasure principle and the struggling consumer involved in an existential quest to find his place as an individual, but within society. The latter is a recurrent theme in many social science disciplines, which we also find under the terms of agency and structure. As noted above through the words of Babcock-Abrahams (1975, pp. 160-161), the Trickster "embodies the fundamental contradiction of our existence: the contradiction between the individual and society, between freedom and constraint." But the Trickster can also overcome (or at least accept) this contradiction. This, we believe, explains in large part why the Trickster is a relevant figure in contemporary consumer society.

To affirm the relevance of the Trickster in consumer society and the narratives it produces, we offer three arguments below. In particular, we stress that the marketplace recounts the story of a liquid life in which consumers are tempted to playfully experiment with life and identity while remaining in a permanent (at least, a much longer) state of liminality.

## #1 Playing with the Rules

The first argument for the relevance of the Trickster figure in contemporary consumer society is that consumers play with the rules. While consumers can play *by* the rules or *with* the rules (Grayson, 1999), consumers-tricksters definitely play *with* the rules. For instance, the streaming platform Netflix's terms of use stipulate that the account should be for "personal and non-commercial use only and may not be shared with individuals beyond your household," but in practice, Netflix tolerates that its customers often play *with* its sharing rules, notably by sharing their account with friends who live in another city (or cities), for example. Another trick carried out by consumers is *wardrobing*, that is, buying items (generally clothes) with the intention to use them for a short and given period before bringing them back to the seller and getting reimbursed. One final example is the yellow rubber duck: The fun and playful tub toy that erases bath fears and stimulates developmental growth during childhood can transform into a river racer to raise funds or a vibrating sex toy. But it is always by playing *with* the rules: Whether Rubber Duckie becomes a red duck with arched eyebrows and horns or an object of sexual pleasure, it remains a floating toy that is used in a water setting. This tricksterlike aspect of playing *with* instead of *by* the rules indicates another tricksterlike tendency to move from *ludus* to *paidia*,[3] from established rules of consumption to a spontaneous desire to play *with* consumption (Alemany Oliver, 2015). For instance, there is a tricksterlike tendency not to visit IKEA stores to buy furniture but to enter IKEA to play hide-and-seek or to transform Disneyland's Splash Mountain ride into an opportunity to take funny and staged pictures of people posing during the ride. Finally, we noted above that, in literature, Tricksters can solve problems within a community but also be subversive—partly thanks to their creativity and freedom. This is visible in consumer society, where consumers-tricksters play, for instance, *with* the meaning and role usually attributed to wooden pallets to transform them into home furniture, cut Canadian bills in half to create a useful new local currency called "le demi" in Quebec's Gaspé region, or develop websites such as Napster in 1999 or The Pirate Bay, which have reversed the power of negotiation between consumers and brands. More generally, protest against traditional visions and tacit rules of society and their violations can be observed in—and partly made possible through—consumer society. But it is also the marketing rules themselves that can be challenged and violated. As Cova, Kozinets, and Shankar (2011) note,

> consumers . . . are not naive about living in their commercial-material world: like Madonna, they are commercial-material boys and girls. They know the game plan; they read the playbooks; they know the strategy. Conscious of a partial manipulation, they decide to what extent they will be manipulated and they manipulate too. (p. 8)

[3] The distinction between *ludus* and *paidia* is originally made by Roger Caillois. Note also that the term *paidia* derives from Greek and means "child."

This is in keeping with the image of the court jester in Shakespeare, who is promulgated as the wise fool, as seen above.

## #2 Experimenting with the Paradoxes of Fluid vs. Fixed, Socially Acceptable vs. Taboo Identity Consumption

The second argument for the relevance of the Trickster figure in contemporary consumer society is the Trickster's ability to navigate among the paradoxes of identity consumption. It is well accepted now that consumers experiment with fragmented and sometimes contradictory identities (Firat & Venkatesh, 1995), which leads to difficulties in managing the consumer as a concept and an entity (Gabriel & Lang, 2008). In sociology, Bauman (1996) highlights how people have moved from being pilgrims during modernity to tourists, strollers, players, and vagabonds during postmodernity, which he later called liquid modernity. What is common among these four liquid figures is the fear of fate and of getting pinned down by society, while we expect, deep inside, to have multiple chances, encounters, identities, and many other life narratives in a single life (we will return to these four figures below). In this sense, we may understand the fragmented identities of the consumer as a sort of tricksterization of the consumer.

While the Trickster reconciles, or at least tries to reconcile, the great paradoxes of humanity, consumer society magnifies some of these paradoxes. For instance, brands sell the illusion of total identity freedom and limitless life by offering to include thousands of different lifestyles in ageless consumers' identity projects. But consumers remain materially, biologically, financially, culturally, socially, and geographically limited. On the one hand, we are fragmented into several idealized and commercialized elements of identity that supposedly help us increasingly be ourselves—and, therefore, different and free from the influence of others; on the other hand, we are desperately seeking a sense of belonging to the point of looking like others and accepting liberticidal social rules. Consumption helps us play predefined roles, like the role of the waiter depicted by Sartre (1943), which ultimately prevents us from being completely free. Whether this is done to belong to a community, out of fear of total freedom, or for any other reason, consumers eventually spend a large part of their time with a romantic mindset: They struggle between idealizing freedom and fully embracing it. They also look for hedonic gratification by consuming daydreams, fantasies, and personal pleasure, which suits consumer society (Campbell, 1987) and pleases the Trickster.

The Trickster is also a romantic figure but does not necessarily suffer from pensive and existential sadness, as we could expect from romantics. The Trickster favors freedom over any social rule and will use imagination to overcome their awareness that, because of their nature, they will never totally meet society's expectations. In this sense, the Trickster does not accept the idea that society will always keep them from living entirely as they wish, so they use creativity and energy to play with the rules of society to ensure it never happens. While conducting fieldwork in Southern California in 2013, Alemany Oliver observed that some of the participants' life narratives, like that of Ava (35, USA) below, reflect certain traits of the Trickster figure. In the case of Ava, the Trickster figure is pervasive as she begins by rejecting society's rules and traditions, experiments with the many options that life has to offer, follows the pleasure principle, and finally uses consumer society's rules and plays *with* them to make a living out of a lifestyle that is often rejected (though fantasized) by society. She says:

> I went to get my master, I was accepted, I went to Paris to do
> an internship because I had to have an internship before starting

my master's. So I did all that... and when I was all ready to go, I had to go to Paris, live there for a year and then come back and start my intense German program because I did not speak very well... and then I was gonna start my regular classes—2 years of Master's but one year in Berlin. This is what I was gonna do... and I went to Paris, I worked a 9-to-5 job, I took the subway... I mean the subway is just as bad as seating in rush hour over here... [...] And I was going to this routine of what people do, and it reminds me... you feel like a zombie cause you're such doing it every day and you feel like just a zombie... and you have no time for yourself... like everybody wants to go to the pub but I have no time for the pub: I've got to go to the gym, I've got to go to the food store... and I'm home at ten. And I've got to get up at seven in the morning to do that again. [...] And I just started realizing that, okay I'm gonna get my master's and I'm gonna do this... I'm gonna be working for "Corporate America" and I'm gonna be a hundred thousand dollars in debt to get my master's and I'm not guaranteed a job... Do I really want this type of lifestyle? Working for somebody else and being miserable... if it wasn't for the travelling and being in Paris... because I had fun... and I said "you know what? That's just what I decided:" because you know I was so driven... I am so driven but I was even more back then and I was just so hard with myself so I say "you know what: I'll just become lazy" not literally but... I decided not to get my master's and it was a very hard decision for me because I was so hard with myself... I came back to the United States, I started my own magazine... but I was doing something on my own. I was doing my little things.
[...]
It began like letting go of society and what they say is right, and what your parents think and religion... Since I let go of religion my life changed for the better immediately. And then it was society, like "oh I can't be a stripper cause... what people will think about me?" Cause I became a stripper. And that was really hard to become a stripper because I was just so worried about... like the future... "I'm nearly like a loser if I become a stripper"... "I'm not gonna make up some story about why I'm stripping... that I'm in school..." you know... what all strippers do because... they do... they don't want to... cause people... many go to strip clubs but still judge you, they want to see you naked but they are like "oh, what do you do... outside of this?" If you tell them "nothing," they're like "oh... so this is really your job?"... "Yes, this is really my job and I love it, I'm proud of it!" And they stop looking at me. So once I let that all go, everything became a lot easier. When you stop caring about what people think about you, then you start living your life, and you do what you want. It's just letting go...

In many respects, this story echoes the Trickster myth of the Winnebago Indians, as noted by Blowsnake (1956). In this myth, the Trickster gradually becomes self-conscious as he engages in encounters and adventures. He transforms himself into a woman, breaks taboos, listens to his drives and his sexual appetite, and creates disorder in society. Later, he becomes a man again, gets married, and has children. The

Trickster becomes a perfect citizen, almost a Senex (i.e., a wise man). At this point, the Trickster symbolizes the birth of the adult, passing from the unconsciousness of the newborn to become a responsible grown-up. He stops following the pleasure principle to consider the reality principle. However, this new situation in which he becomes the man that society asked for makes him suffer from a sort of Baudelaire's (1857) spleen—i.e., melancholia or pensive sadness. While he has become the man that society is waiting for, he finally decides not to have duties toward society and prefers to "go around . . . and visit people" (Blowsnake, 1956, p. 52). As noted by Radin (1956), this decision expresses the protest against society and domestication. This is the Trickster and its most interesting facet: Like Ava above, the Trickster knows the rights and duties of a society very well, as well as everything about the preconceived individual one has to be. They can even adapt to society if they wish to do so. But they decide to play *with* rather than *by* the rules. They decide to follow the pleasure principle simply because it brings a more intense life, no matter what society says. The case of Ava also echoes the work of the novelist Elizabeth Taylor, in which her use of Tricksters highlights a chasm between a sense of identity being naturally fluid and a common conception of people embodying a fixed self—the latter of which she considers to be a false belief enforced by the patriarchal order.

#### #3 Living in Permanent Liminal States

The third argument for conceiving the Trickster as a contemporary consumer figure is the ease with which they evolve in permanent or at least long-term liminal states. Today's consumer society can be described as liquid (e.g., Bardhi & Eckhardt, 2017; Ulver-Sneistrup & Ostberg, 2011) since, as Bauman (2005, p. 1) writes regarding modern liquid society, "the conditions under which its members act change faster than it takes the ways of acting to consolidate into habits and routines." This means people barely have time to understand and master structural and conceptual change in our society when the structures and concepts have already changed. As others have suggested (Alemany Oliver, 2018; Mimoun & Bardhi, 2018), the permanent impermanence that characterizes liquid consumer society leaves room to think of society and consumers as almost permanently stuck in what Turner (1969) calls a liminal state. According to Turner (1969), liminal states can happen during rituals when an individual loses their status without having reached a replacement yet. It is a moment of indistinction, during which the individual is located in an in-between state.

At least three reasons may support the notion that consumer society triggers the possible existence of an almost permanent liminal state. Firstly, consumer society deals in large part with identity projects and identity play—that is, by keeping a stable and harmonious self-concept while exploring and extending it thanks to consumption (Arnould & Thompson, 2005; Belk, 1988). Also, it is generally accepted that developing identity projects through consumption may sometimes lead to such a liminal state, where consumers experience role transitions (Schouten, 1991). In a marketplace that offers us the ability to live out unlimited lifestyles by exploring unlimited roles depending on the signs conveyed by products and services, there is always the possibility of becoming someone else—or always more ourselves—and, then, engaging in perpetual identity work and change, which could trigger liminal states.

Secondly, the market has the potential to trigger permanent liminal states because the conditions in which it puts consumers make them expect that something more is always on the way (e.g., smarter devices, bigger screens, faster connections, greener products, more authenticity, more entertainment, more realistic, cheaper...

and ever more intense experiences). These expectations of the people who have long demanded that they be entertained lead corporations and organizations, in part, to work toward developing pseudo-events—that is, premeditated events conceived in such a way that it gives them value and importance in the eyes of the public (Boorstin, 1962). In his work on news, Boorstin (1962/1992) writes:

> Demanding more than the world can give us, we require that something be fabricated to make up for the world's deficiency. This is only one example of our demand for illusions . . . Every American knows the anticipation with which he picks up his morning newspaper at breakfast or opens his evening paper before dinner, or listens to the newscasts every hour on the hour as he drives across country, or watches his favorite commentator on television interpret the events of the day. Many enterprising Americans are now at work to help us satisfy these expectations. Many might be put out of work if we should suddenly moderate our expectations. But it is we who keep them in business and demand that they fill our consciousness with novelties, that they play God for us. (p. 9)

By increasing the consumers' expectations and meeting their demands, the market has created an intermediate space in which what is available is already outdated because of the simple idea that the market is already working toward a replacement. Consumers want to be at a crossroads rather than on a single road: Just as in *The Idiot* by Dostoyevsky (1869/2003, p. 394), when Ippolit Terentyev explains that "Columbus was happy not when he had discovered America, but when he was about to discover it," what pleases consumers more than actual consumption is the narrative about what is about to happen thanks to consumption. People's great expectations of and interest in what is about to happen echoes Bauman's (1996) four figures of liquid modernity, which we mentioned above, in the sense that these four figures do not want to get pinned down (i.e., caught by life itself). Whether it is the stroller and a life of simulation, the vagabond and a life of freedom and opportunities with no final destination, the tourist and the search for novelty, or the player and a life that perpetually offers new chances and part of luck, Bauman's (1996) figures seem to accept perpetual change with the idea that something new—something more— might always happen.

The last reason for potential permanent liminality might be marketing itself, as an entity that plays with reality and concepts to invite consumers to observe the possibility of otherness—more so than actually embracing otherness. From the image of an orderly but sometimes constraining and boring daily life, marketing proposes vanishing points on this image, which Deleuze and Guattari (1980) call *lines of escape*. These brilliantly marketized vanishing points are created in part by minor transgressions of society's critical rules—transgressions that do not put dominant structures and elements at risk and are more likely to be socially accepted when they occur in the context of consumption, or major transgressions of society's minor rules—so that, in the end, relations of power and dominant constructions do not change.[4] In other words, it is accepted that marketing offers lines of escape and sometimes remains close to the edge of conventional social and moral boundaries, which does not mean it necessarily crosses the boundaries. Marketing can follow dominant social and moral constructions but also enjoys being the entity that

---

[4] It is important to note here that we believe relations of power and dominant social constructions can change in the marketplace, especially with consumers-tricksters, but not with marketing actions alone. While marketing can offer lines of escape, these lines of escape can become subversive only if consumers appropriate these lines and interpret them as calls to action.

offers escapism from these social and moral constructions and suggests or imposes alternative meanings, hierarchies, and arrangements. In fact, while Wiget (1985) considers the Trickster a useful institutionalized principle of disorder, marketing has institutionalized the principle of disorder in the marketplace, the latter becoming an intermediate space between the real and fantasy that gives people enough agency to change their destiny and challenge social constructions. However, because this intermediate space we call the marketplace offers an institutionalized principle of disorder, the disorder can no longer produce disorder: Boundaries are crossed only up to a certain point so that a small amount of disorder allows permanent order in the system. In the end, even if consumers can temporally and locally cross the boundaries and feel the disorder they create can challenge dominant paradigms (Kozinets, 2002), lines of escape are rather lines of dormant potentialities that consumers observe and play with, while they stay in an in-between space (i.e., a crossroad) where the real and the fantasy blur; potentialities rarely come into existence except during momentary acts of consumption, which remain hyperreal moments and, therefore, not real (Baudrillard, 1981). A crossroad from where the presence of multiple roads that consumers never take too far, will reduce the fear of fate and getting pinned down as these roads represent the multiple chances, encounters, identities, and life narratives that they could reach. And as long as marketing offers consumers the opportunity to play the role of the Trickster by experimenting with the different roads while having the sense of freedom, consumers will ask for more while systematically returning to the crossroad to start a new journey. In the end, the apparent disorder created by these multiple roads and lines of escape allows marketing and the capitalist system to endure by keeping consumers locked in this in-between, liminal space.

### Conclusion: A Life of Potentialities

Because of their thirst to live life to the full, even to the detriment of habits and customs, because of the malicious pleasure they take from playing tricks on others, and because of their capacity to overthrow an established order, Tricksters are more or less dangerous or beneficial agitators in society. They reflect the fantasy of being here and there at the same time, not having to choose, or, given the finitude of life, being an incessant becoming—a permanent beginning that constantly reshuffles the cards.

While consumer society promises eternal youth, as well as the multitude of life opportunities and identities that go with it, the Trickster delights in living all these lives and playing by and with the rules imposed on the intermediate area of consumption, while ultimately remaining partly determined by it and also tricked by it—like the folkloric Trickster. If the carnival in the early modern period represented a transient period during which the population could safely challenge order and hierarchies, the same is true of the marketplace today in safer settings. What is generally not tolerated by society (e.g., adult childlikeness) becomes acceptable within artistic and creative realms, as well as the intermediate area of consumption; sometimes, it is even encouraged. The one-day tricksterlike carnivalists of the early modern period transformed into permanent tricksterlike consumers who enjoy— at will—the possibility of escapism and change. Like Falstaff and Touchstone, the Trickster represents a bridge between the artificial and the real, an intermediary or "lord of in-between" (Hyde, 2008, p. 6). Therefore, this figure occupies its rightful place in the marketplace that we have described as an intermediate area of consumption, in-between the fantasy and the real, the inner and outer lives of consumers, and producing liminality. The liminality that characterizes this liquid intermediate area of consumption moves people between two states: their current and imperfect life, on the one hand, and the narrated augmented life that consumption will bring in the near future, on the other hand. This situation is likely to place people in liminal states too, where not being anything yet—rather, they are about to be something else—leads one to imagine oneself as anything because consumption would make it possible.

The exploration of this potential, as we have seen in this chapter, is a task that the Trickster performs brilliantly and is fundamental to consumer activity. It is a task that requires people to be enlivened by a Deleuzian desire for which, we suggest, the Trickster is the very definition. Deleuze and Guattari (1972, 1980) see desire as a positive effect, an intensity that increases our willingness to change. Desire gives rise to elements of becoming; it introduces multiplicity, creativity, and energy into people's lives, as well as our social relationships and society. According to this view, desire is an energy and a pre-personal production (i.e., not internal to a person and already present here) rather than the result of an absence: It is a nomadic and positive intensity. Therefore, there cannot be a state of satiety, since desire is the blood that courses through the veins of any assembled body (Deleuze & Guattari, 1972, 1980). To conclude, there will always be Tricksters if we accept that life relies on this very idea of constant change within assembled bodies comprised of minority and dominant elements. The Trickster represents the energy that minority elements need to deterritorialize their assemblages; it represents becomings. In short, there is no childlikeness without the Trickster.

## References

Aarne, A. (1961). *The types of the folktale: A classification and bibliography*. Academia Scientiarum Fennica.

Alemany Oliver, M. (2015). *A realist(ic) interpretivist approach to childlikeness in consumer research: Neoteny, play, reality, and the reterritorializing adulthood* [Doctoral dissertation, Aix-Marseille Université, IAE Aix]. AMU Campus Library.

Alemany Oliver, M. (2018). L'enfant intérieur, un concept marketing universel ? Exploration du concept aux États-Unis et en France. *Management International, 23*(1), 56–67.

Arnould, E. J., & Thompson, C. J. (2005). Consumer Culture Theory (CCT): Twenty years of research. *Journal of Consumer Research, 31*(March), 868–882.

Artemis, R. (2010). With Orlando in Wonderland. In H. Bloom & B. Hobby (Eds.), *The trickster* (pp. 151–158). Infobase Publishing.

Ashliman, D. L. (2008). Brothers. In D. Haase (Ed.), *The Greenwood encyclopedia of folktales and fairy tales* (Vol.1) (pp. 140–142). Greenwood Press.

Babcock-Abrahams, B. (1975). 'A tolerated margin of mess': The trickster and his tales reconsidered. *Journal of the Folklore Institute, 11*(3), 147–186.

Bakhtin, M. (1963/1984). *Problems of Dostoevsky's poetics*. University of Minnesota Press.

Bakhtin, M. (1968/1984). *Rabelais and his world*. Indiana University Press.

Ballinger, F. (1989/2004). *Living sideways: Tricksters in American Indian oral traditions*. University of Oklahoma Press.

Bardhi, F., & Eckhardt, G. M. (2017). Liquid consumption. *Journal of Consumer Research, 44*(October), 582–597.

Baudrillard, J. (1981/1994). *Simulacra and simulation*. University of Michigan.

Bauman, Z. (1996). From pilgrim to tourist–or a short history of identity. In S. Hall & P. du Gay, *Questions of Cultural Identity* (pp. 18–36), Sage.

Bauman, Z. (2005). *Liquid life*. Polity.

Becker, J. (2010). Making the incomprehensible incomprehensible: The trickery of Kafka's 'A hunger artist.' In H. Bloom & Blake Hobby (Eds.) *The trickster* (pp. 101–108). Infobase Publishing.

Belk, R. W. (1988). Possessions and the extended self. *Journal of Consumer Research, 15*(September), 139–168.

Bell, R. H. (2011). *Shakespeare's great stage of fools*. Palgrave Macmillan.

Belsey, C. (2007). *Why Shakespeare?* Palgrave Macmillan.

Blowsnake, S. (1956/1988). The trickster myth of the Winnebago Indians. In P. Radin (Ed.), *The trickster: A study in American Indian mythology* (pp. 3–61), Schocken.

Boas, F. (1898). Introduction. In J. Teit, *Traditions of the Thompson River Indians of British Columbia* (pp. 1–19). Houghton, Mifflin and Company.

Boorstin, D. J. (1962/1992). *The image: A guide to pseudo-events in America*. Vintage.

Briggs, K. M. (1970). *A dictionary of British folk-tales in the English language, part A: Folk narratives* (Vol. 1). Indiana University Press.

Burton, J. (1988). Folktale, romance and Shakespeare. In D. Brewer (Ed.), *Studies in Medieval English romances: Some new approaches* (pp. 176–205). D. S. Brewer.

Campbell, C. (1987). *The romantic ethic and the spirit of modern consumerism*. Blackwell.

Campbell, J. (1949/2008). *The hero with a thousand faces*. New World Library.

Corrigan, N. L. (2016). Song, political resistance, and masculinity in Thomas Heywood's *The rape of Lucrece*. In L. C. Dunn & K. R. Larson (Eds.), *Gender and song in early modern England* (pp. 139–153). Routledge.

Cova, B., & Cova, V. (2012). On the road to prosumption: marketing discourse and the development of consumer competencies. *Consumption Markets & Culture, 15*(2), 149–168.

Cova, B., Kozinets, R. V., & Shankar, A. (2007/2011). Tribes, Inc.: The new world of tribalism. In B. Cova, R. V. Kozinets, & A. Shankar (Eds.), *Consumer tribes* (pp. 3–26). Routledge.

Currie, M. (2004). *Difference*. Routledge.

Davidson, H. R. E. (1979). Loki and Saxo's Hamlet. In P. V. A. Williams (Ed.), *The fool and the trickster: Studies in honour of Enid Welsford* (pp. 3–17). D. S. Brewer.

Davis, J. M. (2003). *Farce*. Transaction Publishers.

Deats, S. M. (2010). Introduction. In S. M. Deats (Ed.), *Doctor Faustus: A critical guide* (pp. 1–16). Continuum.

Mathieu Alemany Oliver and Lorna Wilkinson

Deleuze, G., & Guatarri, F. (1972/1983). *Anti-Oedipus: Capitalism and schizophrenia.* University of Minnesota Press.

Deleuze, G., & Guatarri, F. (1980/1987). *A thousand plateaus: Capitalism and Schizophrenia.* University of Minnesota Press.

Dostoyevsky, F. (1869/2003). *The Idiot.* Vintage.

Doty, W. G., & Hynes, W. J. (1993). Historical overview of theoretical issues: The problem of the trickster. In W. J. Hynes & W. G. Doty (Eds.), *Mythical trickster figures: Contours, contexts, and criticisms* (pp. 13–32). University of Alabama Press.

Duthie, G. I. (2005). *Shakespeare.* Routledge.

Dynes, W. R. (1993). The trickster-figure in Jacobean city comedy. *Studies in English Literature, 1500-1900, 33*(2), 365–384.

Eliade, M. (1963). *Myth and reality.* Harper & Row.

Firat, A. F., & Venkatesh, A. (1995). Liberatory postmodernism and the reenchantment of consumption. *Journal of Consumer Research, 22*(December), 239–67.

Forti-Lewis, A. (1998). Commedia dell'Arte. In V. K. Janik (Ed.), *Fools and jesters in literature, art, and history: A bio-bibliographical sourcebook* (pp. 146–154). Greenwood Press.

Fox, A., & Woolf, D. (2002). Introduction. In A. Fox & D. Woolf (Eds.), *The spoken word: Oral culture in Britain, 1500–1850* (pp. 1–51). Manchester University Press.

Fox, R. (1994). *The challenge of anthropology: Old encounters and new excursions.* Transaction Publishers.

Gabriel, Y., & Lang, T. (2008). New faces and new masks of today's consumer. *Journal of Consumer Culture, 8*(3), 321–340.

Ghose, I. (2008). *Shakespeare and laughter: A cultural history.* Manchester University Press.

Glasgow, R. D. V. (1995). *Madness, masks, and laughter: An essay on comedy.* Associated University Presses.

Grayson, K. (1999). The dangers and opportunities of playful consumption. In M. B. Holbrook (Ed.), *Consumer value: A framework for analysis and research* (pp. 105–125). Routledge.

Grilli, G. (1997/2007). *Myth, symbol and meaning in Mary Poppins: The governess as provocateur.* Routledge.

Grimm, J., & Grimm, W. (1812/1903). The golden goose. In E. H. L. Turpin (Ed.), *Grimm's fairy tales* (pp. 168–176). Maynard, Merrill and Co.

Grimm, J., & Grimm, W. (1826/2009). The story of the youth who went forth to learn what fear was. In J. Grimm & W. Grimm, *Fairy tales of the brothers Grimm* (pp. 400–141). The Floating Press.

Grover-Freidlander, M. (2005). *Vocal apparitions: The attraction of cinema to opera.* Princeton University Press.

Halio, J. L. (1992). Introduction. In J. L. Halio (Ed.), *The tragedy of King Lear* (pp. 1–94). Cambridge University Press.

Harrison, M. (1998). *The language of the theatre.* Routledge.

Hillman, J. (1983). *Inter views: Conversations between James Hillman and Laura Pozzo on therapy; biography; love, soul, dreams, work, imagination and the state of culture.* Harper & Row.

Hillman, J. (1991). *A Blue Fire.* Harper & Row.

Hirschman, E. C. (2000). Consumers' use of intertextuality and archetypes. In S. J. Hoch & R. J. Meyer (Eds.), *Advances in consumer research, Vol. 27* (pp. 57–63). Association for Consumer Research.

Hyde, L. (1998/2008). *Trickster makes this world: How disruptive imagination creates culture.* Canongate Books.

Hynes, W. J., & Doty, W. G. (1993). *Mythical trickster figures: Contours, contexts, and criticisms.* University of Alabama Press.

Jung, C. G. (1959/1980). *The archetypes and the collective unconscious.* Princeton University Press.

Koepping, K.-P. (1985). Absurdity and hidden truth: Cunning intelligence and grotesque body images as manifestations of the trickster. *History of Religions, 24*(3), 191–214.

Kononenko, N., & Kukharenko, S. (2008). Borat the trickster: Folklore and the media, folklore in the media. *Slavic Review, 67*(1), 8–18.

Kozinets, R. V. (2002). Can consumers escape the market? Emancipatory illuminations from Burning Man. *Journal of Consumer Research, 29*(June), 20–38.

Krupat, A. (2005). Native American trickster tales. In M. Charney (Ed.), *Comedy: A geographic and historical guide* (pp. 447–461). Praeger.

Landay, L. (1998). *Madcaps, screwballs, and con women: The female trickster in American culture.* University of Pennsylvania Press.

Lévi-Strauss, C. (1955). The structural study of myth. *The Journal of American Folklore, 68*(270), 428–444.

Lipovetsky, M. (2011). *Charms of the cynical reason: The trickster's transformations in Soviet and post-Soviet culture.* Academic Studies Press.

Makarius, L. (1993). The myth of the trickster: The necessary breaker of taboos. In W. Hynes & W. Doty (Eds.), *Mythical trickster figures: Contours, contexts, and criticisms* (pp. 66–86). University of Alabama Press.

McCormick, J., McCormick, C., & Phillips, J. (2004). *The Victorian Marionette Theatre.* University of Iowa Press.

Mimoun, L., & Bardhi, F. (2018). Liminality, portals, and narratives of transformation. In A. Gershoff, R. V. Kozinets, & T. White (Eds.), *Advances in Consumer Research, Volume 46* (pp. 214–219), Association for Consumer Research.

Mousley, A. (2013). *Literature and the human: Criticism, theory, practice.* Routledge.

O'Bryhim, S. (2001). Meander and Greek new comedy. In S. O'Bryhim (Ed.), *Greek and Roman comedy: Translations and interpretations of four representative plays* (pp. 83–146). University of Texas Press.

Pelton, R. D. (1980). *The trickster in West Africa: A study of mythic irony and sacred delight.* University of California Press.

Perrault, C. (1697/1993). *The complete fairy tales of Charles Perrault.* Clarion Books.

Pfister, M. (2002). Beckett, Barker, and other grim laughers. In M. Pfister (Ed.), *A history of English laughter: Laughter from Beowulf to Beckett and beyond* (pp.175–190). Rodopi.

Propp, V. (1928/2003). *Morphology of the folktale.* University of Texas Press.

Radin, P. (1956/1988). *The trickster: A study in American Indian mythology.* Schocken.

Ribner, I. (1960). *Patterns in Shakespearian tragedy.* Routledge.

Ricketts, M. L. (1966). The North American Indian trickster. *History of Religions, 5*(2), 327–350.

Sartre, J.-P. (1943/1993). *Being and nothingness: A phenomenological essay on ontology.* Washington Square Press.

Schouten, J. W. (1991). Selves in transition: Symbolic consumption in personal rites of passage and identity reconstruction. *Journal of Consumer Research, 17*(March), 412–425.

Shakespeare, W. (1595/1967). *A midsummer night's dream.* Penguin.

Shakespeare, W. (1595/1968). *Henry IV, part 1.* Penguin.

Shakespeare, W. (1595/2006). *Henry IV, part 2.* Nick Hern Books.

Shakespeare, W. (1599/2012). *As you like it.* W. W. Norton and Co.

Shakespeare, W. (1602/1973). *The merry wives of Windsor.* Penguin.

Shakespeare, W. (1605/2008). *King Lear.* W. W. Norton and Co.

Sheehan, P. (2013). Subterranean folkway blues: Ralph Ellison's mythology of deception. In J. Attridge & R. Rosenquist (Eds.), *Incredible modernism: Literature, trust and deception* (pp. 69–82). Ashgate.

Sinyavsky, A. (2007). *Ivan the fool: Russian folk belief, a cultural history.* Glas.

Storey, R. (1978). *Pierrot: A critical history of a mask.* Princeton University Press.

Storey, R. (1996). *Mimesis and the human animal: On the biogenetic foundations of literary representation.* Northwestern University Press.

Thompson, C. J. (2004). Marketplace mythology and discourses of power. *Journal of Consumer Research, 31*(June), 162–180.

Törnqvist, E. (2015). *The serious game: Ingmar Bergman as stage director.* Amsterdam University Press.

Turner, V. (1969). *The ritual process: Structure and anti-structure.* De Gruyter.

Ulver-Sneistrup, S., & Ostberg, J. (2011). The nouveaux pauvres of liquid modernity. In R. W. Belk, K. Grayson, A. M. Muñiz, & H. J. Schau (Eds.), *Research in consumer behavior, Vol. 13* (pp. 217–232), Emerald.

Vizenor, G. (1989). Trickster discourse. *Wicazo Sa Review, 5*(1), 2–7.

Welsford, E. (1935/1968). *The fool: His social and literary history.* Faber and Faber.

Wiget, A. (1985). *Native American Literature.* Twayne Publishers.

Williams, D. (2012). *The trickster brain: Neuroscience, evolution, and narrative.* Bucknell University Press.

Woodbridge, L. (1993). Patchwork: Piecing the early modern mind in England's first century of print culture. *English Literary Renaissance, 23*(1), 5–45.

Woodford, D. (2004). *Understanding King Lear: A student casebook to issues, sources, and historical documents.* Greenwood Press.

Chapter IV.
# Childlike Minds and Childish Men: Dilemmas of Classical Chinese Fiction[5]
Frances Weightman

The paradox alluded to in the title of this volume, namely the expectation of what a real child would 'do' in a given situation as opposed to romanticized ideals of the 'childlike,' is not confined to European discourse.

The formulation of childhood innocence is often traced to European thinkers such as Locke and Rousseau, and literary corollaries in the Romantic Movement. Disparities between what an imagined child should be like, as opposed to what a real child was like, and the conceptualisation of a child's mind as a blank sheet to be written on, as opposed to one of infinite potential to be tapped, lay at the heart of many of the differences of opinion and debates of the time. Robert Browning's much quoted line, "Genius has somewhat of the infantine: but of the childish not a touch or taint," demonstrates the readiness of Romantic discourse in general to accept uncritically the gap between ideals and reality: being 'of a child' and 'like a child' were two discrete concepts. In Chinese traditional thought, and from a much earlier period, the concept of the childlike is equally conflicted, with connotations on the one hand of purity, single-mindedness, something to be retained and/or retrieved by the grown-up version. On the other hand, the infant was also regularly described as incomplete, requiring enlightenment, and of little worth to society.

Since there are few if any depictions specifically of girls and their path to adulthood in the period I am exploring here, in this chapter I will examine the way that this paradox plays out in the characterization of the adult male in fiction. Recent scholarship has noted that the scholarly-type of male (*wen* 文) in late imperial Chinese fiction was considered no less 'masculine' than the warrior-type (*wu* 武), and has instead been characterised as possessing a 'textuality-based masculinity' in which his ability to produce texts was seen as a defining factor of his manhood (Song, 2004; Louie, 2002; Huang, 2006; Brownell & Wasserstrom, 2002). Song Geng's important study, from which this phrase is taken, concentrates on the widespread characterisation of the scholar hero in Chinese fiction and drama, but if we accept that rather than being purely a fictional creation, this was also a reflection of social expectations of the *wen* male stereotype, then clearly the public recognition of literary ability had a particular urgency. For the overwhelming majority of scholars aiming to obtain an official government post, such recognition, and thus true achievement of "adulthood," could only come from success in the civil service examinations (for more on this, see Weightman, 2004).

Alongside this pressure to gain social recognition and manhood through writing, a debate was on-going in literati circles on the most desirable *manner* of text-production. The sixteenth and seventeenth centuries in China saw the crystallisation of a discourse on the idealisation of childlikeness, the roots of which had been established in pre-imperial times. Factors such as the seemingly unstoppable drift towards syncretism of the three traditions of Confucianism, Daoism and Buddhism, together with the popularity of doctrines of the Wang Yangming School of the Mind, contributed to the currents of spontaneity, romanticism and idealism found in many writings of the latter half of the Ming period (1368-1644). In many of these works

[5] This chapter is a revised and expanded version of a section of my monograph, *The Quest for the Childlike in Seventeenth-Century China*, and the original research for this was in part funded by a grant from the Chiang Ching-kuo Foundation. Unless otherwise noted, all translations are my own.

such trends were, either explicitly or implicitly, linked to the intellectual quest for a return to the perceived innocence of childhood. This was advocated most definitively by Li Zhi 李贽 (1527-1602) in his very influential essay on the childlike mind. Li's writings were to have a major impact on writers of fiction in the decades which followed. Indeed, Chih-p'ing Chou states categorically that Li's "impact on late Ming literature in general and on the three Yuan brothers in particular, was far greater than that of any other writer" (Chou, 1988, p. 21). The nature of this impact is worthy of further investigation.

In literary circles the conflict was keenly felt between, on the one hand, these widely held ideal pursuits of purity, innocence and spontaneity in writing and, on the other, the reality of the pressure on men to write in a manner likely to be successful in the exams. Portrayals, often satirical, of such dilemmas are evident in various guises in much of the fiction of this period.

In what follows, I will consider the way this dilemma, between the childish and the childlike, is reflected in the characterisation of the male scholar, by examining a hugely influential anthology of ghost stories within the context of the sixteenth and seventeenth centuries discourse on childlikeness in China. The anthology, best known in English as *Strange Tales of Liaozhai (Liaozhai zhiyi* 聊斋志异), and which in this chapter I will refer to simply as the *Liaozhai*, was compiled by Pu Songling 蒲松龄 (1640-1715), and is a collection of around 500 tales, dealing with love stories and monstrous anecdotes, featuring ghosts, fox fairies, shrews and the like, and which has remained hugely popular in China throughout the last three centuries, with film and TV adaptations in recent decades.

The *Liaozhai* evidently has some inherently childlike features. A remarkable number of Chinese critics of the *Liaozhai* begin their articles with a personal statement of their own nostalgic affection for the stories, an attachment usually originating in childhood, but undiminished in adult life. In one collection of musings on the *Liaozhai* through the ages, the following well-known intellectuals all begin their articles with a declaration that their love for the collection began in childhood: Ye Shengtao 叶圣陶; Zang Kejia 臧克家; Ge Baoquan 戈宝权; and Yu Jianhua 愈剑华 (Lu & Zhou, 1987). In addition, individual academic studies of the *Liaozhai* by Chinese critics also often begin in this way (Yuan, 1988; Dong, 1976; Yang, 1996; Mu, 1997). In a preface to his edition of the anthology, the well-known commentator Dan Minglun 但明伦 (1795-1853) recalls his secret love of the tales as a child and how, one day, his grandfather discovered what he was reading, and rebuked the boy, saying "How can it be that a child whose knowledge is not yet fixed, likes tales of ghosts and the supernatural?" (reprinted in LZZY, p. 2470). The publication of various children's editions of the tales further demonstrates the continued popularity of the collection among Chinese children today, and many individual tales have been discussed in terms of "children's literature." Several of the tales depict child protagonists overcoming obstacles which defeat the adults around them, a theme which has obvious appeal to young readers and it has even been suggested that, in terms of the artistic value and accuracy of his portrayal of these children, Pu Songling is unrivalled amongst all writers of Chinese classical fiction (Lin, 1989).

The themes of ghosts and animal spirits, transcendence between the animate and the inanimate worlds, and the playfulness inherent in many of the stories are naturally attractive to child readers. Interestingly, however, Charlotte Furth notes that the contemporary medical establishment strongly warned against children reading ghost stories and the like, since it was felt that any such shocks, or frightening experiences, could endanger them physically. The fact that such warnings had to be given, of course, is also evidence of the inherent attractiveness of such subject matter to the very young (Furth, 1987). Moreover, it is indisputable that some of the tales deal with strictly adult themes and the description occasionally borders on the pornographic and thus Pu Songling could never be described primarily as a children's writer.

Several well-known *Liaozhai* tales feature child protagonists with exceptional powers and adult qualities, whether physical strength or wisdom (examples include "The girl from Zhending" 真定女, 1:29; "The trader's son" 贾儿, 1:41; "Crickets" 促织, 3:25; "The Orange Tree," 橘树, 5:24; and "Da'nan" 大男, 8:26). This is in keeping with conventions of children's literature the world over and the transgression of boundaries between childhood and adulthood is standard in works of this type. What is striking, however, in the collection is the number of stories in which these boundaries are crossed in the opposite way: in which the adult protagonists display childlike or childish characteristics.

One of his contemporaries contrasted the way Pu Songling wrote about the supernatural, "using ghosts and spirits for fun" with the didacticism of other such anthologies in which "the ways of ghosts were used as a doctrine to supplement the teachings of the ways of the rites and of kings" (Zhu, 1986, pp. 614-5). Karl S.Y. Kao has also commented that the "*Liaozhai* as a whole has a strong 'frivolous' side to it" (Kao, 1994, p. 202). Playfulness and frivolity, intimately associated with childlikeness, were discouraged by the Confucian educational system, which contrasted it with positive characteristics like diligence. This playfulness, I argue, reflects a broader sense of childlike innocence and purity which pervades the *Liaozhai* and sets it apart from early writings on the strange, which were often didactic in nature.

In their earliest form, supernatural writings set out to prove or disprove the existence of the supernatural, and reality was contrasted with illusion. For Pu Songling, this distinction was not an issue. Indeed, he seems to confront this question deliberately by blurring the very boundaries between human and non-human elements in his tales. The question of external reality is displaced by the notion of internal "realness" or "trueness" as opposed to fakery and hypocrisy, a concept which is entirely subjective and concerns being true to oneself and one's ideals. A concept much discussed by late Ming literati, this sense of genuineness and purity, is closely linked to the idealisation of childlikeness subscribed to by various seventeenth century writers: in many respects, it is the very essence of the naïve or childlike mind which they pursued.

Since the ability to produce literary texts is a defining attribute of the *wen* male-type, then the theories of literary creativity are clearly significant. Below I will outline some of the context behind the debates on retaining one's childlike mind in the creative process, and consider how this discourse became, perhaps necessarily, corrupted by the social realities of the literati's world.

### Towards the Idealisation of the Childlike

Central to the idealisation of the childlike was the concept of the pure, original mind of the child, untainted by the world. Debates about the mind of the newborn infant had occurred in very early philosophical texts and these ideas were to influence later generations of Chinese thinkers (see Weightman, 2006a, for an expanded study of this section).

The infant was essentially seen, particularly in early Confucian sources, as a blank sheet which required education in order to grow and develop into a useful member of society. Confucian writings stress the incomplete nature of the infant, who required systematic training in the classics to achieve his potential, while Daoists focus on the huge capacity, physical perfection, and spiritual superiority of even the unborn child. The vast majority of Confucian texts which have any reference to childhood are in fact treatises on education. Infants need to be enlightened from their original state of ignorance and the means to achieve this is the main theme of these works.

Nevertheless, the tradition of privileging and idealising this state of being began within the Confucian tradition as early as Mencius, in his discussion and idealisation of the infant's mind (*chizi zhi xin* 赤子之心, often abbreviated to *chixin*, sometimes rendered the 'naked mind' but essentially referring to a newborn) which, he believed, a great man never lost (*Mencius*, Li lou xia: 12). In this sense, it is evident that even in the earliest Confucian discourse, there is some conflict between the pure innocence of the unadorned infant's mind, and the requirement for a strict code of education in order to be a 'complete person' (the literal translation of the word for adult, *chengren* 成人) capable of moral judgement. The infant's mind is fundamentally desirable, symbolic of a single-minded purity and sincerity which both gives you an advantage in dealing with complicated affairs of state, but yet also leaves you 'naked' and thus, to some extent, at the mercy of others.

By late imperial times, however, it was the Wang Yangming School of the Mind which contributed most to the discourse on childlikeness. As a result of Wang's key theory of innate knowledge, present from or even before birth, the status of the child was elevated. There is a similarity between the essence of the mind of the child and that of the sage, but the difference, according to Wang, is in experience. The child is still expected to acquire an understanding of appropriate behaviour, in dealing with his superiors. The sage, being more experienced, is therefore able to investigate things and extend his knowledge without effort (Chan, 1963, p. 250). There is no suggestion that he should attempt to return to an infantile *approach* to acquiring knowledge.

Some of Wang's later disciples, however, forgot this point and preached iconoclastic nonconformity, with huge popularity. Such idealisation of the childlike mind, and blurring of any distinctions between naïve innocence and social impropriety, was taken furthest by Li Zhi. Li is representative of the late Ming so-called leftist wing of the School of the Mind. He has been described as "one of the most brilliant and complex figures in Chinese thought and literature" (De Bary, 1991, p. 203). Either blamed by later generations for the collapse of the dynasty or else extolled by them for his contribution to the valorisation of vernacular literature and for his outspoken attacks on the hypocrisy of the orthodox literati, Li Zhi is undoubtedly one of the most controversial figures of the time.

### "On the Childlike Mind"

The essay "On the childlike mind" (*tongxin shuo*) is widely recognised as representative of Li Zhi's philosophy, and forms the backbone for the discourse on ideals of childlikeness. The opening paragraph addresses head-on the perceived conflict between idealised infant purity and improper behaviour.

> This "childlike mind" is the true mind. If you say the childlike mind
> is inappropriate, then you are calling the true mind inappropriate.
> The childlike mind is purely genuine, without falseness, and is the
> original source of all ideas.

This inborn purity can be spoilt, according to Li, "when things are heard and seen through the ears and eyes, and are then taken to be superior to that which is innate," culminating in time with a situation that

> morals, principles and things heard and seen increase day by day,
> then knowledge and perception becomes daily broader; thus from
> this we come to know the goodness of things which have beautiful
> names, and praise them, and the childlike mind is lost; and we
> come to know the ugliness of things which do not have beautiful
> names, and we hide them, and the childlike mind is lost.

Li blames this specifically on "excessive reading," while neglecting to protect the childlike mind.

By accusing the main Confucian educational apparatus (consisting of morals, principles and 'that which is heard and seen') of corrupting this mind, Li Zhi launches a head-on attack on the orthodoxy. It is notable that Li Zhi does not condemn reading in itself ("I don't mean the ancient sages never read!," he claims), even when done to excess, so long as the childlike mind is kept intact, and the reading is not solely motivated by a desire to understand duty and principles.

Thus Li Zhi does not dismiss the need for writings 'of moral worth' but rather stresses that without the childlike mind nothing worthwhile can be achieved. The need for a true 'self,' from which all writing and speech of any value originates, is stressed. Words which are not grounded in this self are, according to Li, false and of no worth. Genuineness (*zhen*), the opposite of this falseness, is the essence of what Li Zhi means by the childlike mind and became a key term and objective for many late Ming writers. Li elaborates on this concept in promotion of his individualist theory of literature, which was to be enormously influential in the late Ming and Qing (1644-1911) periods.

Li goes on to stress the necessity of considering literary works within the context of which they were produced, questioning "Why do poems have to be like those included in the ancient *Anthology of Literature*; why does prose have to be like that of the former Qin?" Such ideas, hardly radical for a modern audience, were very progressive for their day, when the term 'ancient' (*gu* 古) still had near sacred implications, and when the writings and thoughts of the former great literary writers were unquestionably taken as models for guidance and imitation in all writing. Li lists the examination essays as merely the latest new literary genre to emerge whilst in practice the *raison d'être* of these essays was to allow candidates to display their breadth of knowledge of the classics and originality or innovation was generally discouraged. Li Zhi's most controversial comments, however, were saved for the closing paragraph of his essay, where the very authenticity of the Neo-Confucian canon is called into question. Pointing out what he contends many later scholars forgot, namely that these texts were mainly written down by Confucius' disciples from memory, and so are imbued with their own prejudices and exaggerations and as such are unlikely even to bear much resemblance to the master's own ideas, Li ends his essay unequivocally:

> So, then, the *Six Classics*, the *Analects* and *Mencius* are still the pretexts for Neo-Confucianism, and are a hotbed for false people; they plainly cannot be called words from the childlike mind. Alas! How can I find a genuine sage whose childlike mind has not yet been lost and have a talk with him about literature!

By suggesting that the Neo-Confucian commentaries on the Classics, and even the Classics themselves were somehow invalid and inaccurate records of what the sages actually said, Li Zhi is calling into question the foundation of the whole of the Neo-Confucian orthodoxy. Once again, Li decries those who he sees are taking alleged utterances by the sages out of context, and applying them at random. Stephen Owen notes the playful parallel of the final sentence of this essay with the famous line from the Daoist classic the *Zhuangzi* 庄子: "The reason for words is the idea; when you get the idea, you forget the words. If only I could find someone who has forgotten words and have a word with him!" (Owen, 1996, p. 811).

In essence, then, the ideal of the childlike mind which Li extolled represented genuineness, naturalness, innocence and spontaneity. It was heavily introverted, viewing external information with suspicion. It was highly subjective, individualistic and reliant on a specific context and time-frame. Building on the traditions of the ideal of Mencius' *chixin*, Li went further and denied the need to temper the innocence of the childlike ideal with the understanding of social ritual and propriety. In a sense, he denied the boundaries between childlikeness and childishness. As such, the cultivation of the childlike mind ran absolutely contrary to Confucian dictums on the importance of education, social values, and scholastic traditions and on the preservation of a semi-sacred and ageless literary and philosophical canon.

## Childlikeness in Wider Literary Circles

Li Zhi's outspokenness and extreme views had led, in 1602, to his arrest on charges of "daring to promote heterodox doctrine, and of misleading the people," and he committed suicide within a month of his imprisonment (Lin, 1992). However, despite the authorities' attempts to silence him and their threats to punish anyone who published or preserved any of his work, the impact of his writings on the childlike mind had a great deal of influence on his contemporaries, notably on the Gongan school of the Yuan brothers (Yuan Zongdao 袁宗道 [1560-1600], Yuan Hongdao 袁宏道 [1568-1610] and Yuan Zhongdao 袁中道 [1570-1624]), who were themselves tutored by Li, and contributed to a general trend in the late Ming towards the promotion of spontaneity and genuineness in writing, and the elevation of vernacular literature. This movement was to include many very influential writers of the time.

The Yuan brothers' literary circle was concerned with the pursuit of spontaneity and freshness in literature. Like Li Zhi, they believed that traditional canons of literature had become formulaic and empty and, while writing in the classical language themselves, they also championed vernacular works. In one of his most influential essays, a preface to a work entitled *Intuitive Grasp*, Yuan Hongdao discusses the literary principle of *qu* 趣, which can be understood only by those who possess this intuitive grasp, in much the same terms:

> Liveliness (*qu*), when it is achieved from what is natural, is deep; when achieved from study, it is shallow. When one is a child, one knows nothing of the existence of liveliness, but liveliness is present everywhere. The face is never grave; the eyes are never still; the mouth prattles trying to talk; the feet leap up and down and are never still. Life's most perfect happiness is truly never greater than at this time. This is, in fact, what Mencius meant by "not losing the heart of an infant" and what Laozi meant by being "able to be the baby." This is the highest grade of liveliness, its correct enlightenment, its highest doctrine. (Owen, 1996, p. 811).

The privileging of the childlike state is clearly fundamental to these ideas of natural creativity. Late Ming writers were quick to incorporate idealisations of *zhen* (genuineness) and *qu* in their works. The influence of the ideal of the childlike mind in Feng Menglong 冯梦龙 (1574-1646)'s work has been noted by Hsu Pi-ching, in his study of Feng's *Treasury of Laughs* (*Xiaofu* 笑府). Hsu states that, particularly in Feng's preface but also pervading the whole collection, there is a strong underlying conviction that social ambition and success in the examinations are a threat to retaining the childlike mind (Hsu, 1998, p. 1043). In the early Qing anthology *Idle Talk under the Bean Arbour* (*Doupeng xianhua* 豆棚闲话), the influence of these doctrines is equally striking. The fifth chapter extols the virtues of true filiality which is not dependent on gaining high office to bring honour to one's parents, but rather consists of being attentive to their daily needs. The early paragraphs of this chapter closely mirror Li Zhi's ideas, in the way they contrast genuine and natural childlike virtue with the affected and false behaviour of those 'scholars' in office:

> The world today is not a fair place, and the minds of men are unfathomable. Those clever types whose bellies are filled with the books and histories they have read, simply display an ability for mechanical posturing. By the time they reach high office or other lofty position, the initial infant mind of their childhood (*haiti chizi chuxin* 孩提赤子初心) has been completely destroyed. . . . In contrast, are those rustic fellows who have never studied formally, but have both feet grounded firmly in reality, and depend entirely

on the azure sky; they have never heard of the Duke of Zhou, or Confucius, but even in the privacy of their own homes, have not a single careless thought or action. It is rather they who are the embodiment of the uprightness of ancient times and natural goodness for this generation. (Zhang, 1999, pp. 45-46).

Satires on scholars in late imperial fiction are common, the most well-known example being Wu Jingzi's吴敬梓 (1701-1754) novel *The Scholars* (*Rulin Waishi* 儒林外史). The usual theme is one of the corruption and decadence that fast ensues when scholars take up their official posts. Such satirical portrayals would presumably sound particularly poignant to the increasing number of literati who, like Pu Songling, had been excluded from officialdom themselves and whose writings frequently contained satirical attacks on the corrupt bureaucracy and the injustices of the examination system.

## (mis)Interpretations and (mis)Appropriations

In the late Ming period, however, these trends for purity and genuineness caught on so rapidly that they could be said to have become a victim of their own success. While the quest for the childlike was all the rage within the literati classes, the practicalities of career advancement and social aspirations led to irreconcilable contradictions in its practice. After all, who could both act spontaneously, with the heart of an infant, whilst strategically manoeuvring themselves through the examination system? Negotiating the boundary between this widely proclaimed ideal and the realities of the literati workplace led to misappropriations and misinterpretations of the childlike, often far removed from what Li Zhi and the Gongan school would have recognized: either to the posturing parodied in the texts above, where an image of childlike innocence was projected whilst the pursuit of ambition and career success was very much underway, or else to a misguided substitution of childishness for the childlike.

Wilful or otherwise, misinterpretations of childlikeness were commonplace among the literati, as they set out purposefully to acquire this quality in order to comply with the spirit of the age. Ironically, the traits of inner integrity, purity, spontaneity and liveliness for which they were apparently striving often became in practice a superficial means of outward display, nothing more than an integral part of the constructed image which could symbolise intellectual capital in the eyes of their peers. Yuan Hongdao himself comments bitterly in the same article quoted above, "These days people are drawn to the label of *qu* and seek what resembles *qu*" (Owen, 1996, p. 811).

Wai-yee Li and Wu Chengxue 吴承学 have both argued that the pursuit of genuineness became affected by many late Ming writers. Li sees it as part of a 'rhetoric of spontaneity' in the sixteenth and seventeenth centuries, in which this spontaneity becomes an end in itself, leading inevitably, in many later writings, to an artificiality far from what the Gongan theorists had originally intended (Li, 1995). Li cites examples of travel writers who take great pains to describe the spontaneous 'wild shout' of emotion they gave upon seeing a new place, and the self-consciousness and elitism which is present in many of these writings.

In a similar vein, Wu describes such 'truth' as "a purposeful expression, a seeking out, an exaggeration, even a carving out of a kind of 'true' sentiment, for fear of others thinking them not genuine. As such, the flavour of 'truth' is changed" (Wu, 1998, pp. 400-401). It is ironic that this was exactly the sort of falseness that Li Zhi had condemned so strongly.

The true childlike mind was, I believe, further corrupted by the ambiguities of its association with the concept of *chi* 痴 (folly). The widespread use of this term in sixteenth and seventeenth century writings is closely linked to the ideals of childlikeness and, I argue, encapsulates the crossing of boundaries, hinted at by Li Zhi, between the childlike and the childish (indeed the term 'chi' itself often, even in modern Chinese combinations such as *chixiao* 痴小 and *chier* 痴儿, implies associations with the infantile). Of course such associations come naturally within the European romantic tradition, with the most notable defender of folly, the Dutch renaissance humanist Erasmus (1466?-1536), exclaiming "What else is childhood but silliness and foolishness?" (Radice, 1993, p. 23).

One contemporaneous example which demonstrates the ambiguity of this concept is Feng Menglong's series of three anthologies of jokes, entitled *Child's folly* (Tong chi 童痴). For jokes and satire to succeed, the target must be one which the readers can readily relate to and accept without qualification. Folly in general is condoned throughout as a desirable, pure state, with clear overtones of the innocence of the childlike mind. The modern critic Hsu Pi-ch'ing has commented on Feng Menglong's jokes as follows:

> By reversing the worldly practice of praising the socially sophisticated and successful and looking down upon the socially naive and base, the three collections of *Child's Folly* broke the established rules of the mundane world. (Hsu, 1998, p. 1047)

One example from the collection, however, illustrates an alternative view of the foolish man (*chi ren* 痴人). The humour in the anecdote entitled "A foolish man has a daughter (痴人生女)" mocks the protagonist's naiveté and ignorance of the facts of life:

> A foolish man (*chi ren*) got married, but after a long time still did not know how to make love. His wife could not stand it any longer, so held him on top of her and guided him into her, until he was ready to ejaculate. Suddenly he called out "I'm about to wet myself!" She said "Don't worry, just wet yourself inside me." The foolish man did as she said. Later she gave birth to a daughter. "Where did that come from?" he asked his wife. She replied "Don't you remember that time you wet yourself?" At that he suddenly became enlightened. Then he felt regret, and rebuked his wife saying "If by wetting yourself you have a daughter, then if you shit yourself you're bound to have a son. Why didn't you say so earlier?

The innocence of the protagonist in this anecdote is, however gently, ridiculed as ignorance rather than upheld as an ideal to which to attain. He clearly belongs to the category of the childish, rather than the childlike.

I have argued elsewhere that the many references to folly within Pu Songling's writings (a total of 93 times within the tales alone) cover the concepts of idealism and naivete, but also emotional paralysis, worldly incompetence, physical dysfunction (Weightman, 2006b). While idealism and naïveté may encapsulate the genuineness and sincerity advocated by Li Zhi, the latter three categories suggest an inability to relate to others, or to cope in a social setting, an incompetence which tends to the childish rather than the childlike.

### Love Stories of Naïve Men

The majority of the protagonists in the *Liaozhai* are male scholars who display a different but equally misguided interpretation of childlike naïveté. These protagonists embody neither the romantic ideal of the simple rustic fellows endorsed by the likes of the Gongan school, yet nor are they the 'posturers' condemned for their duplicity. Rather, the characterization seems deliberately to confront the childlike/childish dichotomy by displaying a naïveté which, while pure and innocent in motivation as a newborn child, is simultaneously parodied by its ineffectual and dysfunctional nature within the reality of the society. Innocent purity and sincerity is all too often replaced by childish ignorance and incompetence. The characterization is effected in the main by contrasting the naïve male with a worldly wise female counterpart who often, to heighten the satire, is not even of the world, but is rather a fox spirit.

Despite the fact that physical weakness was an expected trait of scholars during this period (Song, 2004), this did not save them from ridicule. Many of the *Liaozhai* tales take the notion of the fragile scholar to extremes in their satirising of an apparently dysfunctional intellectual elite. The reluctance of several physically weak male protagonists to take decisive action, or become involved in a fight, even when morally justified, is contrasted with the macho heroics either of other minor or non-scholarly male characters, or else by powerful women of action.

Foils are provided for weak male counterparts by such women warriors as "Shang Sanguan" (商三官; 2:43), who is required to take on the traditionally male role to avenge her father's death, in place of a man. Similarly strong females are described in "The female knight" (Xia nü 侠女; 2:03) and "The farmer's wife" (Nongfu 农妇; 6:67). However, in none of these tales is the female allowed to retain any sexual desire or role: Shang Sanguan commits suicide before her wedding can take place; the female knight has sex very reluctantly, but explicitly "as a repayment of a debt of gratitude," to provide an heir for her benefactor; and the farmer's wife tries to beat up a nun friend of hers when she discovers she has been having affairs with men. The narrative comment confirms that, as with the portrayals of the shrew mentioned above, this last tale is hardly a progressive piece of feminist writing, by concluding with the rhetorical question wondering "what was her husband like?"

I suggest, therefore, that despite the fact that there are many competent or dominant females within the *Liaozhai* tales, their characters are never fully realised, particularly in terms of their sexuality, and they appear primarily to exist to provide a backdrop to the portrayal of the male scholar.

In what follows, I will look at manifestations of naïveté and immaturity in such adult protagonists, with regard to the three areas most central to the male scholar's daily life: sex, money and studying.

## Sexual Naïveté

The English term 'naïveté' derives from French and Latin roots implying naturalness or innateness, and is defined as: "unaffected, unconsciously artless" or "foolishly credulous, simple;" in reference to art as "straightforward in style, eschewing subtlety or conventional technique;" in the sphere of the medical sciences as "not having had a particular experience before" or "lacking the knowledge to guess the purpose of an experiment." In philosophy, naïve realism is "the belief that an object of perception is not only real but has in reality all its perceived attributes" (*OED*, 1993). Defined in this way, naïveté seems to be the essence of the childlike mind which Li Zhi advocated. It covers both the positive, genuine and unaffected aspects, as well as the inadequacies of ignorance and inappropriate responses to one's physical and social environment. Underlying both is its fundamental characteristic of being a state which is natural, present at birth. When the concept of naïveté is extended to the sexual sphere, however, the childlike/childish contradiction comes to the fore leading us to question what indeed we can mean by sexual naïveté.

Sexual immaturity in the *Liaozhai* is a common feature of the male scholar protagonist, whether in the form of ignorance of the mechanics of sex, or in a physical manifestation of sexual inadequacy or impotence. Sex is something unknown to these protagonists. Even if they are made aware of it, they may not desire it.

The protagonist's sexual ineptitude can lead him to be treated as a child, as someone outside of normal social conventions. The tale "Qing'e" (青娥; 5:27) concerns the relationship between Huo Huan and the eponymous heroine. As an innocent young man, Huo becomes infatuated with Qing'e and uses a trowel given him by a Daoist to dig through the walls in her house, reaching her bedroom, and then simply falling asleep next to her. His desire for Qing'e is a compelling force within him, but is entirely divorced at this stage from any real desire for sex. He simply wishes to be close to her. When confronted angrily by her family the next morning, his reaction is simply to burst into tears and declare: "I'm not a burglar—it was really simply because I was in love with Qing'e and wanted to be close to her sweet fragrance." This leads them to treat him leniently, as a mere child. Thus, the male protagonist is emasculated and thereby avoids social censure for his inappropriate behaviour.

This protagonist's single-minded fantasy to be physically close to the heroine, yet his lack of sexual desire for her, or any awareness of the potential threat of such desire, along with his childish reaction to the confrontation (bursting into tears) all highlight the contradictions of what is meant by 'purity' when applied to the sexual sphere.

Even after the naïve male has been educated about sex, he is not necessarily enamoured with it. Yue Zhong (乐仲; 8:21) is another naïve protagonist, ignorant of the facts of life. He marries late, but is still a virgin, and is horrified on his wedding night, exclaiming: "What men and women do when they sleep together really is the filthiest thing in the world; I certainly don't derive any pleasure from it!" He then divorces his wife and lives alone.

The ignorant naïveté of the male protagonist is often contrasted with the proficiency of a sexually experienced female fox spirit, who frequently adopts the role of sex tutor, or sex doctor. Female superiority in the 'arts of the bedchamber' is a recurring theme in Chinese official discourse on sexual matters, exemplified in the content of many of the medical handbooks. Dangerous as the sexual female is often perceived to be, the ultimate paradox of Confucian gender discourse is the requirement to produce offspring. This ensures the paramount importance of sexual relations within official discourse. The long tradition in China of the compilation of sex handbooks, fundamentally for medical consultation, ascribes a degree of power exclusively to the female, on medical grounds. Several of the handbooks concern the three female sex tutors of the Yellow Emperor, the plain girl (*sunü* 素女) the dark girl (*xuannü* 玄女) and the elected girl (*cainü* 采女), who taught him the joys of sex. In this way, these legendary tutors gave sexual instruction which would ensure female sexual satisfaction, and reinforced this both by presenting the allure of longevity, and by invoking the most compelling Confucian doctrine, that of producing offspring.

The female sex drive is invariably presented as problematic in these handbooks, and not easily understandable for the male. The anxiety that this arouses in the male is taken to extremes in Pu Songling's characterisation of the naïve and sexually ignorant scholar. The setting for a protagonist who is able to learn only from books or teachers, rather than from experience, can neatly be transferred from the study to the bedroom. In the *Liaozhai* tales, the secret of sexual prowess is given primarily to the female fox spirit. Thus, paradoxically, the mortal characters are grounded in naïve idealism while the fantasy characters display experience and worldly wisdom.

An example of the practical nature of advice such a sex tutor from the fantasy world can give occurs in the *Liaozhai* tale 'Hengniang' (恒娘; 7:32). In this case the advice is provided to the mortal female, in the context of reining in her wayward husband. The heroine, Zhu, is initially portrayed as a stereotypical jealous wife, whose husband inexplicably prefers to have sex with his less attractive concubine. At her wits' end, Zhu appears to be following the shrew plot of jealousy-induced concubine-battering for which Pu Songling has become well-known. However, before she resorts to such aggression, Zhu becomes friends with Hengniang, whom she later discovers to be a fox spirit, and pours out her woes to her. Hengniang then proceeds to give Zhu systematic lessons in the art of flirting. Over a sustained period of time, Zhu is taught to stop pestering her husband for sex, and instead to try playing hard to get; to dress shabbily for a period and suddenly stun him with her beauty. This, predictably, works like a charm and Hengniang then continues the lessons, explaining to Zhu how to flirt with him, and, ultimately, how to keep him. By the end of the story, Zhu is in complete control of her husband's sex life. The narrative comment on this tale, while lamenting the trait of human nature which perversely prefers what is hidden to that which is easily available, suggests that the fact that women are able systematically to exploit this human failing is a result of a 'secret knowledge' which has been passed down through the generations.

Of course, the very fact that this story takes place within a male-dominated household, where the husband is allowed the freedom to choose between two sexual partners, while the wife is ultimately subjected to his free-will, is indicative of the limitations of this power. As in the majority of the *Liaozhai* tales, Zhu is allowed a certain degree of sexual autonomy in this story, only so long as she remains within the general male-dominated structures of Confucian society. However, the development of this character of the female sex tutor simultaneously consolidates the character of the naïve male student.

In a literary text, the use of this motif of the omniscient sex tutor instructing an ignorant and innocent student engenders a situation very familiar to many readers in late imperial China, for whom the classroom provided a perpetual backdrop for much of their life. The secrets of the sensual sphere became substitutes for the classical learning formally required of them. While the latter could lead to success in their future career, the former could lead to another kind of personal fulfilment. Moreover, the female fox spirit is substituted for the invariably male academic tutor, and the whole process of gaining sexual experience is thus portrayed in a way which mirrors the pattern of daily life of a seventeenth-century scholar.

Physical sexual immaturity in these tales often takes the form of an inadequate male member. This theme is common among literature of the early Qing, particularly in such works as Li Yu's 李渔 (1611-1680) *The Carnal Prayer Mat* (Rou pu tuan 肉蒲团). In this novel, penis enlargement is a major trope in the plot development. Throughout the novel, it is assumed that female pleasure and satisfaction is in proportion to the size of the male penis. As discussed above, female satisfaction was considered essential for a successful sexual encounter, and thus a small penis was seen as a serious handicap in late imperial China.

The tale "Qiaoniang" (巧娘; 2:11) is perhaps the ultimate reversal of traditional sexual roles. The protagonist, Lian, is described in the opening lines of the tale as being sexually impotent, due to his particularly small penis. His misfortune is further compounded by the fact that this is common knowledge throughout the village, so no woman is willing to marry him. Away from his hometown, he meets the fox spirit Qiaoniang, who attempts to seduce him, but is horrified when she discovers his deficiency. Later, another female fox spirit, to repay a debt of gratitude, brews some medicine to cure him, and he lives out his life in a happy threesome with her daughter and Qiaoniang. The happy ending is condoned by his parents, who then make him show off his sexual prowess, by having intercourse with one of their servants. In this way, a deficiency which had previously made him the laughingstock of the village is cured by female intervention.

The theme of male deficiency cured by the proactive female sex-tutor, is again portrayed in "Xiao Cui" (小翠; 5:46). Here, the root cause of the protagonist's impotency appears to be mental rather than physical. His naïve stupidity is summed up by his inability to distinguish men from women. Xiao Cui, whose reason for marrying is the fulfilment of a previous obligation, initially conforms to the stereotype of the playful fox spirit, who exploits her husband's mental disability by dressing him in different costumes and playing pranks around the house. However, once the debt has been fulfilled, she also cures her husband's impotence. She appears to suffocate him in the bath, and when he revives his simple-mindedness is cured. She then ensures him a sexually fulfilled future by finding him a new wife who is able to bear him children, before leaving him. In this way, Xiao Cui transforms her husband from a social outcast to a family man and active participant in society. Xiao Cui's own misfortune is that, unlike the spirit in "Qiaoniang" whose medical skills are easily evaluated, her contribution is never recognised by her husband's family, who merely tire of her continual pranks and are relieved when she leaves. Sexual impotence and childish stupidity go hand in hand in this tale.

In the above stories, the arts of the bedchamber are the property of the female, to pass on as she wishes. With her superior knowledge of this all-important subject, she is in a position of authority whereby she can control her lover. Whether this control takes the form of tutoring him in the art of making love, or in curing his physical dysfunction, she is ultimately portrayed positively, as opposed to the other type of sexually controlling female construct, the aggressive shrew.

In contrast, when a cure for physical deficiency is sought within the male world, the ending is less than happy. "Medicine Monk" (药僧; 6:56) is a moral tale, a parody of a man's overreaching desire for sexual potency. An itinerant monk sells the protagonist a pill to increase his sexual potency. Delighted with the effect of the medicine as his penis increases in length by a third, he then becomes obsessed, steals more medicine and takes an overdose. Eventually his penis becomes the size of a third leg and he is forced to lie in the street all day, permanently disabled through his obsessive search for sexual supremacy by this means. In this way, Pu Songling suggests the secret to curing male sexual impotency lies with the female alone. This suggestion is closely mirrored in a Ming Dynasty sex handbook, the *Admirable Discourses of the Plain Girl* (Sunü miaolun 素女妙论) [preface dated 1566 AD] in which Sunü warns against the overuse of drugs to combat impotency, advising that "If the emotions of the man and the woman are in harmony and if their spirits are in communion, the size of the male member will increase of its own accord" (Van Gulik, 1974, p. 272). The need to maintain a balance between *yin* and *yang* forces, therefore, invests the female with an authority which places the male entirely at her mercy.

The tale "Yingning" (婴宁; 1:48) is one of the most well-known of the *Liaozhai* tales, and has been studied extensively. It is also the most commonly associated with depictions of naïveté. At first glance it seems to be an exception to my argument above in that in this case, the apparently naïve protagonist is female, and her male partner is the more sexually expert. The personality of the eponymous heroine appears to be very attractive to readers as the epitome of childlike purity and natural happiness. Her name itself, Wai-yee Li notes, "suggests an immediate association with childlike artlessness and innocence (*ying* [baby], *ning-xing-er* [a lovely child). In the story laughter is indeed synonymous with innocence, spontaneity, daring, defiance of ritual and of authority" (Li, 1993, pp. 108-9).

Wang Zifu is a child prodigy, who passes the district exam when he is fourteen. He falls passionately in love with Yingning who is described by her foster-mother as "already sixteen years of age, but just as foolish as an infant" (年已十六, 呆痴裁如婴儿). On meeting Wang, Yingning's immediate reaction is to giggle uncontrollably. When alone with her, Wang tells her of his love, and she persistently misunderstands. Later, when her foster-mother asks them what they were talking about to make them so late for dinner, Yingning replies:

"My cousin wanted me to share his pillow."

In great embarrassment Wang shot her a look at which she smiled and was silent. Luckily the old woman had not heard and repeated her question. Wang made an evasive answer, then whispered a reproach to the girl, who asked, "Did I say something wrong?"

"That's a secret between us!"

"It may be a secret from others, but surely not from my mother. Everybody has to sleep; what harm is there in that?" (Yang & Yang, 1984, p. 47)

Both Wang and the reader are left unsure whether this is a reaction of extreme naïveté, or a manipulative act by Yingning. Wang is very impatient at her foolishness and is frustrated that he has no way to enlighten her. After they get married, he's afraid she'll tell others about their sex life, but she does not. Her laughter endears her to Wang's family, who find her a delight to be around.

However, this changes after an incident with a neighbour, who is entranced by her, and takes her laughter as encouragement. When he tries to have sex with her, he finds she vanishes, leaving a hollow tree trunk, within which is a huge scorpion, which stings the man and kills him. The narrative comment at the end of this story points out that while Yingning's unceasing foolish laughter gives the impression of someone entirely guileless, the trick she played on the neighbour is evidence of her cunning.

This story has been discussed, perhaps, more than any other of the *Liaozhai* tales. It has been dramatised for television, and is consistently included in selective anthologies of the *Liaozhai*. While employing different methods of analysis, commentators on this story seem to agree on at least one point, that Pu Songling's portrayal of Yingning in this tale is broadly positive, despite the fact that she caused the death of a neighbour, confirming the generally perceived fear of female sexuality. As such, Yingning is not genuinely naïve, in the sense of the male protagonists discussed above. She puts on a front of naïveté, but in reality epitomises the generally perceived sexual threat posed by the female. Pretending to be naïve is in fact the very opposite of the true naïveté manifested by the male protagonists.

All of the male protagonists discussed above are depicted as sexually naïve or immature in some way, either mentally or physically. They are usually contrasted with a sexually experienced female spirit who often cures their naïveté, as if guiding them through adolescence. By situating the agents of sexual experience within the fantasy world, the sense of sexual anxiety faced by the male scholar protagonists is further heightened.

The satire is employed on different levels in these tales but, however mild it may be, there is no doubt that Pu Songling is mocking these protagonists. Their innocence and purity is ultimately presented as ignorance, impotence or immaturity which in some cases is cured, in others not. Childish behaviour usurps the childlike mind.

### Financial and Managerial Incompetence

Dealing with money, running businesses and managing household affairs are further skills which require a level of sophistication and worldly wisdom beyond many of the naïve protagonists in the tales. While in the eyes of his peers, the *wen*-type male may have been expected to be weak and fragile, he was after all destined for an official career and thus would have at the very least required administrative skills. This is another sphere in which, it seems, the inadequacy of the late Ming ideology is exposed, the childlike mind is doomed and is replaced by nothing more than childish incompetence.

A general sense pervades the collection of the vulgarity of the naked pursuit of wealth (see, e.g., "Coin Rain," 雨钱, 3:33; "Scholar Zhen," 真生, 7:10; "Zhang Buliang," 张不量, 6:50; "Cattle plague," 牛癀, 5:29). All of these instances condemn the selfish or greedy use of money, and are in line with orthodox Confucian values. Misers are frequent objects of fun in Chinese literature, while rich magistrates who abuse their wealth are roundly condemned. However, money is not despised per se, and the skills of running a household and effective management were also necessary for the Confucian scholar. According to the *Great Learning* (Daxue 大学), one of the four main canons of Neo-Confucian education and, in Ming and Qing times, one of the primary texts upon which the exam papers were based, the different stages and ultimate aim of self-cultivation are set out clearly: the investigation of things leads on to knowledge, which in turn leads to sincerity in mind, and then to rightness of mind, which leads to physical well-being. The reward of this is that now you are able first to set your household/family in order, then to be able to rule the country and finally to pacify all under heaven. Being able to set one's house in order was therefore a prerequisite for candidates wishing to serve their country in higher offices and setting one's house in order inevitably required a level of practicality and financial nous. Ever since the rapid urbanisation of the Song dynasty, the social status of merchants had been gradually improving and by the early Qing, while businessmen were still despised by many among the scholarly elite, the social stigma attached to trading in material goods was far less widespread (Brook, 1998).

Several male protagonists are unable to function effectively with regard to money: some are naïvely generous and trusting of others, and so are repeatedly exploited, even at a cost to their own family; some are unable to work hard, either through laziness or lack of interest; others are simply incapable and do not possess the necessary 'business mindset' or social skills. As in the previous section, naïve males of this type are often portrayed in contrast to highly efficient, socially adept 'others,' usually females, or else non-scholarly males. While superficially pure and innocent, their ineffectiveness precludes them from pursuing their Confucian ideals.

The first-degree graduate Feng Xiangru repeatedly shows himself to be weak and ineffectual in his inability to stand up to any intimidation from others, leaving the fox spirit Hongyu (红玉; 2:16) to take charge. When an old rich lord, Song, tries to buy his wife from him, Feng simply declines politely, suppressing his anger. In the end, Feng's father is killed and his wife commits suicide. Thinking of his young son, Feng still does nothing to avenge the deaths, despite the Confucian imperative to do this. Hongyu then takes action on his behalf and sees that justice is done. She then lives with them, working as the breadwinner and managing all affairs while Feng studies, until he finally passes the provincial examination. While her behind the scenes role throughout the narrative is not always explicit, it is clear that Hongyu is in control. Although to the contemporary readership, it is fair to assume that Feng's behaviour would have been seen as cowardly and weak, *Liaozhai* tales which conclude like this one, with the protagonist proceeding another step up the examination ladder, demonstrate implicit approval of the character.

In the story "Abao" (2:06), the eponymous heroine is depicted as a chaste woman, initially apparently impervious to the affection of the naïve hero, Sun Zichu. Sun is nicknamed "Sun the fool" Sun chi 孙痴 and he is often ridiculed for his naïveté and awkwardness, particularly around women. Abao manages the finances, since "he was a book fool, and did not understand how to manage household affairs." The other view on this contradiction between bookishness and more worldly matters is clear in the advice given by Mrs Liu (刘夫人; 7: 06) to the poor, honest scholar Lian. When she asks him to manage her finances for him, he tries to refuse, worried that, as a mere scholar, he will be unable to cope in the world of finance. She rebukes him saying, "If you plan to study, the first thing to do is to make a living." Unable to function alone, Mrs Liu finds Lian a servant, Wu, to help him and Lian entrusts all the money to him. The combination of Lian's honesty and generosity and Wu's business acumen seems to work well and the business is successful, but Lian never shows much interest in it, preferring to read. At the end of the story, Lian passes the provincial level of the imperial exams. Wu's role, as a socially disempowered servant who is nevertheless a competent, worldly, and wise manager, is constructed similarly to that of the female business-minded characters in the other tales discussed here, and likewise provides a contrast to the honest, but incompetent scholar.

Business dealings and household management require a level of sophistication rarely possessed by these naïve male protagonists. The irony, however, is that while these skills are key both to Confucian maxims and the pursuit of civil service careers, the practice of them often conflicts with attempts to retain childlike honesty and purity. As such, the ideals of the childlike are portrayed as inadequate for successful exam candidates since, in the eyes of their peers, they are nothing but incompetence and childishness. While Pu Songling does not despise merchants or their profession, he repeatedly stresses the virtues of honesty and generosity, and upholds naïveté as a positive virtue, and the trademark of the serious scholar. The male characters in these tales do remain true to themselves, but they are so engrossed in themselves that they are unable to deal with the world around them and so while they may struggle to cultivate themselves, the practicalities of earning a living and running their household finances elude them.

### Studying in an Ivory Dolls' House

Given Pu Songling's own background, and that his immediate audience consisted of other members of the Shandong literary circles, the fact that the vast majority of *Liaozhai* protagonists are described as scholars is hardly surprising. As in Pu's own case, the cyclical process of studying for, and then traveling to sit, the various levels of examination, could take over an individual's whole life. Indeed, in many ways, Pu's repeated attempts to take the provincial level of the exam, attempts which spanned around forty years of his life, encapsulate this, and with it the contradictory elements discussed above about the nature of folly. This is both a positive idealism much in the nature of Li Zhi's doctrines, yet also reflects a detachment from and inability to relate to, or cope effectively with, the reality of the outside world. Twentieth-century Chinese critics have been quick to point this out. Wang Ping 王平, adopting a psychoanalytical approach to the study of Pu Songling's life, has suggested that folly is an attribute both of Pu's attitude to the examination system, and also of his approach to his writing (Wang, 1991). Ma Jigao 马积高 has likewise suggested that for Pu folly was "both an ideal and a guiding principle for one's life" (Ma, 1996, p. 225).

Pu Songling was by no means unique in this dilemma, borne out by the popularity of his fictional portrayals of similarly afflicted candidates. Encouraged by Confucian maxims such as "Study like you will never attain it, as if you are afraid you will lose it" (*Analects* 8:17), obsessive attitudes towards studying were not uncommon among this sector of society. As illustrated in many of the tales, even marriage was often put on hold until the prospective husband had achieved a certain degree.

One comment on education in the late imperial period is particularly illuminating for my study here, since it demonstrates the strong social aspect of teaching and, by implication, studying: "'Teaching' tended generally to mean the production or reproduction of a highly literate elite and the socialization of the far less literate, or even illiterate, common people by means of exhortations and rituals" (Woodside & Elman, 1994, p. 3). The utilitarian aspect of education, of learning to be a social being was always controversial. Confucius himself had lamented that, "In the past people studied for their own sake, nowadays people study for others" (*Analects* 14:24). This controversy is to some extent encapsulated in the perceived contradictions between 'pure' scholarship, and examination success. Such contradictions were clearly an issue for Pu Songling himself. Having gained first place and high praise in the initial stages of the exam system, when he was examined by Shi Runzhang 施闰章 (1618-1683),

an official famed for his open-mindedness, Pu then failed repeatedly at the next stage, when more conventional writing was required (Lu, 1986, p. 9). This conflict between creativity and the practical requirements of the system is a recurring theme in the collection.

In what follows, I will analyse the attitudes and behaviour of some of the many scholar-protagonists in the *Liaozhai*, both with regard to reading and studying *per se*, and in the wider setting of performance in the examinations. Both demonstrate further aspects of the childishness of these male characters.

I have suggested that the naïveté of many *Liaozhai* scholars rendered them unable to deal with practical aspects of life, including dealing with sexual and with financial matters. They were perceived as childish rather than childlike and the romantic ideals of Li Zhi and his followers became the object of ridicule. If the *wen*-type of masculinity was defined as much by a man's ability to produce literary texts as by his sexual prowess, then his approach to reading, writing and sitting the exams was also crucial to his self-fulfilment as an adult man. In these tales, however, the protagonists' linguistic ability is stifled as much as their sexuality and their misunderstandings and blunders are frequent objects of ridicule by more eloquent and quick-witted female fox spirits. Since being able to communicate is the most basic level of socialisation, they are poorly equipped to interact with their surroundings in an adult society.

The different possible levels of interpretation of any given text can indicate varying degrees of maturity or sophistication in readers. For example, children and young readers are often entirely unaware of satirical overtones in novels, reading and accepting them unquestionably as fact. An unsophisticated adult reader may equally well overlook deeper levels of meaning in texts, and this will in no way hamper his ability to memorise and reproduce them. Much criticism of the eight-legged essay (*baguwen* 八股文) requirement in the examinations was precisely that the skills tested were purely those of superficial rote learning and imitation and that creativity, or individual interpretations, were actively discouraged.

However, this type of simplistic approach to reading should be distinguished from the idealised naïveté of Li Zhi's childlike mind. Li argued that the greatness of the sages of ancient times lay in their ability to preserve their childlike mind, however much they read. He contrasted them to the scholars of his day, who read voraciously, but whose purpose in reading was to learn about duty and principles which then distanced them from their childlike mind. As early as the Song dynasty, Lu Jiuyuan and the philosophers of the school of the mind had warned against the limitations of taking things too literally and superficially: "A student must make up his mind. To read books and merely understand their literal meanings means not to have made up one's mind" (Chan, 1969, p.584). As with Wang Yangming later, these philosophers concurred that books were not an end in themselves, and one's mind (however differently they defined this) should not be subjugated to the words on the page.

Many of the *Liaozhai* stories play with literal and non-literal interpretations of language. The relationship between the literal interpretation of characters and their intended meaning is continually challenged. I would further argue that this playful use of language also illustrates another aspect of childlikeness in the collection, a deliberate adoption of interpretations inappropriate to the context.

Some of this wordplay consists of fairly straightforward transferral such as the large number of foxes whose surname is Hu (a phonetic pun on the word for 'fox'), or Scholar Liu (柳生; 5:39) turning out to be the spirit of a willow tree (the literal meaning of his surname). There are also more complex usages, in which the whole tale turns on the deciphering of the linguistic code. In "The Laolong boatmen" (老龙舡户; 8:42) the solution to a multiple murder case depends on the unravelling of a riddle told to the provincial governor in a dream. The four characters of the words 'Laolong boatmen' are described in turn, and the governor eventually works out the riddle, and arrests around fifty boatmen from the Laolong ford, who confess to the crimes. In "Clues from poetry" (诗谳; 6:23) Wu Feiqing, wrongly accused of murder, is told in a dream not to kill himself, as "now there is a good omen inside." Only when his case is overturned by a newly appointed just magistrate and the real murderer arrested, does Wu realise that this refers to the surname of the magistrate, Zhou 周, which includes the ideogram for good fortune 吉. The Chinese script particularly lends itself to these puns and riddles, which can work on the level of a single character, a word, or a whole phrase, and can be based on phonetic similarity or the visual complexity of the characters.

As such, the potential for misinterpretation is great. As any student of Chinese language knows, it is quite possible to understand every character in a sentence, while entirely missing the meaning of the whole. Equally, the sophisticated speaker can exploit the potential of the language at the expense of less eloquent opponents. The numerous instances of poetry composing contests or couplet finishing drinking games demonstrate the priority placed on the witty manipulation of language throughout Chinese fiction. The naïve *Liaozhai* scholar is at a loss when faced with such wit, often demonstrated by a female. In "Fox clique" (狐联; 2:14) a scholar is reduced to a laughingstock by two fox spirits. When he attempts to rebuke them for their inappropriate flirtatious behaviour, they hold an impromptu poetry composing contest, which they then win with ease and leave, laughing. A less heartless depiction of a similar type of female wit can be found in the tale "Fox humour" (狐谐; 3:32). The fox spirit in this case has a secret affair with a young man who is as yet unsuccessful in the exams, reportedly due to bad luck. She amazes his friends by her witty puns, taking particular delight in playing on the characters of their names. In the end, her brothers arrive to take her home and, against the young man's wishes, she goes with them.

This conflict between 'real' understanding and superficial or literal understanding is also an issue in learning in the wider sense. A mature approach to learning would be one which demonstrated interest in long-term education rather than short-term quick gains, and was open to different learning environments, rather than simply relying on books.

One of the most well-known and popular of the *Liaozhai* tales, "The Daoist priest of Mt. Lao" (劳山道士; 1:15), tells the story of the young scholar, Wang, who asks the priest to teach him Daoist arts. Warning Wang of the need to be serious in his study, and not simply to treat the arts as magic tricks, the priest agrees to teach him how to run through walls. As expected, on Wang's return home, he boasts of his skills, attempts to show off to his wife, and injures himself. This tale is very commonly anthologised in collections of children's literature, for obvious didactic reasons. A different learning experience is described in the tale "Fendie" (粉蝶; 8:62). When the protagonist Yang Yuedan's boat capsizes and he arrives at a Daoist paradise island, he meets his late cousin Yan. Yang sees a zither on the shelf and asks to hear some tunes. Yan's wife, Shiniang, asks him what he would like to hear, but he replies that not having read the classic theories on the musical canon, he doesn't know what he would like. There then begins a fascinating dialogue in which Shiniang explains to Yang that music can be composed in the mind, without recourse to books and with no written score. Finally, after practising for some time, Yang is suddenly enlightened and begins dancing spontaneously, having discovered the secret of 'true learning.' The dangers of over-reliance on book learning are thus satirised, leading to a condition symptomatic of a commonly cited criticism of traditional scholars, that the heavy focus on rote learning renders them scarcely able to function independently of the written word. Moreover, the childish dependence on external sources is discarded, and replaced with a spontaneity and genuineness resonant of the childlike. Of course it is hardly coincidental that this is one of the few tales which deal with study in a field (music), unrelated to the examination system and thus one in which the pursuit of such ideals may still be feasible.

According to Kam Louie, "The scholars in literary and artistic dimensions usually have two basic aims in life: to be successful in the civil service examinations and to win a beautiful woman (or women)." (Louie, 2002, p. 59). A recurring theme in the tales is the relationship between these two aims and the compatibility or otherwise of sexual fulfilment and exam success. When Wu Qing'an, a child prodigy, fails the exams, the local court historian promises him the hand of his daughter in marriage if he can succeed within three years. Another temptation is introduced, however, in the form of the immortal Bai Yuyu (白于玉; 2:35), who tries to persuade Wu that reaching immortality is more important than either sex, sons, or success in the exams. Bai himself is a *xiucai* (having passed the first level of the exams) who refuses to learn eight-legged essays and is disillusioned with the mechanisms of the examination system. In the end, Wu's desires are fulfilled when he has sex with an immortal, has a son by her, then retires to become a hermit.

In the story of Zhou Kechang (周克昌; 6:09), sexual fulfilment and success in one's studies are portrayed as somehow incompatible. A spoilt child, Zhou often neglects his studies and plays truant from school, but his parents refuse to scold him. One day he disappears. After a year or so he returns, saying that he was taken away by a Daoist priest, but eventually managed to escape. Thereafter, his studies go very well, he quickly gains the *xiucai* degree, and suddenly many families want to marry their daughters to him. After refusing many proposals, he finally marries the daughter of a top (*jinshi*) degree holder and, while they get along well together, he insists on sleeping alone. Under pressure from his parents to produce a grandson, he eventually leaves, saying that he will send someone who can fulfil their wishes. He disappears, and the next day the real Zhou Kechang returns—he was sold to a rich childless businessman, who has subsequently had his own child, and so has been allowed to return. He is still lax at his studies, but since no-one finds out about the swap, he retains the academic title the imposter has won for him, and has a sexually fulfilling relationship with his wife, producing a child within a year.

A young man, who remains anonymous, marries an intelligent orphan girl, Miss Yan (颜氏; 4:49). Despite her tutoring, he is unable to grasp the intricacies of the eight-legged essay and fails the civil service exams in successive years. In the end Yan persuades him to let her dress up as his younger brother, and sit the exams. At the next sitting, they both take the exams: she gains first place, while he fails outright. She then progresses up the system, gaining a high position, while keeping the secret of her gender hidden, ignoring various marriage proposals. Only after the Ming was overthrown do the couple reveal the truth to a relative. Yan's sex is verified by checking the size of her feet. Thereafter, she passes on her title to her husband, and resumes the life of a woman, dressing in female clothing and remaining indoors. At first reading, this tale is as a positive portrayal of a female who not only assumes the role of tutor to her husband, but further goes on to prove her superiority over him in that very male setting, the examination hall. However, despite Miss Yan's ultimate return to her original character, the gender swap has nevertheless caused them to sacrifice their sexuality –it is noted that Miss Yan never has any children, and her husband does not take a concubine. Once again the perceived incompatibility between success in the examinations and in the bedchamber is exposed.

Prolonged participation in the exam system, studying in isolation for long periods, and then repeatedly confining oneself to the stultifying atmosphere of the examination halls only to meet with successive failures, were all common practice to many literati of the period. Surveying to what extent such conditions did emasculate such candidates, either in their own eyes or in the view of society around them would be a fascinating subject of social historical research. In any case, in these fictional representations, such associations are made repeatedly. The relationship between the pursuit of scholarship and sexuality, which are, in Kam Louie's words, "the two basic aims" of the wen-type of male, is an uneasy one in the *Liaozhai* tales.

### Conclusion ~ "The Book Fool"

The ultimate inept and childish male scholar is the subject of the tale 'The book fool' (Shu Chi 书痴; 7:35), in which ignorance of the sexual act is contrasted clearly with an obsessive thirst for knowledge and books. In many ways this story is itself a study of the conflict between the childlike and the childish, combining and encapsulating many of the themes discussed in this chapter. The specific analogies drawn between educational stagnation and sexual abrogation merit a closer reading and so I have translated and annotated the story in full below, by way of conclusion of my study of childlike minds and childish men.

The title of the tale refers to the male protagonist who is the epitome of the naïve scholar. Described from the beginning as 'foolish' (*chi*), he displays all the elements discussed above of social dysfunction, physical or emotional comatosis, naïveté, and infantile behaviour. In sum, he is entirely introverted and unable to relate to his environment:

> Lang Yuzhu came from Pengcheng, the descendant of a prefect, who had been honest in his post, and did not use his salary to try to accumulate wealth, but instead had amassed enough books to fill his house. Yuzhu himself was particularly foolish (*chi*): his family was impoverished, and he sold absolutely everything, except for his father's book collection, of which he was unwilling to part with a single *juan*. When his father was alive, he had written out the poem "Exhortations to Study" and had pasted it to the right of his seat, and Lang recited this daily; he even covered it with a piece of white gauze, afraid it would fade away.

"Exhortations to study (Quan xue pian 劝学篇)" is the title of a ten-line poem, by the Song emperor Zhenzong 真宗 (r. 998-1022), which reads as follows: "To enrich your household there is no need to buy good fields; in books are stored a thousand kinds of grain. To live peacefully there is no need for lofty halls; in books are found rooms of gold. When you wish to marry don't rue the fact that there are no good matchmakers; in books are found jade-like beauties. When you leave the house don't fret that you lack an entourage; in books chariots and horses are abundant. If a man desires to follow his life's ambition, then he should read the five classics diligently, facing the window" (LZZY, p. 2108). Throughout the tale, Yuzhu repeatedly takes this poem literally, and believes that he will find all the items mentioned physically within his library. When such items seem to appear, he is further confirmed in his naïve faith in the poem. One reason for this poem's influence on Yuzhu is his father's pasting it "to the right of his seat," since "an inscription to the right of one's seat (*zuo you ming* 座右铭)" was a traditional reference to a text which provides instruction and encouragement for a person through his life. Once again, this is a deliberate and playful inversion of a metaphor, which Yuzhu takes unquestioningly at a literal level.

> Not interested in working for the sake of a salary, he literally believed that there really was gold and grain in books. He read by day and by night, regardless of the seasons. Although he was over twenty years old, he still did not seek a marriage partner, hoping for a beauty to emerge from his books. When guests or relatives came to see him, he never knew the correct etiquette of how to greet them, so after saying a few words he would start to recite great works at them, and they would take their leave, in embarrassment. Every time the provincial education commissioner came to give the preliminary inspection, Yuzhu was rated first, but he sadly never passed the provincial exam.

Yuzhu's social ineptitude is encapsulated here, in his incapability even of greeting family members appropriately. Such social etiquette would normally be learnt as part of a child's elementary education, but Lang's studying is entirely introverted and unrelated to his actual environment. As with so many of the *Liaozhai* tales, it is the provincial level exam which proves to be the stumbling block for this naïve protagonist, as it was for Pu Songling himself.

> All of a sudden one day, while he was studying, his book was blown away by a strong gust of wind. Lunging after it, he stumbled and put his foot through a hole in the floor; on further investigation, he found the hole to be full of rotten straw; digging this out, it turned out to be where people of old had once stored grain, but the grain had all decomposed into compost. Despite the fact that it was inedible, it deepened his faith that the 'thousand kinds of grain' theory was not obsolete, and he studied with extra vigour.
>
> One day, at the top of his ladder, he found a miniature golden imperial carriage, about a foot long, among some loose volumes. Delighted, he took this as proof of the 'rooms of gold.' When he took this out and showed it to people, they told him it was only gold-plated, not real gold. Secretly, he bemoaned the ancients for cheating him. Not long after, a man who graduated in the same year as his father became surveillance commissioner of the prefecture. He was an admirer of Buddhism. Someone persuaded Lang to donate the carriage as a stand for a Buddha statue. The commissioner was delighted, and presented Lang with three hundred pieces of gold and twenty-four horses. Lang was pleased, believing that the golden house, the chariots and horses had all been proved, and so became more diligent at his studies than ever. But he was already thirty years old. Someone tried to persuade him to take a wife, but he responded "Since 'in books are found jade-like beauties,' why should I be worried about not having a beautiful wife?" He studied for a further two or three years, but never with anything to show for it, and people all ridiculed him. At that time there was a rumour going round that the Weaving Maid in Heaven had run off. Someone teased Lang, saying "I bet it was you that the granddaughter of Heaven [another term for the Weaving Maid] was running off after!" Lang knew he was joking, so thought no more of it.
>
> One evening, half-way through the eighth volume of the *History of the Han*, he saw a silk cutting of a beautiful girl stuck within the pages. Astonished he exclaimed "Can this be the answer to the riddle of the jade-like beauties contained within books?" He became disheartened. Looking closely at the beautiful woman, she looked real: on her back were the faint tiny characters which said "Weaving Maid." He was incredulous. Every day he placed her on top of that volume, repeatedly gazing or playing so that he forgot to eat and sleep.
>
> One day, just as he was staring at her, the beauty suddenly bent her waist upwards, and sat on top of the book, smiling at him coyly. Lang was terrified, and hid under the desk. By the time he'd got back up, she was already over a foot tall. Even more petrified, he hit his head against the floor. When she got down from the desk and stood before him, he saw that she really was a matchless beauty. Bowing he asked her "Which goddess are you?" The

> beauty replied with a smile: "I'm Yan Ruyu, you've known me for a long time. Having been the object of your daily infatuation, I was afraid that if I didn't make an appearance, no-one this millennium would ever again believe sincerely in the ancients."

Lang's first failure to distinguish real gold from gold-plate is repeated in his confusion about how to interpret the illustration in the book. Since the literal meaning of this girl's name, Yan Ruyu 颜如玉, is 'beauty like jade,' Yuzhu is naturally delighted. The probable significance of her location within the eighth *juan* of the *History of the Han* is in reference to the discussion in this section about the self-sacrificial nature of true love between husband and wife. "Even if there is a catastrophe, the one will risk death to preserve the other. Sincere love is knotted around the heart, and is the extreme of benevolence and generosity" (*Han Shu*, p. 251). Yan's explanation, that her motive for appearing to Yuzhu was to encourage people to 'believe sincerely' in the ancients, is entirely in accord with Yuzhu's naïve sincerity, and he is understandably pleased.

> Lang was delighted, and followed her to the bed. Although they were intimate together, Lang did not know how to make love.

Presumably sensing that Yuzhu's naïveté is such that he is not even yet ready to learn about sex, Yan does not begin to instruct him until later.

> Whenever he studied, he made the girl sit beside him. She warned him not to study, but he wouldn't listen. She said to him "The reason you are unable to gain promotion is simply because of your studying. Look at the rolls of honour for the provincial and metropolitan exams! How many of these people study as hard as you? If you don't listen to me, I'm leaving."

This is a fascinating satirical insight into the conflicting requirements of diligent study and performance in the examinations, one which would doubtless have been appreciated by many of Pu Songling's fellow exam candidates and readers.

> Lang took her advice for a while, but soon he forgot her instruction, and began to recite aloud again. Before long, he looked for her, but she had vanished. At his wits' end, he tried to entreat her with prayers, but could find no trace of her. Suddenly he remembered her original hiding place, took out the *History of the Han* and looked through it carefully, till he reached the same spot as before, and sure enough, there she was. He called out to her but she remained motionless, so he prostrated himself and implored her bitterly. She finally came down and said "But if you don't listen to me again, we'll be parted forever!" She got out the gambling games, and played with him daily. But Lang could not keep his attention on it. When he saw that she was not there, he secretly continued reading. Afraid that the girl would discover this, he took out the eighth volume of the *History of the Han*, and replaced it out of order, in another place to confuse her. One day, absorbed in his book, the girl came in without him noticing; he suddenly saw her, and rushed to cover up the book, but she had already disappeared. Terrified, he painstakingly searched through all the *juan*, but he could not find her; then, he found her once again in the eighth volume of the *History of the Han*, on the correct page. At this he kowtowed to her again, swearing resolutely not to study again. Only then did the girl come down and she began to play Go with him, saying "If you haven't mastered it within three days, then I'll leave again." By the third day, he suddenly beat the girl by two pieces.

By teaching him the rules of Go, Yan is beginning the complex process of socialising her pupil, Yuzhu. He is obviously intelligent enough to learn the game well, but what he is really learning here is the art of interaction with another person, albeit a supernatural one, rather than a book.

> The girl was happy, and began to teach him how to play the zither, demanding that he master one tune within five days. Lang had to put all his concentration onto his hands and his eyes, and he had no time to do anything else: after a long time, he could follow a tune with his fingers, and without realising it, began to feel excited. The girl drank and gambled with him every day, and Lang accordingly started to enjoy himself and forgot about studying.

Although learning to play music is not a social skill *per se*, except when used to entertain others, it requires a creative ability which Yuzhu had never needed before. Together with his new-found hobbies of drinking and gambling, he is now able to interact with others, and has lost much of the foolishness that prevented him from socialising.

> The girl then urged him to go out and made him entertain people.
> From this point on, he suddenly gained a reputation as a playboy.
> The girl said, "Now you can go and take the examinations."

This abrupt juxtaposition of becoming a socialite as a qualification for taking the provincial examination is indicative of the requirement for candidates at this stage in their careers to progress from an idealised, naïve, yet childish state to become a socially adept, worldly, wise 'adult.' Despite the perceived incompatibility, as discussed above, between sexual and intellectual fulfilment for these men, the practicalities of progression up the examination ladder (and particularly past the provincial level, the exam which had formed an unsurpassable hurdle for Pu Songling himself), required scholars to compromise these values and turn away from their books and their bookishness.

> One night Lang said to the girl: "Generally, when a man and a woman live together they produce offspring: I've been living with you for some time, why are we not like that?" The girl laughed and said: "I did tell you studying day after day would do you no good. You've got to the chapter on the relations between husbands and wives, but you're still ignorant of the arts of the bedchamber." Lang asked with surprise "What arts are they?" The girl laughed and did not reply. After a while, she secretly guided him into her. Lang was ecstatic and exclaimed "I had no idea that the joy of a husband and wife was something which could not be transmitted in words."

In this, Yuzhu's next lesson in maturity, he loses his absolute faith in linguistic expression as the sole channel for learning, alongside his virginity.

> Afterwards, he told this to every person he met and everybody had to disguise their laughter. When the girl found out she reproached him. Lang said "If you scuttle about doing shameful deeds, then you must keep it a secret; the joy in a natural human relationship is common to everyone, so why not talk about it?"

Reminiscent of the protagonist in the tale of Yingning discussed above, and having only recently learnt the art of communication itself, Yuzhu is unaware of the social conventions which place restrictions on the appropriateness of topics. Even in his new, enlightened and socialized state, the observance of such social propriety would for Yuzhu mean compromising his true self.

> After eight or nine months, the girl gave birth to a son, and they employed a nurse to raise him. One day, the girl said to Lang: "I've been with you for two years now, and have given you a child, we can now part. If I stay longer I am worried I will bring you disaster, and then it will be too late for regrets." When Lang

heard her words, he collapsed in tears and was unable to get up, saying "Don't you even consider our baby?" The girl was also distraught, and after a long time said "If you really want me to stay, you must throw away all your books." Lang said "These books are your home, and are also my life. Why are you asking me to do that?" The girl did not persist, but said "I also know this is fate, so I can only prewarn you."

Previously, if Lang's relatives ever caught a glimpse of the girl, they were always astonished, and never having heard of her family background, they all interrogated him. Lang could not lie to them, but remained silent. So people became all the more suspicious, and the rumours abounded, until Lord Shi, the district magistrate, heard of them. Shi was from Fujian, and had become a *jinshi* in his youth. When he heard of her he set off, privately wanting to have a look at this beauty and intending to get to her by detaining Lang. When the girl heard of this, she immediately vanished. The prefect was angry and arrested Lang, and stripped him of his *xiucai* degree and put him in shackles, to force the girl's whereabouts out of him. Lang, close to death, said nothing. They tied up his maid, who gave a vague account. The steward thought it was the work of demons, and ordered a carriage and went personally to Lang's house. He saw that the house was filled with books, too many to search through, and burnt them; the smoke in the yard did not disperse, remaining dark, like a heavy cloud.

As his book collection is destroyed, Yuzhu's growing up process also is completed. He now is a fully functioning adult, able to hold an official post and, while still unwilling or unable to tell a lie, he is aware that he cannot talk about the girl's origin. The library, representative of Yuzhu's earlier naïve, isolationist and pure approach to scholarship has proved the final obstacle to his progress in the outside world. He is now finally ready to tackle the provincial level exam.

When Lang was released, he petitioned some of his father's students, and his degree was reinstated. In the Autumn diet of examinations that year he gained the *juren* (the 2nd level) degree, and the following year, the *jinshi* degree. But he held a bitter grudge in his bones. He prayed night and day at Yan Ruyu's memorial tablet, saying "If your spirit is alive, allow me to get a post in Fujian." Consequently, he was indeed made inspector in Fujian. After holding the post for three months, he investigated some of Shi's misdeeds, and confiscated all his household and possessions. At that time his cousin was chief legislator, so he was able to take Shi's favourite concubine, on pretext of procuring a maid for the government office. As soon as the case was closed, Lang sent in his resignation, and returned home with the concubine.

Finally, Yuzhu has learnt how to work the system. By using his contacts, he succeeds in the examinations and ultimately demonstrates that he can even manipulate his power for his own ends. To the very end, Yuzhu retains his integrity, remaining in post only long enough to avenge his loss.

The Historian of the Strange records: "With all things under heaven: hoarding them incites jealousy and admiring them creates demons; the girl's seductive power was the demon created from his books. This matter had already been fairly bizarre, and there was nothing wrong with the way it was dealt with; but surely the ancestral dragon's brutality was cruel enough! How much more did Shi's secret ambitions deserve to be avenged in this vile way.

Alas! What is so strange about that!"

"The ancestral dragon's brutality" (*zulong zhi nüe* 祖龙之虐) refers to the Qin emperor's burning of the books in 213 BC, ordered to suppress criticism of his rule. The Historian argues that since Shi's book-burning was to fulfil his personal, secret ambition, his crime was even greater, and his punishment was even more justified.

The relationship between true scholarship and immaturity satirised within this tale is typical of the *Liaozhai* collection. At the beginning of the tale, the protagonist exhibits naïve and socially improper behaviour, in his lack of etiquette, his persistent misinterpretation of texts and misreading of contexts. He is entirely unable to adapt the knowledge he has from books, to fit the situations in which he finds himself. He 'grows up' as it were, only after discarding his naïve bookishness, and pursuing his official career through the examination system. His initial inappropriate childish mentality is replaced by a fully socialised adult world view. The books which have become a stultifying burden to him, preventing him from developing into an adult male, are sacrificed as he loses his childish foolishness. One of the most optimistic of the tales I have discussed here, by remaining true to himself, the adult Yuzhu is nevertheless ultimately able to retain a degree of the childlike ideal.

# References

## Notes on Primary Sources

Ren, D. 任笃行 (Ed.). (2000). *Liaozhai zhiyi: quanjiao huizhu jiping* 聊斋志异全校会注集评 [*Strange Tales of Liaozhai*: fully collated with annotations and critical commentaries] (3 vols). Qilu shushe.

**Note: I have abbreviated this in the text to LZZY. In all references to *Liaozhai* tales, I state first the number of the *juan*, or volume, and then the story number within it, according to the ordering of the Ren edition.

Zhang, J. 张建业 & Liu Yousheng 刘幼生 (Eds.). (2000). *Li Zhi wenji* 李贽文集 [The collected writings of Li Zhi]. Shehui kexue wenxian chubanshe.

**Note: the core essay by Li Zhi on which much of this chapter is based is entitled "Tongxin shuo 童心说 [On the childlike mind]" and is found in Vol. 1, *Fen Shu* 焚书 [A Book to be burned] pp.91–3.

## Other References Cited

Brook, T. (1998). *The confusions of pleasure: Commerce and culture in Ming China*. University of California Press.

Brownell, S., & Wasserstrom, J. N. (Eds.). (2002). *Chinese femininities/Chinese masculinities: A reader*. University of California Press.

Chan, W-t. (1963). *Instructions for practical living and other neo-Confucian writings by Wang Yang-ming*. Columbia University Press.

Chan, W-t. (Trans. and Ed.). (1969). *A sourcebook in Chinese philosophy*. Princeton University Press.

Chou, C. C. (1988). *Yüan Hung-tao and the Kung-an school*. Cambridge University Press.

De Bary, W. T. (1991). *Learning for one's self: Essays on the individual in neo-Confucian thought*. Columbia University Press.

Dong W., 董挽华 (1976). *Cong Liaozhai zhiyi de renwu kan Qingdai de keju zhidi he songyu zhidu* 从聊斋志异的人物看清代的科举制度和讼狱制度 [The civil service examination system and the litigation system in the Qing dynasty, as seen in characters from *Strange Tales of Liaozhai*]. Chia Hsin Foundation.

Furth, C. (1987). Concepts of pregnancy, childbirth and infancy in Ch'ing Dynasty China. *Journal of Asian Studies, 46*(1), 7–35.

Hsu, P-c. (1998). Feng Meng-lung's *Treasury of Laughs*: Humorous satire on seventeenth-century Chinese culture and society. *The Journal of Asian Studies, 57*(4), 1042–1067.

Huang, M. W. (2006). *Negotiating masculinities in Late Imperial China*. University of Hawaii Press.

Kao, K. S. Y. (1994). Projection, displacement, introjection: The strangeness of *Liaozhai zhiyi*. In E. Hung (Ed.), *Paradoxes of traditional Chinese literature* (pp. 199–230). The Chinese University Press.

Li, W-y. L. (1993). *Enchantment and disenchantment: Love and illusion in Chinese literature*. Princeton University Press.

Li W-y. L. (1995). The rhetoric of spontaneity in Late-Ming literature. *Ming Studies 1995*(1), 32–52.

Lin, H. 临海权 (1992). *Li Zhi nianpu kao lüe* 李贽年谱考略 [Li Zhi's life: a general study]. Fujian renmin chubanshe.

Lin, Z. 林植峰 (1989). Tan *Liaozhai zhiyi* zhong guanyu ertong xinli tezheng de miaoxie 谈聊斋志异中关于儿童心理特征的描写 [On the portrayal of psychological characteristics of children in the *Liaozhai*]. *Pu Songling yanjiu, 2*, 97–109.

Louie, K. (2002). *Theorising Chinese masculinity: Society and gender in China*. Cambridge University Press.

Lu, D. 路大荒 (1986). *Pu Songling nianpu* 蒲松龄年谱 [A Biography of Pu Songling]. In Li Shizhao 李士钊 (Ed.). Qilu shushe.

Lu, T. 鲁童, & Zhou, Y. 周雁翔 (Eds.). (1987). *Liaozhai ti yong* 聊斋题咏 [Inscriptions and Eulogies on the *Liaozhai*]. Baihua wenyi chubanshe.

Ma, J. 马积高 (1996). *Qingdai xueshu sixiang de bianqian yu wenxue* 清代学术思想的变迁与文学. [Literature and the vicissitudes of academic thought in the Qing Dynasty]. Hunan chubanshe.

Mu, H. 牧惠 (1997). *Liaozhai xian kan* 聊斋闲侃 [A frank discussion of *Liaozhai*]. Baihua wenyi chubanshe.

Owen, S. (Trans. and Ed.). (1996). *An anthology of Chinese literature: Beginnings to 1911*. W.W. Norton & Company.

Radice, B. (Trans.) (1993). *Praise of folly* by Erasmus. A.H.T. Levi (Annot). Penguin.

Song, G. (2004). *The fragile scholar: Power and masculinity in Chinese culture*. Hong Kong University Press.

Wang, P. 王平 (1991). *Liaozhai chuangzuo xinli yanjiu* 聊斋创作心理研究 [A psychoanalytical study of *Liaozhai* writing]. Shandong wenyi chubanshe.

Weightman, F. (2004). Milestones on the road to maturity: Growing up with the civil service examinations. *Sungkyun Journal of East Asian Studies, 4*(2), 113–135.

Weightman, F. (2006a). Ideals of childlikeness in Late Imperial China. *Ming Qing Yanjiu*, 14(1), 178–218.

Weightman, F. (2006b). Folly (Chi) in the *Liaozhai Zhiyi*. In P. Santangelo & D. Guida (Eds.), *Love, hatred, and other passions: Questions and themes on emotions in Chinese civilization* (pp. 197–211). Brill.

Weightman, F. (2008). *The quest for the childlike in seventeenth-century China: Fantasy, naivety, and folly*. Edwin Mellen Press.

Woodside, A., & Elman, B. (Eds.). (1994). *Education and society in Late Imperial China, 1600–1900*. University of California Press.

Wu, C. 吴承学 (1998). *Wanming xiaopin yanjiu* 晚明小品研究 [Studies of late Ming vignettes]. Jiangsu guji chubanshe.

Yan, S. 颜师古 (Annot.) (1962*). Han shu* 汉书 [History of the Former Han]. Zhonghua shuju.

Yang, C. 杨昌年 (1996). *Liaozhai zhiyi yanjiu* 聊斋志异研究 [A study of the *Liaozhai*]. Liren Shuju.

Yang, G., & Yang, X. (1984). *Selected tales of Liaozhai*. Panda Books.

Yuan, S. 袁世硕 (1988). *Pu Songling shiji zhushu xin kao* 蒲松龄事迹著述新考 [A new investigation into Pu Songling's life and work]. Qilu shushe.

Zhang, M. 张敏(1999). *Doupeng xianhua* 豆棚闲话 [Idle Talk under the Bean Arbour] by the self-styled Lay Buddhist Aina (*Aina Jushi* 艾衲居士). Renmin wenxue chubanshe.

Zhu, Y. 朱一玄 (Ed.). (1986). *Liaozhai zhiyi ziliao huibian* 聊斋志异资料汇编 [Sourcebook on *Strange Tales of Liaozhai*]. Zhongzhou guji chubanshe.

# Chapter V.
## Childlikeness and Art
### Edwige Comoy Fusaro

> Artists are people to whom society
> grants a certain privilege, that of acting
> ways we do not expect from adults.
> Mike Kelley (2001)

It is well known that there is no consensual definition of art, and we will simply consider art to be that which has been considered as such before, on the condition that the artist was an adult human being. The concept of childlikeness is not much easier to define, although psychologists have demonstrated rather clearly what a child does at different stages of their development until puberty. Puberty is the marker that usually differentiates childhood from the teenage years and, then, adulthood. However, the specific features of child behavior do not disappear with puberty but become less relevant or latent in adult psychomotor dynamics. By and large, movement and emotion are prevalent in children's behavior. First comes the sensorimotor stage: in a baby's brain, because of the prevalence of emotional centers in the limbic system on the prefrontal cortex, the salient features of their behavior are motor impulsivity and affectivity. By contrast, grown-ups temper emotions and motor impulsivity with the filters of reasoning and experience. The child's motivations to act and react are mainly self-centered, whereas an adult may consider other criteria, such as the collective interest or a long-term self-interest. Swiss biologist and psychologist Jean Piaget also identifies a "no stage" between the sensorimotor and the later stage—characterized by the acquisition of moral sense. In the no stage, the child—between the ages of 3 and 6—establishes themselves in an egocentric way through rejection and denial. French psychologist Henri Wallon insists on the centripetal tendencies of this stage, in opposition to the one that follows—between 6 and 10 years of age—when children start considering other points of view than their own and develop intense friendships. Prepubescent children and teenagers return to centripetal tendencies and opposition to the adult system while searching for their own identity.

One can find many features of child behavior in an artistic process. Anticipating Dutch historian Johan Huizinga's theory of *homo ludens*, Sigmund Freud (1959) writes:

> Might we not say that every child at play behaves like a creative writer, in that he creates a world of his own, or, rather, rearranges the things of his world in a new way which pleases him? . . . The creative writer does the same as the child at play. He creates a world of fantasy which he takes very seriously. (pp. 143-144)[6]

Approaching art in a playful way is a salient trend today, as are other childlike features that we will observe in modern and contemporary art, such as centripetal tendencies (just think of tags), the prevalence of motion and emotion (e.g., in action painting), and rejection and denial. Indeed, childlikeness is a key element of contemporary art. It is based on a conception of art that has radically changed since the Second World War and belongs to what Nathalie Heinich (2014) calls "the paradigm of contemporary art." Childlikeness has largely contributed to the rise (and the defining characteristics) of this revolutionary new conception of art, which includes the creative process, the artwork (material or not), the artist, and the beholder.

---

[6] In his essay on Leonardo da Vinci, Freud notes that "the great Leonardo remained infantile in some ways throughout his whole life" (Freud, 1916, p. 110).

Yet, this process is rooted in an older phenomenon, namely, in the words of Alain Vaillant, the "literary crisis" that accompanied Romanticism in the early 19th century in the wake of the industrial revolution. This literary crisis "explains the extraordinary topicality of our 19th century, which, therefore, continues to be the best way to know and analyze contemporary culture" (Vaillant, 2005, p. 7).[7] With this crisis, literary communication is deprived of its traditional intermediate structures and "becomes based on a hero-like face-to-face between the writer and the readership" (Vaillant, 2005, p. 17).[8] This change implies that anyone, whatever their cultural background, is allowed to deal with a piece of art using their own resources. In other words, culture is no longer a requirement to approach art; the relationship between childlikeness and art involves not only the artists and the art as a product but also the image or the idea of art among the recipients of the artwork.

With Romanticism and modernity, from the pre-industrial world to our current post-romantic and post-modern era, the idea of what a child is has also shifted significantly from that of a non-finished human being to that of an unknowing master to learn from, for the child is supposed to be closer to nature. In this perspective, the child has not the savage nature of an animal to be tamed but the gentle nature of a genuine human being; the purer they are, the freer from cultural patterns and filters they are. Such an evolution originated with schooling and the concentration of the social and affective life within the family nucleus, when children started to be isolated from adults, as shown by Philippe Ariès. Ariès (1973, p. 134) teaches that in the Middle Ages there was no "sense of childhood" defined as "an awareness about the child specificity."[9] In the 14th century, a new "sense of childhood" regarding the child's ingenuity, kindness, and funniness emerged, but it was only in the 18th and 19th centuries, thanks to moralists and educators, that our current "sense of childhood" was born. Since then, the child's specificity has piqued psychological interest and drawn moral concern. As a result of this "school and sentimental revolution" (Ariès, 1973, p. iv),[10] artists started to portray children.

Art is a sponge and a lens. It has anticipated, reflected, and crystallized these fundamental changes that have been brought about and fueled by the development of child psychology, pedagogical approaches, and the questioning of anthropocentrism, Western-centrism and adult-centrism. The new trend of praising childhood appeared and paved the way for childlikeness. One root was probably the idea of non-corrupt nature *versus* a corrupt and corrupting civilization, as well as the myth of the noble savage,[11] which emerged in the wake of Jean-Jacques Rousseau's philosophy and led to the modern, positive understanding of the concept of wilderness, for example thanks to the oeuvre of Henry David Thoreau. Another root was the recognition of extraordinary talent among artists in their childhood or at a very young age, such as Wolfgang Amadeus Mozart and Victor Hugo. The decisive step was taken in the 20th century, with the developing sciences of anthropology, psychology, and educational sciences, especially with the child-centered approaches to education promoted by Ellen Key from Sweden, Maria Montessori from Italy, and Célestin and Élise Freinet from France.

[7] Translated from French. Original version: "explique l'extraordinaire actualité de notre XIX<sup>e</sup> siècle, qui demeure, pour cette raison, le meilleur instrument pour connaître et analyser la culture contemporaine."
[8] Translated from French. Original version: "La communication littéraire se résume désormais au face-à-face héroïsé entre l'écrivain et le public."
[9] Translated from French. Original version: "le sentiment de l'enfance n'existait pas. Le sentiment de l'enfance . . . correspond à une conscience de la particularité enfantine." My translation is literal. Hugh Cunningham (1998 p. 1197) stresses the official translation — "the idea of childhood" — as being quite far from the original author's concept.
[10] Translated from French. Original version: "révolution scolaire et sentimentale."
[11] See Cronon 2009. The paper resumes the study published in 1995: *Uncommon ground. Rethinking the human place in nature.*

The 20th century continued to build a positive image of childhood with an approval of transgression. In the journey described by Gianni Celati in *Verso la foce* (1989), the author refers to the story told by the bar owner of Borgoforte about a countess widow:

> Afterward she never wanted to sell the "fruit produce" from her husband's land; merchants come asking to buy her pears and apples and walnuts, but she chases them away "with even bad words." If however some children come to steal fruit from the trees, "be assured that if the countess sees them, she hides and watches them without saying a thing, and seems rather happy."
> (Celati, 2018, p. 27)

The reasons why the countess never wanted to sell the fruits of her late husband are unclear, as are those why she is happy to see the children stealing them. What matters to us in this anecdote is that, when it happens, she secretly watches them and enjoys what she sees. Celati is very clear about the mischievous nature of the behaviors of both the thieves (the children) and the spy (the countess). In so doing, the countess behaves like a child. Adults, especially aristocrats, are supposed to behave properly, following common rules of sociability and morality. Stealing and spying are not part of these rules. The character's misbehavior is even more surprising—childlike— since, as a countess, she is supposed to also conduct herself in a very different way that certainly precludes the pleasure of transgression.

A few years ago, Dutch artist Niels SHOE Meulman, founder of Calligraffiti, made *Crime Time*, a work that consists of two words painted with spray cans and plays on the expression "Prime Time." He sought to blame watching TV as a leisurely evening activity and to encourage people, instead, to spray-paint in the streets, even if—or especially because—it is illegal. Shoe tightly links creativity to transgression, as if art could not exist within the lines of the law. (But the praise for crime-art, in this case, is a bare assertion: the work, executed on a regular canvas, was put up for sale and ended up being sold.) Celati's countess and Shoe's artwork belong to what Matt Mason (2008, p. 31) calls "pirate mentality" and, even more, "pirate culture," which originated in the punk movement and rose up through "punk capitalism," whose landmarks include: "1. Do It Yourself . . . 2. Resist Authority . . . 3. Combine Altruism with Self-Interest." This new culture, which has been fully implemented in contemporary art, is based on the individual's behavior as a pirate towards the community that is perceived as restricting the individual's freedom and personality: the latter two characteristics appear to be intrinsic to childhood, since a child is not liable for misbehaving. Thus, it comes as no surprise that childlikeness has become a main value of art, for childhood represents both wildness and transgression.

Literature was prophetic, and fine arts came later to childlikeness, but *ut pictura poësis*: painting is similar to poetry. Hence, the chapter, which has two parts, outlines this evolution in both literature and the plastic arts from the mid-19th century—with a significant prevalence of the former—before focusing exclusively on the situation in (mostly contemporary) art over the past few decades. For reasons related to my personal background and field of expertise, the body of work on which the survey was conducted consists entirely of Western (especially Italian) artworks and focuses mainly on literature and the plastic arts to the exclusion of other disciplines such as dance and music.

## Children and Childlikeness in Modern Art

From the second part of the 19th to the early 20th century, literature experimented with changing points of view in new narrative voices, from the implicit choral voice in Giovanni Verga's later novels to unreliable and ideologically alien narrators (like in Bertold Brecht) and James Joyce's stream of consciousness. These new ways of telling expressed the authors' curiosity about otherness, which involved neurosis, madness, and childhood. Far from being alone in this endeavor, writers shared this curiosity with their contemporaries (i.e., during this period, the emergence of several new scientific disciplines); as a result, there were similar developments in the fine arts. The child first became a character, then a master. Childhood embodied by children as characters is external to the writer or the artist, whether the child is treated as an object (from the adult's view) or as subject (from the adult's memory). These two steps would lead to an internal perception of childhood, hence creating childlikeness: the phenomenon of an adult feeling, thinking, and behaving as a child would do. Then some writers and artists tried to put themselves in children's shoes by initiating innovative ways of artistic expressions embedded in a brand-new conception of childhood, which has remained into adulthood.

### The Child as a Character: Who Adults are Looking at

The Italian literary and artistic movement of Scapigliatura, which emerged in the aftermaths of Italy's unification in 1860 (at least in the first geographical draft of the country's territory), was the first movement to take an interest in children as objects of representation. While its authors were drawn more and more to adolescent-like characters, literally or metaphorically through figures of orphans and/or neurotics, *scapigliati* painters like Tranquillo Cremona and Daniele Ranzoni, and later also the sculptor Medardo Rosso, repeatedly chose children as their favorite topics. Good examples include *I due cugini*, the nickname given to *Schizzo dal vero*, an oil on canvas painting that Cremona made around 1870 with Cremona's personal technique of *sfocato* or *vaporoso* (blurred), and Ranzoni's *Ritratto del bambino William Morisetti*, also known as *Willy* or *Ritratto di bambino*, painted around 1885 and exhibited in 1890, one year after Ranzoni's death. Ranzoni captures the child's internal life through his peeled eyes and relaxed facial muscles while suggesting movement by using an even more elaborate blurring technique than that of Cremona. The *Willy* portrait looks like a snapshot and expresses the moment-to-moment and constantly moving way of living that typifies childhood.

Meanwhile, literature was questioning the prevailing Positivism, which was exclusively scientific and rationalist, and exploring an alternative epistemology and axiology based on intuition and irrationality. In the pre-*verista* novella entitled *Rosso Malpelo* (1878), Giovanni Verga's eponymous child protagonist is still seen from an external point of view, but the narrative voice has become a collective one, namely that of the Sicilian miners' community of the time: in so doing, Verga (1878) also reflects Rosso's voice because the child is part of this community and the community's voice is also becoming his. The story begins with this sentence: "He was called Malpelo [evil-haired] because he had red hair; and had red hair because he was a mean and bad boy." The apparently logical link between the description that he "had red hair" and the judgment that he "was a mean and bad boy," which implies a causal relationship between the boy's malice and his red hair, is obviously misleading. The author expresses the mining community's point of view, informed as it is by irrational beliefs. But even though Rosso is the scapegoat of this same social environment, he shares the point of view. Therefore, for the reader, who belongs to another community (one that is educated), Verga's novella not only opens a window onto the child's world and life and stresses the heavy influence of adults' world and lives on him but also reflects a childlike, pre-logical thinking. At the time, it was a common belief that the thinking of children, as well as that of non-educated people, is irrational and similar to so-called primitive men. In a series of papers published between 1866 and 1899, Ernst Heinrich Haeckel, professor of zoology in Jena, formulated the "fundamental biogenetic law," according to which the development of a human being reproduces the development of the human species in natural history; ontogeny resumes phylogeny.[12]

---

[12] See Rossi (1989). Italian scientists endorsed this theory, see Comoy Fusaro (2007, p. 186).

In the late 19th century, scientists also conceived the primitive state as being deprived of "moral sense," morality. In Italy, Cesare Lombroso, founder of the School of Criminal Anthropology and an advocate of the degeneration theory initiated in France by Bénédict-Augustin Morel (1857), based his conception of the human being upon this principle. He explains:

> The seeds of moral madness and delinquency lie, not exceptionally, but normally, in the first ages of mankind, like some constant features of the fetus are monstrosities in an adult; so that the child would represent a sort of a man deprived of moral sense, which is named moral madness by alienists, born-offender by us [criminal anthropologists]. (Lombroso, 1884, p. 112)[13]

In literature, children also started being portrayed with a transgressive side. This type of point of view came from Carlo Collodi, in the 1880s. Collodi published *Le avventure di Pinocchio* (1881-1883) without seeking to deliver any moralistic lesson, especially in the first version of the novel, in which Pinocchio ends up hanged by the fox and the cat. Indeed, in this version, the wooden puppet does not really learn anything: *Le avventure di Pinocchio* is not a *Bildungsroman*. Collodi's first version fully expresses the child's views, without any internal moralistic obstacles to counteract the ever present urges to follow his own pleasure. In psychoanalytic terms *ante litteram*, one would say that Pinocchio has no superego and remains driven only by the id. But there is no need to call in Doctor Freud, since Lombroso's generation had clearly assessed the natural amorality of the primitive man and the normal immorality of the child.

Cremona, Ranzoni, Verga, and Collodi only look at children as case studies and narrative matters, and from adults' voices and points of view. Other authors and artists take two steps towards childlikeness—first by reminiscing about their childhood and then by reviving the child they used to be.

The second part of the 19th century is the moment when children also emerge as subjects. The first chapters of Ippolito Nievo's posthumous novel *Confessioni di un italiano* (1867) provide a good example of this category. Even though the narrator is explicitly an 80-year-old man, albeit very similar to the young author Nievo, who was 27 years old when he wrote the novel (left unpublished because of his early death at the age of 29), he describes his childhood by adopting, from time to time, the child's point of view. Around the same time, the then 19-year-old Carlo Dossi opted for an exclusive child's point of view in *L'altrieri. Nero su bianco* (1868). He coins a fully personal language that expresses this childlike vision and

> recreates the short-sightedness (not the blindness) of a child, their ability to do one thing at a time, to focus only on the enjoyment by ignoring the disruptive elements. The joyful literary world is not obscured by the consciousness of the inevitable fall because it is not filtered by the adult's vision and only recreates the child's vision, that of a magic world. Ultimately, through the images of childhood, Dossi expresses the nostalgia for carelessness, the ability to seize the day, in an osmotic contact with reality. (Comoy Fusaro, 2015, p. 338)[14]

[13] Translated from Italian. Original version: "i germi della pazzia morale e della delinquenza si trovano, non per eccezione, ma normalmente, nelle prime età dell'uomo, come nel feto si trovano costantemente certe forme che nell'adulto sono mostruosità; dimodochè il fanciullo rappresenterebbe come un uomo privo di senso morale, quello che si dice dai freniatri un folle morale, da noi un delinquente nato." Lombroso also refers to Moreau, *De l'homicide chez les enfants* (1882) and Perez, *Psychologie de l'enfant* (1882).
[14] Translated from Italian. Original version: "ricrea la miopia (non la cecità) del bambino, la sua capacità di fare una cosa alla volta, di focalizzarsi sul piacere in sé, prescindendo dagli elementi perturbanti. Il mondo letterario gaudente non è oscurato dalla coscienza dell'inesorabilità della caduta perché non è filtrato dallo sguardo dell'adulto ma restituisce il solo sguardo del fanciullo, la sua visione di un mondo magico. In ultima analisi attraverso le immagini dell'infanzia Dossi esprime a mio avviso la nostalgia dell'incuranza, la capacità di vivere l'istante presente, in contatto osmotico con gli oggetti naturali."

The ever autobiographical protagonist of Dossi's narratives, the "top-hatted child" (*bimbo-in-cilindro*) as written in *Vita di Alberto Pisani* (1870), embodies not only the failures of the usual character of a loser of that time but also new esthetics, gnoseology, and ethics. According to Dossi, one can only get to know reality by being oneself, and one can only be oneself by getting rid of all things coming from education, that is, cultural tradition and society: thoughts, habits, beliefs, opinions, values, knowledge, etc. The child is in a spontaneous osmotic relationship with natural objects, and this relationship is not only joyful but also the only way to genuinely be oneself.

Dossi belongs to the Scapigliatura movement, which was reluctant to admit scientists' dogmas and keen to promote non-scientific, non-rational, non-logical values and methods (despite the movement's intrinsic contradictions, which were influenced by Lombroso and colleagues). Whereas the other *scapigliati* rather focused on marginal figures such as loser artists and neurotics, he first identified in his own childhood a key to apprehending reality differently, maybe better. Dossi intuitively presented the child as a master: he confined his investigation to his own case but forged a path for others.

### The Child as a Master: As an Adult Should Do

Dossi's top-hatted child was an adult remembering his childhood and writing from time to time as a child would do. In this part of the study, we focus on childlikeness as an unreachable ideal. Here, childhood is an image embodied by iconic holy children who have little to do with reality. Indeed, unlike the characters of children briefly examined above, the child in these images is a symbol of morality and wisdom. Thus, it is about what an adult should do.

In Elsa Morante's novel *La storia* (1974), Useppe, just like the child in Vittorio De Sica's film *The Bicycle Thieves* (1948), is not the main character but symbolically embodies the emotional thread of the plot. Unlike De Sica's child, however, Useppe's natural joy seems not to be corrupted by his cruel environment (the Second World War). He is happy regardless of what happens; he is the holy child. But in the world of *La storia*, Useppe-likeness is impossible: indeed, he ends up being the scapegoat, the innocent victim of the insane violence of the world of the adults. Referring to tragic images, Olivier Duhamel (1993) writes:

> As soon as the child is shown, the image is there. The one of the kid with the bloody headband will symbolize the Bosnian horror for a long time. Just as, some time ago, the young Vietnamese girl running away from the napalm explosion, or recently the white-shirted Chinese boy on Tiananmen Square. Some people fear that the image trivializes the unbearable. On the contrary, it shows it and carves it into our collective memories. Without the image of the wounded child, Srebrenica was at risk of being slaughtered. The image of a bombed child contains all the hate. No one who saw it could still believe that mankind is good, naturally good. Auschwitz and the Gulag did not make many people immune.[15]

To this list, we could add "The vulture and the little girl," which appeared in *The New York Times* on 26 March 1993 (11 years after Nick Ut's *The Terror of War*), for which South African photographer Kevin Carter won the Pulitzer Prize. We could also think

---

[15] Translated from French. Original version: "L'enfant montré, l'image est là. Celle du môme au bandeau ensanglanté symbolisera durablement l'horreur bosniaque. Comme jadis la petite Vietnamienne fuyant le napalm, naguère le Chinois en chemise blanche de la place Tiananmen. D'aucuns craignent que l'image ne banalise l'insoutenable. A l'inverse, elle le montre, et l'inscrit dans les mémoires collectives. Et, sans l'image de l'enfant blessé, Srebrenica risquait d'être massacrée. L'enfant bombardé, toute la haine est là. Aucun de ceux qui l'ont vu ne croira plus jamais que l'homme est bon, naturellement bon. Auschwitz ou le goulag n'ont pas vacciné grand monde."

of Etienne Carjat's famous portrait of Arthur Rimbaud (1871), "living icon of youth" (Leon, 2008 p. 119),[16] where the highly symbolizing image of a child (rather, a very young man) refers little to the reality of childhood but refers substantially to the image of childhood in the mind of an adult. Here children are mere objects, used as symbolic signs of something lacking in the world, which, by definition, is the world to which children do not belong because they do not make the rules—they endure them. In these images, children are portrayed as the opposite of adults (even though each adult was a child once) and used to implicitly denounce all the flaws in our world: injustice, violence, inequality, and so on.

The contemporary Italian hyperrealist painter Mauro Maugliani regularly portrayed children as symbols, like the anonymous children killed during the Shoah in the *Stelle cadenti* exhibition. One of his final works, exhibited in the *Contamination* show in Nice in the autumn of 2019, represents the then-16-year-old Greta Thunberg, the famous environmental activist whose voice could surely grab a global audience because of her young age (see Figure 1). Truth comes out of the mouths of babes, as the saying goes. However, these iconic holy children are images in adults' scale of values; they embody adults' guilty conscience. Childlikeness appears as difficult as going back to a remote vision of life where values and principles counter to the ongoing organization of the real world would be implemented. It is a very unlikely aim. Yet, a step towards this goal was taken with the idea of the inner child.

**Figure 1. Mauro Maugliani, Greta, 2019**

### The Inner Child: Adults' Childlikeness

When Chinese photographer Wang Wenlan was asked, "What is your philosophy in taking photographs? What makes a photograph an exceptional one?," he answered:

> I like things that pass away immediately, or things that are changing. Something that is not yet born, or undergoing changes, such as a child. I also like something about to vanish. In a nutshell, the moment of change. (Briel, 2016, p. 86)

As Baruch Spinoza already understood in the 17th century, an adult is nothing but a child who has grown up, and the transformation or development from childhood to

[16] Translated from French. Original version: "icône vivante de la jeunesse."

adulthood is to be seen not as a death–birth dialectic but rather as a process involving a preservation of the first stages.[17] In other words, the child that one used to be remains inside the adult that one has become.

According to Charles Baudelaire (Baudelaire, 1863 p. 8), "genius is nothing but childhood recaptured at will."[18] As for the child, the artist needs to revive the primitive and primary ignorance and openness to the external world (that of the second stage of childhood, according to cognitive sciences, around the third and the fourth year of life, when everything looks new to their curious, ignorant eyes). Dossi tried to forget his adultness during the creative process to express only the childness in his memory and deep in his brain; other authors, like Alberto Savinio in *Tragedia dell'infanzia* (1937), later tried to meet the challenge of reviving their inner child. Its theorization had been shaped a few decades earlier by Giovanni Pascoli in the essay "Il fanciullino," first published in *Il Marzocco* in 1897 and then included in *Pensieri e Discorsi* (1907). A little child endowed with a serene ability to be amazed "is inside us," "then we grow up, but he stays small," he states (Pascoli, 1946, p. 5).[19] Like Baudelaire, Pascoli praises a poetics of the inner child based on the myth of *tabula rasa*. The poet is "the eternal child, who sees everything with amazement, as if for the first time" (Pascoli, 1946, p. 16).[20] Pascoli's poems can, therefore, be considered former products of childlikeness in poetry because in the creative process he tried to evict his adultness and only let the inner child write. The *fanciullino* is very different from Pinocchio: he is peaceful, loving, and imaginative, easily interacts and plays with others, is happy in nature and his natural environment, and naturally listens to and reproduces the music of nature, especially birdsongs. He is simple, humble, emotional, easily scared, contemplative rather than active, sensitive, and unable to think rationally. Pascoli's poetry is intrinsically sensual, analogical, intuitive, and focused on small, simple elements of the natural world: it is, he says, "the harvest, fully innate, of the perennial, primordial psyche." It is a poetry of things, where the words that are used to say things come second. The poet's goal is to "go back to and melt into nature, which he comes from" (Pascoli, 1946, pp. 36, 55).[21]

As usual, theory came after practice: Pascoli (in his *Myricae*, first released in 1891), as well as some other artists of that time and even earlier, had already implemented these principles before they were theorized. Special mention has to be made of an often unduly ignored novella by *scapigliato* writer and musician Arrigo Boito: *La musica in piazza* (1870-1871). In this work, through the character of troubadour Barbapedàna, Boito (1996, p. 229) promotes "street music" in contrast to the "music in a cage."[22] The only genuine poetry (in a general meaning, including all sorts of art) comes from freedom: the modern minstrels are "everlasting nomads,

[17] Pascal Sévérac explains: "The development from childhood to adulthood is a real transformation—from one nature to another; but this transformation is also a preservation; moreover, it is based on a partial yet real commonality between the child and the adult" ["Le développement de l'enfant en adulte est bel et bien une transformation—un passage d'une nature à une autre ; mais cette transformation est aussi une conservation ; bien mieux, elle se fonde sur une communauté, partielle mais réelle, entre l'enfant et l'adulte"] (Sévérac, 2018).
[18] Translated from French. Original version: "le génie n'est que l'*enfance retrouvée* à volonté."
[19] Translated from Italian. Original version: "È dentro noi un fanciullino;" "antica serena maraviglia;" "quindi noi cresciamo, ed egli resta piccolo."
[20] Translated from Italian. Original version: "fanciullo eterno, che vede tutto con maraviglia, tutto come per la prima volta."
[21] Translated from Italian. Original version: "la coltivazione, affatto nativa, della psiche primordiale e perenne;" "riconfondersi nella natura, donde uscì."
[22] Translated from Italian. Original version: "musica in piazza;" "musica in gabbia." See Bonelli (2020).

migrants, hobos," and Barbapedàna is compared to "a poor little bird, independent, wild, with no boss nor millet" (Boito, 1996, pp. 232-233).[23]

In line with a new awareness of the pervasiveness of images not only as external objects surrounding the subject but also as internal objects corrupting sight and filtering our approach to reality, Philippe Hamon (2007) has studied the revolution in 19th-century literature. He situates the turning point

> somewhere between Baudelaire, Verlaine, Flaubert, and Rimbaud, all of whom, in different ways, look for a new eye, that of the savage or the barbarian (Rimbaud), or that of the child, which is clean, naïve, ingenuous, virginal. (Hamon, 2007, p. 36)[24]

Thus, the question is how to get back to the child's virginal eye fascinated by the "primitive toy," to borrow from Baudelaire, or how to "see with the eyes, not with the neck," as French painter Gustave Courbet put it (in Hamon, 2007, p. 31).[25] The answer that authors found was to import materials into the literary text that were originally from the non-literary world—(industrial and popular) images, in particular. This is how what Hamon (2007, p. 35) calls "pop-art literature"[26] was born.

It took more time for visual artists to become involved with pop art. In the meantime, other experiments tried to get rid of academic conformism and social rules—that is, culture and restriction on individualism. They were called *avant-gardes*. "It took me a whole lifetime to learn how to draw like children," Picasso said (in Kerlan & Robert, 2013, p. 286).[27] Even if a big part of avant-garde research in art was inspired by science, which belongs to the adult world (e.g., Carlo Carra's later works and Giacomo Balla's work studies on light and speed), the core principles of the Italian avant-garde and Futurism were motion, presence, and opposition. This is clear from, for example, the habit of throwing tomatoes onto the theatre stage. There was also a forceful rejection of the old and sentimental way of doing art ("Let's Kill the Moonlight!").[28]

The growing interest in childhood, which led to the emergence of childlikeness in cultural communities in Europe from the mid-19th to the early 20th century, was a sign of a general curiosity about otherness, but it also came from a general disappointment. It expressed nostalgia for the pleasurable characteristics of childhood, such as carelessness, moment-to-moment living, freedom, and spontaneity—in sum, an action—and emotion-based way of living. It expressed the feeling or the idea that culture may be a hindrance: the myth of the *tabula rasa* took over the principle that education was necessary, which had previously held sway. The counterpart of the idea of a child's ignorant wisdom (not only for self-enjoyment and self-development but also for social wellness and ecology, as the model-seeking pattern reveals) is the child's compulsion to transgress, which is an idea that binds childlikeness to either self-centered motivations (the personal pleasure principle—Freud, 1998) or anarchy-like visions of social organization (the pirate syndrome). In both cases, however, the father's or adult's law—or the reality principle, in Freud's words—is transgressed. Indeed, the gesture of rejection is central to childlikeness and especially to contemporary art.

[23] Translated from Italian. Original version: "sempre nomadi, migranti, vagabondi;" "un augelletto povero, indipendente, selvaggio, senza padrone e senza miglio."
[24] Translated from French. Original version: "quelque part entre Baudelaire, Verlaine, Flaubert et Rimbaud, qui invoquent tous, sur des modes différents, un nouveau regard, celui du sauvage ou du barbare (Rimbaud), ou celui de l'enfant à l'œil décrassé, naïf, niais, vierge."
[25] Translated from French. Original version: "voir par les yeux et non pas par la nuque."
[26] Translated from French. Original version: "littérature pop-art."
[27] Translated from French. Original version: "Il m'a fallu toute une vie pour apprendre à dessiner comme les enfants."
[28] *Uccidiamo il Chiaro di Luna!* is the title of the second manifesto written by the founder of Futurism (Marinetti, 1909, pp. 9-20).

## The Childlike Turn and Childlikeness in Contemporary Art

Even though there have been some radical changes, such as the emergence and development of punk culture over the course of time (Mason, 2008), a merely chronological approach would paint a misleading picture of art in the 20th and 21st centuries since, as Nathalie Heinich brilliantly demonstrates, contemporary art is a paradigm rather than a period in the history of arts. It is "not a common pattern . . . but a cognitive base shared by all of us" and is radically different from the previous modern paradigm; therefore, one is justified in talking about a "revolution" (Heinich, 2014, pp. 43-44).[29]

Contemporary art questions and plays with (especially but not exclusively ethical, juridical, and esthetic) limits. It breaks away from the conception of art product as an object and makes it a set of narratives and ideas around and about the—often, if not primarily—dematerialized artwork; that is, the frameless artwork, if "frame" is intended as the artwork's "material border" as much as its "nonphysical boundaries," whether it be "the institutional frame, the perceptual frame, the semiotic frame, or the gendered frame," or the "ideological frame" ("the frame as signifier of value"—Paul Duro, 1996, pp. 1-4).

Contemporary art was surely a revolution when it first appeared; nonetheless, regarding the conception and assumption of childlike characteristics, what it accomplished had been prepared by earlier generations dating to the industrial or post-industrial era (depending on the geographical area): Baudelaire, Rimbaud, Dossi, Collodi, Pascoli, and others. *Volens nolens*, Picasso, Duchamp, Marinetti, and all other founders of the art revolution were implementing an old recipe. Therefore, in this second part of the study, we will recognize patterns inherited from the 19th century, at the start of the history of childlikeness in art. The two outstanding features we will dwell on first are, on the one hand, the myth of the *tabula rasa* and nature observable in primitivist artists and movements throughout the 20th century and, on the other hand, the rejection of rules and limitations, the no phase that we will depict on the basis of a case study: the work of Italian artist Maurizio Cattelan. Finally, we will focus on street art, which rounds up all the characteristics of childlikeness in art, some old and many others new to the extent that it sets up a milestone that I shall call the Childlike Turn.

### The Myth of Nature: Primitivisms

In this category of 20th-century art, childlikeness encompasses an artistic practice and esthetics based on a myth of nature as being better than culture, which praises the values of ignorance (artists are self-taught or pretend to be so or try to get rid of their knowledge) and spontaneity; the idea(l) is to reach the purity—both the innocence and the authenticity—of a child's gesture, or a child's feeling and thinking. However, let us mention that the concept of nature underlying the search for genuineness is a myth

---

[29] Translated from French. Original version: "non tant un modèle commun . . . qu'un socle cognitif partagé par tous." Heinich borrows this definition of a paradigm from Thomas Kuhn's *The Structure of Scientific Revolutions* (1962). Hence, for instance, "Duchamp's ready-mades are emblematic of contemporary art, whereas his *Nu descendant l'escalier* fully belongs to modern art. . . . This is a question of artistic practice, along with an axiological question, . . . a question that deals with institutions, organization, economics, logistics, etc." ["les ready-mades de Duchamp sont emblématiques de l'art contemporain, alors que son *Nu descendant l'escalier* appartient de plein droit à l'art moderne. . . . C'est une question de pratique artistique, ainsi qu'une question axiologique, . . . une question institutionnelle, organisationnelle, économique, logistique, etc."]. (Heinich, 2014, p. 34). Similarly, she also writes, Pollock's drippings belong to modern art, whereas the art of Rauschenberg, Murakami, and Klein from the same time belong to contemporary art.

because, as recent research in ecology has shown with its neologism *natureculture*, in the wake of some pioneering studies that are sadly often unquoted or forgotten (especially the work of Edgar Morin—see Morin, 1973), nature and culture are intertwined in such a way that they cannot be separated (Malone & Ovenden, 2017).

Naïve art, Fauvism, Art brut (raw art), Action painting, Abstract Expressionism, then Cobra, Art informel (informal art), Tachisme (stain art), Neo-expressionism, outsider art, and other terms were given to different groups and movements that all rejected the academic tradition of fine art and favored a childlike simplicity of vision and execution. Whereas the first 19th-century forms of primitivism were intended to revive pre-Rinascimento art features that were thought to be incorruptible and pure, primitivism in the 20th century became "an interest in or study of societies and cultures that have an ostensibly less developed notion of technological, intellectual, or social progress,"[30] and the practice of an "art that celebrates certain values or forms regarded as primal, ancestral, fertile, and regenerative:"[31] in sum, it described "the fascination of early modern European artists with what was then called primitive art" and "means the search for a simpler more basic way of life away from Western urban sophistication and social restrictions."[32] In the early 20th century, French painter, printmaker, and sculptor Paul Gauguin "sought to achieve a 'primitive' expression of spiritual and emotional states in his work"[33] by being inspired by Oceanic art and real environment and opting for roughness of execution and violence of colors. The same was true for Pablo Picasso and some artists of the avant-garde in the first decades of the century. Jean Dubuffet was a "strong supporter of Art brut, which fascinated him because it made no reference at all to art history" (Pradel, 1996, p. 14).[34] In 1948, along with André Breton and Jean Paulhan, he established the movement to "advocate a different art, an art of subversion and a rejection of all esthetic forms of conformism" (Pradel, 1996, p. 14).[35]

After the Second World War, many other artists based their method of work on childlike spontaneity and experimentation: the Cobra artists drew inspiration from children's drawings; Tachists tried to present painted marks as being unmediated by the conscious mind; inspired by Dubuffet, raw (or outsider) artists were often inspired by patients at psychiatric hospitals, as well as prisoners and children, as they sought to incorporate the raw expression of their vision and emotions into art. Later, in the late 1960s and beyond, Arte povera (literally "poor art") rejected technological and artificial tools and aimed to regain a daily experience of nature and to make works of art with nature by using poor, raw materials. Here, "art becomes an awareness of the expressive possibilities that lie inside the matter, either vegetal or animal, including elementary—childlike—mental processes."[36]

The spontaneous gesture and childlike ways of formal execution continued to be favored in the last decades of the 20th century, with artists like Keith Haring, Jean-Michel Basquiat, and Ben. But the most significant phenomenon in the Childlike

[30] This is the definition provided by Encyclopedia (available here: https://www.encyclopedia.com/literature-and-arts/art-and-architecture/art-general/primitivism).
[31] This is the definition provided by Google Arts & Culture (available here: https://artsandculture.google.com/entity/primitivism/m06s0d7?categoryId=art-movement).
[32] This is the definition provided by Tate (available here: https://www.tate.org.uk/art/art-terms/p/primitivism).
[33] Retrieved from the biography of Paul Gauguin in the Britannica Encyclopedia (available here: https://www.britannica.com/biography/Paul-Gauguin#ref728095).
[34] Translated from French. Original version: "fervent défenseur de l'art brut qui le fascine par l'absence de référence à l'histoire de l'art."
[35] Translated from French. Original version: "prônant un art autre, un art de subversion et de refus de tous les conformismes esthétiques."
[36] Translated from Italian. Original version: "l'a[rte povera] si pone come presa di coscienza delle possibilità espressive insite nella materia vegetale, animale, minerale o persino in un processo mentale elementare" (http://www.treccani.it/enciclopedia/arte-povera/)

Turn of contemporary art happened when unauthorized artworks started covering the walls inside cities, directly (but not only) inspired by the first writers (initially without any artistic intentions): Graffiti Writing and street art. A few European artists like Ernest Pignon-Ernest and Gérard Zlotykamien had already made unauthorized interventions in the public space since the 1970s and had both artistic and political motivations. Some of them, like Zlotykamien, opted for minimalistic features, and the speed at which they were illegally created in the streets contributed to characterizing them as childlike.

The revolution of street art inside the revolution of contemporary art highlighted the leap of the Childlike Turn, which came along with a radically new vision of life and lifestyle, including the experience of art, with computerization and globalization, from the 1990s on. The modern art myth of nature and the *tabula rasa* paved the way for the contemporary art approach to art as rejection, transgression, and play (*versus* approval, tradition and institution, and work); within this contemporary art paradigm, along with street art, a brand-new way of conceiving and experiencing art emerged—one that is democratic and childlike. Before addressing this crucial, final stage, let us observe how childlikeness has been breeding contemporary art by examining the case study of Cattelan.

## The No Phase: Maurizio Cattelan[37]

Maurizio Cattelan was born in Padua in 1960. He started his work as an artist around 1990 and quickly gained fame and success. In 1993, he was already invited to the Venice Biennale. His celebrity has not faded, and for the past few years, he has been the best-rated living Italian artist. In May 2016, for example, at Christie's, an artist's proof of *Him* sold for $17,189,000 (hammer price).

Childlikeness is at the core of Cattelan's artworks and art gestures, although a substantial number of his works have had a political aspect to them, especially since 2000. For instance, in the trilogy *La nona ora* (1999), *Him* (2001), and *Franck & Jamie* (2002),[38] there is criticism of ideologies and "the rhetoric of power," as Massimiliano Gioni (2003, p. 180) puts it.[39] In previous works, especially those from the 1990s, his criticism targeted art institutions, as in *Una domenica a Rivara* (1996), an installation made of sheets tied to each other and hanging from an open window in the Castello di Rivara of Turin (Italy), the headquarters of the Centro d'Arte Contemporanea, and in another installation from 1997, which is untitled and consisted of a rectangular pit dug inside the Consortium Museum in Dijon (France). The meaning of such artworks is clear: the white cube—gallery, exhibition place, museum—is a prison or a grave. Similar motivations inspired him in 1999 for the non-exhibition of the Sixth Caribbean Biennale and the exhibition of gallerist Massimo De Carlo glued to the wall in *A Perfect Day*. He suggested that the role played by art institutions—both material and immaterial, from promotional posters to exhibition

---

[37] This part of the chapter was first released as an oral presentation, *The Artist as a Child. The case study of Maurizio Cattelan*, at the conference of The Arts in Society, June 14th-16th 2017, Paris (FR).

[38] *La nona ora* is an effigy of Pope John Paul II struck by a meteorite and lying on a red carpet on the ground. The title ("The Ninth Hour," "ennatos" in ancient Greek, corresponds to 3 p.m. in our division of time) refers to the division of time in force in the gospel: "And at the ninth hour Jesus cried with a loud voice, 'Eloi, Eloi, lema sabachthani?' which means, 'My God, my God, why have you forsaken me?'" (Mark 15:34, English Standard Version). *Him* is a 40-inch sculpture representing a kneeling Hitler. *Franck & Jamie* are two lifelike dummies positioned head down and wearing police uniforms. All sculptures consist of polyester resin, wax, pigment, human hair, clothes, and accessories.

[39] Criticism also engages capitalism, like in *L.O.V.E.* (2010), which is a gigantic hand pointing its middle finger at the Italian Stock Exchange in Milan.

openings and deals with collectors and gallerists—is as important as the artworks themselves, perhaps even more. In an interview, Cattelan stated that

> Art is what's left between a fax to a gallery, a phone call to a collector and a reservation at some hip restaurant in Tribeca. This doesn't mean I subscribe to the cynical idea that art is just a matter of visibility, promotion and public relations. What I'm trying to say is that art is a collision of different systems and levels of reality. And I wish our biennial could reflect all this. (Di Pietrantonio, 1988, p. 142)

Nevertheless, the way the artist expresses his opposition is always humoristic and rooted in a punk-like, "fuck-it-all attitude,"[40] a childlike rejection of any kind of authority or limitation. In Cattelan's provocative humor, *vis comica* has the flavor of *vis tragica*: "I'm interested in the tragi-comical element," he said.[41] This bitter laughter deals with childhood at two levels: individual and collective. At a personal level, childhood refers to the real period of his life as a child, which is both an image of nostalgic desire because it symbolizes freedom and a painful memory because it is the age at which he first experienced the trauma of violence and constraint. As suggested by Sévérac (2018),

> it may well be that in times (ours) when childhood is not considered a necessary evil but a real good, the feeling to fight is no longer the sadness of pity (*commiseratio*) because of a present evil but has become the sadness of regret (*desiderium*) because of a good that is lacking: regret because childhood is over, perhaps also regret because childhood went bad.[42]

Before observing this personal, sweet-and-sour facet of Cattelan's childlikeness, let us consider its collective dimension in his work, where childhood refers to the metaphorical position of the artist and his generation in the context of art and cultural history.[43] As a postmodern heir of the multifaceted revolutionary 20th-century art, from ready-made and appropriation to action art and performances, as Gioni (2003) says,

> [l]ike many artists of his generation, Cattelan always seems to start off with a declaration of impotence . . . Art is bound to play with what is already there in an endless series of permutations, as if reality and its spectacle could only be rearranged, never reinvented. Indeed, today's art largely relies on a systematic practice of recycling, thriving on the ruins of the present. (pp. 183-186)[44]

[40] "Grouped together in what the artist describes as a trilogy against any form of ideology, these three works [*La nona ora*, *Him*, and *Franck & Jamie*] not only share the same punk, fuck-it-all attitude; they also participate in the same ritual of exorcism against the spectres of history and authority" (Gioni, 2003, p. 181).

[41] Casavecchia, 1999, p. 139. In another interview, the artist said that the English word *morbid* might have something to do with the Italian word *morbido*, which literally means sweet and soft, and defines his work "between softness and perversity" (Ruiz, 2002, p. 156).

[42] Translated from French. Original version: "Il est bien possible qu'à une époque (la nôtre) où l'enfance n'est plus considérée comme un mal nécessaire mais comme un bien véritable, l'affect à combattre soit devenu non plus la tristesse de la pitié (*commiseratio*), devant un mal présent, mais la tristesse du regret (*desiderium*), pour un bien absent : regret que l'enfance soit passée, regret aussi parfois qu'elle se soit mal passée."

[43] Cattelan is aware of expressing not only a personal issue but the crisis of his generation: "My face is a mask, a prop. I use my own face as a way to generate sympathy from the viewer, who sees my face and imagines that it is literally me who must be suffering. That connection creates a sense of empathy," he said in an interview (Ruiz, 2002, p. 150).

[44] The term "spectacle" clearly alludes to the concept of "*société du spectacle*" by Guy Debord, founder of Situationism. See Marcolini (2012).

This is the meaning of the installations *Mini-me* (1999) and *La rivoluzione siamo noi* (2000). In the former, a 14-inch-tall puppet resembling Cattelan himself sits among art books on a bookshelf. The puppet looks puzzled and a bit scared. Its small size suggests the artist feels inferior to the artists referred to in the books. In the latter, a 50-inch-tall dummy resembling Cattelan and wearing the typical Joseph Beuys grey felt suit hangs from a coat rack like an old, useless piece of clothing. The tribute to the German artist is also a tribute to the previous times in which political commitments and collective actions were still possible: as in the early 20th century, when Pellizza da Volpedo represented the growing working class in *Il Quarto Stato* (1901), the painting from which Beuys made *The Revolution Is Us* in 1972. Considering the position of Cattelan's dummy, the work also looks like self-deprecation, as if to say that in 2000, art no longer has any impact on society. Cattelan always depicts himself with "self-deprecating irony," "chronic pessimism and troubled self-esteem" (Gioni, 2003, pp. 186-188).[45] Self-deprecation is also obvious in *Senza titolo* (1996), an ambiguous tribute to Lucio Fontana (see Figure 2) in which the rip of the canvas forms the letter Z, resembling the signature of Zorro, an icon of pop culture or subculture:

> In my art, I use things which surround me from the society I live in. These are my objects. My message is that we can find a philosophical idea through the television we watch every day. (Di Pietrantonio, 1988, p. 112)[46]

Recurring motifs such as theft, usurpation, and a breach of rules and laws are other means that Cattelan uses to express this feeling: "his whole artistic praxis is a continuous infringement on the canonical established system" (Manacorda, 2006, p. 81).[47] Indeed, an early work (1992) shows an authentic report of theft at the spot where a piece of art was supposed to be exhibited. The theft (of an artwork) was fake, but the exhibition of the police document in the art exhibition was real. In 1996, with *Another Fucking Readymade*, he exhibited a copy of an artwork exhibited in the next gallery.[48] The motifs of incompetence, usurpation, and breach of the rules are merged in the untitled installation made in 2001 in a room of the Museum Boijmans Van Beuningen in Rotterdam: The usual dummy gets his head out of a hole in the floor and looks, circumspectly, at the old paintings on the walls. It is not only Catellan who is engaged in this deception but his entire generation. Elisabeth Wetterwald (2003, p. 46) interprets *La rivoluzione siamo noi* as a sign of the "transition from the great determination of the Sixties to a contemporary lack of determination,"[49] and Francesco Bonami (2003, p. 50) also comments: "He personifies a culture born too late to be part of the cultural revolution of the 1960s and too early to be lured by the aestheticization of media and communication developed in the 1980s."

---

[45] Cattelan says it himself in interviews: "I don't think I have anything interesting to say . . . I am not an artist. I really don't consider myself an artist. I make art, but it's a job" (Spector 1999, p. 79); "I really don't deserve much attention" (Ruiz 2002, p. 151).

[46] "For Cattelan, design and advertising are as attractive as contemporary art. He sees all these aesthetic disciplines as tools of equal status, with which to extract the best from the aesthetic process" (Bonami, 2003, p. 58).

[47] Translated from Italian. Original version: "la sua pratica artistica in generale si rivela come effrazione continua nel canonico sistema stabilito"

[48] Bonami comments: "While the output of artists such as Sherrie Levine, Peter Nagy or Jeff Koons was defined in the mid-1980s as 'appropriation art,' Cattelan's strategy is simply robbery" (Bonami, 2003, p. 69). Elisabeth Wetterwald expresses a smoother opinion, saying that thefts, piracy, and cheating are "common in the art world and in society in general" ["monnaie courante dans le milieu artistique, dans la culture et dans la société en general"] and that Cattelan only highlights taboos (Wetterwald, 2003, p. 47).

[49] Translated from French. Original version: "passage des grandes volontés des années 60 aux menus vouloirs contemporains."

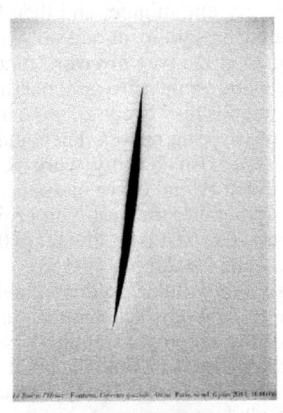

**Figure 2. Le Jour ni l'Heure 5350: Lucio Fontana, 1899-1968, Concetto spaziale, Attesa (1960), photograph Renaud Camus (2014)**

Maurizio Cattelan is a late baby boomer and feels irremediably confined to a non-growing position of being childlike, an outlaw, compared with the previous generation that included Pop Art, conceptualism, minimalism, hyperrealism, land art, arte povera, transavanguardia, the young British artists, and so on. Furthermore, as Paco Barragán (2016) wrote in the wake of McLuhan's theory:

> Society has shifted from a word-based culture to an image-based culture, a shift that occurred sometime in the late 1960s. The advent of hyper-consumerism, pop culture, mass media, celebrity politics and entertainment industries signals this new paradigm. (para. 3)

This image-based culture is linked to childlike patterns that started prevailing in mass media communication by the time Cattelan reached adulthood.

Childlikeness is also a relevant characteristic of his art in relation to his own childhood. On many occasions, Cattelan's works make reference to the childhood of their creator. The artist regularly puts himself in the figure of the bad boy, the spoiled brat, the poor pupil. With the installation *Charlie* at the Venice Biennale in 2003, Cattelan questions the art institution while representing an image of joy, play, and freedom. Charlie, his *alter ego* as a child, looks like an impertinent boy having a lot of fun driving his tricycle toy through the rooms of the Corderie and the Giardini. The enjoyment comes from the pleasure of riding his tricycle and also from the thrill of defying authority, since it is forbidden to ride a bike inside an art space. An untitled installation from 1997 also depicts an image of happiness: It consists of three stuffed mice sitting on a long chair, chilling out under a beach umbrella. One of the mice is a little one, a projection of the artist as a child. Indeed, Cattelan explained in an interview in 1999 that, in his works, animals are "self-referential" (Spector, 1999, p. 87). With this, he implicitly deprecates the value of work and stresses instead the value of laziness, chilling out, having fun, and playing.

But the image of happiness itself is constructed by the adult. The child's full happiness is nothing but a mental image. As Bonami (2003, p. 65) puts it, "All the work he has produced since 1990 is a slow march back home. But this is not the home he left when he was eighteen years old; he is seeking a home he never had." Cattelan explained:

> I think childhood, for example, is a confusing time; feelings seem clearly divided between good and evil and yet behind this clear-cut distinction lies a universe of doubt. A child, for example, can love

his mother very intensely one minute, and then hate her terribly the next over something insignificant and silly. Maybe this kind of confusion is reflected in the way my work functions: I like my images to be very clear and straightforward, but the more you look at them the more ambiguous they become . . . To me childhood is a fiction, one of many possible narratives. There may be an element of autobiography, if you wish, but my work is more about the way you reconstruct memory and relive moments of your life in a new way. When you remember the past, you project an image of yourself as you are now. The past is an invention that always takes place in the present. (Ruiz, 2002, pp. 149-150)

This is why childlikeness is also tightly linked to the critical part of his production.

The first institution to embody schematism and authority, power and ideology, is not the art institution but school. In Cattelan's oeuvre, school impinges on personal development and freedom. The first time the artist used the figure of Charlie was in the late 1990s, with *Charlie Don't Surf* (1997). The scene is tragic: the boy has both hands nailed to a school table by two pens. According to Francesco Manacorda (2006, p. 58), the image "transforms the desk into something like a cross. The title refers to punishment as a limitation of the space of play allegedly with the goal of integrating the individual into adult society."[50] Before he had fun on his tricycle, Charlie had to endure school but gained little from it, if we interpret the title of the 1997 installation—*Charlie Don't Surf*—as a schoolboy's grammar mistake: "don't" instead of "doesn't."

In an untitled work from 1991, Cattelan uses a schoolboy grid sheet covered with the sentence "Fare la lotta in classe è pericoloso" [*Struggle in classroom is dangerous*]. This looks like punishment, but there is more: the preposition "in" is systematically crossed out with red ink and replaced with "di" so that the allegedly correct sentence reads "Fare la lotta di classe è pericoloso" [*Class struggle is dangerous*]. The artist questions not only an educational system rooted in repetitive punishment but also, by ironically referencing the Marxian interpretation of society, the ideological content of what is taught at school. Moreover, the schoolboy's "mistake" and the teacher's correction show the gap in communication between the two. Francesco Bonami (2003, p. 66) sees in these pieces a criticism of the culture of guilt: "These works are a melancholic analysis of the sense of guilt encouraged by society in individuals from their first contact with the structured world, represented here by the school system."

*Bidibibodibiboo* (1996) is another famous early Cattelan artwork: it shows a miniature working-class kitchen, where a stuffed squirrel has just shot itself (its inert head on the table, a gun on the floor below). The squirrel, inspired by Walt Disney's chipmunks, embodies Cattelan as much as the environment represents his childhood: "[t]he squirrel's kitchen is my parents' kitchen," according to him (Spector, 1999, p. 88). The title of the work recalls the Disney film *Cinderella* (1950), inspired by Charles Perrault's book, in which one fairy sings *Bibbidi-Bobbidi-Boo* while transforming the pumpkin into a carriage, thereby making Cinderella's dream come true.[51] Cattelan's version is antithetical: there is no hope for a better life for the little

---

[50] Translated from Italian. Original version: "trasforma il banco nell'equivalente della croce. Il titolo ci illumina sulla punizione quale limitazione dello spazio del gioco finalizzata alla presunta integrazione nella società adulta." According to Francesco Bonami, the work comes from an episode in the real Cattelan's childhood: The young Maurizio allegedly nailed a pen into a classmate's hand: "Writing and its tools, such as the ballpoint pen with which he had once stabbed a school friend's hand, became a kind of obsession, which transmuted much later into some of his most poignant works" (Bonami, 2003, p. 43).

[51] The stuffed animals of Cattelan's works *Loves Saves Life* (1995) and *Love Lasts Forever* (1997) are also inspired by Jacob and Wilhelm Grimm's fairy tale *Two Musicians of Bremen*.

hero.[52] Suicide is the desperate answer to the violence perpetrated on the individual by social systems, whether family, school, art institution, or whatever else—in short, adulthood. The miniaturization of the scene, the playful characteristics of the staging, and the disguise as an animal probably all allow the artist to defuse the anxiety through creation. Indeed, a "theatrical element pervades all of Cattelan's work" (Gioni, 2003, p. 164), and dramatization—in the etymological sense—triggers catharsis.

In consumer behavior, Mathieu Alemany Oliver (2013, 2015) shows that childlikeness is a relevant trend of consumers today: they act like children or in the name of their inner child. Such a trend is due to both a negative perception of adulthood and an emphasized childhood. The analysis shows that consumer childlikeness is

An act of resistance against disenchanted and constrained adulthood, and an act of existence dedicated to the quest for a more authentic self, that are both made possible thanks to playful consumption and the making of intermediate realities it can trigger. (Alemany Oliver, 2015, p. 184)

Isn't *Bidibibodibiboo* an "act of resistance," as Agnès Violeau (2016) explicitly construed Cattelan's exhibition at La Monnaie de Paris as an "iconography of resistance"? Isn't the Biennale's *Charlie* an "act of existence"? Isn't art an "intermediate reality" in which "self-esteem is increased within role play" (Alemany Oliver, 2015, p. 194)?

Considering the relevance of the image of childhood in Cattelan's works and his childlike behavior or gesture as a trickster, it is reasonable to apply it to his art, which is also a big market. Indeed, the four dimensions of consumer childlikeness identified by Alemany Oliver (2015) (i.e., escapism, reality conflict, stimulus-seeking, and aggressiveness) fit Cattelan's artworks. Stimulus-seeking and aggressiveness echo Cattelan's provocation, like with *Him* (the kneeling Hitler). The reality conflict dimension that "captures the struggle that consumers have with the complexities and responsibilities of adult reality" (Alemany Oliver, 2015, p. 99), reflects the discouragement and despair that are often expressed—for instance, in *Bidibibodibiboo* (the suicide squirrel) or *Untitled* (2004), which is made up of three life-size children-like open-eyed dummies hanging from the oldest tree in Milan. Finally, escapism describes many works of pure rejection, like *Una domenica a Rivara* (sheets tied to each other like a rope hanging from the museum window).

Of course, although art is not (only) to be consumed, it has a lot to do with consumption, since art is generally first and foremost what is sold in galleries and at auctions, especially with regard to the recipient, who has become a consumer and a user much more than a beholder. After the Second World War, and along with anticipating Walter Benjamin's interpretation of art in the massified modern society after the loss of the "aura" and the shift of the artwork as a product of consumption, a new conception of art and a new approach to art emerged, thus germinating the seeds of a century-long process, promoting easiness, simplicity, ready-made, and empathic "reading." Indeed, during the second part of the 20th century, artists widely used the tools and strategies of the society of consumption, which was becoming more and more popular. Andy Warhol and pop art arrived on the scene with acid colors, ready-made images, and the mass reproduction and marketing of these transformed images as artworks. With pop culture, references to the temples of consumption and so-called subcultures, like comics and films, arose. Acid colors, black outlines, and schematized figures were the milestones of the new esthetics, similar to the visual regime of toys and other artifacts produced for the children. Since the 1930s, Alexander Calder's colorful mobiles were already "strongly promising a better world, reconciled with the imagination

---

[52] "For the title, I thought about magic words like "bibeddy bobbedy boo", which could transform something, make something better. That time, however, the magic didn't work" (Spector, 1999, p. 88).

and poetry of a childhood dream" (Pradel, 1996, p. 22);[53] the blossoming of pop art made references to a child's world even more explicit, with direct influences from comics and animated movies in Roy Lichtenstein's works, for instance (see Figure 3). From the end of the 20th century, brands and designers applied the same recipe to the world of appliances and daily products of consumption, such as cars (Renault Twingo, introduced in 1992), kitchen tools (Alessi's series "Family Follows Fiction," launched with Stefano Giovannoni's *Fruit Mama* in 1993), personal computers (the iMac G3, the first consumer-facing Apple computer with colored plastic, was sold in 1998). The most popular artworks today still largely apply the pop recipe (one need only think of Jeff Koons) and often expect (or pretend to expect) a childish or childlike reception. Significantly, the image chosen by Italian art curator Francesco Bonami to illustrate the cover of his book *Lo potevo fare anch'io. Perché l'arte contemporanea è davvero arte* shows not only *Sunflower* (1996) by Keith Edmier but also a person looking at it; this person happens to be a child. The reason probably lies in scaling the gigantic artwork, but it is no accident that the scale is a boy, who is supposed to be the favored recipient.

The value of childlikeness is also primarily relevant in street art, which (just like Cattelan) emerged in the 1990s and has been developing to such an extent that it has become the main movement—or rather, phenomenon—of contemporary art today.

**Figure 1. Roy Lichtenstein by leafar, photograph Raphaël Labbé (2008)**

## The Childlike Turn: Street Art

With street art, childlikeness becomes fully, consciously, and explicitly central to the whole artistic process: not coincidentally, a French artist famous for using fire extinguishers to paint-bomb the shop windows of luxurious trademarks calls himself Kidult. The conception of childhood established and promoted by street art is rooted in the previously highlighted characteristics and values of movements from primitivisms to contemporary art: genuineness and transgression. However, street artists add other facets and dimensions by transforming humor (dark in Cattelan's work) into playfulness, rule-opposing topics into illegal execution, and the search for values related to childhood into explicit, figurative motifs; moreover, they turn the art product into a life experience, which means transforming the beholder into a user and involving them in the process of childlikeness.

Transgression is carved into the genes of the global phenomenon. As I write elsewhere:

[53] Translated from French. Original version: "lourds des promesses d'un monde meilleur, réconcilié avec l'imaginaire et la poésie d'un rêve d'enfance" (Pradel, 1996, p. 22).

> Strictly speaking, street art is a type of art made with a wide range of different techniques but with two essential characteristics: it is situated in the public space (generally urban) and is accessible by (and intended for) whoever happens to find themselves in this space. It comes in part from various trends and movements: graffiti (whose origins are lost in the mists of time), Graffiti Writing (originally North American), Mexican muralism, and different movements of Western contemporary art (especially Futurism, Lettrism, Cobra, Situationism, Dada, Fluxus, Pop Art). It is different from graffiti because of the polysemy of its content and its formal features, in other words, because of its artistic dimension; it is different from Graffiti Writing because of its immediate readability (not cryptic) and global destination (not clannish); it is different from Urban Art—a recent genre or under-genre of Public Art—because of its freedom of execution since street artworks are not made to order nor for a fee. (Comoy Fusaro, 2019b, p. 7) [54]

No canvases nor white cubes for street artists: the city is their playground. This is not a metaphor. With street art, more obviously and systematically than in contemporary art, making art is like playing. It is like "transforming the city into a huge playground . . . Their [urban hackers'] subversion is joyful: it merges with the freedom of reinventing the world at every step" (Pujas, 2015, p. 7).

As American street artist Swoon puts it, street art is about "this feeling of just wanting to create the surprise, this kind of openness, this beautiful moment that people are not expecting to find" (Bürger & Cantu, 2009). Urban hacking, which integrates elements of the urban environment into the artwork, like aped traffic signs by French artist Clet Abraham (see Figure 4) or city pals transformed into penguins by Italian artist Pao, is an excellent illustration. There is transgression, a violation of public rules, but it is peaceful, playful, and often humorous.

**Figure 4. No entry sign with Pac-Man by Clet Abraham, Piazza Santa Croce, Florence (2013), photograph LivornoDP (2014)**

[54] Translated from French. Original version: "*Stricto sensu*, le street art est une forme d'art aux techniques variées dont les deux caractéristiques essentielles sont de se situer dans l'espace public (généralement urbain) et d'être accessible (et adressée) à quiconque traverse cet espace. Elle est issue en partie du graffiti (dont les origines se perdent dans la nuit des temps) et du Graffiti Writing d'origine nord-américaine (dont il est aussi contemporain), du muralisme mexicain et de certains mouvements de l'art contemporain occidental du XXe siècle (notamment Futurisme, Lettrisme, Cobra, Situationnisme, Dada, Fluxus, Pop Art). Il se distingue du graffiti par la polysémie de ses contenus et son élaboration formelle, c'est-à-dire par sa portée artistique, du Graffiti Writing par sa lisibilité immédiate (et non cryptique) et sa destination universalisante (et non clanique), et de l'art urbain—nouvelle forme ou sous-genre de l'art public—par la liberté de son exécution, puisqu'il n'est pas réalisé sur commande ni contre retribution." It is reductive to mention only Mexican muralism, since many other types of muralism have existed and still exist in other countries, like in the area of Orgosolo, in Sardegna (Italy), or in Dakar (Senegal). See Leduc-Gueye (2016).

In contemporary art, the child's mind is still perceived as a precious source of inspiration for many artists, and some artist residencies even propose living with children (Kerlan & Robert, 2013). Many people think that an artist at work is like a child who is playing.[55] Indeed, among the various values that characterize the contemporary paradigm in art, French sociologist Nathalie Heinich has rightly nailed down that of play. The "playful dimension," she writes,

> surely deals with childhood, of course, both with activities for children and with a specific genre such as comics or animated movies; it also deals with adult entertainment (light comedies at the theater and the cinema), and with fiction of any shape, as well as with sports, which triggers *agon*, competition. As we can see, this playful dimension is very important: it is required in all kinds of circumstances to assess words and behaviors. (Heinich, 2017, p. 251)[56]

**Figure 5. Robi the Dog, Untitled, Berlin, 2014, photograph**
**Edwige Comoy Fusaro**

The intrinsically childlike method of doing street art, which is transgressive and playful, often comes with recurrent representations of animals and children, presumably as symbols of wilderness and/or nastiness, as in many of the paste-ups of Swiss street artist Robi the Dog (see Figure 5), who died prematurely in 2016. But they can also convey innocence and dreams, as in the stencils of Italian street artist Alice, for instance, or in an artwork signed Bouchon on a wall in Rennes (Brittany, France), which depicts the body of a baby wearing men's briefs that are way too big and sport the Superman logo. Children often appear as victims of harmful societies because, to some extent, street art always has political intentions. Juvenile figures are also often self-portraits, like in

---

[55] "This is a children's game played by an adult—the artist at work," writes the journalist reporting on Mike Kelley's retrospective exhibition in Amsterdam (Searle 2012).
[56] Translated from French. Original version: "concerne bien sûr le domaine de l'enfance, tant avec les activités enfantines qu'avec les genres dédiés de la bande dessinée ou du cinéma d'animation ; mais aussi le domaine du divertissement pour adultes (théâtre de boulevard, comédies cinématographiques…), et la fiction sous toutes ses formes, ainsi que le sport en tant qu'il relève de l'*agon*, de la compétition. C'est dire l'importance de ce registre ludique, sollicité dans toutes sortes de circonstances pour évaluer paroles et comportements."

Seth's artworks (some unauthorized, many authorized since the French artist has gained worldwide popularity and become a successful urban artist rather than a street artist). In an unauthorized piece on a wall in Paris, for example, he represented the hooded figure of a boy (his face hidden as if it was inside the wall, as usual) holding a spray can. Artists' self-portraits as animals (often rats and monkeys) and kids make at least three statements. First, they proclaim their marginalization (from the current system, the society of consumption, and the major issues that it creates, especially regarding social inequalities and environmental issues), that is, their opposition to the world they live in; second, they declare that anyone has the right to make art, following their vision of a non-pyramidal, non-organized, and non-commercial usage of shared places; and third, they state that art comes first and foremost from emotions—specifically, from the hippocampus, the most primitive part of the human brain.

Authorized works of urban art, either executed on big walls in public space (murals) or on movable supports such as canvases (gallery art using street and urban art esthetics), are also full of portraits of children, generally in criticizing roles. *Revolution*, presented at the 9th edition of the Pow! Wow! festival held in Hawaii in 2019 by Japanese artist RoamCouch, portrays a helmeted child surrounded by animals standing on a police car that they have obviously wrecked with colorful splashes of paint. French artist Kurar regularly features children in desolate environments, clearly denouncing the damage caused by pollution and savage capitalism.

Finally, childlikeness in street art also subsists in the implicit invitation to do what a child would do—not only from the artist's side but also from that of the user-beholder. If a large part of public art is made up of statues representing people who we reckon play a valuable part in history, it is not only to honor these late individuals' memory but also to hold them up as models for us to follow. The flowering of portraits (from Amy Winehouse to Che Guevara, to cite only two examples) in street art, urban art, and contemporary urban art demonstrates the relevance of the model-seeking trend. Niels SHOE Meulman's *Crime Time* (see Figure 6) seeks to encourage people to leave their homes and create in a shared and playful way. With street art, art becomes an experience rather than a product—an experience for the producer of the artwork (or its initiator, since the authorship is questionable), who tries to recapture the child he/she was—his/her inner child—in the creative process conceived as knowledge obtained through practice, which includes trial and error (for the etymological meaning of *experience*, from the Indo-European *peri*, trial).[57] It is also an experience for the recipients of the artwork because they are invited to an unexpected game of hide and seek on their way through the city, transforming their limited A-to-B route through public space into a playful and participatory art experience.

## Conclusion

In the mid-19th century, the child became a topic of interest in literature and the plastic arts, and some artists tried to understand and express the child's point of view. In the same period, youth started to become a symbol of wild beauty, purity, vain rebellion, and victimhood, along with an intuitive comprehension of the world. Starting in the mid-20th century, while new patterns valuing childlike behaviors and preferences (such as playfulness) were gradually prevailing in design, advertisement, and (more recently) working environments and habits, the art world was doing the same by praising self-taught artists and childlike esthetics and practices. And then, in the last decade of the century, the Childlike Turn emerged.

The street art esthetics of a (delusionary) natural, spontaneous creative gesture binds these artists to the modern art trend of childlikeness, whereas the exaltation of the juvenile and playful side of art, along with anti-institutional

[57] Significantly, the word "pirate" also has this root (Garrus, 1996, p. 258).

motifs, binds them to contemporary art practices. Yet, whereas contemporary artists' childlikeness mainly concerns the artists themselves, in street art it significantly involves the beholder-consumer-user of art. Thus, the openly undertaken guerilla model and the advocacy of horizontal, one-to-one communication and collaborative, democratic yet not seldom anarchist-like agency allow street artists to best embody childlikeness in art.

Childlikeness does not apply to all contemporary art, but it does to a large part of it, especially when we pay attention to how it is received. Nowadays, museums have become a playground offering playful activities to visitors: for instance, the Columbus Museum of Art (Ohio, USA) proposes to "Experiment with twist ties. Take your creation home or leave it on the wall for others to enjoy."[58]

But after the results comes the discussion. Now, by doing art, an artist focuses not only on play, emotion and motion, a search for identity, and a search for primitiveness but also reactivates the no-stage of child development: this is probably a way to express the nostalgia of self-centeredness, non-liability, and freedom. But even if art-making conveys childlike features, who is creating is still an adult and when the time comes to deliver the work, the artist is surely not playing any longer. This is why Freud (1958) writes that art combines the pleasure principle with the reality principle:

> An artist is originally a man who turns away from reality because
> he cannot come to terms with the renunciation of instinctual
> satisfaction . . . He finds the way back to reality, however, from
> this world of phantasy . . . [he moulds] his phantasies into truths
> of a new kind, which are valued by men as precious reflections of
> reality. (p. 224)

An artwork is a cultural product; it cannot belong to the merely sensorial approach to life and the state of epiphany, wonder, amazement, and enjoyment that supposes a full presence in the world. Instead, an artwork requires *art* (i.e., *techné*, technique, which has often become idea with the new paradigm of contemporary art) and *work* (artifact, often a result of scholarly labor and/or physical effort): as such, it is a cultural construction. Therefore, childlikeness is necessarily a limited part of an artwork. At its extreme, it would concern an artist doing *unintentionally* as a child would do at each step of the art-making process, from conception to implementation, but thereby necessarily excluding the final stages of promotion and, perhaps, sale.

Finally, as with all new paradigms and revolutions, the Childlike Turn may be linked to a major technological change: in this case, the revolution in the world of personal computers and the Internet in the 1990s. Without IT, street art would not have been the global phenomenon it has been in the 2000s and the 2010s. No one knows how art will develop with Generation Z, especially after the Covid-19 pandemic, but in all likelihood, childlikeness will remain firmly embedded in the virtual if not the real world.

---

[58] Another activity is "Tag it!": "In this exhibition you will discover many different ways in which dogs are depicted. Some look playful, others are fierce. Some seem goofy, others appear noble. What do you think? Select one or more tags from the bin. Look for a dog in a work of art that best represents the word on the tag. Hang the tag on the hook." These activities (and many others) were offered in April 2017.

# References

Alemany Oliver, M. (2013). Wait... was I supposed to grow up? Consumers' adventures in Wonderland. In S. Botti & A. Labroo (Eds.), *Advances in consumer research, vol. 41* (pp. 441–442). Association for Consumer Research.

Alemany Oliver, M. (2015). A realist(ic) interpretivist approach to childlikeness in consumer research: Neoteny, play, reality, and the reterritorializing adulthood [Doctoral dissertation, Aix-Marseille Université, IAE Aix]. AMU Campus Library.

Ariès, P. (1973). *L'enfant et la vie familiale sous l'ancien régime*. Seuil.

Barragán, P. (2016). Push to flush: Pop culture versus high art (Reflections about an undialectical dialectics). http://artpulsemagazine.com/push-to-flush-pop-culture-versus-high-art-reflections-about-an-undialectical-dialectics

Baudelaire, C. (1863). Le peintre de la vie moderne. https://edisciplinas.usp.br/pluginfile.php/14785/mod_resource/content/1/BAUDELAIRE_le%20peintre.pdf

Boito, A. (1996). La musica in piazza. Ritratti di giullari e menestrelli moderni. In *Opere letterarie*. Istituto Propaganda Libraria.

Bonami, F. (2003). Static on the line: The impossible work of Maurizio Cattelan. In F. Bonami, B. Vanderlinden, M. Etkind, & N. Spector (Eds.), *Maurizio Cattelan*. Phaidon.

Bonami, F. (2007). *Lo potevo fare anch'io. Perché l'arte contemporanea è davvero arte*. Mondadori.

Bonami, F. (Ed.) (2008). *Italics. Art italien entre tradition et révolution (1968-2008)*. Mondadori.

Bonelli, F. (2020). Su alcuni motivi scapigliati ne *La musica in piazza* di Arrigo Boito. *Arrigo Boito cent ans après | Arrigo Boito cent'anni dopo, Loxias*, 70.

Briel H. (2016). Every picture should be unique. A Conversation with Wang Wenlan. *The IAFOR Journal of Cultural Studies, 1*(1). http://iafor.org/archives/journals/iafor-journal-of-cultural-studies/10.22492.ijcs.1.1.pdf

Buchmann, M. C., Kriesi, I. (2011). Transition to adulthood in Europe. *Annual Review of Sociology*, 37, 481–503.

Bürger, A., Cantu, B. (2010). *Street art: The ephemeral rebellion* [video]. https://www.youtube.com/watch?v=gALbQeZriFU

Cairns, R. B., Valsiner, J. (1984). Child psychology. *Annual Review of Psychology, 35*, 553–577.

Casavecchia, B. (1999/2003). Interview of Maurizio Cattelan. In F. Bonami, B. Vanderlinden, M. Etkind, & N. Spector (Eds.), *Maurizio Cattelan* (2003). Phaidon.

Cattelan, M. (2004). *Maurizio Cattelan*. Paris-Musées

Comoy Fusaro, E. (2019a). Where is street art? In E. Comoy Fusaro (Ed.), *Framing graffiti & street art* (pp. 7–14). SAUC.

Comoy Fusaro, E. (2019b). Introduction. In E. Comoy Fusaro (Ed.), *Street art, récit et poésie* (pp. 7-12). EUD.

Comoy Fusaro, E. (2015). *Poliorama. Le immagini di Carlo Dossi*. Chemins de traverse.

Comoy Fusaro, E. (2007). *La nevrosi tra medicina e letteratura. Approccio epistemologico alle malattie nervose nella narrativa italiana (1865-1922)*. Polistampa.

Cooper, D. (2019). Paul Gauguin. In *Encyclopaedia Britannica*. https://www.britannica.com/biography/Paul-Gauguin#ref728095

Cronon, W. (2009). Le problème de la wilderness, ou le retour vers une mauvaise nature. *Écologie & Politique, 38*, 173–199.

Cunningham, H. (1998). Histories of childhood. *The American Historical Review, 103*(4), 1195–1208.

Di Pietrantonio, G. (1988/2003). Interview of Maurizio Cattelan. In F. Bonami, B. Vanderlinden, M. Etkind, & N. Spector (Eds.), *Maurizio Cattelan* (2003). Phaidon.

Duhamel, O. (1993). L'enfant de Srebrenica. *L'Express*. https://www.lexpress.fr/informations/l-enfant-de-srebrenica_605303.html

Duro, P. (Ed.) (1996). *The Rhetoric of the frame. Essays on the boundaries of the artwork*. Cambridge University Press.

Freud, S. (1916). *Leonardo Da Vinci: A psychosexual study of an infantile reminiscence*. Moffat, Yard & Company.

Freud, S. (1958). Formulations on the two principles of mental functioning. In *The standard edition of the complete psychological works of Sigmund Freud*, vol. 12 (pp. 218–226). Hogarth Press.

Freud, S. (1959). Creative writers and day-dreaming. In *The standard edition of the complete psychological works of Sigmund Freud, vol. 9* (pp. 143–153). Hogarth Press.

Freud, S. (1993). Un souvenir d'enfance de Léonard de Vinci. In *Œuvres complètes, vol. 10* (pp. 79–164). Presses Universitaires de France.

Freud, S. (1998). Formulations sur les deux principes de l'advenir psychique. In *Œuvres complètes, vol. 9* (pp. 11–21). Presses Universitaires de France.

Freud, S. (2007). Le poète et l'activité de fantaisie. In *Œuvres complètes, vol. 8* (pp. 159–171). Presses Universitaires de France.

Garrus, R. (1996). *Etymologies du français. Curiosités étymologiques.* Belin.

Gioni, M. (2003). Maurizio Cattelan—Rebel with a Pose. In F. Bonami, B. Vanderlinden, M. Etkind, & N. Spector (Eds.), *Maurizio Cattelan.* Phaidon.

Hamon, P. (2007). *Imageries. Littérature et image au XIXe siècle.* José Corti.

Heinich, N. (2014). *Le paradigme de l'art contemporain. Structures d'une révolution artistique.* Gallimard.

Heinich, N. (2017). *Des valeurs. Une approche sociologique.* Gallimard.

Heinich, N. (2019). Le street art, de l'artification à l'art contemporain. In E. Comoy Fusaro & H. Gaillard (Eds.), *Street art. Récit et poésie* (pp. 75–81). EUD.

Holland, O. (2019, May 16). Jeff Koons' $91M 'Rabbit' sculpture sets new auction record. *CNN.* HTTPS://EDITION.CNN.COM/STYLE/ARTICLE/JEFF-KOONS-RABBIT-AUCTION-RECORD/INDEX.HTML

Kang, S. K., & Bodenhausen, G. V. (2015). Multiple identities in social perception and interaction: challenges and opportunities. *Annual Review of Psychology, 66,* 547–574.

Kerlan, A., & Robert, A. D. (2013). Enfance, art, modernité et postmodernité. *El Futuro del Pasado, 4,* 277–293.

Key, E. (1909/2018). *The century of the child.* Public domain—Available online at: http://www.gutenberg.org/files/57283/57283-h/57283-h.htm

Laïdi, Z. (2000). *Le sacre du présent.* Flammarion.

Leduc-Gueye, C. (2016). Du *Set Setal* au *Festigraff* : L'évolution murale de la ville de Dakar. *Cahiers de Narratologie, 30,* https://doi.org/10.4000/narratologie.7461

Léon, P. (2008). L'écrivain et ses images, le paratexte photographique. In J.-P. Montier, L. Louvel, D. Meaux, P. Ortel (Eds.), *Littérature et photographie* (pp. 113–126). Presses Universitaires de Rennes.

Lipovetsky, G. (1987). *L'empire de l'éphémère. La mode et son destin dans les sociétés modernes.* Gallimard.

Lombroso, C. (1876/1884). *L'uomo delinquente in rapporto all'antropologia, giurisprudenza ed alle discipline carcerarie.* F.lli Bocca.

Malone, N., & Ovenden, K. (2017). Natureculture. In Augustín Fuentes (Ed.), *The International Encyclopedia of Primatology* (pp. 848-849). John Wiley & Sons.

Manacorda, F. (2006). *Maurizio Cattelan.* Mondadori Electa.

Marcolini, P. (2012). *Le mouvement situationniste. Une histoire intellectuelle.* L'échappée.

Marinetti, F. T. (1909/1994). *Marinetti e i futuristi.* Garzanti.

Mason, M. (2008), *The Pirate's dilemma. How hackers, punk capitalists and graffiti millionaires are remixing our culture and changing the world.* Allen Lane.

Morel, B. A. (1857). *Traité des dégénérescences physiques, intellectuelles et morales de l'espèce humaine et des causes qui produisent ces variétés maladives.* Baillière.

Morin, E. (1973). *Le paradigme perdu : La nature humaine.* Seuil.

Pascoli, G. (1907/1946). *Il fanciullino.* In *Prose. Vol. I: Pensieri di varia umanità.* Mondadori.

Pinto, R. (1991). Interview of Maurizio Cattelan. *Flash Art, 164.*

Pradel, J.-L. (1996). *L'art contemporain depuis 1945.* Bordas.

Pujas, S. (2015). *Street art. Poésie urbaine.* Tana.

Rossi, P. (1989). Il paradigma della riemergenza del passato. In F. M. Ferro, M. Di Giannantonio, G. Riefolo, & M.C. Tonnini Falaschi (Eds.), *Passioni della mente e della storia. Protagonisti, teorie e vicende della psichiatria italiana tra '800 e '900* (pp. 309–317). Vita e Pensiero.

Ruiz, A. (2002/2003). Interview of Maurizio Cattelan. In F. Bonami, B. Vanderlinden, M. Etkind, & N. Spector (Eds.), *Maurizio Cattelan* (2003). Phaidon

Searle, A. (2012, December 18). Mike Kelley: The nonconformist's whole life is here. *The Guardian.* https://www.theguardian.com/artanddesign/2012/dec/18/mike-kelley-nonconformist-whole-life-here

Sévérac, P. (2018). L'enfant est-il un adulte en plus petit ? Anthropologie et psychologie de l'enfance à partir de Spinoza, *Astérion, 19,* http://journals.openedition.org/asterion/3406; DOI : 10.4000/asterion.3406

Shanahan, S. (2007). Lost and found: The sociological ambivalence toward childhood. *Annual Review of Sociology, 33*, 407–428.

Sirmans, F. (2010). *Maurizio Cattelan: Is there life before death?* New Haven Publishing.

Spector, N. (1999/2005). Interview of Maurizio Cattelan. In *Pressplay: Contemporary artists in conversation.* Phaidon.

Thoreau, H. D. (1862/2014). *Marcher.* Le mot et le reste.

Tierney, A. L., & Nelson, C. A. (2009). Brain development and the role of experience in the early years. *Zero Three, 30*(2), 9–13.

Tobelem, J.-M. (2005). *Le nouvel âge des musées. Les institutions culturelles au défi de la gestion.* Armand Colin.

Vaillant, A. (2005). *La crise de la littérature. Romantisme et modernité.* ELLUG.

Verga, G. (1878/2015). Tutte le novelle. Einaudi.

Violeau, A. (2017). Maurizio Cattelan: Plus grand le visage, plus grand le revers. *Inferno,* 8.

Wetterwald, E. (2003). *Rue sauvage.* Les Presses du réel.

# Chapter VI.
## Consumer Childlikeness
### Mathieu Alemany Oliver and Russell W. Belk

On her popular blog entitled *Hyperbole and a Half*, which has been turned into a *New York Times Bestseller* book that Bill Gates described as "funny and smart as hell," Brosh (2013) humorously relates her attempt to be a real adult and how she ultimately came to realize that she will never be one. According to her, being "a real adult" involves being responsible, stopping procrastinating about cleaning the house, paying the bills, having schedules, and cooking. Contemplating the endless tasks, she finally decides to rebel and remain a kidult. One year after Kiley (1984) had introduced the Peter Pan syndrome to describe a growing number of people who do not want to grow up, Martin (1985) coined the word *kidult* to refer to adults who take advantage of adulthood while simultaneously being reluctant to embrace it fully— more specifically, by refusing the obligations, seriousness, and duties it is thought to entail. Brooks (2007) called it *adultolescence*, while Cross (2008) dubbed the men who best exemplify this delayed adulthood "boy-men" or "basement boys," after the associated trait of continuing to live with their parents well into their twenties.

Kidults delay traditional markers of adulthood like "leaving home, completing one's education, starting work, getting married, and becoming a parent" (Kimmel, 2008, p. 24). In 1960, 77 percent of women and 65 percent of men had reached these markers by age 30; in 2000, only 46 percent of women and 31 percent of men had done so (Brooks, 2007). And 55 percent of men aged 18 to 24 were still living with their parents even before the global recession made their move outside the home even more uncertain (Cross, 2008). The pattern is not unique to the USA but is also found in Italy (Cavalli, 1995) and Japan (Bosker, 2014; Demetriou, 2011), among others. In Asia, the Middle East, sub-Saharan Africa, Central America, and South America, many adolescents now live with extended family members rather than their parents (Patton et al., 2016). In this context, a growing number of researchers are calling for a re-evaluation of adulthood, whose current form is quickly disappearing (Cook, 2016; Mary, 2014; Quill, 2011). For example, Patton et al. (2016) suggest that, based on puberty patterns, delayed marriage and childbirth, and continuing higher education, adolescence now ranges from ages 10 to 24, which includes almost a quarter of the world's population. In the same vein, Arnett (2000) suggests adding a life stage called "emerging adulthood" between adolescence and adulthood. While this additional life stage is not without its critics (Côté, 2014; Hendry & Kloep, 2011), it nonetheless underlines the current difficulty in defining what our societies call adulthood, just as it prompts an interest in how consumers interpret and appropriate their adulthood (Alemany Oliver, 2015; Weinberger, Zavisca, & Silva, 2017).

Following Cross (2008), who considers the phenomenon of prolonged adolescence a contemporary lifestyle rather than a life stage, we argue that prolonged adolescence is a cultural phenomenon that reveals a growing social acceptance of childlikeness in our cultures. In particular, we believe that kidults are part of a wider phenomenon that takes the form of childlikeness and contributes to both the reterritorialization of adulthood and a change in the practices of consumers of any age. In dictionaries and in this book, childlikeness means the state or quality of behaving in a "childlike" manner as an adult. While it can have biological, cognitive, and emotional aspects, this chapter mainly considers childlikeness as a cultural phenomenon in the sense that certain cultures sanction, condemn, or promote such behavior more than others do. Many terms have been used to label childlike persons (e.g., kidult, adultescent, rejuvenile); in this chapter, we call them the Childlikes. Furthermore, we define childlikeness as *a particular hedonistic mentality—or mode of thought*. Childlikeness brings consumers toward what is socially constructed as the child's realm. The child's realm includes an emphasis on play, non-rational thinking, risk-seeking, non-seriousness, lightness in life, instantaneous pleasure, exploration, and, more generally, that which is considered to run counter to the socially acceptable adulthood guiding a majority of adults' everyday behavior in society.

Childlikeness is a topic that remains distinctly understudied and undertheorized, although it has previously been referred to (Alemany Oliver, 2015, 2018; Belk, 2000; Cross, 2002, 2004, 2008; Holbrook, 2001) and is considered part of popular culture (Noxon, 2006; Porterfield, Polette, & Baumlin, 2009). Aspects of childlikeness have entered consumer research in less recognized ways, such as experiential consumption, magical thinking, anthropomorphism, desire, extreme sports, and play (Aaker, 1997; Arnould and Price, 1993; Belk, 2014; Belk, Ger and Askegaard, 2003; Brown, 2010; Holbrook and Hirschman, 1982; Holbrook et al., 1984; Holt, 1995; Kim & McGill, 2011; St. James, Handelman & Taylor, 2011; Scott, Cayla, & Cova, 2017; Thompson, 2004). Somewhat more explicitly, Belk (2000) examines the infantilization of adults in Las Vegas, Brown (2011) and Brown and Ponsby-McCabe (2014) deal with playful brand *mascots*, and connections with avatars as virtual selves in online games have been compared to playing with dolls (Bogost, 2006; Wang, Zhao, and Bamossy, 2009). Consumer childlikeness also emerges during certain holiday celebrations in the West, such as New Year's Eve, Halloween, and Mardi Gras or Carnival, when adults dress in costumes, pretend, and act with childlike abandon (Belk, 1994; Derrett, 2003; Weinberger & Wallendorf, 2012).

Because the concept of childlikeness still needs to be delineated in consumer research, the objective of this conceptual contribution is to describe what childlikeness is, how it relates to other concepts used in consumer research, and how the understanding of childlikeness can help us revise our understanding of some consumer and marketing practices. To that end, we propose a framework that sees childlikeness as a consequence of consumers' adjustment to the world, as well as a potentially consequential phenomenon of consumer and marketing practices. Inspired by the general philosophy of the Annales School[59] regarding social and cultural history, we begin with an overview of childlikeness in popular cultures and academic literature. This overview advances the contradictions and conflicts that these constructions can produce in people's lives. They also constitute, according to the Annales School, the conditions under which a particular mentality such as childlikeness becomes possible at a particular moment in time. More specifically, we deal with positive and negative views of childlikeness, fashionable childlikeness in Western and East Asian consumer cultures, as well as the appeals of advertisements that cater to various aspects of childlikeness. The second section draws from the representations of childlikeness mentioned in the previous section to theorize how childlikeness today is reflected in the constructions of nature, the self, and society. We argue that nature is perceived as a state outside of civilization and close to what we imagine we have already experienced in childhood prior to

---

[59] The Annales School is a school of thought founded by the French historians Lucien Febvre and Marc Bloch in the 1920s in reaction to the positivist and dominant paradigm of the time. This school favors the inclusion of other social science disciplines such as psychology, economics, sociology, and geography to focus on people's daily lives and beliefs, social norms, and, more generally, societies rather than their rulers and the wars that have shaped them. It is interested not only in the ideas and opinions of societies of the past but also in those of contemporary societies.

being socialized. With the same logic, who we truly are—our authentic self—is a contemporary quest that can be easier to undertake if we remember the child we once were, who was not socialized and constrained. We also speculate that society reflects childlikeness when it displays polymorphously perverse relationships that privilege instant and omnipresent gratification. The third and final section presents the possible implications of childlikeness for consumer and marketing practices regarding authenticating acts, the appeal of the adolescent figure, and adulthood. But before any such developments, we will briefly explain what we mean by viewing childlikeness as a *mentality* and provide a framework for studying it and then provide a short historical account of the social constructions of the child and childhood in the West that have influenced the meanings of childlikeness.

### [Preliminary section I] A Framework for the Study of Childlikeness in Consumer Research

Childlikeness is defined here as a mentality, that is, a mode of thought resulting from the interaction between the social world and the more personal feelings and intellectual experiences of reality and existence. It is interchangeable with the concept of worldview, which similarly involves the way people make sense individually and collectively of their relationship with the physical and spiritual world around them. To historians of mentalities, a mentality is the socialized aspect of mental life that underlines the contextual character of ideas and opinions without underestimating the individual experience of existence (Bloch, 1949; Bloch & Febvre, 1930; Burke, 1990; Febvre, 1952; see also the Annales School). As shown in Figure 1, which we develop in the next sections, mentalities/worldviews are reflected by both collective and individual assumptions about nature, the self, and society (Geertz, 1973) and influenced by the many and constantly changing material, technical, social, legal, and political conditions of existence. To Febvre (1952), mentalities are mental tools adjusted to these conditions of existence in order to provide people with ways of thinking, feeling, and doing. In other words, reality is constructed from the dialectical relationship between individuals and their environment, and socialization is defined by this relationship much as this relationship is defined by socialization. Finally, mentalities are barely perceptible by people and rather implicit in both thought and action. Consequently, we draw from historians of mentalities' general idea of observing and analyzing collective phenomena and conceptualizations, as well as their will to study not only historical events but also contemporary phenomena (Bloch & Febvre, 1930; Febvre, 1952).

To avoid any misunderstanding, it is important to note that the study of mentalities neither determines nor fixes any particular way of thinking but limits what it is conceivable for a given period and in a given place. Along the same lines, integrating insights from anthropology, sociology, economics, or psychology is not done in order to provide a coherent literature review that would construct a clear narrative about childlikeness but rather to gather the different and sometimes contradictory pieces of knowledge found in academic literature and popular cultures that possibly shape perceptions, discourses, and applications of childlikeness in consumer society. Childlikeness, as it is presented here, is not necessarily or strictly followed by the Childlikes. Because mentalities are shaped by both collective representations and individual experiences, childlikeness depends on the time and place but also the individuals. In other words, a consumer may reveal childlikeness in some contexts and activities and display a very *adult* consumer behavior at other times.

**Figure 1. Framework for the study of consumer childlikeness**

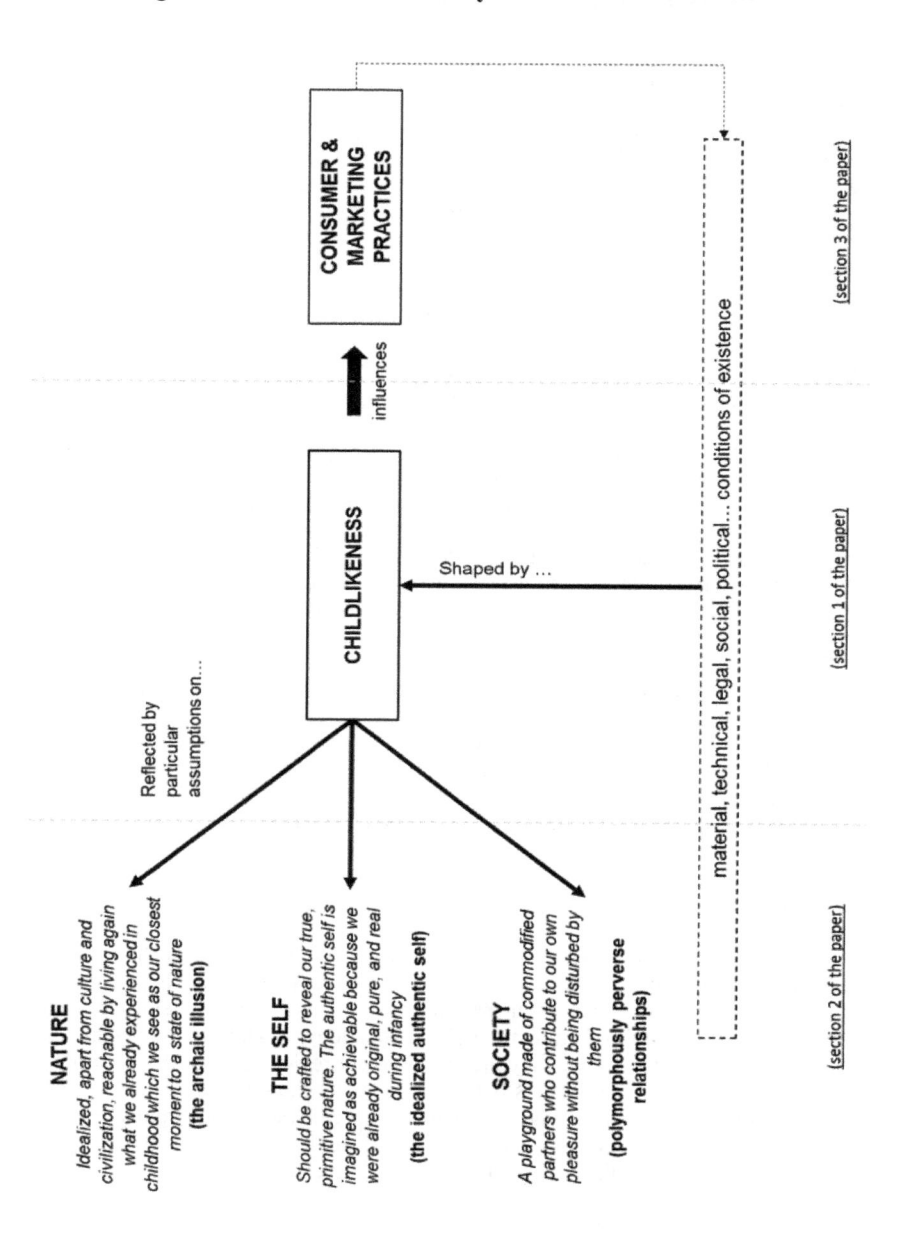

**[Preliminary section II] The Social Construction of the Child and Childhood**

The constructions of childlikeness that we present below are directly shaped by our understanding of the child and of childhood. From a social constructionist perspective, childhood is primarily composed of myths, stories, and visual representations constructed by adults and made meaningful by culture (James, Jenks, & Prout, 1998; Stainton-Rogers & Stainton-Rogers, 1992). As such, the history of childhood is more a history of adult attitudes toward children than a real history of children (Steedman, 1998).

Childhood has not always been a meaningful concept and has evolved, just like childlikeness. History reveals a perpetual debate about Western concepts and conceptualizations of childhood. For example, Ariès (1960) contends that medieval societies did not have any concept of childhood. This is suggested by the lack of organization and discipline within the few schools that existed and in Giotto's paintings in which children are depicted as tiny adults. However, Hanawalt (1993) highlights a recognition of the concept of childhood in early scientific and medical work, as well as folk terminology. For instance, Londoners conceptualized childhood as "wild and wanton," whereas adulthood was perceived as "sad and wise" (Hanawalt, 1993, p. 6). The same debate appears during the early period of Modernism and the Enlightenment era with a Lockean view of childhood that, together with the economic forces behind child labor, started shaping what would become our Western conceptualization for more than 300 years. Locke (1693) associated childhood with ignorance, errors, confusion, vulnerability, and the need for protection. In his view, a child's mind at birth is a blank slate that has to be filled by adults. This conception lies between a pessimistic Hobbesian view of human nature that regards children as inherently selfish and a more celebratory Rousseauian view that emphasizes the innate purity of children. Despite these divergences, the Enlightenment period drew attention to the need to differentiate childhood from adulthood and to stop looking for the man in the child (Rousseau, 1762). The image of purity in children was also influenced by religion. The paintings of the 14th century illustrate how Christian societies started devoting themselves to the Christ Child and made the figure of the Child a privileged intercessor between God and humans.

This figure of the Divine Child was fed by 19th-century Romanticism, which idealized childhood and considered it a source of inspiration (Heywood, 2001). By the mid-19th century, the urban middle class in the USA had already adopted the notion of the priceless child (Zelizer, 1985). This romantic vision of the child was politicized and institutionalized in the USA and Europe throughout the 20th century and encouraged families—including the working class—to favor the child's sentimental value over their monetary worth and promote the gradual end of child labor (Steedman, 1998; Zelizer, 1985). Another consequence of romanticizing childhood is the increasing number of studies on child development in psychology. The theories of Piaget (1927, 1966) and Vygotsky (1978) are among the best-known and most-used theories in developmental psychology (Duncan, 1995; Glassman, 1995) and consumer research (John, 1999). These theories highlight the importance of childhood in cognitive development and suggest paying special attention to the child (Postman, 1982). One main conclusion that society may have reached because of Piaget's and Vygotsky's popular theories is that children are not tiny adults; on the contrary, they must be protected and

**Table 1. Overview of childlikeness**

| Approach | Childlikeness can be associated with… |
|---|---|
| **Philosophy** | In Ancient Greece and Rome: aionic (vs. chronological) experience of time (i.e., qualitative experience), naivety, savagery, and weakness<br>In 15th-century China: the true and authentic self<br>From the Enlightenment to the 21st century in the West: immaturity, lack of reason, transcendental illusion |
| **Sociology, Anthropology** | Possible response to feelings of anxiety caused by uncertainty and/or social and moral suffocation<br>The result of pervasive youth culture<br>Coolness and cuteness<br>Mutability, plasticity of identity, instability, and flexibility<br>Irresponsible behavior, a temporary state before adulthood |
| **Mythology** | The Child and the Trickster figures are heads and tails of the same coin<br>The Child reflects society's expectations about what adulthood should be and accepts responsibility, rationality, or the idea of citizenship (having rights and duties toward others); the Child is the hero figure<br>The Trickster reflects taboo and prohibited behaviors and society's expectations about what adulthood should NOT be, and it does not accept responsibility, rationality, or citizenship; the child is the antihero |
| **Psychoanalysis** | Pleasure principle over reality principle<br>Preference for youth, enchantment, daydreams, freedom<br>The result of temporal regression, visible through playful and fantasy behaviors<br>The free inner child is associated with adventure, art, imagination, energy, disinhibition, and a rebellious life<br>The constrained inner child is associated with anxiety, arrogance, defensiveness, dependence, nervousness, and complaints |
| **Advertising** | Magical thinking<br>Imagination and hedonism<br>Playful behavior, entertainment |
| **Consumer Research** | Particular relationship to nature, the self, and society<br>Malleable and enchanted reality influenced by the pleasure principle<br>Need for authentic/true self<br>*Social/moral suffocation in parallel with a need for an original relationship with the natural world/state of nature*<br>*Transformation of social and personal roles that become transactional games to play* |

educated in a logic of joyful discovery fostered by tolerant adults and children with more advanced cognitive abilities, who accept that each child develops at their own pace. This dominant discourse leads Rose (1984) and Zornado (2001) to view the child as someone who is totally dominated by adults. In their view, stories told to children implicitly consist of propaganda that serves the purpose of reinforcing adult domination over children and sanctions the adult punishment of emotional outbursts. Adults and children engage in power relations that are both repressive and productive, leading adults to maintain their authority and moral superiority (Buckingham, 2000; Cox, 1996; Foucault, 1985).

Modernity, with its focus on production, has made childhood a time to prepare to assume the adult-producer role. The child is, then, both a king and a target, requiring an investment by a society that has faith in its future (Gauchet, 1985). The modern individual was born a pilgrim and pursues the ideal of progress (Bauman, 1996). While childhood is preparation for this journey, adulthood is the journey, which is considered real life. James, Jenks, and Prout (1998, 62) contend that "Western childhood has become a period in the life course characterized by social dependency, asexuality, and the obligation to be happy, with children having the right to protection and training but not to social or personal autonomy." And yet, according to these authors, children are potentially active agents. This is illustrated by deMause's (1974/2006, p. 52) arguments that parents have adopted a "helping mode" in recent decades, with the implicit idea that "the child knows better than the parent what it needs." This particular view of the child is emblematic of a romantic and sacralized image of the child that contributes to the conceptualization of childlikeness and its celebration.

Today, childhood in the West continues to be influenced by, on the one hand, a modern and productivist view that emphasizes the preparation of the child to undertake the adult journey and, on the other hand, the romantic view that makes childhood an idealized moment of happiness, discoveries, and freedom (but also a source of inspiration for adults).

## Childlikeness in Popular Cultures and Academic Literature

To define and contextualize childlikeness, attention is given here to the central part of Figure 1 before developing, in the second section, the possible assumptions that reflect this hedonistic mentality and have consequences for consumer research. We underline different aspects of childlikeness found in popular cultures and academic literature. These many different collective perceptions, constructions, and applications of childlikeness have been shaped by the various material, technical, social, legal, and/or political conditions of existence, and they potentially construct the current collective understanding of consumer childlikeness. Table 1 compartmentalizes the different constructions of childlikeness that we mention in this section and also includes mythological and psychoanalytical understandings that are developed elsewhere in this book (see chapter II by Rohde-Brown and chapter III by Alemany Oliver and Wilkinson).

## Childlikeness: For Better or Worse

As we noted above, childlikeness has long been shaped by constructions of the child and childhood. Childlikeness has had different meanings depending on the time, place, and culture. For example, in the ancient Greco-Roman world, childlikeness was associated with naivety, savagery, and weakness but also with an aionic (vs. chronological) experience of time that corresponds to a qualitative (vs. quantitative) experience (Cicero, -44; Golden, 2015; Kohan, 2015; Plato, -360). In Mesoamerica, the Aztecs differentiated adults from children because of their ability to discipline the body and its appearance (Joyce 2000), thus making the Childlike the one who is incapable of self-control. In China, 16th- and 17th-century philosophers, including Mencius (2003) and Li (2016), shaped thinking about childlikeness. They conceived of *chizi zhi xin*, or *chixin*, the infant's mind, as something that an adult never loses completely (Weightman, 2008). Li (2016) considers the childlike mind to be the true and authentic mind that allows the true self to blossom. Similarly, the neo-Confucian Luo believes that the yang forces are mainly the forces of the child and that they weaken during adulthood, while the more adult yin forces gain strength (Huang, 1987; Lee, 2012). Therefore, it is critical for adults to keep the yang forces strong in order to achieve an equilibrium of forces. One way to do this is by recovering a child's heart-mind and accepting the spontaneous expression of feelings (Lee, 2012).

From a practical standpoint, childlikeness seems to respond to feelings of anxiety caused by uncertainty and/or social and moral suffocation. This was visible, for example, in the *Beat Generation* with its Trickster behavior and in the French *Zazou* subculture during World War II, which protested against an ultra-conservative morality and difficult times by showing childlike recklessness and adopting a fun morality. Similarly, Romanticism, exemplified by romantic literature and the *Sturm und Drang* movement, which advocated giving free rein to emotions and subjectivity, appeared as a protest movement against the Enlightenment and rationalization. In Japan, a theater company called *Chelfitsch* "represents the baby-like disarticulation of the English word 'selfish.' It is meant to evoke the social and cultural characteristics of today's Japan, not least of Tokyo" (Chelfitsch.net, June 27, 2016). Varney, Eckersall, Hudson, and Hatley (2013, p. 112) write that this theater company's "work has been connected to experiences of loss and fragmentation in Japan's historical identity, to questions of political inertia—questions that seem to haunt Japan in the decades of economic malaise since 1991," when the Japanese bubble economy burst.

While some see childlikeness as freeing, others continue to vilify the notion. To Barber (2007), brands and capitalism can be blamed for spreading an infantilist ethos by asking consumers to remain childlike and impetuous in their tastes so that marketers can keep launching new products at a steady pace. This infantilist ethos is spurred by a "forever young syndrome" that helps marketers make youth culture the main engine spreading consumer culture, notably through advertising (Danesi, 2003; Patton et al., 2016). Bernardini (2014) argues that the Childlikes are characterized by spontaneity, dependency, doubt, a preference for instant pleasure, an emphasis on rights rather than obligations, and tendencies toward egocentrism, narcissism, insecurity, individualism, and conformity. Mazur (2015, p. 144) characterizes the presence of childlikeness and infantilization as a "dangerous" replacement of civic duty by hedonism and immaturity nourished by the marketplace. Adult immaturity, according to Cataluccio (2006), is the disease of our time and characterizes the crisis of fatherhood. In line with these claims, the marketplace often tells consumers that they are the center of attention and that impulsivity is not socially prohibited. It transforms disciplined leisure and purposive play into "childish playfulness" and highlights easiness, simplicity, and speed over difficulty, complexity, and slowness (Barber, 2007, p. 42). The result, according to authors like Aboujaoude (2011) and Twenge and Campbell (2009), is a regressive, narcissistic, and infantile ego that forgets its duties and responsibilities.

**Fashionable Childlikeness in Western and East Asian Consumer Cultures**

Western consumer culture emerged as part of an exaltation of youth. Kjeldgaard and Askegaard (2006, p. 233) underline how "youth culture and marketing have been historically intertwined, representing a transnational market ideology of youth." The rise of Hollywood movies in the 1910s through the 1930s showed a "preference for 'little girls with curls,'" as illustrated by Shirley Temple (Addison, 2006, p. 8). This coincided with the decline of child labor and the targeting of children by toy and clothing marketers who no longer treated them as little adults (Cook, 2004). Meanwhile, identity projects became more individualistic (Giddens, 1991), leading Western consumers to become more flexible, mobile, and liquid in their pursuit of such identities (Bauman, 2004). Salinger's 1951 novel *The Catcher in the Rye* already voiced regret about those who grew up and lost the purity of youth. It was an expression of youthfulness evolving from being considered a life stage and becoming regarded as a lifestyle (Cross, 2008).

Such an exaltation of youth is part of the childlikeness impulse. Observing its presence in the media, Porterfield, Polette, and Baumlin (2009) suggest that American culture has been in arrested development, and they contend that the media nourishes a quest for perpetual adolescence. Examples are quite easy to find and include successful TV series such as *Friends, Seinfeld, How I Met Your Mother, The Big Bang Theory*, and *Two and a Half Men*, as well as the success of late-night shows in which Jimmy Fallon and Conan O'Brien play in a childlike manner with singers, actors, and other entertainment artists. The media celebrates and legitimizes childlike behavior by singing the praises of today's heroes who never forgot and kept their childlike personas strong, which allows them to approach life in the most experiential ways possible. A thread connecting all these TV actors and presenters is the omnipresence of coolness. Considered today as an alternative status system to the orthodox, "adult," social class system (e.g., Belk, Tian, & Paavola, 2010; Poutain & Robins, 2000; Warren & Campbell, 2014), coolness has spread across the world's marketplaces as an alternate form of youth rebellion (Frank, 1997). Being cool, or hip, was embraced by consumers wishing to set themselves apart from the standardized market economy. During his time in office, U.S. President Barack Obama frequently greeted people with a high-five or a fist bump, went to basketball games where he sipped beer while dressed in casual attire, and made claw hands and monster faces during the annual White House Easter Egg Roll, thereby becoming rather emblematic of the institutionalization of cool youth culture.

In East Asian marketplaces, childlikeness is particularly visible and fashionable in the form of kidult fashion, girlishness, and kawaii subculture, which are elaborated on below (Aoki, 2001). In South Korea, kidult fashion is characterized by the pursuit of fashion, exciting emotions, a girlish image (among both boys and girls), a preference for anime, manga, and fantasy characters, and the pursuit of fun, fantasy, and nostalgia (Cha & Hong, 2007; Lee & Yoo, 2007). Cha and Hong (2007, p. 1373) also emphasize that kidult fashions do not represent "the attachment to the past but [rather a] positive expression of self and individuality." Regarding girlishness, a gendered and pejorative definition refers to "a socially constructed, often playful childlike pose, spoken or acted out, that explicitly displays the vulnerability of approval seeking" (Maynard and Taylor, 1999, p. 40). According to these two authors, girlishness is indicative of conformity, non-aggressiveness, non-competitiveness, and vulnerability. Warren-Crow (2014) partly explains the increasing presence of girlishness in media by its perfect fit with our digital era: the mutability, plasticity of identity, and instability and flexibility that characterize the process of becoming. In Japan, girlishness is part of the shōjo imagery that reflects the contradictory assemblage of youth, femininity, innocence, budding sexuality, and autonomy and takes an idealized form in the character of Lewis Carroll's Alice (Monden, 2014).

Lastly, *kawaii* is the Japanese word for cute but has a broader meaning (Miller, 2004). For example, it is possible to talk about not only baby and infant cuteness but also adult cuteness, pornographic cuteness, and authoritative cuteness (McVeigh, 2000). For Granot, Brashear-Alejandro, and Russell (2014), cuteness takes the form of feminine revenge, via consumption, over the masculine cool culture. Maynard (2002) suggests that the Japanese population, by being immersed in a cult of cuteness culture, has become socialized to adore playful childlikeness. According to Kinsella (1995), Japan witnessed a growing desire for more than just a youthful look in the 1970s as a form of resistance to assuming rigid adult roles in Japanese society (Field 1995). Fashion magazines started displaying childlike looks and asked their readers to play and be cute. Kawaii clothes are "deliberately designed to make the wearer appear childlike and demure" (Kinsella, 1995, p. 229). Kinsella (1995) observes that Japanese people also understand kawaii as *natural* and *genuine*. Finally, she argues that the move to Japanese cuteness among those in their teens and twenties "romanticized childhood in relation to adulthood," just as "Disney romanticized nature in relation to industrial society." The result is an implicit indictment of adulthood as "an individualized and limited way of condemning society generally" (Kinsella, 1995, p. 241).

**The Advertised Childlike**

In the West, advertising sometimes uses the inner child concept with explicit messages to indulge in childlike consumption practices. For example, in Australia, *McDonald's* asks consumers to "feed [their] inner child," a *Mercedes-Benz* dealer in Hagerstown, Maryland, USA, calls for drawing on one's inner child in order to better experience the sound and speed of its latest car models, and in France, *Nestlé* urges consumers to "save the child" that is sleeping inside the adult. But most of the time, messages invoking childlike characteristics are more implicit, as with *Evian*'s global advertisements— reproduced in Figure 2—showing people child versions of themselves.

**Figure 2. Evian's global "live young" campaign (since 2013)**

Advertisements that use childlikeness often use magical thinking to attribute supernatural powers to products. For example, a man's deodorant can have incredible effects on women (e.g., *Axe*), or a magic wand can allow friends to share a good time (e.g., *Hyundai*). More generally, advertising is a source of magic that consumers use in hopes of moving toward happier mental states (Jhally, 1989; Otnes & Scott, 1996). By offering specific rituals and invoking animist acts, advertising also recalls aspects of the savage or prelogical mind as described by Lévi-Strauss (1962) and Lévy-Bruhl (1910). These aspects have long been pejoratively associated with indigenous populations and childhood but are perpetuated during adulthood at a lower level, in particular when a person shows signs of imitation, fear, or desire (Fernandez & Lastovicka, 2011; Piaget, 1927; St. James, Handelman, & Taylor, 2011).

A second critical element of the childlikeness depicted in or encouraged by advertising is the use of a childlike imaginary. Imaginary worlds develop and become limitless as soon as magic allows consumers to believe in a world of endless possibilities. A good example is the mobile company *Three*'s campaign in the UK in 2013–2014. In its advertisements, *Three* promoted childlikeness and offered consumers entry into a wide universe that breaks free from the normal surroundings and turns into imaginary scenes. Imagination and fantasy play a critical role in consumption (Holbrook & Hirschman, 1982; Martin, 2004). According to Campbell (1987), the hedonist is like an artist of the imagination, fine-tuning a daydream in order to envision a perfect vision of life. Although imagination exists in adulthood (Belk, 2001), it is traditionally attached to the child, who invents imaginary friends, draws, pretends, or otherwise escapes for hours from the real world. It has been accepted that imagination "enters . . . into all children's pastimes" (Sully, 1896, p. 50) and has long been regarded as a "master of error and falsehood" (Pascal, 1670/1995, p. 9) or as involving a "fool who is pleased to play the fool" (Malebranche, 1997, p. 4) in a society that focuses on reason-driven experience and observation. Therefore, imagination becomes stigmatized as the focus of children and a primary topic in educational psychology (Harris, 2000; Vygotsky, 1930). Often associated with play (Singer & Singer, 2005; Sutton-Smith, 1997), imagination is not regarded as part of ordinary working adulthood (Wyness, 2012). Nevertheless, it is an important part of the creative process (Hirschman, 1985; Holbrook & Hirschman, 1982).

Playful behavior is the third element regularly found in Western advertisements invoking childlikeness. Play has always been part of the human species: We are homo ludens (Huizinga, 1944). However, it has also long been relegated to "the work of the child" (Cross, 2001, p. v) and to leisure time in adult life (Bauman, 2005; Gelber, 1999; Giddens, 1964). Wyness (2012) stresses that, despite the difficulty of finding a definition for play, almost all Western societies agree that play is synonymous with childhood, while adulthood is synonymous with work. For instance, the United Nations recognizes play as "the right of every child" (General Assembly Resolution 44/25 of November 20, 1989). Another example is the Japanese and Chinese character for play, which represents a child floating on water while another child wanders around (Kiuchi, 2009). Taking a Derridean perspective, Edwards (1998, p. 17) underlines that play "affirms freedom and possibility against restriction, resignation and closure . . . the joyous affirmation of play of the world and of the innocence of becoming, the affirmation of a world of signs without fault, without truth, and without origin which is offered to an active interpretation." Imaginative play is a key element in the transition between past and future identities (Schouten, 1991; Vygotsky, 1978; Winnicott, 1971), particularly because it connects inner and outer realities (Bettelheim, 1988; Winnicott, 1971). It can also be viewed as a parody of emotional vulnerability that helps individuals remove the limits of everyday life and create positive outcomes (Sutton-Smith, 2003).

Consumer society can only celebrate play since play is at the very heart of consumer desire and object seduction. As Belk, Ger, and Askegaard (2003) remind us, many consumption processes are derived from consumer desire and the related seduction game that is played in which consumers readily agree to participate (Deighton and Grayson, 1995)—what Belk et al. (2003) call auto-arousal. From the moment consumers react to brands' messages, they engage in a self-seduction game that opens up desire. In this context, the overlap between consumption and play becomes visible (Grayson, 1999; Holbrook et al., 1984; Holt, 1995; Kozinets et al., 2004) and leads to a kind of legitimacy of playfulness in the realm of consumption that is often interpreted as childlike. As illustrated by the recent success of the *Pokémon Go* game, which involves augmented reality on mobile phones, consumer society is now a playground where technological toys react to and interact with us (Pesce, 2000). It is a playground that relies on illusion and is "governed by a form of magical thinking" (Baudrillard, 1970/1998, p. 31). The occasional intentional humor of the Siri and Alexa voice-interactive digital assistants or the Pepper and Sofia humanoid robots is another example.

—

This first section provided an overview of the different collective perceptions, constructions, and applications of childlikeness as they are shared in popular cultures and academic literature. To sum up, childlikeness often represents human potentialities. Associated with an as yet unsocialized mode of thought, childlikeness is socially constructed around a logic of action and adaptation to provide change and growth. By providing the opportunity for freedom and authenticity of individuals, this lifestyle allows Childlikes to sidestep social and moral constraints, which some see as a positive liberation and others as a threat to society. In the field of consumption, this section offers the first elements for an understanding of what consumer childlikeness might be. More precisely, consumer childlikeness can be seen as a hedonistic mentality that, with the help of marketing, creates the conditions to reach feelings of freedom and authenticity vis-à-vis society. By combining magical thinking, imagination, and play, brands convey a discourse that puts childlikeness at the service of the pleasure principle. Since this perfectly fits the imperatives of marketing and the capitalist economy, it is tempting to speculate how marketing has exploited and nurtured childlikeness to better offer what is at the heart of marketing: seduction, desire, fantasy, and the possibility for change. After having been regarded as misbehavior for a long time, childlikeness has begun to be supported by marketing—notably, through the appeal to eternal youth—to finally become more and more acceptable and spill over into the media, fashion, and even the White House in the USA. Brands exploit childlikeness and encourage the consumer to be childlike, tricksterish, cool, fun, cute, and authentic. The childlike consumer is one of the contemporary heroes of consumer culture, the charismatic ruler that societies willingly follow and believe in (Maffesoli, 2000). Emblematic of this phenomenon, the American artist Matt Starr in 2015 suggested moving to a babycore look—that is, dressing in adult-sized babywear.

### Childlikeness's Possible Reflections in Nature, the Self, and Society

The previous section offered an overview of the collective perceptions, constructions, and applications of childlikeness. We will now dig a little further into consumer childlikeness by moving to the left-hand side of Figure 1. Following Geertz (1973), who suggests that mentalities are reflected by assumptions about nature, the self, and society, we consider childlikeness within these three constructs.

### Nature—Contemporary Savagery and the Archaic Illusion

As Canniford and Shankar (2013) remind us, consumers may want to perpetuate a view of nature as something apart from culture and civilization by assembling it through romantic experiences that overcome the potential tensions arising when the ideal of nature is contested. This experience of nature allows consumers to step back from everyday bureaucracy and society more generally (Arnould & Price, 1993; Belk & Costa, 1998; Kozinets, 2002). It is also important to stress that, in contrast to Canniford and Shankar (2013, p. 1052), who understand nature as "the opposite of modern culture," nature is the opposite of the idea of civilization itself more than modern culture. In this vein, only the poor, the primitive, the violent, and the oppressed—those excluded from civilization—are considered real, authentic people (Trilling, 1972). As Ellis (1997) suggests when discussing Tacitus's (98) description of the Germanic people, the idealization of nature is not idealization per se but a rejection of civilization that we find even before the romantic movement and still find today:

> [Someone] disillusioned and even embittered by the flaws, inconsistencies, and retrogressions of a great civilization, deludes himself that a world of primitive innocence and natural goodness exists in peoples who are untouched by the advances of that civilization. So intense are his hostile feelings toward his own society that he is unable to see the one he compares it to with any degree of realism: whatever its actual qualities, it is endowed with all of the human values that he misses in his own. (Ellis, 1997, p. 14)

One of the figures that best illustrate this disillusionment is the Noble Savage (Belk & Costa, 1998; Price, 1989; Torgovnick, 1990). The Noble Savage is the idealization of man living in a state of nature, even if, as Lévi-Strauss (1955/2012, p. 316) stresses, it is a state that "no longer exists, has perhaps never existed, and probably will never exist." The romantic label of Noble Savage has long been used to describe cultural practices and mentalities that are different from the existing and dominant social and economic structures of our own civilization. Because it represents the idealization of a state of nature that has not yet been corrupted by civilization, the Noble Savage is not only a romantic figure but also a timeless mythological character that we already find, for example, in Montaigne (1580) or, as we have already seen, even earlier in Tacitus (98).

With such a view of nature, childlikeness can be seen as a form of contemporary savagery. One reason might be that it shares with savagery the idea of undomesticated worlds and mentalities. Savagery, as Lévi-Strauss (1955) underlines, withstands time. We see it today in contemporary "Tough Mudder" competitions in which participants defile and degrade themselves (Scott, Cayla, & Cova, 2017). Referring to *Lord of the Flies* (Golding, 1954), the Oxford English dictionary defines savagery by concluding that "without adult society, the children descend into savagery." As early as the 16th century, when the figure of the Noble Savage started to spread in literature, French explorer Cartier (1535) associated Canadian natives with innocent people who have a soul as pure as children. To Lévi-Strauss (1949), this association of the savage with the child is explained by an archaic illusion, a naive evolutionary vision that rocks our societies. According to Lévi-Strauss (1949), child thinking, which is devoid of social norms and representations, constitutes a sort of universal substrate that easily (and wrongly) makes a connection between the savage or undomesticated mind and the as yet unsocialized mind of a child. Just as the Noble Savage figure is praised in romantic primitivism, we saw in the previous section that childlikeness is today being hailed by popular culture. If Romantics are savages because "any action not in keeping with tradition is mere romanticism" (Sartre, 1945/2007, p. 19), then Childlikes are savages because any action not in keeping with standard adulthood is mere childlikeness. By being associated with savagery, childlikeness reveals consumers' wish to get back to an original state where, in existentialist terms, existence precedes our essence. It also bears witness to our Western fascination with the primitive, especially when it comes to dealing with identity crises (Torgovnick, 1990).

As for the Romantics, the Childlikes' desire is to experience what is thought to have existed before social contracts and to indulge the fantasy of connecting with our true nature. The success of naturism is one of the best illustrations of this wish to get closer to the very first hours of our presence on Earth (Barcan, 2004). Likewise, Paleolithic diets and Bear Grylls's reality television series may indicate a fascination with what was already here before *us civilized* people. But compared with Romanticism, we suggest that childlikeness has a low temporal distance with idealized nature since childhood is something that we have all experienced. Despite our conscious inability to go back to a state of nature, we can feel that we come closer to it by living again what we already experienced in childhood, which we see as our closest moment to a state of nature. In this context, childlikeness appears as the ultimate state before the true and authentic self is reached.

**The Self—The Idealized Authentic Self**

Authenticity has become an absolute value in contemporary life and "one of the cornerstones of contemporary marketing" (Brown, Kozinets, & Sherry Jr, 2003, p. 21; Gilmore & Pine, 2007). It is defined as original, pure, and real (Lindholm, 2008), and there is probably nothing more original, pure, and real than the newborn who is considered a tabula rasa. This echoes Christian writings, which ask their faith community to become like little children in order to enter the kingdom of heaven (Matthew 18:3). Translations of Chinese philosopher Li's (1590) *A Book to Burn* use the concepts of childlikeness and authenticity interchangeably. For example, where Weightman (2008) writes that losing the childlike mind is equivalent to losing the true mind, Saussy's 2016 translation of *A Book to Burn* (Li, 2016*)* says that the person vanishes when the mind loses its authenticity. By idealizing the authentic self as being close to what a newborn must experience, childlikeness suggests an authentic self that is free from moral and social strains and stains. In this vein, it might not be a coincidence that an individual's inner world—the only world available during early childhood (Freud, 1923; Winnicott, 1971)—has been regarded as the ultimate source of freedom in contemporary myths (Lahire, 2013). The inner world offers a refuge for those confronted with an all too present society imposing regimes of self-governance on the populace (Foucault, 1985). Similar negative feelings are also found in what Wrong (1961) calls the oversocialized conception of adulthood, which eventually increases the perceived gap between imaginative and innocent childhood, on the one hand, and corrupted adulthood, on the other hand (Bauman, 2005).

Childlikes' search for authenticity—and, more generally, the crafting of an authentic self—may reflect an advanced form of individualism in Western cultures that marks other more collective experiences and goals as mere enclaves of unreality (Belk & Costa, 1998). This relationship between childlikeness, authenticity, and individualism can be visible, for instance, in the frontier myth, which has long nurtured the idea that wilderness is the last bastion of rugged individualism, "the ultimate landscape of authenticity," where we can escape the strict rules of civilization and be true to ourselves (Cronon, 1996, p. 16). Quite characteristic of this individualism, Foucault (1976) suggests a general acceptance that truth is deep inside our most secret nature and yearns to be revealed. Illouz (2008) notes that being able to share an authentic and unique self through therapeutic narratives—created in a confessional style and broadcast through blogs and on TV shows—has become critical for people today who are in search of psychological health, self-esteem, and self-actualization.

Self-construction and therapeutic narratives are highly visible in American culture, where the successful self is an independent and emancipated entity that provides a feeling of control over crumbling institutions (Illouz, 2008; Moisio & Beruchashvili, 2010). Among the different therapeutic tools offered by pop psychology magazines and blogs, the inner child is promoted as an opportunity for adults to rediscover their individualities. Inner child therapy is lauded as a personal journey consisting of finding, awakening, healing, nurturing, feeding, listening to, and liberating the child we once were. It is the unsocialized part that still acts spontaneously and intuitively and eventually reveals who we truly are: the authentic self.

Ironically, this individuation process calls for activities offered by the same consumer society that presumably contributed to the loss of authenticity through the mass production of non-original and standardized products offered in highly artificial and hyperreal worlds (Boorstin, 1962; Baudrillard, 1981; Eco, 1990; Miller, 2008). In the eyes of many critics, the pursuit of authenticity is bound to be in vain, if not a mere status game through which consumers attempt to one-up one another (Boyle, 2004; Orvell, 1999; Potter, 2011). Childlikeness can also be considered a status game. We have seen that it can be advertised, made fashionable (Kinsella, 1995), and related to coolness, which is itself considered an alternative to the adult status system (Belk, Tian, & Paavola, 2010). However, childlikeness cannot be reduced to a social game only. An extreme example is ageplay, that is, adults roleplaying being a different age (Rulof, 2011). Usually, ageplay involves adults taking on the role of children by acting physically, mentally, or/and emotionally like children. Viewed by the medical community as a paraphilic disorder totally unrelated to pedophilia (Aggrawal, 2008; Doshi, Zanzrukiya, & Kumar, 2018), ageplay is hardly tolerated in our societies. Yet, in a survey of almost 2,000 male and female members of an ageplay community (i.e., ABDL community—Adult Baby and Diaper Lover), Zamboni (2018) concludes that many age role-players are comfortable with their practices and do not require therapy. Illustrative of this gap between ageplayers' and society's attitudes toward this practice, one can easily find online communities of ageplayers in many U.S. cities. Several Amazon pages sell related books, but there is only one brick-and-mortar store in the USA (Michelson, 2017). Even some ordinary childlike activities like fandom, cosplay, and furry communities remain socially unacceptable in the eyes of many adult consumers (Alemany Oliver, 2015; Kozinets, 2001; Seregina & Weijo, 2016). This sometimes leads Childlikes to remain hidden or create dedicated enclave communities in which they can be true to themselves (Healy & Beverland, 2013, 2016).

### Society—Polymorphously Perverse Relationships

Under the influence of seduction and in the absence of well-developed socialization, young children find undifferentiated sexual pleasure from any part of their bodies but also from a large variety of external objects: They become polymorphously perverse (Freud, 1905). In Freud's (1905) view, sexuality covers much more than genital heterosexuality and includes anything that can help in achieving pleasure. In adulthood, people can display the characteristics of a polymorphously perverse mind, for instance, by desacralizing sexual intercourse, having virtual sex, or, as with some Japanese, having no sex life at all (Bosker, 2014; Demetriou, 2011). Marcuse (1955), drawing on the Marxist concept of freedom from alienation, invited people to be more open to sexual experimentation and more polymorphously perverse. According to Marcuse (1955), we must accept the regression involved in the reactivation of erotogenic zones since pleasure is the authentic expression of being-in-the-world. In this context, the pleasure principle is no longer dominated by the reality principle and the logic of production. Instead, it is supplanted by the logic of exploration, in which sexuality becomes an end in itself that allows consumers to step aside from the domination of the performance principle. Drawing on Foucault's (1976) work on sexuality while keeping to the general Freudian view of sexuality as any form of stimulation that helps to achieve pleasure, we can see how mass consumption cultures have institutionalized sexuality as they have also furthered the control, shaping, and commodification of sexuality and desire. Such a commodification of sexuality and desire is visible through consumer socialization around the logic of instant and polymorphous gratification that extends to consumer childlikeness. With the help of an information-based economy, marketplaces reduce the waiting time to provide immediate gratification. For example, many companies today provide a 24/7 chat service, online sales, and e-mail auto-responses. *Amazon* sometimes offers customers the digital version of the first few sections of the book they have just bought to make the time they have to wait for the hard copy more bearable. The website *Booking.com* offers a city guide after an online reservation is made, and some brands like *Ray-Ban* allow consumers to virtually try on their products.

In the context of high individualism that childlikeness may represent, this instant and polymorphous environment of gratification is likely to influence the quantity and quality of Childlikes' relations to others, with more and more short interactions being deprived of involvement. Selman (1980) calls the stage that corresponds to momentary physical interaction, like when children gather with nearby playmates, the level zero of friendship. In this stage, children decide who else may or may not play in order to keep things their way, and they do not try to understand each other. All that matters is to have fun and play. A very recent example is the app *LegalFling*, which records sexual consent in a legally binding agreement. In a sense, this app contributes to the acceptance and playfulness of lust without shame. It symbolically legitimizes the idea that society has the right to have pleasure *for the sake of* pleasure and not commitment or reproduction (Blackburn, 2004). This app codifies a momentary physical interaction based on polymorphous perversity, where playmates are just here to have fun through superficial and apathetic relationships. It also shows a highly developed form of commodification of people who are less game partners than objects with a precise role: contributing to one's own pleasure without being disturbed. Regarding digital consumption and virtual groups, Turkle (1995) suggests that a connected society looks for intense but short moments of pleasure without any true involvement. Another view shared by Turkle (2011), which is related to Selman's (1980) level zero of friendship, is people's need to feel in control and omnipotent, which is associated with a disengagement in relationships and leads to *being alone together*. An example that illustrates this level zero of friendship is Bardhi and Eckhardt's (2012) study of Zipcar consumers who engage in opportunistic behaviors and negative reciprocity without collaborating with other Zipcar participants.

Polymorphous gratification is particularly visible in consumers' play with products that are becoming more ludic. While describing the particular relationship that Americans can sometimes have with their possessions, Brown (2003) wonders

> Why do you find yourself talking to things—your car, your computer, your refrigerator? Do you grant agency to inanimate objects because you want to unburden yourself of responsibility? Or because you need to mark how overwhelmed you are by your material environment? Or is it simply because you're lonely? Because, unlike a child, you don't have a toy to talk with? (p. 12)

Today, more and more brands like Tesla and Apple display a childlikeness mentality by *toyifing* objects (Noxon, 2006) and providing consumers with a toy that they can talk to and can even be given agency and responsibility. Writing about Japanese technological toys, Allison (2006) considers polymorphously perverse pleasure key to the appeal of Japanese play products and the construction of fantasy. She also notes the relationship between capitalism, Japanese Shinto-influenced techno-animism, and polymorphous perversity:

> Key here are the two qualities of polymorphous perversity (continual change and the stretching of desire across ever-new zones/bodies/products) and techno-animism (the forefronting of technology that is animated into spirits, creatures, and intimacies of various sorts). What emerges is a fantasy of perpetual transformation (humans who morph into Rangers, icons that "grow" into virtual pets) that, extended into the cyberfrontier, promise (New Age) companionship and connectedness albeit in a commodity form. Resonant with the fluctuation, fragmentation, and speedup facing postindustrial youth across the world, such a fantasy also becomes addictive, compelling players to keep changing and expanding their play frontiers through a capitalism of endless innovation, information, and acquisition. (Allison, 2006, p. 277)

Similar sorts of interpretations have been offered regarding the appeal of Japanese science fiction and anime (Bolton, Csicsery-Ronay, & Tatsumi, 2007). As Turkle (2011) reminds us, intelligent electronic devices are humans' closest neighbors today. As the example of cyborgs illustrates very well, both subject and object vanish or merge in an age of advanced technology. Human beings are reduced to flexible raw materials and, as machines, are increasingly composed of exchangeable pieces (Zimmerman, 2000). In this context, we get fully interpellated within technologies and behave according to the requirements of technology instead of being autonomous, self-conscious agents (Zimmerman, 2000). In this view of a society that makes human interactions look like level zero of childhood friendships and considers non-human others to be our closest neighbors, consumers' search for authenticity might well be found through technology. As illustrated in Spike Jonze's film *Her* or the Swedish TV series *Äkta Människor* (*Real Humans*), machines sometimes seem to care more about us than anyone else does. While Kelts's (2006) book on Japanese pop culture suggests that technology will play a more and more decisive role in Japanese relationships, we can already see Japanese consumers starting to engage with their robots. Kahn et al. (2010) even suggest the possibility of being deeply, psychologically intimate with robots in the future. Sex with robots is also emerging as an incentive to adopting robotics, just as pornography was to the more widespread usage of VHS tapes, CDs, DVDs, and the Internet (e.g., Levy, 2007; Scheutz, 2012; Yeoman & Mars, 2012). Since consumers can find flavors of authenticity in childlikeness, the next step may be the era of robots because they represent, in a way, blank slates that cannot be influenced by society. Moreover, for the moment, creating robots gives consumers the ability to shape them as works of art (Foucault, 1982) and, therefore, provide the experience of authenticity experienced by craftspeople (Bergadaà, 2008).

—

We hypothesized that childlikeness is expressed by a view of nature that is idealized, apart from culture and civilization, and reachable by reliving what we believe we have already experienced in childhood. This is premised on seeing childhood as our closest moment to a state of nature. Regarding the self, we have proposed that the Childlikes are searching for an authentic self that can be attained through therapeutic narratives, myths of wilderness, and other experiences that make it possible to set us apart from civilization. This is especially the case when we see these experiences getting us closer to the unsocialized child that is, therefore, considered as original and pure. Finally, childlikeness may be expressed in views that treat people as commodified game partners who contribute to our own pleasure without really having to engage with them. These more individualistic interactions are close to what Selman (1980) calls the level zero of friendship in children and are visible in adults through their need to feel in control and omnipotent, which eventually leads them to disengaged relationships (Turkle, 2011).

## Possible Implications for Consumer Behavior Theory and Research: A Discussion

Based on the different collective perceptions, constructions, and applications of childlikeness (suggested in the first section of this chapter), as well as the assumptions about nature, the self, and society that reflect childlikeness (suggested in the second section of this chapter), we now pay attention to the right-hand side of Figure 1: the implications for consumer and marketing practices. First, we suggest that childlikeness echoes a more impulse-oriented and unsocialized view of self-authenticity, which leads to simpler mechanisms and processes of authentication in which instincts and desires are celebrated. Second, we propose that the adolescent figure symbolizes a critical liminal moment during which it is still possible to relinquish oversocialized adulthood while retaining the child's purity and non-socialized traits. In this view, Childlikes are likely to follow the adolescent figure and enter liminoid spaces of consumption in which they renegotiate time and identity for the benefit of the authentic self. Finally, we consider future constructions of adulthood, especially if robotization provides adults with as much time to play as children have.

### Processes and Mechanisms of Authentication

Childlike consumption may represent what some call an authenticating act (Abrahams, 1986; Arnould & Price, 2000), that is, the expression of the "true self, our individual existence, not as we might present it to others, but as it 'really is,' apart from any roles we play" (Handler, 1986, p. 3). In this context, what are the conditions for this act to be successful? Do the Childlikes use particular processes and mechanisms? Arnould and Price (2000) suggest that authenticating consumers can either produce their own objects or customize them in accordance with self-narratives. Moreover, they speculate that the intrinsic valuing of action, spontaneity, and feelings of uniqueness and surprise favor the production of authenticating acts.

These enabling orientations fit with childlikeness and the idea that identity is defined no longer by material possessions and social position but by creative and active participation in life and the production of objects and experiences. This view echoes previous research on consumers' quest for authenticity that underlines how authenticity is constructed through consumption practices, regardless of whether these practices are mental or physical (Belk & Costa, 1998; Beverland & Farrelly, 2010; Rose & Wood, 2005). In saying this, these authors underline that it is not the object that makes consumers feel authentic but the consumers themselves through their actions. It is the goal of motivating consumption that reveals the authenticity of a product or person. Also, it is important to note that products' inauthenticity does not necessarily have an impact on the authenticity of an experience or, in a larger sense, the self (Crăciun, 2014). One can consume replicas, narratives, or replicas of replicas and narratives of narratives and yet be in the middle of an authenticating act. This echoes Turner and Schutte (1981), who argue that authenticity is an affective, phenomenological experience and that it can be more important to feel that something (or someone) is authentic rather than to know whether it is (or they are) actually authentic or not. In this context of consumers' active participation in the production of authenticating acts, Childlikes' abilities to easily enter the realm of magic, the imaginary, and play might facilitate the authenticating process even more. Like a child playing with a plastic toy and using magical thinking and imagination to reinvent the object, consumers can find authenticity through replicas because they actively participate in understanding and exploring themselves and others (Miller, 1987). For instance, replica guitars can trigger authenticating acts by letting the players live out their private fantasies and thereby experience self-transformation (Fernandez & Lastovicka, 2011). Cosplayers use costumes and other replica accessories to freely live out their fantasies (Kozinets, 2001; Seregina & Weijo, 2016). Or a Moleskine notebook—a replica of earlier artists' notebooks covered in faux leather—can help users craft and explore their identities (Alexis, 2017).

The research referenced in the previous paragraph suggests that consumers plan authenticating acts and develop a priori narratives about them. In contrast to this idea, childlikeness can also underline a certain absence of self-consciousness in consumers in the sense that we intellectualize our actions and feelings not necessarily by relating them to the self but by relating to them through a more immediate search for pleasure, the avoidance of pain, and other more instinctive behaviors. This echoes the more impulse-oriented and unsocialized view of self-authenticity that stresses how abandoning institutional routines "in order to do only what one wants to do, just because one wants to do it," can help us discover our authentic self (Turner & Schutte 1981, p. 12). For example, people can recognize their authentic self in their experience of undisciplined desire (Turner, 1976). This absence of intellectualization is also close to the social construction of "primitive" thought. Speaking of primitive and prelogical thinking as Lévy-Bruhl (1910) did is, as Douglas (1975/2003, p. 108) says, "unfortunate" and connotes negativity despite Lévy-Bruhl's attempts to explain himself (he later replaced "prelogical" with "magical"). However, "the general problem [that Lévy-Bruhl underlines] still stands" (Douglas, 1975/2003, p. 108). Moreover, it may partially explain why childlikeness and primitive thought can be associated with each other in consumers' minds and facilitate feelings of authenticity. As we have seen, savagery or primitivism is a social construct that "can be—has been, will be—whatever Euro-Americans want it to be" (Torgovnick, 1990, p. 9). In other words, the needs of the present eventually shape the primitive figure, and primitive thought only denotes the modes of thought that are not central to our societies but common to all cultures. As long as so-called primitive thought is circumvented by "we, the civilized," who "sort matters out analytically," unlike "they, the savage," who "wander about in a hodgepodge of concrete images, mystical participations, and immediate passions" (Geertz, 1983/2000, p. 148), primitive thought will represent our true, authentic mode of thinking, which has not been domesticated. Similarly, childlikeness represents impulsive behaviors and non-rational modes of thinking that are still excluded from Western ideal practices. By concentrating these non-rational modes of thinking, childlikeness not only provides feelings of authenticity but also decenters Cartesianism by considering it as one historically and culturally particular mode of thinking among many others that is not always relevant when living a more hedonistic life. In a way, consumer childlikeness de-complexifies primitive thinking by displaying it without shame and challenging the so-called civilized Cartesianism. This is particularly visible in a consumer society, where consumers have used magical thinking and have embraced experiential consumption (Holbrook & Hirschman, 1982; St. James, Handelman, & Taylor, 2011).

While marketing and consumer research use dominant thinking processes and, thus, often put forward, for example, ways that consumers paradoxically deal with authenticity and inauthenticity (Chalmers & Price, 2009) or incoherent ideologies and identities, a possible alternative view is that childlikeness represents a contemporary form of primitivism that goes against dominant rational thought and its underlying mechanisms and processes. In this view, the Childlikes do not deal systematically with paradoxes because they do not really care about finding coherence. Like informants sometimes say to the researcher, we behave in a particular way *because we like it, because it is fun* (Holbrook & Hirschman, 1982). Sometimes there is no need to rationalize consumers' thinking more than necessary and search deeper than these motivations. While childlikeness can surely be associated with elaborated mechanisms and processes of authentication, as Arnould and Price (2000) suggest, it can also stress simpler mechanisms and processes involving instincts and desires. This forgetting of one's self might be what constitutes a basic form of authenticity: the idea is that the more we intellectualize the self, the less authentic it becomes.

## The Adolescent Figure and Liminoid Consumption Spaces

We stated in the introduction that prolonged adolescence reveals a growing social acceptance of childlikeness in our cultures. In many respects, the adult construction of the adolescent journey is similar to the Childlikes' search for an authentic self. For instance, it is seen as a moment when one should connect who one really is with how one appears in society while avoiding role confusion (Erikson, 1950). In both situations, the main existential issue remains the same, that is, how to preserve agency to be ourselves once we enter stifling social structures that eventually turn us into *das Man* (Heidegger, 1927). Both the Childlike and the adolescent might represent this common wish to resist social structures and better dedicate themselves to self-fulfillment projects. This is exemplified in their common fascination with the primitive and the wilderness, which is stronger in times of identity confusion (Torgovnick, 1990; 1997) and often likened to moments of in-betweenness (liminality) and becoming (Turner, 1974). Thrust into a society that idealizes childhood and makes adulthood a disenchanted period of life (Bauman, 2005), adolescence became a privileged life period in the 20th century (Ariès, 1960). In literature, popular works such as *Alice in Wonderland* (Carroll, 1865), *Peter Pan* (Barrie, 1911), *The Wonderful Wizard of Oz* (Baum, 1900), and *The Little Prince* (Saint-Exupéry, 1943) have underlined this difficult passage from childhood to adulthood and the idea of adulthood as being corrupt. What potentially makes the adolescent such an appealing figure to the Childlikes is that it symbolizes a privileged state in which people can benefit from the extension of childhood into an adult world that is open to them but without having to deal with its responsibilities and social imperatives (yet). If actual adolescence is far from this idealized adolescence and much more complex, "the average person . . . feels that this period [i.e., adolescence] is the time of one's life when one is carefree and has no responsibilities" (Côté & Allahar 1996, p. 107). Teen movies often depict adolescence as a life period when one is still allowed to defy authority, institutions, and civilization at large while simultaneously enjoying the rights and vices of adulthood—for example, by driving, traveling alone, drinking, smoking, or having sex (Boutang & Sauvage, 2011). These movies contribute to the creation of a defined and hermetic space in which adult conventions are rejected and the pleasure principle is widely followed. In some respects, this space is related to what Bey (1991) calls a temporary autonomous zone (TAZ): a territory in which people evolve in a totally free environment. These delimited and autonomous moments and spaces of freedom can also be understood as liminal states, moments when people are "neither here nor there . . . betwixt and between the positions assigned and arrayed by law, custom, convention, and ceremonial" (Turner 1969, p. 95). To many (e.g., Drenten, 2014; van Gennep, 1909; Waller, 2009), adolescence is a characteristic of this moment of in-betweenness and becoming. It was constructed as a moment charged with rituals through which children become adults. Therefore, in our current Western societies that privilege childhood, adolescence represents a pivot point from which the child who transforms into a corrupted adult will not be able to turn back. In this view, adolescence symbolizes the last chance to remain as free and authentic as the child is supposed to be.

Behind the media and marketing portrayal of this adolescent lifestyle (Noxon, 2006; Porterfield, Polette, & Baumlin, 2009), we suggest that it is the liminal state provided by adolescence, as well as the possible re-enactment of this liminal state through consumption, that the Childlikes covet. As we have seen above, polymorphous perversity partly nurtures a fantasy of perpetual transformation (Allison 2006) that can be made possible through liminality. Liminal states are likely to be triggered by the marketplace, which makes consumers want to linger in them as long as possible (Koops & Zuckerman, 2003). As Turner (1974, p. 86) writes, "bars, pubs, some cafés, social clubs, etc." constitute "permanent liminoid settings" that help individuals reach individual freedom and self-perfection. The marketplace can use the myth of adolescence and the mechanism of liminality to offer consumers the opportunity to experience this feeling of omnipotence again by being neither here nor there (Turner, 1969), neither adult nor child, socialized enough yet still wild enough to use and play with cultural narratives and imagine all sorts of futures and means of self-achievement (see chapter III by Alemany Oliver & Wilkinson). Succumbing to the marketed sirens of perpetual adolescence and youth may contribute to entering liminal moments during which one is not bounded by the child/adult frontier but, on the contrary, evolves in a no man's land that gives permission thanks to the absence of society. Ironically, this suspension of social norms and values offered by marketed liminality can help consumers feel freer and closer to their "authentic" selves, insofar as brands can market a standardized narrative of authenticity that eventually keeps consumers away from genuine authenticity.[60] The importance of these liminoid spaces in the marketplace seems all the more plausible since Western societies have moved into identity societies in which people try less and less to reach specific socially sanctioned goals in life. Instead, they are searching more and more for identities and roles that they hope will eventually reveal their true nature (Giddens, 1991; Glasser, 1972).

The ambiguity and the uncertainty of liminality deconstruct hierarchies and liberate people from socially defined roles and statuses (Turner & Turner, 1978). Therefore, liminality potentially offers consumers a moment outside the structures that regulate social life and facilitates non-fixation and role play within a quest for authenticity. This is visible, for instance, in the mountain men rendezvous (Belk & Costa, 1998), where participants evolve in a bounded space from which they experience personal transformation outside the ordinary structures regulating social life. In the case of childlikeness, the myth being consumed is not that of the mountain man but that of childhood; it is a myth offering symbols such as purity (i.e., unsocialized), spontaneity, and playfulness with which to authenticate oneself. The strength of the childhood myth, as we have emphasized, is its low temporal distance, as all of us believe that we have once already lived the myth for real by being children. We also believe that we can experience it again, especially at a moment when consumer culture promotes youth and life as an experience that knows no age boundaries. This renegotiation of the meaning of time makes it seem that there is a preference for a more aionic (vs. chronological) experience of time that was, as we have seen, associated with childlikeness in the ancient Greco-Roman world. Deleuze (1969) sees this aionic experience of time as the extra-temporality of an ideal present, the time for pure instants that open up unlimited futures. In the same vein, Bauman (2007), Bertman (1998), and Maffesoli (2000) underline how consumers and people at large embrace a culture of the *here and now* that gives power to instant gratification and makes life the sum of eternal instants. To Maffesoli (2000), this culture is pervaded by the mythological figure of the eternal child, who contributes to a re-enchantment of the world.

**Reconstructing Adulthood**

Most scientific research in the social sciences deals with adult subjects. And yet, we seldom explicitly conceptualize or consider this taken-for-granted life stage. As we have implicitly underscored in this chapter, adults are conceived as representatives of a higher authority because of the rational-legal and traditional statuses of domination that they occupy. From ancient times to the present day, adulthood has been the moment of maturity and independence dedicated to citizenship—that is, having rights in and responsibilities toward society and the community. The concept of citizenship and the related concept of responsibility are deeply rooted in what Blatterer (2007) calls a "standard adulthood," which is still in force in Western societies. For instance, markers

---

[60] For existentialists, authenticity is not a given, predefined self waiting to be discovered.

of adulthood, as well as rituals of transition, remain close to the modern conception of adulthood: Adulthood happens when we have left our parents' home, graduated from or left school, gotten married, had a child, and become financially independent (Furlong & Cartmel, 2007; Furstenberg et al., 2004). However, these markers are increasingly being altered or delayed in both Western and Eastern countries (Allison, 2013; Goldscheider & Goldscheider, 1993; Tian, 2016). Adulthood appears to be close to what Beck (2001) calls a zombie concept: one that is still routinely in use even though it is no longer relevant or meaningful.

One possible scenario is that the legitimization of childlikeness—through its promotion by marketing actors—can enable society to find a legitimate structure, namely the market, from which to reterritorialize adulthood by including more childlikeness. This would allow adults to maintain their rational-legal and traditional Weberian authority and, thus, continue to dominate in an official capacity (Weber, 1922). If we accept this scenario, childlikeness may open up new perspectives and questions about tomorrow's adulthood and its relationship to consumption. For instance, how will the patterns of behavior of tomorrow's consumer adults relate to polymorphous perversity and new technologies? Which rituals related to adulthood transition are likely to appear, transform, or simply disappear? Is childlikeness a mentality that will be favored by specific social classes? And thus, as Weinberger, Zavisca, & Silva (2017) started to investigate, how can social classes possibly influence and facilitate a transition to adulthood if childlikeness becomes a form of cultural capital? If we accept that many jobs will likely be robotized even more than they are today, and consumers in some countries may receive a universal basic income allowing them to increase their leisure time (Ford, 2015; Kaplan, 2015), the role of consumption is a particularly important topic. In this case, what would become of the childhood/adulthood dualism and adults' legitimate authority in a society that has long associated childhood with play and adulthood with work (Wyness, 2012) and eventually sees its adult population having as much time as children to play and learn, and where work is no longer necessary to receive an income? This would lead to societies where production and consumption interpenetrate even more deeply than they already do (Firat & Venkatesh, 1995), while work and play will increasingly overlap. Maciel & Wallendorf (2012) suggest that manual labor undertaken during leisure time can be understood as a marker of social privilege. In this scenario of almost fully robotized production, human work could represent the ultimate practice of the privileged and educated classes. Craftsmanship would then be regarded as art and labor that liberate the self. This post-work society would likely be a post-consumer society, too, in which heavy consumption as we know it would be considered the mark of *enslaved, too domesticated* people and is, therefore, relegated to the lower classes. This is the thesis of Frederick Pohl's (1954) science-fiction story *The Midas Plague*. A preview of this post-consumer society might also be found in voluntary simplicity and the appreciative expression of materialism it relates to (Kramarczyk & Alemany Oliver, 2020). As Arnould (2007) reminds us, voluntary simplicity and other anti-consumption movements that resist the market can often be afforded only by wealthy consumers and, therefore, strengthen social classes. Craig-Lees and Hill (2002) observe that voluntary simplifiers generally have access to wealth and education, along with well-paid jobs. And yet, they spend their leisure time undertaking manual labor whose output replaces objects they simply could have bought. This is all the more possible in individualistic societies in which people strive to reach an authentic self.

### Concluding Remarks

Because the idea that "nobody knows how to be a grown-up anymore" is accepted by an increasing number of adult consumers (Scott, 2014, p. 38), we wrote this chapter to provide a better understanding of the understudied phenomenon of consumer childlikeness and what we define as a hedonistic mentality. At the collective level, we have seen that childlikeness has often been a symbol of humans' best and worst potentialities. Depending on the time and place, childlikeness is associated with an as yet unsocialized state, the pleasure principle, weakness, and savagery, as well as the pursuit of an authentic self, coolness and cuteness, possibility for change, enchantment, and freedom in a constraining society. Finally, through advertising, brands often display and promote magical thinking, imagination, and playful behavior that appeal to childlikeness while being perfectly suited to capitalist requirements. From these perceptions, constructions, and applications of childlikeness, we speculated about childlikeness' expressions in nature, the self, and society. More specifically, we suggested that childlikeness reflects itself through idealized views about primitiveness in which the figure of the Childlike replaces that of the Noble Savage. Idealization of nature and primitivism are also visible through the quest for an authentic self, which can be reached if we de-socialize ourselves to better listen to our desires and instincts. Additionally, we proposed that childlikeness transforms this same constraining society into a playground in which consumers commodify others and make them game partners. From the perspective of both Childlikes and marketers, society is here to provide pleasure without disturbing or involving Childlikes too much. Finally, we underlined that childlikeness might have consequences for the way consumers seek authenticity if the adolescent figure is followed and given the coming social reconstructions of adulthood in a future world where adults may have as much time to play as children.

In her book *A Consumer's Republic*, Cohen (2004) calls for the revival of a consumers' society, harking back to the post-World War II era in which consumers were also citizens whose main concern was not only "am I getting my money's worth" (Cohen, 2004, p. 397) but also "safeguarding the general good of the nation" (Cohen, 2004, p. 18). Childlikeness might not fit well with this notion of citizenship insofar as it is influenced by the pleasure principle. In the eyes of Mennell (1990), childlikeness indicates a de-civilizing trend in the West that does not reverse the civilizing process but interrupts it in the short term. In a similar manner to that of DeLillo's (1986) *White Noise*, consumers and marketing professionals are perceived here as actors in a society where no one is responsible or in control of anything. It is a society where children are presented as almost more competent and responsible than their parents, and childlikeness is interpreted as a kind of regression that leads consumers to abandon life and dive into a disintegrated society fed by violence and a consume-or-die mentality. In our view, this interpretation of childlikeness remains overly simplistic and pejorative. In times of anxiety, we believe that consumers need to escape not only from the everyday but also to liminal spaces where they feel relatively safe to play with redefined rules and recreate a world of possibilities. In this context, consumer childlikeness appears as a potential means to find such spaces and to absorb the playful and innovative character of these spaces by triggering what Featherstone (1991/2007, p. 58) calls "controlled de-control." Childlikeness illustrates our eternal struggle between the inner and outer worlds—between our idealized true, savage, instinctive nature, on the one hand, and the socialized and technical version of ourselves, on the other hand, which can prevent us from having agency and can suffocate us. Unlike what DeLillo (1986) might suggest, we conclude that consumer childlikeness is not the result of a social failure that necessarily leads to darker ages. As Freud (1908/1995, p. 191) indicates, there is a limit beyond which people "cannot comply [anymore] with the demands of civilization." This is probably why tragedy implies an interplay between order and chaos and leads Apollo and Dionysus to go hand in hand (Nietzsche, 1872). But it is also why childlikeness seldom represents an integral part of a consumer's behavior.

## References

Aaker, J. L. (1997). Dimensions of brand personality. *Journal of Marketing Research, 34*(August), 347-356.

Aboujaoude, E. (2011). *Virtually you: The dangerous powers of the e-personality.* W.W. Norton.

Abrahams, R. (1986). Ordinary and extraordinary experience. In V. Turner & E. Bruner (Eds.), *The anthropology of experience* (pp. 45-73). University of Illinois Press.

Addison, H. (2006). Must the players keep young? Early Hollywood's cult of youth. *Cinema Journal, 45*(Summer), 3-25.

Aggrawal, A. (2008). *Forensic and medico-legal aspects of sexual crimes and unusual sexual practices.* CRC Press.

Alemany Oliver, M. (2015). *A realist(ic) interpretivist approach to childlikeness in consumer research: Neoteny, play, reality, and the reterritorializing adulthood* [Doctoral dissertation, Aix-Marseille Université, IAE Aix]. AMU Campus Library.

Alemany Oliver, M. (2018). L'enfant intérieur, un concept marketing universel? Exploration du concept aux Etats-Unis et en France. *Management International, 23*(1), 56-67.

Alemany Oliver, M., & Wilkinson, L. (2021). The Trickster figure in literature and consumer society narratives: Potentialities and liminality. In M. Alemany Oliver & R. W. Belk (Eds.), *Like a child would do: An interdisciplinary approach to childlikeness in past and current societies.* Universitas Press.

Alexis, C. (2017). The symbolic life of the Moleskine notebook: Material goods as a tableau for writing identity performance. *Composition Studies, 45*(2), 32-54.

Allison, A. (2006). *Millennial monsters: Japanese toys and the global imagination.* University of California Press.

Allison, A. (2013). *Precarious Japan.* Duke University Press.

Aoki, S. (2001). *Fruits.* Phaidon.

Ariès, P. (1960/1962). *Centuries of childhood: A social history of family life.* Vintage Books.

Arnett, J. J. (2000). Emerging adulthood: A theory of development from the late teens through the twenties. *American Psychologist, 55*(May), 469-480.

Arnould, E. (2007). Should consumer citizens escape the market? *The Annals of the American Academy of Political and Social Science, 611*, 96-111.

Arnould, E. J., & Price, L. L. (1993). River magic: Extraordinary experience and the extended service encounter. *Journal of Consumer Research, 20*(June), 24-45.

Arnould, E. J., & Price, L. L. (2000). Authenticating acts and authoritative performances: Questing for self and community. In S. Ratneshwar, D. G. Mick, & C. Huffman (Eds.), *The why of consumption: Contemporary perspectives on consumer motives, goals, and desires* (pp. 140-163). Routledge.

Barber, B. R. (2007). *Consumed: How markets corrupt children, infantilize adults, and swallow citizens whole.* Norton.

Barcan, R. (2004). Regaining what mankind has lost through civilisation: Early nudism and ambivalent moderns. *Fashion Theory, 8*(1), 63-82.

Bardhi, F., & Eckhardt, G. M. (2012). Access-based consumption: The case of car sharing. *Journal of Consumer Research, 39*(December), 881-898.

Barrie, J. M. (1911/2004). *Peter Pan.* The Modern Library.

Baudrillard, J. (1970/1998). *The consumer society: Myths and structures.* Sage.

Baudrillard, J. (1981/1994). *Simulacra and simulation.* University of Michigan Press.

Baum, F. (1900/1996). *The wonderful wizard of Oz.* Dover.

Bauman, Z. (1996). From Pilgrim to Tourist—Or a Short History of Identity. In S. Hall & P. du Gay (Eds.), *Questions of cultural identity* (pp. 18-36). Sage.

Bauman, Z. (2004). *Identity.* Polity.

Bauman, Z. (2005). *Liquid Life.* Polity.

Bauman, Z. (2007). *Consuming Life.* Polity.

Beck, U. (2001). Interview with Ulrich Beck. *Journal of Consumer Culture, 1*(July), 261-277.

Belk, R. W. (1994). Carnival, control, and corporate culture in contemporary Halloween celebrations. In J. Santino (Ed.), *Halloween and other festivals of death and life* (pp. 105-132). University of Tennessee Press.

Belk, R. W. (2000). May the farce be with you: On Las Vegas and customer infantilization. *Consumption Markets & Culture, 4*(2), 101-124.

Belk, R. W. (2001). Specialty magazines and flights of fancy: Feeding the desire to desire. In A. Groeppel-Klein & F.-R. Esch (Eds.), *European Advances in Consumer Research - Vol. 5* (pp. 197-202). Association for Consumer Research.

Belk, R. W. (2013). Extended self in a digital world. *Journal of Consumer Research, 40*(October), 477-500.

Belk, R. W. (2014). Objectification and anthropomorphism of the self: Self as brand, self as avatar. In S. Brown & S. Ponsonby-McCabe (Eds.), *Brand Mascots* (pp. 19-34). Routledge.

Belk, R. W., & J. Costa (1998). Modern mountain men: A contemporary consuming fantasy. *Journal of Consumer Research, 25*(December), 218-240.

Belk, R. W., Ger, G., & Askegaard, S. (2003). The fire of desire: A multisited inquiry into consumer passion. *Journal of Consumer Research, 30*(September), 326-351.

Belk, R. W., Tian, K., & Paavola, H. (2010). Consuming cool: Behind the unemotional mask. In R. W. Belk (Ed.), *Research in Consumer Behavior - Vol. 12* (pp. 183-208). Emerald.

Bergadaà, M. (2008). Craftsmen of art, and their craft: The experience of authenticity and its materialization in the places where craftspeople and enlightened clients meet. *Recherche et Applications en Marketing, 23*(September), 5-24.

Bernardini, J. (2014). The infantilization of the postmodern adult and the figure of kidult. *Postmodern Openings, 5*(June), 39-55.

Bertman, S. (1998). *Hyperculture: The human cost of speed.* Praeger.

Bettelheim, B. (1988). *A good enough parent: A book on child-rearing.* Random House.

Beverland, M. B., & Farrelly, F. J. (2010). The quest for authenticity in consumption: Consumers' purposive choice of authentic cues to shape experienced outcomes. *Journal of Consumer Research, 36*(February), 838-856.

Bey, H. (1991/2011). *T.A.Z.: The Temporary Autonomous Zone, ontological anarchy, poetic terrorism.* Autonomedia.

Blackburn, S. (2004). *Lust.* Oxford University Press.

Blatterer, H. (2007). *Coming of age in times of uncertainty.* Berghahn.

Bloch, M. (1949/1953). *The historian's craft.* Vintage.

Bloch, M., & Febvre, L. (1930). Au bout d'un an. *Annales d'Histoire Economique et Sociale, 5,* 1-3.

Bogost, I. (2006). *Unit operations: An approach to videogame criticism.* Massachusetts Institute of Technology Press.

Bolton, C., Csicsery-Ronay Jr., I., & Tatsumi, T. (Eds.) (2007). *Robot ghosts and wired dreams: Japanese science fiction from origins to anime.* University of Minnesota Press.

Boorstin, D. J. (1962/1992). *The image: A guide to pseudo-events in America.* Vintage.

Bosker, B. (2014, January 21). Meet the world's most loving girlfriends — Who also happen to be video games. *The Huffington Post.* http://www.huffingtonpost.com/2014/01/21/loveplus-video-game_n_4588612.html.

Boutang, A., & Sauvage, C. (2011). *Teen Movies.* Vrin.

Boyle, D. (2004). *Authenticity: Brands, fakes, spin and the lust for real life.* Harper.

Brooks, D. (2007, October 9). The odyssey years. *The New York Times.* http://www.nytimes.com/2007/10/09/opinion/09brooks.html, last accessed December 3, 2016.

Brosh, A. (2013). *Hyperbole and a half.* Simon & Schuster.

Brown, B. (2003). *A sense of things: The object matter of American literature.* University of Chicago Press.

Brown, S. (2010). Where the wild brands are: Some thoughts on anthropomorphic marketing. *The Marketing Review, 10*(August), 209-224.

Brown, S. (2011). Show me the mascot: Corralling critters for pedagogic purposes. In R. W. Belk, K. Grayson, A. Muñiz, & H. J. Schau (Eds.), *Research in Consumer Behavior - Vol. 13* (pp. 39-56). Emerald.

Brown, S., & Ponsonby-McCabe, S. (Eds.) (2014). *Brand mascots and other marketing animals.* Routledge.

Brown, S., Kozinets, R. V., & Sherry Jr, J. F. (2003). Teaching old brands new tricks: Retro branding and the revival of brand meaning. *Journal of Marketing, 67*(July), 19-33.

Buckingham, D. (2000). *After the death of childhood.* Polity.

Burke, P. (1990). *The French historical revolution: The Annales School 1929-1989.* Stanford University Press.

Campbell, C. (1987). *The romantic ethic and the spirit of modern consumerism.* Blackwell.

Canniford, R., & Shankar, A. (2013). Purifying practices: How consumers assemble romantic experiences of nature. *Journal of Consumer Research, 39*(February), 1051-1069.

Carroll, L. (1865/1993). *Alice's adventures in Wonderland.* Dover.

Cartier, J. (1535/2000). *Voyages au Canada.* Lux.

Cataluccio, F. M. (2006). *Inmadurez: La enfermedad de nuestro tiempo.* Siruela.

Cavalli, A. (1995). Prolonging youth in Italy: 'Being in no hurry.' In A. Cavalli & O. Galland (Eds.), *Youth in Europe* (pp. 23-32). Pinter.

Cha, J.-H., & Hong, K.-H. (2007). A study on the characteristics and the buying behaviors of kidult fashion purchasers—Kidult fashion emotion and socio-psychological variables. *Journal of the Korean Society of Clothing and Textiles, 31*(9-10), 1373-1383.

Chalmers, T. D., & Price, L. L. (2009). Perceptions of authenticity in advertisements: Negotiating the inauthentic. In A. L. McGill & S. Shavitt (Eds.), *Advances in Consumer Research - 36* (pp. 72-75). Association for Consumer Research.

Cicero, M. T. (-44/1909). *Cato the Elder on old age.* P. F. Collier & Son. Available online at: http://www.bartleby.com/9/2/

Cohen, L. (2004). *A consumers' republic: The politics of mass consumption in postwar America.* Vintage.

Cook, D. (2004). *The commodification of childhood: The children's clothing industry and the rise of the child consumer.* Duke University Press.

Cook, E. E. (2016). Adulthood as action: Changing meanings of adulthood for male part-time workers in contemporary Japan. *Asian Journal of Social Science, 44*(3), 317-337.

Côté, J. E. (2014). The dangerous myth of emerging adulthood: An evidence-based critique of a flawed developmental theory. *Applied Developmental Science, 18*(4), 177-188.

Côté, J. E., & Allahar, A. L. (1996). *Generation on hold: Coming of age in the late twentieth century.* New York University Press.

Cox, R. (1996). *Shaping adulthood: Themes of uncertainty in the history of adult-child relationships.* Routledge.

Crăciun, M. (2014). *Material culture and authenticity: Fake branded fashion in Europe.* Bloomsbury.

Craig-Lees, M., & Hill, C. (2002). Understanding voluntary simplifiers. *Psychology and Marketing, 19*(2), 187-210.

Cronon, W. (1996). The trouble with wilderness, or, getting back to the wrong nature. *Environmental History, 1*(1), 7-55.

Cross, G. (2009). *Kids' stuff: Toys and the changing world of American childhood.* Harvard University Press.

Cross, G. (2002). Valves of desire: A historian's perspective on parents, children, and marketing. *Journal of Consumer Research, 29*(December), 441-447.

Cross, G. (2004). *The cute and the cool: Wondrous innocence and modern American children's culture.* Oxford University.

Cross, G. (2010). *Men to boys: The making of modern immaturity.* Columbia University Press.

Danesi, M. (2003). *Forever young: The teen-aging of modern culture.* University of Toronto Press.

Deighton, J., & Grayson, K. (1995). Marketing and seduction: Building exchange relationships by managing social consensus. *Journal of Consumer Research, 21*(March), 660-676.

Deleuze, G. (1969/1993). *The logic of sense.* Columbia University Press.

DeLillo, D. (1986). *White noise.* Penguin.

deMause, L. (1974/2006). The evolution of childhood. In L. deMause (Ed.), *The History of Childhood* (pp. 1-74). Rowman and Littlefield.

Demetriou, D. (2011, December 11). 'She feels as real as my real girlfriend': Love Plus captures hearts in Japan. *The Telegraph.* http://www.telegraph.co.uk/women/sex/8940765/She-Feels-as-Real-as-My-Real-Girlfriend-Love-Plus-captures-hearts-in-Japan.html.

Derrett, R. (2003). Making sense of how a community's festivals demonstrate a sense of place. *Event Management, 8*, 49-58.

Doshi, S. M., Zanzrukiya, K., & Kuma, L. (2018). Paraphilic infantilism, diaperism and pedophilia: A review. *Journal of Forensic and Legal Medicine, 56*(May), 12-15.

Douglas, M. (1975/2003). *Implicit meanings.* Routledge.

Drenten, J. (2014). The role of market-mediated milestones in negotiating adolescent identity tensions. In R. W. Belk, L. L. Price, & L. Peñaloza (Eds.), *Consumer Culture Theory - Research in Consumer Behavior—15* (pp. 97-122). Emerald.

Duncan, R. M. (1995). Piaget and Vygotsky revisited: Dialogue or assimilation? *Developmental Review, 15*(December), 458-472.

Eco, U. (1990). *Travels in hyperreality*. Harcourt.

Edwards, B. (1998). *Theories of play and postmodern fiction*. Routledge.

Ellis, J. M. (1997). *Literature lost: Social agendas and the corruption of the humanities*. Yale University Press.

Erikson, E. H. (1950). *Childhood and society*. W.W. Norton & Company.

Featherstone, M. (1991/2007). *Consumer culture and postmodernism*. London: Sage.

Febvre, L. (1952/1992). *Combats pour l'histoire*. Armand Colin.

Fernandez, K., & Lastovicka, J. (2011). Making magic: Fetishes in contemporary consumption. *Journal of Consumer Research, 38*(August), 278-299.

Field, N. (1995). The child as laborer and consumer: The disappearance in contemporary Japan. In S. Stephens (Ed.), *Children and the Politics of Culture* (pp. 51-78). Princeton University Press.

Firat, A. F., & Venkatesh, A. (1995). Liberatory postmodernism and the reenchantment of consumption. *Journal of Consumer Research, 22*(December), 239-267.

Ford, M. (2015). *Rise of the robots: Technology and the threat of a jobless future*. Basic Books.

Foucault, M. (1976/1998). *The history of human sexuality: The will to knowledge*. Penguin.

Foucault, M. (1982). The subject and power. In H. L. Dreyfus & P. Rabinow (Eds.), *Michel Foucault beyond structuralism and hermeneutics* (pp. 208–28). University of Chicago Press.

Foucault, M. (1985). *The history of sexuality - Vol. 2. The use of pleasure*. Random House.

Frank, T. (1997). *The conquest of cool: Business culture, counterculture, and the rise of hip consumerism*. University of Chicago Press.

Freud, S. (1905/2000). *Three essays on the theory of sexuality*. Basic Books.

Freud, S. (1908/1995). *Creative writers and day-dreaming*. Yale University Press.

Freud, S. (1923/1990). *The ego and the id*. Norton.

Furlong, A., & Cartmel, F. (2007). *Young people and social change: New perspectives*. Open University Press.

Furstenberger, F. F. Jr, Kennedy, S., McLoyd, V. C., Rumbaut, R. G., & Settersten, R. A. (2004). Growing up is harder to do. *Contexts, 3*(August), 33-41.

Gauchet, M. (1985/1997). *The disenchantment of the world*. Princeton University Press.

Geertz, C. (1973). *The interpretation of cultures*. Basic books.

Geertz, C. (1983/2000). *Local knowledge*. Basic Books.

Gelber, S. (1999). *Hobbies: Leisure and the culture of work in America*. Columbia University Press.

Giddens, A. (1964). Notes on the concepts of play and leisure. *The Sociological Review, 12*(March), 73-89.

Giddens, A. (1991). Modernity and self-identity: Self and society in the late modern age. Stanford University Press.

Gilmore, J., & Pine, B. J. (2007). *Authenticity: What consumers really want*. Harvard University Press.

Glasser, W. (1972). *Identity society*. Harper & Row.

Glassman, M. (1995). The difference between Piaget and Vygotsky: A response to Duncan. *Developmental Review, 15*(December), 473-482.

Golden, M. (2015). *Children and childhood in classical Athens*. Johns Hopkins University Press.

Golding, W. (1954/2003). *The lord of the flies*. Penguin.

Goldscheider, F., & Goldscheider, C. (1993). Whose nest? A two-generational view of leaving home during the 1980s. *Journal of Marriage and the Family, 55*(4), 851-862.

Granot, E., Brashear Alejandro, T. B., & Russell, LT. M. (2014). A socio-marketing analysis of the concept of cute and its consumer culture implications. *Journal of Consumer Culture, 14*(March), 66-87.

Grayson, K. (1999). The dangers and opportunities of playful consumption. In M. B. Holbrook (Ed.), *Consumer value: A framework for analysis and research* (pp. 105–25). Routledge.

Hanawalt, B. A. (1993). *Growing up in medieval London: The experience of childhood in history*. Oxford University Press.

Handler, R. (1986). Authenticity. *Anthropology Today, 2*(February), 2-4.

Harris, P. L. (2000). *The work of the imagination*. Blackwell.

Healy, M. J., & Beverland, M. B. (2013). Unleashing the animal within: Exploring consumers' zoomorphic identity motives. *Journal of Marketing Management, 29*(1-2), 225-248.

Healy, M. J., & Beverland, M. B. (2016). Being sub-culturally authentic and acceptable to the mainstream: Civilizing practices and self-authentication. *Journal of Business Research, 69*(1), 224-233.

Heidegger, M. (1927/2008). *Being and time.* HarperPerennial.

Hendry, L. B., & Kloep, M. (2011). Lifestyles in emerging adulthood: Who needs stages anyway? In J. J. Arnett, M. Kloep, L. B. Hendry, & J. L. Tanner (Eds.), *Debating emerging adulthood: Stage or process?* (pp. 77-104). Oxford University Press.

Heywood, C. (2001). *A history of childhood: Children and childhood in the West from medieval to modern times.* Polity.

Hirschman, E. (1985). Scientific style in the conduct of consumer research. *Journal of Consumer Research, 12*(2), 225-239.

Holbrook, M. B. (2001). Times Square, disneyphobia, hegemickey, the ricky principle, and the downside of the entertainment economy. It's fun-dumb-mental. *Marketing Theory, 1*(June), 139-163.

Holbrook, M. B., Chestnut, R. W., Oliva, T. A., & Greenleaf, E. G. (1984). Play as a consumption experience: The roles of emotions, performance, and personality in the enjoyment of games. *Journal of Consumer Research, 11*(September), 728-739.

Holbrook, M. B., & Hirschman, E. (1982). The experiential aspects of consumption: Consumer fantasies, feelings, and fun. *Journal of Consumer Research, 9*(September), 132-140.

Holt, D. B. (1995). How consumers consume: A typology of consumption practices. *Journal of Consumer Research, 22*(June), 1-16.

Huang, T.-H. (1987). *The records of Ming scholars.* University of Hawaii Press.

Huizinga, J. (1944/1949). *Homo ludens: A study of the play-element in culture.* Routledge.

Ilouz, E. (2008). *Saving the modern soul: Therapy, emotions, and the culture of self-help.* University of California Press.

James, A., Jenks, C., & Prout, A. (1998). *Theorizing childhood.* Polity.

Jhally, S. (1989). Advertising as religion: The dialectic of technology and magic. In I. Angus & S. Jhally (Eds.), *Cultural politics in contemporary America* (pp. 217-229). Routledge.

John, D. R. (1999). Consumer socialization of children: A retrospective look at twenty-five years of research. *Journal of Consumer Research, 26*(December), 183-213.

Joyce, R. A. (2000). Girling the girl and boying the boy: The production of adulthood in ancient Mesoamerica. *World Archaeology, 31*(February), 473-483.

Kahn Jr, P. H., Ruckert, J. H., Kanda, T., Ishiguro, H., Reichert, A., Gary, H., & Shen, S. (2010). Psychological intimacy with robots? Using interaction patterns to uncover depth of relation. In P. Hinds & H. Ishiguro (Eds.), *Proceedings of the 5th ACM/IEEE International Conference on Human-Robot Interaction* (pp. 123-124). IEEE.

Kaplan, J. (2015). *Humans need not apply: A guide to wealth and work in the age of artificial intelligence.* Yale University Press.

Kelts, R. (2006). *Japanamerica: How Japanese pop culture has invaded the U.S.* Palgrave Macmillan.

Kiley, D. (1984). *The Peter Pan syndrome: Men who have never grown up.* Avon Books.

Kim, S., & McGill, A. L. (2011). Gaming with Mr. Slot or gaming the slot machine? Power, anthropomorphism, and risk perception. *Journal of Consumer Research, 38*(June), 94-107.

Kimmel, M. (2008). *Guyland: The perilous world where boys become men.* Harper.

Kinsella, S. (1995). Cuties in Japan. In L. Skov & B. Moeran (Eds.), *Women, media, and consumption in Japan* (pp. 220-254). University of Hawaii Press.

Kiuchi, Y. (2009). Japan. In R. P. Carlisle (Ed.), *Encyclopedia of Play in Today's Society,* (pp. 335-338). Sage.

Kjeldgaard, D., & Askegaard, S. (2006). The glocalization of youth culture: The global youth segment as structures of common difference. *Journal of Consumer Research, 33*(September), 231-247.

Kohan, W. (2015). *Childhood, education and philosophy: New ideas for an old relationship.* Routledge.

Koops, W., & Zuckerman, M. (2003). *Beyond the century of the child cultural history and developmental psychology.* University of Pennsylvania Press.

Kozinets, R. V. (2001). Utopian enterprise: Articulating the meanings of Star Trek's culture of consumption. *Journal of Consumer Research, 28*(June), 67-88.

Kozinets, R. V. (2002). Can consumers escape the market? Emancipatory illuminations from Burning Man. *Journal of Consumer Research, 29*(June), 20–38.

Kozinets, R. V., Sherry Jr., J. F., Storm, D., Duhachek, A., Nuttavuthisit, K., & Deberry-Spence, B. (2004). Ludic agency and retail spectacle. *Journal of Consumer Research, 31*(December), 658-672.

Kramarczyk, J., & Alemany Oliver, M. (2020), Accumulative vs. appreciative expressions of materialism: Revising materialism in light of Polish simplifiers and new materialism. *Journal of Business Ethics,* https://doi.org/10.1007/s10551-020-04628-9.

Lahire, B. (2013). *Dans les plis singuliers du social : Individus, institutions, socialisations.* La Découverte.

Lee, P. C. (2012). *Li Zhi, Confucianism and the virtue of desire.* SUNY Press.

Lee, S. J., & Yoo, T. S. (2007). Study on the consumer characteristic and the facter of goods as well as the type of goods image in kidult fashion goods. *Journal of the Korean Society of Clothing and Textiles, 31*(2), 225-235.

Lévi-Strauss, C. (1949/1969). *The elementary structures of kinship.* Beacon.

Lévi-Strauss, C. (1955/2012). *Tristes Tropiques.* Penguin.

Lévi-Strauss, C. (1962/1966). *The Savage Mind.* University of Chicago Press.

Levy, D. (2007). *Love + sex with robots: The evolution of human-robot relationships.* Harper Perennial.

Lévy-Bruhl, L. (1910/1985). *How natives think.* Princeton University Press.

Li, Z. (2016). *A book to burn and a book to keep (hidden).* Columbia University Press.

Lindholm, C. (2008). *Culture and authenticity.* Blackwell.

Locke, J. (1693/1996). *Some thoughts concerning education and of the conduct of the understanding.* Hackett.

Maciel, A. F., & Wallendorf, M. (2012). Leisure consumption as conspicuous work. In Z. Gürhan-Canli, C. Otnes, & R. Zhu (Eds.), *Advances in consumer research volume 40* (pp. 644-645). *Association for Consumer Research.*

Maffesoli, M. (2000). *L'instant* éternel. Denoël.

Malebranche, N. (1837/1997). *Dialogues on metaphysics and on religion.* Cambridge University Press.

Marcuse, H. (1955). *Eros and civilization.* Beacon.

Martin, B. A. S. (2004). Using the imagination: Consumer evoking and thematizing of the fantastic imaginary. *Journal of Consumer Research, 31*(June), 136-149.

Martin, P. (1985, August 11). Coming soon: TV's New Boy Network. *The New York Times.*

Mary, A. (2014). Re-evaluating the concept of adulthood and the framework of transition. *Journal of Youth Studies, 17*(3), 415-429.

Maynard, M. L, & Taylor, C. R. (1999). Girlish images across cultures: Analyzing Japanese versus US *Seventeen* magazine ads. *Journal of Advertising, 28*(Spring), 39-48.

Maynard, M. L. (2002). Friendly fantasies in Japanese advertising: Persuading Japanese teens through cartoonish art. *International Journal of Comic Art, 4*(Fall), 241-260.

Mazur, J. (2015). Кідлат - як явище постмодернізму. Молодь і Ринок, *7*(126), 143-146.

McVeigh, B. J. (2000). *Wearing ideology: State, schooling and self-presentation in Japan.* Bloomsbury.

Mencius (2003). *Mencius.* Penguin Books.

Mennell, S. (1990). Decivilising processes: Theoretical significance and some lines for research. *International Sociology, 5*(2), 205-223.

Michelson, N. (2017, March 21). Inside the misunderstood world of adult baby diaper lovers. *The Huffington Post.*

Miller, D. (1987). *Material culture and mass consumption.* Basil Blackwell.

Miller, D. (2008). *The comfort of things.* Polity.

Miller, L. (2004). You are doing burikko! Censoring/scrutinizing artificers of cute. In S. Okamoto & J. S. Shibamoto Smith (Eds.), *Japanese language, gender, and ideology: Cultural models and real people* (pp. 148-165). Oxford University Press.

Moisio, R., & Beruchashvili, M. (2010). Questing for well-being at weight watchers: The role of the spiritual-therapeutic model in a support group. *Journal of Consumer Research, 36*(5), 857-875.

Monden, M. (2014). Being Alice in Japan: Performing a cute, 'girlish' revolt. *Japan Forum, 26*(2), 265-285.

Montaigne (de), M. (1580/1993). *The complete essays.* Penguin.

Nietzsche, F. W. (1872/2000). *Basic writings of Nietzsche.* Modern Library.

Noxon, C. (2006). *Rejuvenile: Kickball, cartoons, cupcakes, and the reinvention of the American grown-up.* Three Rivers.

Orvell, M. (1999). *The real thing: Imitation and authenticity in American culture, 1880-1940.* University of North Carolina Press.

Otnes, C., & Scott, L. M. (1996). Something old, something new: Exploring the interaction between ritual and advertising. *Journal of Advertising, 25*(Spring), 33-50.

Pascal, B. (1670/1995). *Pensées.* Penguin.

Patton, G. C., Sawyer, S. M., Santelli, J. S., Ross, D. A.,... Viner, R. M. (2016). Our future: A Lancet commission on adolescent health and wellbeing. *The Lancet, 387*, n°10036, 2423-2478.

Pesce, M. (2000). *The playful world: How technology is transforming our imagination.* Ballentine.

Piaget, J. (1927/1997). *The child's conception of the world.* Routledge.

Piaget, J. (1966/2000). *The psychology of the child.* Basic Books.

Plato (-360). *Timaeus.* Massachusetts Institute of Technology (Internet Classics Archive). Available online at http://classics.mit.edu//Plato/timaeus.html

Pohl, F. (1954). The Midas plague. *Galaxy, 8*(April), 6–58. Available online at: https://archive. org/stream/galaxymagazine-1954-04/Galaxy_1954_04#page/n59/mode/2up

Porterfield, S. F., Polette, K., & Baumlin, T. F. (2009). *Perpetual adolescence: Jungian analyses of American media, literature, and pop culture.* SUNY Press.

Postman, N. (1982/1994). *The disappearance of childhood.* Vintage Books.

Potter, A. (2010). *The authenticity hoax: How we get lost finding ourselves.* HarperCollins.

Poutain, D., & Robbins, D. (2000). *Cool rules: Anatomy of an attitude.* Reaktion.

Price, S. (1989). *Primitive art in civilized places.* University of Chicago.

Quill, L. (2011), The disappearance of adulthood. *Studies in Philosophy and Education, 30*(4), 327-341.

Rose, J. (1984). *The case of Peter Pan or the impossibility of children's fiction.* University of Pennsylvania Press.

Rose, R. L., & Wood, S. L. (2005). Paradox and the consumption of authenticity through reality television. *Journal of Consumer Research, 32*(September), 284-296.

Rousseau, J.-J. (1762/1979). *Emile or on education.* Basic Books.

Rulof, P. (2011). *Ageplay: From diapers to diplomas.* Nazca Plains.

Saint-Exupéry (de), A. (1943/2000). *The little prince.* Harcourt.

Salinger, J. D. (1951). *The catcher in the rye.* Little, Brown and Company.

Sartre, J.-P. (1945/2007). *Existentialism is a humanism.* Yale University Press.

Scheutz, M. (2012). The inherent dangers of unidirectional emotional bonds between humans and social robots. In P. Lin, K. Abney, & G. Bekey (Eds.). *Robot ethics: The ethical and social implications of robotics* (pp. 205-222). Massachusetts Institute of Technology.

Schouten, J. W. (1991). Selves in transition: Symbolic consumption in personal rites of passage and identity reconstruction. *Journal of Consumer Research, 17*(March), 412-425.

Scott, A. O. (2014, September 14). The death of adulthood in American culture. *The New York Times - Sunday Magazine.*

Scott, R., Cayla, J., & Cova, B. (2017). Selling pain to the saturated self. *Journal of Consumer Research, 44*(1), 22-43.

Selman, R. L. (1980). *The growth of interpersonal understanding.* Academic.

Seregina, A., & Weijo, H. A. (2017). Play at any cost: How cosplayers produce and sustain their ludic communal consumption experiences. *Journal of Consumer Research, 44*(June), 139-159.

Singer, D. G., & Singer, J. L. (2005). *Imagination and play in the electronic age.* Harvard University Press.

St. James, Y., Handelman, J. M., & Taylor, S. F. (2011). Magical thinking and consumer coping. *Journal of Consumer Research, 38*(December), 632-649.

Stainton-Rogers, W., & Stainton-Rogers, R. (1992). *Stories of childhood: Shifting agendas of child concern.* University of Toronto.

Steedman, C. (1998). *Strange dislocations: Childhood and the idea of human interiority.* Harvard University Press.

Sully, J. (1896). *Studies of childhood.* Appleton.

Sutton-Smith, B. (1997). *The ambiguity of play.* Harvard University Press.

Sutton-Smith, B. (2003). Play as a parody of emotional vulnerability. In D. E. Lytle (Ed.), *Play and educational theory and practice* (pp. 3-17). Praeger.

Tacitus, C. (98). *Agricola. Germania. Dialogue on oratory.* Harvard University Press.

Thompson, C. J. (2004). Marketplace mythology and discourses of power. *Journal of Consumer Research, 31*(June), 162-180.

Tian, F. F. (2016). Transition to adulthood in China in 1982-2005: A structural view. *Demographic Research, 34*(1), 451-466.

Torgovnick, M. (1990). *Gone primitive: Savage intellects, modern lives.* University of Chicago Press.

Torgovnick, M. (1997). *Primitive passions: Men, women, and the quest for ecstasy.* University of Chicago Press.

Trilling, L. (1972). *Sincerity and authenticity.* Harvard University Press.

Turkle, S. (1995). *Life on the screen: Identity in the age of the internet.* Simon and Schuster.

Turkle, S. (2011). *Alone together: Why we expect more from technology and less from each other.* Basic Books.

Turner, R. H. (1976). The real self: From institution to impulse. *American Journal of Sociology, 81*(5), 989-1016.

Turner, R. H., & Schutte, J. (1981). The true self method for studying the self-conception. *Symbolic Interaction, 4*(Spring), 1-20.

Turner, V. (1969). *The Ritual Process: Structure and Anti-Structure.* Aldine.

Turner, V. (1974). Liminal to liminoid, in play, flow, and ritual: An essay in comparative symbology. *Rice Institute Pamphlet - Rice University Studies, 60*(3), 53–92.

Turner, V. & Turner, E. (1978). *Image and pilgrimage in Christian culture.* Columbia University Press.

Twenge, J., & Campbell, W. K. (2009). *The narcissism epidemic: Living in the age of entitlement.* Free Press.

van Gennep, A. (1909/1960). *The rites of passage.* University of Chicago Press.

Varney, D., Eckersall, P., Hudson, C., & Hatley, B. (2013). *Theatre and performance in the Asia-Pacific: Regional modernities in the global era.* Palgrave Macmillan.

Vygotsky, L. S. (1930/2004). Imagination and creativity in childhood. *Journal of Russian and East European Psychology, 42*(January-February), 7-97.

Vygotsky, L. S. (1978). *Mind in society: The development of higher psychological processes.* Harvard University Press.

Waller, A. (2009). *Constructing adolescence in fantastic realism.* Routledge.

Wang, J., Zhao, X., & Bamossy G. (2009). The sacred and the profane in online gaming: A netnographic inquiry of Chinese gamers. In N. Wood & M. Solomon (Eds.), *Virtual social identity and consumer behavior* (pp. 109-123). Sharpe.

Warren, C., & Campbell, M. (2014). What makes things cool? How autonomy influences perceived coolness. *Journal of Consumer Research, 41*(2), 543-563.

Warren-Crow, H. (2014). *Girlhood and the plastic image.* University of New England Press.

Weber, M. (1922/1978). *Economy and society.* University of California Press.

Weightman, F. (2008). *The quest for the childlike in seventeenth-century Chinese fiction: Fantasy, naivety and folly.* Edwin Mellen.

Weinberger, M., & Wallendorf, M. (2012). Intracommunity gifting at the intersection of contemporary moral and market economies. *Journal of Consumer Research, 39*(June), 74-92.

Weinberger, M., Zavisca, J., & Silva, J. (2017). Consuming for an imagined future: Middle-class consumer lifestyle and exploratory experiences in the transition to adulthood. *Journal of Consumer Research, 22*(August), 332-360.

Winnicott, D. W. (1971/1982). *Playing and reality.* Routledge.

Wrong, D. H. (1961). The oversocialized conception of man in modern sociology. *American Sociological Review, 26*(April), 183-193.

Wyness, M. (2012). *Childhood and society.* Palgrave Macmillan.

Yeoman, I., & Mars, M. (2015). Robots, men and sex tourism. *Futures, 44*(4), 365-371.

Zamboni, B. D. (2018). Partner knowledge and involvement in adult baby/diaper lover behavior. *Journal of Sex and Marital Therapy, 44*(2), 159-171.

Zelizer, V. A. (1985). Pricing the priceless child: The changing social value of children. Princeton University Press.

Zimmerman, M. E. (2000). The end of authentic selfhood in the postmodern age? In M. A. Wrathall & J. Malpas (Eds.), *Heidegger, authenticity, and modernity: Essays in honor of Hubert L. Dreyfus* (pp. 123-148). Massachusetts Institute of Technology Press.

Zornado, J. L. (2001). *Inventing the child: Culture, ideology, and the story of childhood.* Garland.

# Chapter VII

# From Playborers and Kidults to Toy Players: Adults Who Play for Leisure, Work, and Pleasure[61]

Katriina Heljakka

**Figure 1. How many kidults can you see engaged in play in the sprinkle pool at the Museum of Ice Cream, San Francisco?**

In the Christmas 2018 advertising campaign of a well-known Finnish supermarket chain, adults were shown practicing playing with children's toys. The slogan of the imaginary play university, which served as a teaching facility, reflected the significance of play for human well-being by stating that "The world is healthy when it plays." While the holiday advertising campaign[62] was running on the screens of Finnish

[61] The author wishes to express her gratitude to The Strong National Museum of Play, where she acted as a Research Fellow in 2017 to explore the Brian Sutton-Smith Library & Archives of Play in search of material on toyification and adult play. She is especially thankful to Christopher Bensch and Julia Novakovic, who provided their kind assistance during and after the many visits to the library and archives in association with her doctoral and post-doctoral research.
[62] "Joulun hittilelut löydät Prismasta" [You'll find Christmas Hit Toys at Prisma] (2019). https://www.youtube.com/watch?v=HkM0jScps_o

television viewers, the customs authority at Vancouver airport asked me about my research topic. After hearing that it is play, the clerk asked, "What is play?"

Traditionally, play is understood as a particular type of leisure activity (Giddens, 1964) that is easy to recognize but often challenging to define or measure. Because "the complexity of play makes it difficult or impossible to define exactly what constitutes play itself" (Lockwood & O'Connor, 2017, n.p.), the best we can do is probably to indicate or illustrate play (Johnson et al., 2015, p. xiii). Moreover, conventional understandings of what constitutes play are largely shaped by personal experiences of play and societal expectations of appropriate spaces and activities for play. Therefore, the "definition of play must rather be broad than narrow" (Sutton-Smith, 1997, p. 218).

Contemporary play may take many forms. It can be solitary or social, embedded in the physical, digital, or imaginative, and engaged in by players of different ages, even between individuals of different generations. To the working adult, play is most often perceived as a form of recreation. Stressful work life may promote apathy and depression, which are widespread in modern life and may have negative consequences for health and work. "In regard to them, play's indirect ability to motivate a zestful life perhaps entitles us to claim for it a restorative function" (Sutton-Smith, 2017, p. 123). Firat and Venkatesh (1997, 1995) compare the concept of play with that of consumption, noting their similarities in relation to the public and private, home and workplace, labor and leisure, and child and adult. Indeed, a great deal of play in the 21st century involves the consumption of various structured play materials and activities. However, at the same time this engagement also manifests as creative and thus productive acts involving handicrafts and technologies. Further, one may play with or without playthings in particular areas dedicated for play or by transforming mundane environments into playgrounds with the help of imagination, props, and peer players.

The aim of this chapter is to present and problematize current understandings of playfulness, play, and playthings in relation to adults in the contexts of pleasure, leisure, and work by arguing that creation, consumption, and production all co-exist in contemporary forms of play as the traditional boundaries between leisure, recreation, and work break down to give space to new perspectives on adult play. This new perspective challenges former simplistic views on adult play as the primary source of "fun morality," according to which "fun, from having been suspect, if not taboo, has tended to become obligatory" (Wolfenstein, 1998, p. 198; Wolfenstein & Leites, 1950). By exploring play as theorized and empirically scrutinized in earlier scholarly perspectives on human development and activities, the chapter aims to arrive at a new view of seeing the contemporary adult not only as a consuming kidult but also as a creative toy player and productive playborer. The theoretical underpinnings of these multidimensional perspectives are grounded in earlier work of play theorists, educationalists, developmental psychologists, sociologists, and the ideas presented by researchers of toy cultures and consumer research.

### Foreword on the Concepts of Play and Playfulness

Play is defined as an activity that is (1) self-chosen and self-directed, (2) intrinsically motivated; (3) guided by rules; and (4) imaginative and conducted in an active, alert, but relatively nonstressed frame of mind (Gray, 2015, p. 125). Any form of play may be investigated by examining its ludic (goal-driven, even competitive) or paidic (open-ended, unstructured) qualities (Caillois, 1961). The relationship between free play and the playing of games is often described, with the difference being that rules condition game play, whereas open-ended play is a more free-form activity without preexisting goals. Homo ludens, the playing human being, engages both in games and open-ended play activities throughout life. Unstructured "free play" and structured game play can merge into free-form play, with the "game-like" regularities and goals characteristic of social activities developing through the interplay between players.

How we understand and value play is largely defined based on how much importance play has been accredited during each period of time. Our attitudes towards play reflect our ideologies, educational backgrounds, and related rhetorics (Russell & Ryall, 2015). For instance, play is particularly respected in cultures that celebrate individualism, creativity, technological innovation, and social resilience. More generally, play exists in and is conditioned by contexts that are psychological, biological, environmental, social, and cultural (Henricks, 2015). Play is ubiquitous in all mammalian orders and other classes of animals and allows them to learn and acquire useful skills to adjust to the world (Bjorklund, 2021, chapter 1 in this volume; Burghardt, 2005). For humans, play is an enjoyable activity in which all age groups engage and is beneficial in many ways. It is simultaneously useless and fun and is crucial for our mental well-being and self-expression. Indeed, play deprivation may have serious outcomes for human health. Stuart Brown lists the consequences of long-term play deprivation for adults as a "lack of vital life engagement, diminished optimism, stuck-in-a-rut feeling about life with little curiosity or exploratory imagination to alter their situation, predilection to escapist temporary fixes . . . alcohol, excessive exercise (or other compulsions), [and] a personal sense of being life's victim rather than life's conqueror" (Brown, 2014, n.p.). However, play is not only useful for human development but is meaningful as well. For instance, Gordon (2014) presents what she describes as the adaptive advantages of play—its necessity in the development of metacommunication, finding meaning in experience, emotional stability, flexibility in identity, creative expression, symbolic representation, the ability to form and communicate narratives, social bonding, and collaboration. These skills significantly impact an individual's well-being and begin to develop at a very early stage (Gordon, 2014). Johan Huizinga (1938/1971), historian and philosopher of play, states that culture itself arises from play.

At this point, and for the sake of clarity, it is worth differentiating play from playfulness. Where playfulness manifests itself as an intrinsic attitude toward the world and is sometimes considered a personality trait (Proyer, 2017), play is something even more. Play is behavior; it is a voluntary, pleasure-driven, and creative interaction with different instruments, people, spaces, and environments and is either interactive with others or interactive with the activity itself (Van Vleet & Feeney, 2015). Interestingly, research on play in adulthood is more scarce than research on playfulness. Despite the belief that play stimulates creativity and promotes the physical, mental, and social well-being of individuals of any age, scholars interested in play tend to approach the phenomenon either exclusively through children's play or by focusing on the playfulness of the young and of adults. Barnett (1990) defines playfulness as a mental propensity to engage in playful behavior that consists of five dimensions—physical spontaneity, social spontaneity, cognitive spontaneity, manifest joy, and sense of humour, and as "the predisposition to frame (or reframe) a situation in such a way as to provide oneself (and possibly others) with amusement, humour, and/or entertainment" (Barnett, 2007, p. 955).

Bundy's Model for Playfulness (1997) suggests that playfulness can be determined within any transaction of the evaluation of three elements: (1) source of motivation (from intrinsic to extrinsic), (2) perception of control (from internal to external), and (3) the suspension of reality (from free to not free). "As play is different from other primary occupations, this model suggests that it may be more important to assess playfulness than the individual's performance" (Bundy, 1997). As the model illustrates, playfulness is a suitable concept when evaluating an individual's predisposition to various phenomena, including play itself. Playfulness is integral to play (Lockwood & O'Connor, 2017) and due to its attitudinal aspect can be encouraged in everybody (Lieberman, 1977), particularly in situations where spontaneity and freedom from evaluation are allowed (Tegano & Moran, 2015).

According to Rubin et al. (1983), playful adults: (a) are guided by internal motivation and are oriented toward process, (b) attribute their own meanings to objects or behaviors and are not bound by what they see, (c) focus on the pretend and seek freedom from externally imposed rules, and (d) are actively involved. However, when it comes to adulthood, actual play seems less permissible than for children (Ariès, 1962). For example, Article 31 of the United Nations Convention on the Rights of the Child (adopted by the General Assembly of the United Nations on November 20, 1989) states that the child has a right to leisure, play, and participation in cultural and artistic activities. No similar declaration exists for adult play. Yet, according to Schylter (1976), adults often have an insatiable need for play. This need might be partly explained by the neotenous nature of humans (see Bjorklund, 2021 in this book). This means we retain the juvenile ability to play from our distant ancestors. Moreover, humans and many other species progress to maturity through acts of play (Henricks, 2015). According to one popular saying, "We don't stop playing because we get older. We get older because we stop playing."[63] "Perhaps the very existence of youth is largely for the sake of play," philosopher and psychologist Karl Groos states (1892, p. 76). Interestingly, the United Nations (2013) distinguishes the free play of children from play that is more directly led by adults and from recreation, such as "functional" activities related to art, sport, or community engagement. Sutton-Smith (1997, p. 7) notes how in Western cultures it is more of a tradition to think that children play, while "adults only recreate." Nevertheless, as Wilson notes, leisure is present in childhood as well; the child engaged in play or daydreaming is by definition leisured (Wilson, 1981). In fact, the world of leisure and the world of childhood cannot be "stronger or more evident than in the sphere and spirit of play" (Wilson, 1981, p. 298). Everyone from children to the elderly enjoy leisure in their own ways, but there has been a reluctance to use the label "play" for adolescents and adults (Barnett & Owens, 2015). Indeed, while children are assigned the role of players, adults are considered workers (Firat & Venkatesh, 1997). Giddens (1964, p. 85) notes this undeniable relationship that adult play has with the occupational sphere of life, stating "Adult play is not psychologically identical with the play of children, since its character is determined partly by its juxtaposition with work."

Adult play has usually been disguised as entertainment, recreational sports, leisure and tourism (Sutton-Smith, 2009; Henricks, 2015), hobbying, or collecting (Rogan, 1998) in order to camouflage play or avoid the stigma associated with adult play (Heljakka et al., 2018). However, the motivation to play in adults seems to be much more complex than a quest for leisurely entertainment or lighthearted amusement, as the functions and meanings of play may range from pure nonsense to deeply existential matters of human life, depending on the situation. As Frappier (1976, p. 179) notes, "all is not lightness and sweetness. Existential dilemmas of possibilities versus limitations crop up naturally in adult play." For adults, play may offer the same psychological functions as it does for children—the possibility to dissipate personal tensions through its cathartic function and to provide the satisfaction of achievement and self-realization (Giddens, 1964). Sutton-Smith (2017, p. 75) believes play performances to form "a different kind of reality" where play represents itself partly as fantastic, and partly as lifelike, mimicking reality. However, he also thinks that

---

[63] The "We don't stop playing" quote is attributed to Benjamin Franklin, Oliver Wendell Holmes (Sr. or Jr.), Herbert Spencer, or George Bernard Shaw but may originate in the work of play theorist Karl Groos' titled *Die Spiele der Thiere* (The Play of Animals, 1896, p. 68), where he writes: "die Thiere spielen nicht, weil sie jung sind, sondern sie haben eine Jugend, weil sie spielen müssen." ("The animals do not play because they are young, but they have a youth because they must play.") For reference, see https://liturgy.co.nz/let-us-play-tag.

play "is seldom a carbon copy of quotidian experience." For example, some kinds of play may serve to provide satisfactions that are denied expression in other activities (Giddens, 1964).

For some adults, playing is an activity that when considered childish could mean judgement from the perspective of other adults (Nicholson & Shimpi, 2015). Ernst Lurker has observed how, when referring to play, "there is a staggering amount of euphemisms used to camouflage this joyful human activity" (Lurker, 1990, p. 147). If the association with immaturity is not enough to affect the undervalued status of play, associating it with enjoyment and uselessness is likely to arouse suspicion (Frappier, 1976). It is precisely this linkage between adult play(fulness) and the non-utilitarian nature of play that presents a problem for many. Supposedly, adults should use their time productively in the spirit of the Protestant Ethic (Weber, 1930; Wilson, 1981). Nevertheless, Giddens notes that there is no reason to start calling it "recreation" rather than "play" (1964). Historically, in fact, Lieberman explains that play has been more an activity of adults than children. During the Middle Ages, the Renaissance, and even the Age of Enlightenment, childhood play not only was minimal within an individual's lifespan but was accorded little importance in human development. She notes that "If play was emphasized—and written and sung about, it was the play of the adult, and particularly the play of the adult in the leisure class" (Lieberman, 1977, pp. 143-144). In modern times, ideas about who is entitled to and has the right to play have shifted towards the early years of human life. Robert E. Neale perceived ambivalence in modern man's attitude towards play in the late 1960s and commented that "Any culture oriented toward work will find play to be incomprehensible and dangerous: a few people will respond favorably to the possibility of play, but many more will respond unfavorably; the vast majority will respond ambivalently" (Neale, 1969, p. 12).

In this way, play is traditionally contrasted to work, but according to psychologist and founder of the National Institute for Play, Stuart Brown (2009), the opposite of play is not work but boredom and depression. Philosopher Bertrand Russell (1996) states that the opposite of boredom is not pleasure but excitement. Caillois classifies play according to four categories—agôn (competition), alea (chance), mimicry (simulation), and ilinx (vertigo). The quest for excitement may be one of the key drivers for adults to engage in play related to competition (e.g., games and sports), chance (e.g., gambling), and vertigo (e.g., amusement park rides). In a similar vein, Alemany Oliver (2015) notes that current times may well be theorized as akin to the search for experiences combining two of Caillois' categories, namely simulation and vertigo. He states that "the simulation-vertigo combination is a time for illusion and disruption with regular perception" (Alemany Oliver, 2015, p. 654). But there are adults whose appetite for play is guided more by experiences that are enabled by creationist practices involving playful objects, environments, and player-generated cultures than by the excitement that stems from gaming, e-sports, or participation in other dynamic spectacles.

This movement away from the competitive forms of play, such as the playing of games, towards the imaginative and more fantasy-driven realm of play becomes visible when considering how adults are positioned and labelled as a particular segment of consumers of play and playful products in the marketplace (kidults) and how playing adults actually create their own cultures around objects traditionally viewed as belonging almost exclusively to childhood (toys).

In what follows, the chapter argues for how playfulness, play, and playthings all come to influence not only the leisured or working adult but consumption, prosumption, and produsage (Toffler, 1971; Bruns, 2008) during playbor, activities that blend elements previously perceived to belong in the separate areas of play and work. These developments are scrutinized in more detail in the following parts of this chapter.

## From Leisure to Playification and Playborers

As we have seen above, adult play has long been relegated in the West to moments spent outside of work as a leisure activity or recreational moment. Illustrative of the leisure economy that arose in the 20th century to let adults play without shame, tourism—considered a form of play, as the tourist becomes a player (Heynders & Van Nuenen, 2014)—is still today one of the most popular forms of adult entertainment. What has changed since the advent of tourism is the current pervasiveness of play in people's lives in a world that uses technology to always become more play-oriented. Perhaps the most notable and studied phenomenon of what Sutton-Smith (1997) calls a ludic era is gamification. Gamification is originally "a process of enhancing a service with affordances for gameful experiences in order to support user's overall value creation" (Huotari & Hamari, 2012). However, gamification today can also employ elements familiar from games to enhance work, with the idea that play is extremely productive for the lives of the playing groups involved (Sutton-Smith, 1986) and therefore promises increased motivation, effectivity, and productivity (see also Fuchs et al., 2014 for a critical perspective on gamification). What has also changed is that play entered the realm of work. Through processes of gamification and more generally playification (Scott, 2012), companies engage in play to increase employee motivation, creativity, and commitment to the organization (Butler et al., 2011), notably through a growing interest in playful physical working environments (De Souza e Silva & Sutko, 2005; West et al., 2017), most prominently at leading global companies such as Google (Koeners & Francis, 2020).

An illustrative example of contemporary forms of adult play activity is found in social media and the sharing of photographs. Enabled by evolving mobile technology, visual play is increasingly practiced in connection with the use of cameras, photo-management services, and the selfie culture. In what some call the post-digital age (Cramer, 2015),[64] photography can also be seen to be associated with a kind of "collection" of sometimes playful experiences. With Pinterest, for example, it is possible to compile various treasure maps and visual guidebooks for a wide variety of hobbies. The adult thus enjoys playing with picture-based cultures and in the company of like-minded people, for example, through Instagram. In this way, the play of adults is both documented and produced as photographs. Playful production cultures are also on display on YouTube, which has been described as the largest showcase of toy cultures of our time, for example, in the form of unboxing videos. Moreover, an adult player seems to be interested in the play activities of peers; spectating and consuming the play of others through audiovisual content has become part of socially shared and communal play of both young and mature players.

Contemporary forms of play, such as sharing photographs on social media, highlight the tendency for play to enter every aspect of a consumer's life but also the realm of production. The productive aspect of play is visible, for instance, in the consumption of fashion, which is considered by some people as a conduit for creative, self-expressive, and resource-intensive play activities related to a variety of dress styles, beauty enhancements, and hairstyles. In this case, homo ludens is also a homo faber—someone who creatively reinvents personal aesthetics by the manipulation of physical appearance. Another area of playful and productive activity that also combines visual and material culture and that has had a recent upsurge in popularity is the so-called "maker culture"—the creative tinkering, customization, and production (including 3D printing) of objects, accessories, and instruments as a form of material play. While consumers-producers have been called prosumers in the field of marketing (Kotler, 1986), the importance of play in prosumption today should

[64] The post-digital condition suggests a move to complete merging of fluid and dynamic flows between the analogue and digital worlds (Cramer, 2015).

rather make us talk of playful prosumption or playbor (i.e., play+labor) (Kücklich, 2005). Playbor highlights how leisurely play itself can become professionalized and production-driven. Sutton-Smith notes how the ability to join or lead the entertainment of others has become a valued and direct form of adaptation. He considers this ability in adults a metaplay function because it involves professionally playing with play (Sutton-Smith, 2017). One example of metaplay is the creation and consumption of "doll dramas" with adult players who transform into playborers and who act both as content creators and game hosts by providing viewers and other players with content created through their own play (Heljakka & Tuomi, 2020). Contemporary doll dramas, which are built up as soap opera-like serial narratives, act as a prime example of how play transforms into playbor via persuasion strategies, such as participation through entertaining content creation, and into consumption through active viewership.

We have so far seen that play has entered the different realms of adult life. Adult play in the 21st century can be both solitary and social in the private and public spheres (work included), but it can also be hybrid, intertwining material tools and physical environments with digital technologies and can be seen as productive activity. Perfectly fitting the capitalist system, gamification and playification processes follow the logic of profits by improving consumer experience and performance at work. In a more subtle way, they also legitimate adult play and childlikeness by making them business partners that are no longer contradictory to work. In such a context, we show in the next section that marketing has given birth to a consumer segment consisting of playful adults, namely kidults.

### Kidults—Labelling the Playful Adult Consumer

In current times, a prolonged childhood is often perceived as the most significant factor explaining adult interest in play. Issues such as age compression (Kurnit, 2009) and infantilization (Barber, 2007) have been highlighted as causing anxiety in both sociology and the toy industry, as the potential anarchy and creative chaos generally associated with childhood play present risks for the responsible adult. Neil Postman argued in the 1990s that children are more like adults, while adults are becoming more like children (Postman, 1994). On one hand, previous literature has expressed how the age of childhood has been shortened (Bernardini, 2014) and has identified the tendency of adults staying younger longer (ASYL) as a counterweight to children, who mature earlier (kids growing older younger or KGOY).[65] Barber (2007) observes that the narrowing differences between children and adults in modern culture is not new. In *No Sense of Place*, Meyerowitz (1985) argues that in modern culture children are becoming more adult-like and adults are becoming more child-like.

The acronym KGOY entered the marketing field in the early 1990s when marketers began to talk about a shift in the behavior of young consumers (Kurnit, 2009). Children's aspirational age has increased, while that of adults has fallen, according to Chudacoff (2007). On the threshold of the new millennium, "preschoolers were beginning to act like kids," as age compression became the new reality among young consumers; as Kurnit states, "They would cast off their preschool toys and adopt play patterns and product requests" (Kurnit, 2009, n.p.).[66]

[65] More recently, this development has, for example, also been coined under the notion of "adulkids," referring to kids that look and behave like adults and who are consuming products such as cosmetics and spa services (see Kalbi, 2018).
[66] Notably, in the same article, Kurnit (2009) revises his drastic view on age compression by stating that in the end, kids still want to be kids. He writes: "Kids growing older younger is now counter balanced by kids staying younger longer (KSYL)."

Hayward (2013) introduced the concept of "life stage dissolution" (and its bi-directional processes of "adultification" and "infantilization"), meaning that it is increasingly difficult for young people to differentiate and disassociate themselves from the generation immediately ahead of them, and vice versa. To exemplify how this trend has been employed by companies operating in the consumer market, Hayward observes how Anglo-American advertising and marketing practices in particular employ themes previously associated with children's culture, such as cartoon tropes. The consequence of the presented life-stage dissolution is that "the postmodern adult is by now characterized by an unprecedented infantilist nature" (Bernardini, 2014, p. 40). This ethos of infantilization has worked to sustain consumer capitalism, which according to some leads to an undesirable social situation. An infantilized person, in many cases a man described as surrounded by inexhaustible entertainment and toys, poses a threat to our civilization (Barber, 2007).

In his posthumous work, Sutton-Smith (2017) considers the existence of adult play and speaks of ludic liberation mainly as an individualistic project and a consumption-related activity. Alemany Oliver (2015, p. 654) highlights the existence of a playful consumer society that allows adult consumers to play without shame and describes the shift from ludic to paidic consumption as a move from "established rules of consumption to spontaneous desire to play with consumption."[67] According to Cross (2008), adult men want to immerse themselves in an adventure that is all about never-ending play, living "an artificial youthness as infinite potentiality" (Bernardini, 2014, p. 48). Whereas this extreme manifestation of the contemporary (male) homo ludens, driven by paidic desires, presents potential risks for performance-oriented Western societies, it also presents lucrative opportunities for the marketplace. These possibilities may be considered under the rubric of "rejuvenated adulthood," as new adulthood is constructed based on understanding play as an integral part of this construct (Alemany Oliver, 2015).[68]

In adulthood, games, sports, and perhaps entertainment more generally seem to be extensions of the play of early childhood (Oatley et al., 2006), but imagination-driven fantasy play is often thought of as childish in the general debate. However, with rejuvenated adulthood, cross-over genres of entertainment seem to have experienced an upswing in popularity among adults in the 2010s. As Morace (2005) points out, the phenomenon of the Forever Kids was reported some time ago by the Future Concept Lab. The trend can be exemplified, for example, by the growing success of cartoon books and films for adults. This trend is visible in how children's literature provides audiences of all ages with adventure narratives (e.g., the Harry Potter series), in how coloring books offer experiences of living in the present and of mindfulness to adults, and in how luxury Christmas calendars containing, for example, miniature cosmetics are increasingly targeted to mature players who wish to be surprised and delighted. As children are assumed to grow and develop faster beyond the reach of companies serving the youth market, adults are reciprocally forming an even more significant group of buyers and consumers for new play experiences, products, and services. According to the Urban Dictionary, "A kidult is an adult that prefers items that society deems are for a younger person. An adult who plays with toys or games." Bernardini states that this figure "is the archetype of an encouraged regression to facilitate the promotion of goods which are only apparently addressed to young people and children" (Bernardini, 2014, p. 41). For example, a case study by Martin and Schouten

[67] According to Alemany Oliver (2015) "Paidic play can be found: beer pong, paintball battles, flea markets, logo parodies, and so forth. These all have a common preference for spontaneity as opposed to organization."

[68] In fact, play can be seen to develop in an even more "ageless" direction. For instance, some play products are today recommended for players of all ages from 5 to 105. Some are even marked with the symbol for eternity, ∞ (Dash, "The original STEM learning robot" by Wonder Workshop. For reference, see https://www.makewonder.com/robots/).

(2014) on minimotos (miniature motorcycles used for racing and originally targeted to children) shows how new markets may also emerge from consumption activity. It has been acknowledged that kidults are consuming play in more varied forms than toys alone (like the aforementioned minimotos); therefore, we next elaborate on toys as a particular area of products understood to attract this consumer market-identified segment.

One of the first signs of interest in kidult players from the industry side was shown by the organizers of the Hong Kong International Toy Fair in January 2013. The theme of the fair focused on adults—"collectors and other toy aficionados." The trend towards "kidult" play was envisioned to present the toy industry with "opportunities of historic proportions" (HKTDC, 2013). As it was stated,

> this target group has plenty of money to spend and expects a very high level of product quality, which is why many companies have already introduced two lines of the same product groups. The products exhibited at the event will include toy cars, collectible dolls, trains and other mechanical toys.

Interestingly, the kidult theme accentuated at the Hong Kong fair concentrated mainly on toy categories that have been seen as male-oriented; action figures, scale models, and magic tricks were chosen to represent what kidults are mainly playing with. Nevertheless, the kidults of today represent both male and female consumers with an interest in character toys, miniature environments, transmedia-related playthings, etc. To exemplify, Hwang (2013) notes how the respondents to a survey stated that 80.4% of the participants had a positive view of the kidult phenomenon. Of the respondents who claimed to be kidults, 50.9% were interested in animation and comic books, 27.6% in plamodels (known in Japan as plastic die-cast models, kits, or similar merchandise), 18.9% in remote control vehicles, 18.2% in character products such as Winnie the Pooh and Hello Kitty, 17.1% in figures and miniatures, and 13.5% in puzzles.

According to Leclerc, Dean, and Cuni (2007), some 50% of all toys sold in the US, the EU, and Japan are consumed by adults. Over £230 per year per person (some 290 euros in 2012) is spent on toys purchased for people over 18, and two thirds of that is spent by men. In the majority of markets, the percentage of traditional toys and games that target adults (population aged 20 and over) remains below 10% (Tansel, 2013). In Japan, however, which is also one of the major sites for new characters and thus character/designer toy development, toys targeted to those over 20 years of age accounted for more than 23% of all traditional toy sales. An NPD Group (an international company specializing in market research and information) study showed there has been a two-thirds increase in the purchase of toys by adults for personal use in the last five years. The market research analysts at the NPD Group observed a 21% increase in 2016 alone. Moreover, the kidult market has been growing rapidly in South Korea (Kalbi, 2018), where the Korea Creative Content Agency has reported that the Korean market for kidults is worth more than one trillion won (US$880 million) as of 2016.

Kidults range across many age categories. Looking at the purchasing power of various age groups, however, the Millennials (18-34-year-olds) account for approximately half of the spending among adults buying toys for themselves, followed by Generation X (35-54-year-olds) at approximately a third. Of the Baby Boomer generation (over 55), 18% buy toys for themselves. Adults without children spend more money on toys for themselves than adults with children and are also more likely to buy on impulse, for instance, when browsing in a toy department (Spielwarenmesse, 2019).

The kidult trend has grown into a notable megatrend accentuated at toy industry-related events, most recently at the Nuremberg International Toy Fair in February 2019, where this consumer group for toys was highlighted as having significant buying potential. Adults playing also means that it is the adults who are paying; they are actively searching for, acquiring, and repeating purchases as returning toy customers and are bringing their toy enthusiastic peers into the growing consumer base. The role of media—and social media in particular—is crucial in highlighting how mature adults who play with toys who are outside the traditional consumer base for toys are growing in number. "If kidults are recognised as their own target group, there are millions of new toy purchasers who are still young at heart and enjoy playing to be reached" (Spielwarenmesse, 2019). According to another toy industry publication, the products that interest the adult consumers do not necessarily belong to established toy lines of big toy companies but are more akin to high-end lifestyle products and are "decorative," "design-oriented," and even "collector's items:"

> Toys 4 Kidults: design-oriented and game-oriented products intended for those who, no longer a child, want to relax by escaping the stress of everyday life or keeping alive a childhood memory. Wooden objects by well-known designers with which to create compositions to keep in the office or at home, building kits from thousands of pieces, tracks of vintage cars, characters and heroes that can occupy a "privileged" place in the home: products for all tastes which for some become decorative or design elements, for other collector's pieces or for other dreams that are realized. (Licensing Magazine, 2019)

While the (toy) market-formulated notion of the kidult attempts to define the adult as a playful consumer, it fails to extend the definition to the cultural significance of the phenomenon, that is, what it means to be a kidult and to grasp the activity beyond purchasing, decorative displaying, or collecting and to connect kidults with the realm of play. Therefore, the conception of kidult must lead to more flexible formulations on adult play. In this chapter, we suggest using the term adult toy player, which more accurately describes the demographic and the sort of plaything being used without compromising play in the equation. Before introducing the profiles of adults as players of actual toys, we illustrate the broad dimensions of the current concept of toys that extends beyond the traditional understandings of artefacts linked to childhood, namely adult "toys," and the tendency to introduce products and services with toy-like characteristics through toyification.

## Adult "Toys" and Toyification

The products used in play, such as games and toys, are historical and material manifestations of play. According to Caillois, toys do not change their form but their social function (Caillois, 1961). "Toys are a barometer of sorts for the culture," argues Mohler (2006, n.p.), meaning that toys are moral and cultural markers of the age. They represent an important aspect of our material culture, as noted by Yrjö Hirn in the early 1900s (1918, p. 7):

> It is hardly possible in our day to write a complete history of civilization without devoting one's own chapter on toys in it; nor did the organization of a complete historical museum take place without giving at least a few cabinets to the objects that illuminate the children's playful occupations. However insignificant toys may seem to insiders in the opinion of chroniclers, they have begun to attract more attention from recent research.[69]

Anthropologists, economists, scientists, historians, educators and psychologists, folklorists, and philosophers all have different stories to tell us about the meaning of toys. Adults were considered the primary audience for artifacts we now recognize

---

[69] Translated from Finnish by the author.

as toys, such as doll houses (see, e.g., Stewart, 1993) and fashion dolls, one of the most popular categories of dolls in contemporary toy culture devised by Parisian costumiers as early as the 14th century (Daiken, 1963). However, during the 19th and 20th centuries toys have mainly been acknowledged as playthings intended for children.

Mainly due to the sociotechnological developments of the early 21st century, such as the increased popularity of the Internet and, most importantly, the growing popularity of social media platforms as popular playgrounds, we are witnessing the gradual strengthening emergence of the once ephemeral phenomenon of adult toy aficionados, enthusiasts, and more precisely, players. A voyage into the virtual toy boxes on the Internet reveals that toys of the current time do not only represent children's material and digital or hybrid culture. Instead, it reveals the active and visible nature of the existence of adult toy play.

The concept of "toy" is very broad, as it continues to expand with the diversifying cultures of play and the growth of the audience of players, such as the segment of kidults discussed earlier in the chapter. In addition to traditional play equipment linked to children, sex toys, cars, cameras, kitchen utensils, and other technical equipment are often referred to as "toys." Perhaps the most prominent category of adult toys from this listing are toys connected to intimate and sensuous bodily play—sex toys. Following the definition given by the Oxford English Dictionary, a sex toy is a "device or object designed for sexual stimulation (as a dildo, vibrator, etc.) or to enhance sexual pleasure or performance." Juffer (1998, p. 83) states that "sex aids have more recently come to be understood in terms of recreation. They have become 'toys' just as sex has lost its significance as a form of reproduction or relationship and become a form of 'play.'"

Metaphorically, the concept of toy has entered the adult market in relation to toy-like products and services, for example, in the category of utensils (such as kitchenware), but also other types of lifestyle products, cosmetics, and fashion apparel (Heljakka, 2013). Moreover, toys or "toyish" attributes and elements are constantly being used in advertising to communicate what is generally considered "cute" or "playful." Often, so-called family brands are marketed in a playful manner, and the advertisements are designed to provoke positive emotions through the use of familiar toy characters, such as teddy bears, or cartoonish manifestations thereof (Hayward, 2012). Furthermore, toy-like objects feature as a regular type of decoration in chain stores, and there are even hotels that refer to themselves as toy hotels (Heljakka, 2013).

The embellishment of cultural products with playful elements emerged at the end of the 20th century. Architecture, design, fashion, and in fact most cultural phenomena have become more playful in the past decade or two (Lurker, 1990). Through toyification, these playful products of culture are being introduced with plasticity, modularity, customizability, and participatory affordances. As defined by Thibault and Heljakka (2018), toyification refers to the use of aesthetics and functionality familiar from toys applied to the use of other aspects of culture, such as sex toys, games, fashion, the furniture industry, kitchen utensils, household appliances, and even technology, for example, in the form of toyified devices such as robots. Most prominently, toyification becomes visible in living spaces and, for example, playful office settings through furniture-like objects and utensils. An example of a toyified lifestyle product is designer furniture such as Eero Aarnio's sculptural Puppy, Dino, Pony, and Tipi characters that are an intersection between furniture and toys and that are disguised as interior elements. Known for its kitchen utensils, the Italian brand Alessi is identified by its playful design philosophy that has given many of the company's products a toy-like character known from the world of toys. Toyification is also seen in wearables. In fashion, the toy-oriented collections designed by designer Jeremy Scott for the sports brand Adidas and the fashion house

Moschino speak to the toyification of fashion. Designer Minna Parikka's footwear represents the same aesthetics that draw on toy cultures, where playful design is combined with a wearable item using elements reminiscent of various toys, such as bunny ears and illustrations of Hello Kitty and My Little Pony characters. In addition to the toyification in fashion and everyday objects, it is possible to observe toyifying features related to, for example, immersive selfie museums, such as the Museum of Ice Cream (see Figure 1) and Happy Place. Indeed, this designed, character-based, and even cutified aesthetic and photogenic playfulness speaks to the mature consumer of play who seems attracted not only to enhancing their living and working environments with decorative design objects and collector's items as a dis-player but who is also drawn to wear the toys and to gain experiences in toyified spaces. What still needs further clarification, however, are the dimensions of play related to adult engagement—consumption and production and their various manifestations—with toys as the original, playable objects that, according to the traditional and strikingly narrow understanding, belong only to the sphere of childhood play.

### Profiling the Adult Toy Players

Today, the toy industry represents a professional arena within the larger sphere of the entertainment supersystem (Kinder, 1991), a (sub)division of the industries of play concentrating on the production of playthings and an agent in the ecosystem, or 'supersystem' of contemporary play (Heljakka, 2013), which mainly recognizes mature toy enthusiasts as collectors and not as players. However, adult toy players vary in their taste as much as children do. Adults choose their play materials from an abundance of different toys—collectables, designer (or art) toys that are limited in number, and unique handcrafted items but also mass-produced toys familiar from childhood play. Play has an essential role in the lives of these adults. An adult may have a second childhood if he or she has an appreciation of toys, a good memory, and is an active player, claims Stevanne Auerbach also known as "Dr. Toy" in the Anglo-American toy industry (Auerbach, 2004). Besides enabling a 'second childhood,' toys are once again becoming an increasingly important object of adult interest, collection, and play. Therefore, the romantic notion of the toy-playing child (Sutton-Smith, 1997) has been challenged in the 21st century as toys become identified as objects of adult fandom (Geraghty, 2014) and play.

Dolls, dollhouses, action figures and movie memorabilia, other artifacts linked to transmedial storytelling (contrasting collectors' editions, such as collectors' edition Barbies), are often distinguished as "children's toys." It is sometimes still difficult for adults to call or even recognize their own activities with either of these types of toy play, even if they understand the playful nature of their "collectors' items" or "vinyl," sometimes spoken of as "non-toys" using the phrase "This is not a toy." The possibility of play is further avoided by using euphemisms and, for example, by calling activities related to various dolls a hobby or "dolling." The discourses of hobbying, fandom, and collecting as substitutes for the concept of play in toy-related activities all tell something about the difficulty and avoidance that adults often encounter in relation to play. For example, one Pullip doll enthusiast says that "The doll is expensive and not intended for play. That's why it has a 15-year 'recommended age' limit" (Aaltio, 2018). At the same time, adult toy play is publicly displayed more than ever, as it is located in the digital world and is ingrained in the use of mobile devices and social media, similar to other forms of play that occur in physical, public environments, such as engaging with location-based adventure games and immersive (pseudo)museum spaces.

In earlier studies, we profiled adult toy players in four subgroups—toy collectors, toying artists, toy designers, and "everyday players" (Heljakka, 2013).

While toying artists use toys as inspiration or raw material for their artistic creations and toy designers are responsible for the creation of new toys, toy collectors and everyday players do not have a professional reason to engage with toys. It is on these latter two profiles that we will now focus. However, it is first important to note that these four profiles of adult players are not necessarily mutually exclusive. On one hand, collectors may express a significant interest in, for example, storytelling with their collected toys, just like everyday players might be keen to add items to their toy collections in addition to their narrative and customizing activities. On the other hand, in many ways toying artists and toy designers also display similar play patterns with toys as the other profiled adult toy players. In fact, as illustrated in earlier research (Heljakka, 2013), most of the profiled adult toy players own some sort of toy collection, a resource that allows various creative activities to take place.

**Toy Collectors**

In terms of toys, adults have for a long time been mainly acknowledged as collectors. "Toy-collecting adult" is a recognized, cultivated, and common term used in reference to the mature toy enthusiasts of the Western world. Larry Bernstein famously stated that "Collectors are a pimple on the elephant's ass" (Miller, 1998), referring to the trivial interest toy companies previously had in adult toy enthusiasts. Some 20 years later, this statement has proved untrue, as, for example, Funko (maker of Funko "Pops!" vinyl collectibles) mostly caters to the adult market. For these toys, adult collectors may in fact represent the main target group.

Collecting as a formalized type of play behavior, a subcategory of object play, can be further categorized in terms of its aims. Collectors are interested in creating a collection but doing so based on their own motivation and principles. Collecting and speculating are part of our culture and are even recognized as interesting forms of play (Lurker, 1990). Furthermore, collections serve psychological functions even for the mature, as collections may be seen as transition objects (Winnicott, 2005) or security blankets for adults (Belk, 1988, p. 154).

Recognizing the adult player as a toy collector or "builder" is one (additional) way for the toy industry to label the adult toy player. For example, a significant number of LEGO "builders" are adults, but rather than players of these toys, they are diplomatically referred to as adult fans of LEGO (AFOL). When asking Howard Roffman, head of Lucas Licensing, about how consciously new Star Wars toys are developed with the adult player in mind, he answered that "The adults would certainly not admit to playing with the toys. When the products are right for kids, the products are also right for adult collectors" (Heljakka, 2013, p. 230). Thus, the most common subcategory identified, accepted, and recognized by the toy industry as an adult toy activity is still collection, although adult-toy relationships often extend beyond collecting and are colored by a wide range of functionalities, such as creative activities. As a collected object, the toy is distinguished from many other collectibles by its creative manipulation, that is, object play based on modifying the toy's essence, as illustrated in the practices of everyday players.

**Everyday players**

As social media allows for the rapid and efficient sharing of all kinds of stories, toys have also become a medium in their own right—a tool that is used in world-building and in storytelling. At the same time, the toy is a creative tool for players of all ages to tell their own stories and therefore to extend their sense of self into the toy (Belk, 1988). Play promotes the mixing of reality and fantasy (Brown, 2009), just as consumers blend fantasy and reality (Kozinets et al., 2004). In playing, children master emotions by bridging internal fantasy worlds with external realities (Bettelheim, 1972).

Imagination plays an essential role in the definition of play (Piironen, 2004). The child inherently has a desire to come up with fables, a desire to create parallel realities and fabricate stories (Heinonen, 2004). For a child, therefore, a toy can be the key to reality and for an adult an unreal object that leads to the world of fantasy. In toy play, both for a child and an adult, there is a dialogue with the toy object, a projecting of one's own world of experience already lived or in the form of a dream. For example, in doll play, toys meet imagined worlds; this expands into visual storytelling as they come to showcase the fantasies of their players through, for example, photography.

Objects in our possession literally can extend the self, allowing us to do things that we would otherwise be incapable of (Belk, 1988). Toys are one example of tools for everyday players and are often considered as central in children's creative, imaginative, and self-expressive play. Almost exclusively (with the exception of those who collect toys as investments), the activities of an adult toy collector are also accompanied by imaginative and creative play, such as displaying toys as part of dioramas, room boxes, or doll houses. Nonetheless, dolls like the aforementioned Pullip doll play a major role in the creative activities of adult toy players, such as photoplay or toy photography (Heljakka, 2013). In toy play, adults hone skills through collecting, customizing, and photoplay and build both physical and fantasy-based worlds for toy characters. Character toys that serve adult play preferences, such as the Blythe dolls, Star Wars action figures, My Little Pony, Sylvanian Families figures, and various plush toys, seem to act as prompts, objects inviting and pushing adults to play. They crack open the doors to imaginative worlds in more ways than do other consumer products. With toys, as illustrated in the chapter, adult imagination seems to become more effortlessly materialized and made visible through play than through the flirtation with playfulness evoked by toyified entities, such as interaction with utilitarian artefacts that carry a toyified aesthetic, such as bunny-eared sneakers, Darth Vader toasters, or unicorn-inspired hair colors. This is because toys are objects that are the primary playable instruments—things specifically designed and crafted for the purpose of play.

As anthropologist Jean-Pierre Rossie has noted, a toy only comes to life when it is played with (Rossie, 2005). Even in adult play, toys are "brought to life"—a metamorphosis from plastic and plush objects into role-playing characters in various stories. In addition to useful perspectives and purposefulness related to skill-building and socialization around toys, adult toy play also serves storytelling needs. In fact, storytelling becomes part of the toy character already at the beginning of its design process. While the narratives—from the name of the toy to its backstory—are given by the toy designers, the stories shaped by the players themselves play an even more important role. Media influences toy play as well. Children take topics from, for example, televised content or games in their playing, but every occasion of play is different (Karimäki, 2007). It is the same for adult toy players, as stories from popular culture are mimicked and re-played with toys. Homo ludens and homo faber are thus also homo narrans, a storytelling person, when playing.

**Conclusion: Towards a Paidic (R)Evolution Through Intergenerational Play**

In this chapter, we attempted to demonstrate how views on the formerly rigid assumptions about children's progressive play and adults' regressive play need to be reconsidered. By introducing earlier work on playfulness and play, it was shown how playfulness stands as a flexible, mental stance and attitude towards the world that is applicable to various phenomena, while play as behavior, such as a consumption activity was earlier considered an antithesis to work and other productive activities.

While liberating adult play from its previous boundaries related to seeing play purely as consumptive leisure, this chapter aimed to show how the different dimensions of play co-exist in adult play. In essence, play in the contemporary world plays a part not only in leisure but also in work and not solely as an unproductive activity but also as a productive one. A healthy approach to play recognizes and values all of its dimensions, and a happy adult seeks to find balance between the axis of freedom and regulated forms of play and preferences to engage in play during pleasure, leisure, and work.

Free-form or paidic play based on physical play equipment and a human presence is needed to counterbalance competition and performativity—the ludus of the technological, gamifying world. Moreover, it is appropriate to question whether it is time for the ludic turn to give way to paidic (r)evolution and a realization that playing in the contemporary sense means more than participation in gamification—to enjoy the excitement of alea and agon, as formulated by Caillois (1961). In fact, as Alemany Oliver (2015) states, current preferences in play seem to lean towards ilinx and mimicry, a vertigo-simulation approach, the forms of play highlighted in this chapter.

With the privilege of play in the 20th century, it has become possible to think of all the ways in which we escape from the bonds of work to the joys of pleasure. We have come to idealize these forms of pleasure; sports, games, play, and toys have all become vehicles for this idealization (Sutton-Smith, 1986). Contrary to this, 21st-century play is to be understood as an activity with both entertaining and pleasurable elements, as well as serious connotations relating to self-expression and self-realization, even overall well-being. In summary, play is both useless and useful, unproductive and productive, and an activity that centers around the manipulation and modifying of physical materials and environments extended by the technological possibilities afforded by the post-digital age. There is no place for regression in imaginative and creative, sometimes even rule-breaking—paidic—play, as imagination and creativity are fundamental virtues of the playing individual, no matter the age.

Just like play, consumption has previously been considered antithetical to work. However, "when one considers consumption as play, it ceases to be the end, but becomes the moment where things happen, where strategies are planned and employed, where, in fact, learning and production and preparation toward the future begin" (Firat & Venkatesh, 1997, pp. 298-299). Play has been moving from ludus to paidia (Caillois, 1961), from established rules of consumption to a spontaneous desire to play within consumption (Alemany Oliver, 2015). If consumption is to be understood as play, it is better to define adult play as an activity in which creation, consumption, and production co-exist. This thought aligns with Sutton-Smith's (1993, p. 104) idea of the complexity of future play. He states that "if play does prepare for the future, then it seems to do so most obviously by preparing the players to play more complexly in the future."

The era of the ludic turn would seem to give way to a paidic (r)evolution more open to embracing the progressive aspects of play in adults than regressive ones. The emergence of adult players in the paidic turn through work and production as playborers, through the commercial and public sphere of the marketplace as kidults, and through the creative cultures of toys as toy players has begun, and adults seem to use a large variety of tools, instruments and environments in their play. Adults engage in playful exercise culture, covet luxurious Christmas calendars with beauty products, jump at the opportunity to dive into ball pits, and interact with other playable installations and environments in urban locations targeted specifically at adults. In addition to play activities in sports, theatre, visual arts, and games, adults are notably and increasingly looking for playful tools that are both physically and digitally manipulable and previously associated with children's culture—that is, toys.

The spread of play from the field of leisure to the arena of working life seems ongoing. Play is no longer limited to children's culture but has become a pastime for all ages. At the same time, there is a constant effort to harness play for more useful purposes, such as education, cultural services, and organizational management. The role of the toy as an object related to toy cultures is in a state of transformation in the paidic-oriented era and is colored by activities on digital and social media. Increasingly visual and shared play shapes our perceptions of how toys are progressively becoming a significant, interactive, and attitude-shaping media. Indeed, contemporary play is characterized by its determination and multidisciplinary nature; research on toy play will at the same time reveal the diverse and assertive nature of adult toy play. The toy play in all its diversity that is practiced by contemporary adults would seem to question and dismantle dated assumptions and attitudes about play as an exclusive activity of children. As the chapter has demonstrated, toys are already a tool for adult interest, collecting, and creative play activities. The transition to adulthood does not have to mark the end of toy play. The emergence of a permissive attitude towards adult toy play is exemplified in connection with doll play; as Henna Kiili, a social media influencer who plays with Barbie on her Instagram account, says "I want to send a message to children: you never have to stop playing" (Sychold, 2018).

Garry Chick calls for emerging perspectives that unite evolution, culture, and the environment as complementary rather than competing explanatory variables with respect to both child and adult play (Chick, 2015). One of the interesting research topics concerning play as an "ageless" activity is intergenerational play, the joint play activity of players of different generations, which has already proven popular in games, both board games and digital games. Earlier studies on play between generations point to the benefits and rewards of shared play experiences between older and younger participants (Cohen & Waite-Stupiansky, 2016).

Finally, following Henricks (2015, pp. 386-387), the play of adults is understood to be critical to maintaining 'a good society'—a happy and healthy society. "Play articulates the values, social divisions, and problems of communities. It provides ways for persons and groups to display their character, abilities, and standings before others and to explore the implications of alternative statuses." In today's world, we are all childlike in our preferences to engage with toys and toy-like objects and environments. To an increasing extent, we share similar toys and patterns of play between generations, thus increasing togetherness through shared play experiences. A recent example of play involving both adults and children relates to toy play conducted during the first lockdown period of the COVID-19 pandemic in the spring of 2020. In a play pattern called the "teddy challenge," players of different ages displayed toys in windows and gardens to spread a playful message of hope and solidarity to everyone affected by the lockdown and physical social distancing. Identified as "communal playing for the common good" (Heljakka, 2020), this intergenerational play pattern involved mature players as the displayers of teddy bears and other stuffed animals and children and youth as players who try to spot the toys in the windows of their neighborhoods. The teddy challenge presented a hybrid approach to play, making use of physical and digital play media, and it engaged representatives of homo ludens of many ages. In this way, pandemic toy play as a joint form of play between adults and children, as was common in agricultural societies (Dyson, 2015), reunites the generations in the digitalizing era. Furthermore, play of this kind presents itself as much as a solitary and an individual pastime as a way of social and communal celebration, a necessity for a healthy life. Play is powerful in its tendency to liberate and unify. "For sensitivity, inner strength and personal equilibrium, playing appears to have definite survival value" (Frappier, 1976, p. 196). Therefore, we should stop associating adult play with shame and guilt and begin to perceive it more positively. As Lurker (1990) states:

> Nobody is advocating that we now should all become players and
> should forget about the rest. But it is definitely an unfortunate and
> unhealthy situation when we are inhibited and at odds with play,

> when we are ashamed and allow feelings of guilt and inferiority to interfere with our play. All the negative attitudes and opinions that play is infantile, undignified, trivial, frivolous, superfluous, a sinful waste of time, or even the source of evil are really unnecessary. (p. 164)

Perhaps the time has come at last to recognize the adult player as not separated from the playing youth but instead as a "childlike," co-playing agent. Following this thought, it becomes possible to envision how the future of play will be more paidic and intergenerational. Indeed, the examination of adult play has revealed the unnecessary age-based division and has shown how the assumed risks associated with infantilization can be mitigated. Children and adults should be seen as similar beings, constantly evolving in our minds, playing in the world, and playing with the opportunities offered by the world freely and creatively without losing our ability to act responsibly and respectfully. We know you, the adult reader of this book, are playing in some way for pleasure, leisure, or work. But with what tools, technologies, and environments and with whom? And which toys?

## References

Aaltio, M. (2018, October 12). Näille nukeille et ole koskaan liian vanha. *Satakunnan Kansa*, 8–9.

Alemany Oliver, M. (2015). Rejuvenated territories of adulthood. In K. Diehl & C. Yoon (Eds.), *Advances in Consumer Research, Vol. 43* (pp. 654-655). Association for Consumer Research.

Ariès, P. (1962/1996). *Centuries of childhood*. Random House.

Auerbach, S. (2004). *Smart play, smart toys. How to raise a child with a high play quotient. How to select and use the best toys*. Educational Insights.

Barber, B. R. (2007). *Consumed: How markets corrupt children, infantilize adults and swallow citizens whole*. Norton.

Barnett, L. A. (1990). Playfulness: Definition, design, and measurement. *Play & Culture, 3*, 319-336.

Barnett, L. A. (2007). The nature of playfulness in young adults. *Personality and Individual Differences, 43*(4), 949-958.

Barnett, L. A., & Owens, M. (2015). Does play have to be playful? In J. Johnson, S. Eberle, T. Henricks, & D. Kuschner (Eds.), *The handbook of the study of play* (pp. 453–459). Rowman & Littlefield.

Belk, R. W. (1988). Possessions and the extended self. *Journal of Consumer Research, 15* (September), 139-168.

Bernardini, J. (2014). The infantilization of the postmodern adult and the figure of kidult. *Postmodern Openings, 2*(5), 39-55.

Bettelheim, B. (1972). Play and education. *The School Review, 81*(1), 1-13.

Brown, S. (2009). *Play: How it shapes the brain, opens the imagination, and invigorates the soul*. Penguin.

Brown, S. (2014). Consequences of play deprivation. *Scholarpedia, 9*(5), 30449.

Bruns, A. (2008). *Blogs, Wikipedia, Second Life, and beyond: From production to produsage* (Vol. 45). Peter Lang.

Bundy, A. C. (1997). Play and playfulness. What to look for. In L.D. Parham & L. S. Fazio (Eds.), *Play in occupational therapy for children* (pp. 52-66). Mosby-Year Book Inc.

Burghardt, G. (2005). *The genesis of animal play: Testing the limits*. MIT Press.

Butler, N., Olaison, L., Sliwa, M., Meier Sørensen, B., & Spoelstra, S. (2011). Play and boredom. *Ephemera, Theory & Politics in Organization, 11*, 329-335.

Caillois, R. (1961). *Man, play and games*. University of Illinois Press.

Chick, G. (2015). Anthropology and the study of play. In J. Johnson, S. Eberle, T. Henricks, & D. Kuschner (Eds.), *The handbook of the study of play* (pp. 71-84). Rowman & Littlefield.

Chudacoff, H. P. (2007). Children at play. An American history. New York University Press.

Cohen, L. E., & Waite-Stupiansky, S. (2016). Play for all ages: An exploration of intergenerational play. In M. Patte & J. Sutterby (Eds.), *Celebrating 40 years of research: Reflecting on our past, exploring the present, and playing into the future. Play and Culture Studies, Vol. 13* (pp. 61-80). Rowman & Littlefield.

Cramer, F. (2015). What is 'post-digital?'. In D. Berry & M. Dieter (Eds.), *Postdigital aesthetics: Art, computation and design* (pp. 12-26). Palgrave Macmillan.

Cross, G. (2008). *Men to boys. The making of modern immaturity*. Columbia University Press.

Daiken, L. (1963). *Children's toys throughout the ages*. Spring Books.

De Souza e Silva, A., & Sutko, D. (2005). Playing life and living play: How hybrid reality games reframe space, play, and the ordinary. *Critical Studies in Media Communication, 25*(5), 447-465.

Dyson, J-P. C. (2015). Play in America. A historical overview. In J. Johnson, S. Eberle, T. Henricks, & D. Kuschner (Eds.). *The handbook of the study of play* (pp. 41-50). Rowman & Littlefield.

Firat, A. Fuat, & Venkatesh, A. (1995). Liberatory postmodernism and the reenchantment of consumption. *Journal of Consumer Research, 22*(December), 239-267.

Firat, A. Fuat, & Venkatesh, A. (1997). 'The play is the thing...': Comments on Ben Fine's 'Playing the consumption game.' *Consumption, Markets and Culture, 1*(3), 297-302.

Frappier, P. (1976). *The playing phenomenon in adults*. University of Quebec Press.

Fuchs, M., Fizek, S., Ruffino, P., & Schrape, N. (2014). *Rethinking gamification*. Meson Press.

Geraghty, L. (2014). *Cult collectors*. Routledge.

Giddens, A. (1964). Notes on the concepts of play and leisure. *The Sociological Review, 12*(1), 73-89.

Gordon, G. (2014). Well played: The origins and future of playfulness. *American Journal of Play, 6*(2), 234-266.

Gray, P. (2015). Studying play without calling it that. In J. Johnson, S. Eberle, T. Henricks, & D. Kuschner (Eds.), *The handbook of the study of play* (pp. 121-138). Rowman & Littlefield.

Groos, K. (1892). *The play of animals*. Kessinger Publishing Co.

Hayward, K. (2013). 'Life stage dissolution' in Anglo-American advertising and popular culture: Kidults, lil' Britneys and middle youths.' *The Sociological Review, 61*(3), 525-548.

Heinonen, S.-L. (2004). Draamaleikkiä päiväkodissa. In L. Piironen (Ed.) *Leikin Pikkujättiläinen* (pp.92-97). Helsinki: WSOY.

Heljakka, K. (2013). *Principles of adult play (fulness) in contemporary toy cultures: From wow to flow to glow* [Doctoral dissertation, Aalto University].

Heljakka, K. (2020, May 11). Pandemic toy play: Teddy bears, window-screens and playing for the common good in times of self-isolation. *WiderScreen*. http://widerscreen.fi/numerot/ajankohtaista/pandemic-toy-play-against-social-distancing-teddy-bears-window-screens-and-playing-for-the-common-good-in-times-of-self-isolation/

Heljakka, K., Harviainen, J. T., & Suominen, J. (2018). Stigma avoidance through visual contextualization: Adult toy play on photo-sharing social media. *New Media & Society, 20*(8), 2781-2799.

Heljakka, K., & Tuomi, P. (2020). Gamified doll-dramas: Provocations, playbor and participatory play practices in the age of iTV. In A. Veloso, O. Mealha, and L. Costa (Eds.), *21st International Conference on Intelligent Games and Simulation* (pp.67–70). EUROSIS-ETI.

Henricks, T. S. (2015). Where are we now: Challenges for the study of play. In J. Johnson, S. Eberle, T. Henricks, & D. Kuschner (Eds.), *The handbook of the study of play* (pp. 381-391). Rowman & Littlefield.

Heynders, O., & Van Nuenen, T. (2014). Tourist imagination and modernist poetics: The case of Cees Nooteboom. In G. Lean, R. Staiff, & E. Waterton (Eds.), *Travel and imagination* (pp. 103-118). Ashgate.

Hirn, Y. (1918). *Leikkiä ja taidetta*. WSOY.

HKTDC. (2013, January 7). Product development and business opportunities of kidult toys [Seminar session moderated by R. Gottlieb]. *2013 Hong Kong Toys & Games Fair*, Hong Kong.

Huizinga, J. (1938/1971). *Homo ludens: A study of the play-element in culture*. Beacon Press.

Huotari, K., & Hamari, J. (2012, October). Defining gamification: A service marketing perspective. In A. Lugmayr, H. Franssila, J. Paavilainen, & H. Kärkkäinen (Eds.), *Proceeding of the 16th international academic MindTrek conference* (pp. 17-22). The Association for Computing Machinery.

Hwang, S.-J. (2013, September 2). Kidult phenomenon in Korea. *Kookmin Review*. https://english.kookmin.ac.kr/kookmin/special/169?pn=15

Johnson, J. E., Eberle, S. G., Henricks, T. S., & Kuschner, D. (Eds.). (2015). *The handbook of the study of play*. Rowman & Littlefield.

S-ryhmä (2018, November 29). *Joulun hittilelut löydät Prismasta* [Video]. YouTube. https://www.youtube.com/watch?v=HkM0jScps_o

Juffer, J. (1998). *At home with pornography: Women, sex and everyday life*. New York University Press.

Kalbi. (2018, January 14). Line between Korean kids and adults blurs. *Koreancultureblog.com*. https://koreancultureblog.com/2018/01/14/line-between-korean-kids-and-adults-blurs/

Karimäki, R. (2007). Media leikin innoittajana. In L. Pentikäinen, A. Ruhala, & H. Niinistö (Eds.) *Mediametkaa! Osa 2-Kasvattajan matkaopas lasten mediamaailmaan* (pp. 40-47). Mediakasvatus Metka ry.

Kavanagh, D. (2011). Work and play in management studies: A Kleinian analysis. *Ephemera, Theory & Politics in Organization, 11*(4), 336-356.

Kinder, M. (1991). *Playing with power in movies, television and video games: From Muppet babies to teenage mutant ninja turtles*. University of California Press.

Koeners, M. P., & Francis, J. (2020). The physiology of play: Potential relevance for higher education. *International Journal of Play, 9*(1), 143-159.

Kotler, P. (1986). Prosumers: A new type of consumer. *The Futurist, 20*, 24–28.

Kozinets, R. V., Sherry, J. F. Jr., Storm, D., Duhachek, A., Nuttavuthisit, K., & Deberry-Spence, B. (2004). Ludic agency and retail spectacle. *Journal of Consumer Research, 31*(December), 658-72.

Kurnit, P. (2009). KGOY reconsidered: Kids just want to be kids. Executive insight. *Young Consumers, 10*(3), https://doi.org/10.1108/yc.2009.32110cab.002

Kücklich, J. (2005). FCJ-025 Precarious playbour: Modders and the digital games industry. *The Fibreculture Journal, 5*, https://five.fibreculturejournal.org/fcj-025-precarious-playbour-modders-and-the-digital-games-industry/

Licensing Magazine. (2019, January 31). *The traditional toy market closes with a turnover of -1% compared to last year*. https://www.licensingmagazine.com/2019/01/31/the-traditional-toy-market-closes-2018-with-a-turnover-of-1-compared-to-last-year/?lang=en

Lieberman, N. J. (1977). *Playfulness. It's relationship to imagination and creativity*. Academic Press.

Liturgy. (2018, October 10). Let us play—TAG. https://liturgy.co.nz/let-us-play-tag

Lockwood, R., & O'Connor, S. (2017). Playfulness in adults: An examination of play and playfulness and their implications for coaching. *Coaching: An International Journal of Theory, Research and Practice, 10*(1), 54-65.

Lurker, E. (1990). Play art: Evolution or trivialization of art? *Play & Culture, 3*, 146-167.

Marks-Tarlow, T. (2010). The fractal self at play. *American Journal of Play, 3*(1), 31-62.

Martin, D. M. & Schouten, J. W. (2014). Consumption-driven market emergence. *Journal of Consumer Research, 40*(February), 855-870.

Meckley, A. M. (2015). A student's guide for understanding play through the theories of Brian Sutton-Smith. In J. Johnson, S. Eberle, T. Henricks, & D. Kuschner (Eds.), *The handbook of the study of play* (pp. 393-405). Rowman & Littlefield.

Meyerowitz, J. (1985). *No sense of place: The impact of electronic media on social behavior*. Oxford University Press.

Miller, W. G. (1998). *Toy wars. The epic struggle between G.I. Joe, Barbie, and the companies that make them*. Adams Media Corporation.

Mohler, Albert. (2006, December 20). "KGOY"—or kids growing older younger: The message of Barbie and Bratz. *Albertmohler.com*. https://albertmohler.com/2006/12/20/kgoy-or-kids-growing-older-younger-the-message-of-barbie-and-the-bratz

Morace, F. (2005). The challenge of the forever kids. *Modo Magazine*, 246.

Neale, R. E. (1969). *In praise of play: Toward a psychology of religion*. Harper & Row.

Nicholson, J., & Shimpi, P. M. (2015). Guiding future early childhood educators to reclaim their own play as a foundation for becoming effective advocates for children's play. *Early Child Development and Care, 185*(10), 1601-1616.

Oatley, K., Keltner, D., & Jenkins, J. M. (Eds.) (2006). *Understanding emotions*. Blackwell Publishing.

Urban Dictionary (2005, June 28). Kidult, by B. O'Keefe. In *Urbandictionary.com*. Retrieved from https://www.urbandictionary.com/define.php?term=kidult

Piironen, L. (2004). Leikin voima taidekasvatuksessa. In L. Piironen (Ed.), *Leikin pikkujättiläinen* (pp. 316-325). WSOY.

Postman, N. (1994). *The disappearance of childhood*. Random House.

Proyer, R. T. (2017). A multidisciplinary perspective on adult play and playfulness. *International Journal of Play, 6*(3), 241-243.

Rogan, B. (1998). On collecting as play, creativity and aesthetic practice. *Etnofoor, 11*(1), 40-54.

Rossie, J-P. (2005). *Toys, play, culture and society: An anthropological approach with reference to North Africa and the Sahara*. International Toy Research Center.

Rubin, K. H., Fein, G., G., & Vandenberg, B. (1983). Play. In P. H. Mussen, & E. M. Hetherington (Eds.), *Handbook of child psychology: formerly Carmichael's manual of child psychology, Vol. 3* (pp. 693-774). Wiley.

Russell, B. (1930/1996). The conquest of happiness. W. W. Norton & Company Ltd.

Russell, W. & Ryall, E. (2015). Philosophizing play. In J. Johnson, S. Eberle, T. Henricks, & D. Kuschner (Eds.), *The handbook of the study of play* (pp. 139-159). Rowman & Littlefield.

Schylter, B. (1976). *Leikit ja leikkikalut*. Tammi.

Scott, A. (2012). Meaningful play: How play is changing the future of our health. In Industrial Design Society of America. *IDSA Educational Symposium, 2012 White paper*. www.idsa.org/sites/default/files/Scott.pdf

Shen, X. S., Chick, G., & Zinn, H. (2014). Playfulness in adulthood as a personality trait: A reconceptualization and a new measurement. *Journal of Leisure Research, 46*(1), 58-83.

Smith, P. (2010). *Children and play*. Wiley-Blackwell.

Smith, P. K., & Vollstedt, R. (1985). On defining play: An empirical study of the relationship between play and various play criteria. *Child Development, 56*, 1042-1052.

Spielwarenmesse. (2019). *Why adults represent a relevant target group for traditional toys.* https://www.spielwarenmesse.de/magazine/article-detail/kidults-traditional-toys-for-grown-ups/language/1/

Stewart, S. (1993). *On longing. Narratives of the miniature, the gigantic, the souvenir, the collection.* Duke University Press.

Sutton-Smith, B. (1986). *Toys as culture*. Gardner Press.

Sutton-Smith (1993). Suggested rhetorics in adult play theories. *Play Theory & Research, 1*(2), 102-116.

Sutton-Smith, B. (1995). Conclusion: The persuasive rhetorics of play. In A. Pellegrini (Ed.), *The future of play theory: A multidisciplinary inquiry into the contributions of Brian Sutton-Smith.* (pp. 275-295). State University of New York Press.

Sutton-Smith, B. (1997). *The ambiguity of play*. Harvard University Press.

Sutton-Smith, B. (2009). Toying with history: A response to Vonèche. *Archives de Psychologie, 74*(288/289), 107.

Sutton-Smith, B (2017). *Play for life: Play theory and play as emotional survival*. The Strong.

Sychold, L. (2018). Ellie ja minä olemme feministejä. *Kodin Kuvalehti, 1*, 46-47.

Tansel, U. (2013, March 8). Why should toy manufacturers focus more on adults? *Global Toy News.* https://globaltoynews.com/2013/03/08/why-should-toy-manufacturers-focus-more-on-adults/

Tegano, D. W., & Moran, J. D. III. (2015). Play and creativity: The role of the intersubjective adult. In J. Johnson, S. Eberle, T. Henricks, & D. Kuschner (Eds.), *The handbook of the study of play.* (pp. 175-186). Rowman & Littlefield.

Thibault, M., & Heljakka, K. (2018). Toyification: A conceptual statement. In G. Brougère & M. Allen (Eds.), *Proceedings of the 8th International Toy Research Association World Conference.* International Toy Research Association (ITRA).

Leclerc, R., Dean, P., & Cuni, B. (2007). *Think, Make, Play: Toy Design Booklet.* Toy Manufacturer's Association of Hong Kong/The Hong Kong Polytechnic University.

Toffler, A. (1971). *Future shock*. Pan.

UN Committee on the Rights of the Child (2013). *General comment No.17 on the right of the child to rest, leisure, play, recreational activities, cultural life and the arts (art. 31).* United Nations.

Van Vleet, M., & Feeney, B. C. (2015). Play behavior and playfulness in adulthood. *Social and Personality Psychology Compass, 9*(11), 630-643.

Weber, M. (1930). *The Protestant ethic and the spirit of capitalism*. Scribner's.

West, S., Hoff, E., & Carlsson, I. (2017). Enhancing team creativity with playful improvisation theater: A controlled intervention field study. *International Journal of Play, 6*(3), 283-293.

Wilson, R. N. (1981). The courage to be leisured. *Social Forces, 60*(2), 282-303.

Winnicott, D. W. (1971/2005). *Playing and reality*. Routledge.

Wolfenstein, M. (1998). Fun morality. An analysis of recent American child-training literature. In H. Jenkins (Ed.), *The children's culture reader* (pp. 199-208). New York University Press.

Wolfenstein M. & Leites, N. (1950). Movies: A psychological study. Free Press.

Chapter VIII.
# Click to Disable: Infantilization in Terminal Interactions and/at Work
Simon Gottschalk

*For the first time in history, a society has felt its economic survival demands a kind of controlled regression, a culture that promotes puerility rather than maturation.*
Barber (2008)

*Americans can no longer think of one another as grown-ups.*
Konigsberg, quoted in Daly and Wice (1995)

*Men dress up like children and children dress up like superheroes.*
Baumbach (2010)

In this chapter, I discuss contemporary infantilizing trends in the domain of work. To do so, I first review the problematic concept of infantilization and discuss infantilizing trends in various institutions of contemporary society. Because participation in everyday institutions, and especially work, increasingly requires that we interact with computer terminals, the second section of this chapter suggests that four unique and interrelated affordances of terminals further induce, normalize, and reward infantile dispositions in adult users. Those are: dependence and coercion, personalization, simplification, and surveillance. Throughout this discussion, I point at similarities and tensions between the infantilization induced by those four affordances and broader cultural trends that characterize the hypermodern present. I conclude by calling attention to a number of risks presented by those trends.

Before continuing, two caveats. First, I use the word 'terminal' to refer to desktops, laptops, tablets, smart phones, GPS, Apple watches, and a variety of other devices that enable (and force) users to go online where they interact with others and with content (Gottschalk, 2018). Since the adjective 'terminal' also connotes a stage in the life of organisms, objects, and processes, its use will allow for (hopefully interesting) double-entendres that synonymous adjectives such as 'virtual,' 'cyber,' or 'digital' do not. Second, I discuss here four affordances that infantilize users, needless to say that terminals provide many more affordances and that those also have many beneficial effects on users (Belk, 2013).

## The Infantilist Ethos

In his book *Consumed*, Barber (2008) discusses an 'infantilist ethos' that seems increasingly pervasive in contemporary culture and politics. Referring to the common-sense assumptions we (un)consciously embrace and everyday practices we (un)consciously enact as we participate in various social institutions, this ethos favors easy over hard, simple over complex, and fast over slow. The infantilist ethos should not be dismissed as benign because, as Barber reminds us, "infantilism's preference for simple, easy, and fast gives it an affinity for certain political forms over others." And those are typically not intelligent ones (Nigam, 2018).

At first glance, it seems that what constitutes adult or infantile behaviors, emotions, cognitions, and aptitudes is most relative. After all, the ancient Israelites considered that a thirteen-year-old male was a man who was fully responsible for his actions.[70] Mohandas Gandhi married at thirteen; in colonial America, girls as young as seven were considered fit for marriage, and girls are routinely married around that age in several contemporary societies. On one hand, therefore, historical and anthropological research provide us with intriguing reminders of the arbitrariness of our mental categories about the stages of the life cycle, and the norms we attach to them. On the other hand, it seems that in most societies, members typically distinguish between behaviors, emotions, cognitions, and aptitudes that are considered fitting different stages of the life-cycle—however they slice it—and typically notice those that are not. Thus, for example, while the stages of the life-cycle are organized differently in today's America than they were around 57 A.D. in the Middle East, Corinthians (13: 11) is still clear about important distinctions between them. As the famous quote reminds us: "When I was a child, I talked like a child, I thought like a child, I reasoned like a child. When I became a man, I put childish ways behind me." Accordingly, an infantile individual is a person who does not enact the behaviors, emotions, cognitions, and aptitudes that are considered age-appropriate in his or her society, and who enacts instead those s/he acquired in a less mature stage of development. The infantile individual is thus a regressive one.[71] Of course, spontaneous and intermittent childlike behaviors among adults are far from being inherently problematic. As Maslow (1962) suggested, such behaviors can—in context—be therapeutic, enriching, and facilitating interactions between adults, and between adults and children. In addition, children's orientations include many positive traits, such as curiosity, and openness to experience, traits that are valuable among adults as well. But spontaneously occurring and intermittent childlike behaviors among adults are quite different from regressive orientations that are systematically induced by the underlying assumptions and routine practices that organize those contemporary institutions that adult citizens experience as the everyday.

What can explain this infantilist ethos? In contemporary Western society, young and not so young individuals find the traditional criteria of adulthood (marriage/parenting work, and independent living) uninspiring and poorly adapted to existing socio-economic conditions. Accordingly, Blatterer (2007) proposes that new criteria of adulthood, such as risk-taking, commitment to short-term projects, and flexibility across contexts, might be more pertinent to establish a sense of adulthood in the accelerating and destabilized present. However, while these criteria seem indeed adaptive for individuals who are trying to navigate turbulent hypermodern currents, they are also self-centered. They do not seem motivated by the basic drive to interact with others in order to develop with them a mutually nurturing and co-evolving relationship, which is ultimately the basic drive of a healthy social and psychological existence. Accordingly, if adulthood is a relative concept that urgently needs re-definition, we must still acknowledge that leading psychological theories as well as major philosophical-spiritual systems rooted in vastly different cultures have consistently understood maturity as a complex of other-oriented dispositions. Empathy,

[70] Hence, the ritual celebrations of the Jewish bar-mitzvah and bat-mitzvah, which announces the passage to an adult life-stage.

[71] One can also fail to act one's age in the reverse direction, for example, when a young person enacts behaviors appropriate for adults (see Hayward 2012, 2013).

compassion, patience, care, love, responsibility, trustworthiness, dependability, humility, honesty, loyalty, self-sacrifice, forgiveness, and commitment to others rather than greater than oneself all evoke adult dispositions that are oriented to others rather than individualistic and self-serving aptitudes one performs for no one in particular.[72] By promoting individualistic and self-oriented skills or aptitudes, these new criteria of adulthood seem to reproduce the very immaturity adults are generally expected to transcend.

### Regressive Institutions

Visiting America, Claude Lévi-Strauss (1946) already commented on the distinctively (and often endearing) childlike traits he noticed in American culture. Contemporary cultural critics and scholars note, however, that such traits have become noticeably less charming and are contaminating a growing number of institutions. For examples, infantilist trends have been documented in contemporary art (Hebdige, 2003), in the treatment of Las Vegas tourists (Belk 2000), in architectural trends such as Disney's planned communities (Dery, 1999), and in the 'dumbing down' tendencies that are distinctive of contemporary higher education (Berman, 2006, p. 27),[73] sound bites from political figures, literature, and the mass media, among others (Hayward, 2012, 2013; Nigam, 2018; Williams, 2014). The link between post World War II capitalism and infantilizing mass media has been the topic of an especially rich scholarship. As Jappe (1999, p. 107) reminds us:

> the infantilization of the spectator is no mere side-effect of the spectacle and the culture industry, but the embodiment of their anti-emancipatory goals: for Adorno, the ideal of the culture industry is to reduce adults to "the level of twelve-year-old;" for Debord, "the need to imitate that the consumer experiences is a truly infantile need."[74]

This infantilization in the mass media is echoed, normalized, and amplified by parallel trends in more 'serious' institutions, such as education, health, and, as developed below, work. To wit, the infantilist ethos that reaches well beyond the walls of the Furedi (2004) calls a "therapy culture" that reaches well beyond the walls of the psychologist's office. As he explains, such a culture promotes a view of adults as vulnerable, weak, and fragile subjects whose troubles qualify them for a 'permanent suspension of moral sense,' and whose successful prognosis requires the continuous dependence on a therapist's expert knowledge that helps them overcome the obstacles they stumble upon in the trenches of everyday life. This statement does not deny the importance and benefits of therapy. On the contrary, the stories we tell about who we are, what ails us, and why matter a great deal for how we understand ourselves and what we believe we can accomplish. In Furedi's (2004) opinion, however, to insist that unfortunate childhood experiences so powerfully shape adult life absolves grown-ups from adult responsibilities, erodes their trust in their own adult experiences and insights, weakens their social networks, and fundamentally shapes how they relate to others.

For sociologist Lipovetsky (2006), infantilizing trends are perhaps most conspicuous in contemporary consumption patterns:

> If old people want to look like young people, the young refuse to grow up. While the market for regressive consumption develops,

---

[72] While there exist cultures where members associate adulthood with dispositions such as manipulation, rigidity, domination, dishonesty, and a paranoid worldview, these seem to be the exception rather than the rule.
[73] See also Dnes (2017), Furedi (2017), and Kennedy (2020).
[74] See also Plass (2009).

the refusal to grow up starts increasingly earlier, as young adults
seem to want to live in the eternal prolongation of their childhood
or adolescence. (p. 65)

Bernardini (2014) detects infantile tendencies in other aspects of this new form of consumerism: it is easily suggestible, driven by individualistic, irrational, and almost exclusively playful desires, aimed at objects that have no utilitarian purpose, and is typically oblivious of others' needs. Brisman and South (2015, p. 216) also accuse this 'anti-social' consumption for its "promotion of, and obsession with, the individualized and infantilized consumer who is given permission to think only about 'me' and to do so 'now.'" Thanks to technologies of communication, this infantile ethos has fast traveled to and shaped other cultures. It has been documented in popular culture, news broadcasts, and the discourse on crime in the UK (Hayward 2012, 2013), consumption patterns in Italy (Bernardini, 2014), and linguistic patterns in Russia (Martynnova & Glukhov, 2015), Spain (Guzman, 2015), and France (Barus-Michel, 2005).

Well-adapted to the needs of an 'affective capitalism' (Andrejevic, 2013), the regressive orientations celebrated in the spheres of culture and consumption are unsurprisingly replicated in the sphere of production. Here, this infantilization operates on three interrelated levels. On a first level, having fun and playing seem to have become de rigueur in many a corporate office. For example, journalist Mark Labasch (2008) documents workplaces where "there are rubber chickens, Frisbee tosses, mustache-growing contests, pet psychics, interoffice memos alligator-clipped to toy cars, and ceremonies that honor employees for such accomplishments as having 'the most animated hand gestures.'"[75]

On a second level, those kindergarten-style interior designs, toys, and rituals conceal more insidious ideological shifts in corporate culture and in the subtle control of adult employees, more generally. Thus, the 'boarding school syndrome' is also manifest in "organizations that are creating and holding employees development"[76] (Herbert, 2019), in managers who "don't trust adults to make the right decisions" (MacLellan, 2019), and who "insist on telling people when to arrive at work, where to sit, what to do, how to dress, how to behave and so on" (Borges, 2018). Unsurprisingly, notes Borges (2018), "when companies treat adults like children or teenagers who cannot entirely think for themselves, then that's exactly how they will behave."

On a third level, corporations can also—purposefully or not—encourage what sociologist Max Pagès (2005, p. 230) calls "massive collective regressions." For example, documenting *The Google Life*, hacktivist and Reddit co-designer Aaron Swartz (2006) remarked that:

It's about infantilizing people . . . Give them free food, do
their laundry, let them sit on bouncy brightly-colored balls. Do
everything so that they never have to grow up and learn how to live
life on their own . . . The dinosaurs and spaceships certainly fit in
with the infantilizing theme, as does the hot tub-sized ball pit that
Googlers can jump into and throw ball fights. Everyone I know
who works there either acts childish (the army of programmers),
enthusiastically adolescent (their managers and overseers), or else
is deeply cynical (the hot-shot programmers). But as much as they
may want to leave Google, the infantilizing tactics have worked:
they're afraid they wouldn't be able to survive anywhere else.

Similarly, researchers Mühlhoff and Slaby (2018) warn that the 'fun' and immersive architectural designs of Google and other companies of its ilk do not simply encourage infantile tendencies and dependency but are also instrumental in manipulating the much more volatile realm of (especially young) employees' affective relations and investments:

---

[75] See also Hebert (2019) and Teodorescu (2017).
[76] See also Eriksen (2001) and Gustavvson (2005).

> [they] are exemplary of a local arrangement designed to immerse employees with their personal and affective potentials, relations and impulses into a productive apparatus of human relations, thus making their energies exploitable for company benefit. While teamwork stimulates and harnesses affective bonds of co-workers around the felt qualities of reciprocal reliability, guilt, appreciation, insecurities, shared commitment, the affective arrangement of a "life at Google" additionally stimulates a "play instinct," and, by that means, "creativity" (Mühlhoff & Slaby, 2018, p. 166).

The authors also critically examine the subtle and implicitly coercive dimension of those affective arrangements that may—emotionally—'lock in' employees more forcefully and cunningly than conspicuously authoritarian work regimes (Cabanas & Illouz, 2019).

In sharp contrast to the young hip Silicon Valley employees who are encouraged to have fun, to play, to bond, to express themselves, and to be creative, less fortunate workers are more likely to be strictly disciplined and threatened. Commenting on the working conditions that are—ironically—imposed on Disneyland employees, Cultural Studies scholar Dick Hebdige (2003) describes this infantilization as:

> a process whereby employees . . . bludgeoned into submission by downsizing, deskilling and temporary contracts—are made to audition for their jobs on a daily basis, are expected, on pain of summary dismissal, to defer automatically to all 'superiors,' to stay 'in role,' 'on script' and 'in view'—subject to surveillance by company-appointed supervisors for however long the shift lasts at the work-place. (p. 161)

This work regime extends beyond the Magic Kingdom and organizes other sectors of the economy as well (Ehrenreich, 2011; Van Maanen, 1991; Van Maanen & Kunda, 1989). Thus, a 2015 research published by the RAND corporation (2017) finds that 20 percent of American workers report abuse or harassment at work and that 36 percent have no say in setting their work hours.

### Terminal Regressions

Manuel Castells (2006, p. 60) defines the contemporary 'network society' as "the social structure resulting from the interaction between the new technological paradigm and social organization at large." In his analysis, the digital networks of communication are as much the 'backbone' of the network society as the power networks were the infrastructure of the industrial one.

The colonization of everyday life by terminals is by now well documented. In 2017, a Pew Research Center report found that nearly nine-in-ten Americans were online, that roughly three-quarters owned a smartphone, and that nearly three-quarters had broadband service at home (Smith, 2017). In 2019, the total number of computers in the world was 2 billion.[77] That same year, another Pew Research Center report indicated that a third of all American adults are "almost constantly online" (Perrin & Kumar, 2019). That same year, research found that there were 8,918,157,500 active connected devices and about 5,123,988,900 unique mobile subscribers, which adds up to 65.65 percent of the planet's inhabitants being connected.[78]

The terminal colonization of our institutional, socio-cultural, and physical environments extends to our mental ones. To quote Marshall McLuhan, we shape our technologies and they, in turn, shape us. Whether it's a microscope or Microsoft, technologies have 'preferred encodings;' they are designed to be used in prescribed

[77] Source: SCMO
[78] Source: Quora

ways, and have—to quote Zygmunt Bauman—"manipulated probabilities" (Bauman & Lyon, 2013, p. 79). To operate those technologies efficiently, users must adjust certain skeletal, muscular, sensory, cognitive, or neural movements to them, and such adjustments necessarily transform them.

Technologies necessarily also concretize, normalize, and promote particular perceptions of reality. They are "genuine social indicators of what a society thinks of itself, how it represents itself, and hence realizes itself" (Carr, 2011, p. 45). This is especially true of mental technologies, as they both embody "an intellectual ethic, a set of assumptions about how the human mind works or should work," and transmit those into the minds and culture of its users (Dubey, 2005, p. 275). For Levy (2011),

> Technology has become a major component of my ideology and of most people's, at least in the sense of "ideology" that refers not to a set of opinions but to actual behaviors and rituals that integrate people into social structures. Insofar as electronic devices determine our actual behavior on a day-to-day basis, it is not too much to say that ideology is engineered.

Accordingly, "machines can and do accelerate trends, magnify cultural weaknesses, and fortify certain social structures while eroding others" (Baym, 2010, p. 44). And while they do not "make history by themselves, "some kinds of machines help make different kinds of histories and different kinds of people than others" (Baym, 2010, p. 44)

The multiplying affordances presented by our terminal devices require different kinds of adjustments in various categories of users. Among those, I am especially interested in those adjustments that infantilize adult users, and thus, especially workers.

**Terminal Work**

Today, most American workers are employed in the service sector, and their activities often entail interacting with terminals, often from a variety of locations, across different time zones, and on the go. According to a 2017 Brookings Institution report (Muro et al., 2017), "the share of jobs requiring high digital skills had jumped to 23 percent. The share requiring medium digital skills rose to 48 percent. And in a huge shift, the share of jobs requiring low digital skills fell from 56 to 30 percent." In contrast to the agro-industrial economy that was located in the workplace (the factory plant, the field, the ocean, the mine), the hypermodern one is located in worktime. For many workers in Western and other societies, the important question is less where we work, but for whom and how. This temporal and spatial dislocation of work is significant on many levels. If the factory or the office are concrete physical spaces that can foster solidarity among physically co-present workers, worktime on terminals encourages solitarity— the freedom to personalize one's labor according to one's lifestyle, preferences, and predilections, often in isolation from other co-workers who are becoming increasingly invisible and absent. While working from a mobile terminal is evidently convenient for many and has countless advantages, this dislocation of workplace to worktime is transforming both the life-project of work and the interpenetration between work and personal life. Thus, if a growing number of white-collar and knowledge workers can increasingly leave the office, now the office never leaves them. They are given more freedom to manage the time and space of their labor, but they are also simultaneously expected to work more, and often during their newly gained 'free' time. As a familiar example, many corporate workers are now unofficially expected to attend to work-related e-mails, messages, and phone calls after hours, on weekends, and on holidays (Jauréguiberry, 2014, 2005, 2004, 2003a, 2003b).

Where Marx indicted an industrialist order that brutalizes workers' bodies, the digital one rewires workers' brains—their thoughts, perceptions, emotions, dispositions, and even neural activity (Bauerlin, 2011; Carr, 2011; Turkle, 2011; Vannini, Waskul, & Gottschalk, 2011). Where the industrial order is oppressive, concrete, and repetitive, the digital one is user-friendly, symbolic, and rapidly mutating. Where the conspicuous factory is the concrete space of the industrial apparatus, the terminal is the mobile and miniaturized node of the digital one. Where power rests in the hands of those who own of the means of production in an industrial order, it rests in the hands of those who own the means of virtual interaction and surveillance in the digital one. In such conditions, terminal workers do not live an alienated existence only because they have lost control over the conditions under which they must labor, but also because they have lost control over their relations to time, space, the tools with which they work and interact, and the rules they must follow to do so (Rosa, 2013). To complicate the picture, the current stage of capitalism also witnesses the rise of an entirely new category of 'prosumers' who are exploited as both consumers and producers, and who produce/consume mostly at terminals (Ritzer, 2015; Ritzer & Jurgenson, 2010).

The idea that interactions with terminals infantilize workers (and adult citizens more generally) might sound technologically deterministic. However, guided by the symbolic interactionist axiom that individuals can only develop as individuals through interactions with others, one must acknowledge that in the hypermodern present, the terminal is becoming an increasingly important 'other' with which/ whom workers must interact and through which they interact with others. Routinely interacting with terminals requires users to adjust to four unique and interrelated affordances that infantilize them: Dependence and coercion, personalization, simplification, and surveillance.

## Dependence and Coercion

On an immediate level, an infantile mindset is already invited in the childlike design of many webpages, logos, lettering, colors, icons, and brand names (Bunz, 2015). According to neuropsychologist Greenfield (2017), the very software, apps, and interfaces that power the terminal "are infantilizing the brain into the state of small children who are attracted by buzzing noises and bright lights, who have a small attention span and who live for the moment." More importantly, however, terminals infantilize users by the combined effects of dependence and coercion. Today, in order to participate competently in society, we must access a terminal. Whether we want to locate a journal article or apply for a job, purchase music or book a trip, select a doctor or register for a conference, there is no escape and no relief. As Hassan (2009, p. 134; 2012) puts it, we are increasingly becoming victims of digital slavery, and are growing dependent on terminals because "we need to be connected to live and work and to be part of the 'normal' mainstream of networked life." It is useful to remember that pre-digital technologies such as televisions, telephones, or typewriters were neither necessary for participation in everyday life nor pervasive. Individuals could function quite effectively for long periods of time without using them, some lived without them altogether, and they were not perceived to suffer from social exclusion, boredom, boorishness, or deprivation as a result. As we increasingly interact with terminals to meet a growing catalog of needs, it becomes near-impossible to imagine society, interactions, and everyday life that are free of their presence. Thus, a third of a sample of American adults report that their mobile devices are 'something they can't imagine living without,' with almost half deeming their attachment to these devices 'an addiction'[79] (Bodford et al., 2017, p. 320).

We confront our dependence on digital technologies especially in those instances when we find ourselves paralyzed because there is no internet connection, because 'computers are slow,' our batteries are empty, or 'the system is down.' These

[79] See also Rainie and Anderson (2017).

moments of paralysis remind us that "our ability to perform the everyday competently is now contingent on the widest range of obscure factors" about which we understand very little (Greenfield, 2017) and over which we have no control. We also experience this dependence when we confront our inability to understand their functioning, to master their capacities, to manage the power they bestow, and the risks they present. As a result, the smarter they become, the stupider we feel (Rosa, 2013). To soften the alarming realization of this total dependence, routine interactions with terminals remind users that:

> there is no need to understand the forces and interests that have created those bright colourful surfaces. Cheerful design sets users free from second thoughts about the complexity of the technological apparatus, or about the complexity of the world we live in. The user does not need to understand, but just needs to try it: go create. No need to think twice. Simply do as you are invited, and play along happily, dear child. (Bunz, 2015, pp. 197-198)

These recurring experiences of dependence and coercion always already position users as certain kinds of subjects who find their capacity to make informed decisions, to exercise free will, and to develop a sense of efficacy degraded to a lower stage of development (Keen, 2012).

Interactions with terminals further infantilize users in a more implicit but significant manner. Terminals are uniquely interactive in at least two senses. First, because they enable users to interact with others who are not physically co-present, and that is one of their two main functions. Second, because terminals interact with us. Unlike, say, Ernest Hemingway's Corona typewriter or Annie Leibovitz's Cannon Mark III camera, we do not interact with terminals by simply pressing on mechanical keys or carefully rotating lenses. Our terminals ask us questions, require that we make particular decisions and perform particular gestures, to which they respond in an emerging and potentially endless dialogue. In other words, we must interact with (rather than operate) terminals in order to use them efficiently. In this sense, terminals are not solely coercive because we must interact with them to participate in everyday life, but because we must obey their inflexible rules of interaction. Those rules do not serve human needs or dispositions but articulate a constraining digital logic. The routine experience of submitting to inflexible digital rules might also cultivate in users the habit of all too easily surrendering to technological authority. This habit inevitably reduces adults' range of (and belief in their) capacities, sense of autonomy, of agency, and trust in their abilities to guide the outcomes of interactions.

## Personalization

Although our enforced interactions with terminals should prompt spirited resistance, it does not. On the contrary, we love our terminal devices. We never leave home without them and bring them with us wherever we go. We interrupt whatever we are doing and compulsively turn towards them whenever they indicate that someone or something is summoning us. We talk to them, listen to them, and teach them to recognize our voices. We conspire with them and entrust our memories and secrets to them. We rely on them to remember important information and consult them when making vital decisions. We protect, accessorize, and decorate them. We feel panic when we lose them, violated when others access them without our permission, and experience a condition akin to brain damage when they no longer respond.

On one hand, we are attached to our terminals because, as we saw above, we simply depend on them to accomplish a growing number of basic functions that were once easily performed without the assistance of complex (or any) devices. On the other hand, we are also attached to them because we personalize them to our unique proclivities and preferences. Scholars of the internet consider this affordance of personalization as the game changer that launched Web 3.0—the third internet revolution. Introduced in 2009 to improve the performance of the Google search engine, this second affordance of personalization has evolved considerably and is rapidly re-organizing all our interactions with terminals. We experience this personalization on at least three levels.

### Appearance

Personalization refers, first, to our ability to customize the very appearance of our terminal devices. We can, for example, decide on the number, types, location, and animations of the icons that populate our screen. We adjust the screen's brightness and haptic sensitivity. We select the screensavers, the background images, the window sizes and the color intensity. We calibrate the speed of the mouse's clicking, scrolling, and tracking. We choose the fonts, assign the shortcuts, and set the toolbars. We schedule back-up functions and pick our 'security' and 'privacy' parameters. On all our terminal devices, our preferences become the default settings and are concretized into a visible (virtual) reality that we can continuously alter. In addition, and under the constant threat of hacking, we are urged to personalize our terminals even more by encoding secret passwords, sweeping patterns, fingerprints, or facial recognition that will protect them and us. Of course, although generous, this affordance to personalize the physical appearance of the terminal is not limitless. It is still encoded by certain rules to which we must submit, and which we cannot change, at least not without a great deal of specialized knowledge. Still, this palpable ability to personalize the appearance of the terminal constitutes a profound revolution in our relation to objects.

### Content

Our ability to personalize the terminal's appearance extends to its content. Tripped by enigmatic algorithms, our terminal records the kinds of information we are likely to pay attention to and daily 'recommends' newspapers we'd probably like to read, music we'd probably like to listen to, movies we'd probably like to watch, food we'd probably like to taste, places we'd probably like to visit, people we'd probably like to 'friend,' and political causes we'd probably like to support.[80] In addition, if we are offended, irritated, or bored by any type of content, we can easily delete it, report it, and avoid all future similar ones.[81] Unsurprisingly, this 'filtering' disposition also guides our treatment of the 'real' people we encounter at the terminal. Here also, we can summarily block, ignore, un-friend, un-follow, or crop out of our lives those who have displeased us, those whose attitudes, poor taste, or belief systems offend us, those who irritate us, and those who bore us. As we increasingly personalize our terminal experience and as it records our choices, mirrors those back to us, and continuously fine-tunes them, we withdraw into what Eli Pariser (2012) calls a 'filter bubble.' As he notes,

> Ultimately, the proponents of personalization offer a vision of a custom-tailored world, every facet of which fits us perfectly. It's a cozy place, populated by our favorite people and things and ideas . . . If we never click on the articles about cooking, or gadgets, or the world outside our country's borders, they simply fade away . . . We're never bored. We're never annoyed. Our media is a perfect reflection of our interests and desires (Pariser, 2012, pp. 12, 125). [82]

---

[80] Although there are some recommendation systems that try to educate users and broaden their tastes. Those, however, can also be controversial. See Karakayali, Kostem, and Galip (2018).

[81] Except, as always, commercial ads, unless we pay.

[82] In his farewell address, president Obama also recognizes this withdrawal as one of the three main challenges America faces today.

Psychologist Watzlawick (1977) famously stated that believing that one's view of reality is the only reality is the most dangerous of all delusions. Yet, the terminal's increasingly precise algorithms normalize this delusion; by adjusting the terminal to our self, we are also adjusting our self to the terminal (Pariser, 2012).

Social psychologists of various stripes have long established that a person's ability to self-reflect accurately from the perspective of an increasingly complex, abstract, diverse, and distant other is key to mental-moral maturity, to emotional and social intelligence, and—more generally—to sanity. However, self-reflection requires intelligent role-taking—an adult aptitude that typically entails empathy. Paradoxically, however, while the terminal has multiplied the number of people with whom users could potentially self-reflect and role-take, Sherry Turkle's (2011) research suggests that today's youth are both decreasingly capable of role-taking, and of finding much value in the ability to do so.

However, as our interactions with terminals are becoming increasingly personalized and responsive, our interactions with humans are becoming increasingly uncivil and aloof (Bauman, 2000),[83] and one suspects that those two trends are related. In contrast to the cornucopia of options we can select to better personalize our terminal experience, those real individuals we meet both at the terminal and face-to-face typically neither instantly adjust to our moods nor anticipate our constantly changing preferences. Switching back and forth between those very different mindsets requires skills such as intuition, mutual perceptiveness, sensitivity to context, and, as we'll see below, patience. But those are categorically not the sorts of adult aptitudes one can learn and nurture in terminal interactions. To wit, Balbus (2005, p. 117) notes that such interactions facilitate the three fundamental—and infantile—narcissistic fantasies "of the grandiose self: the fantasy of total control, the fantasy of perfect recognition, and the fantasy of immortality." As a result, perhaps, "a quarter of Americans report having no close confidantes, double the number who reported such a degree of isolation in 1985" (Jackson, 2009, pp. 59-60). Similarly, in a recent *New York Times* editorial, Khullar (2016) reports that the percentage of Americans who say they feel lonely has recently doubled to 40 percent. As he notes, such a condition is literally killing many of those so afflicted.

### Operation

"All the Power You Want. All Day Long," promises the commercial ad for the Mac Book Air. "Rule the Air," a printed Verizon commercial ad exhorts viewers. Terminal interactions also induce the experience of personalization by normalizing the regressive expectation of constant and instant gratification. Whether we want to access our GPS, listen to music, play a video-game, send someone a joke, call a friend, or launch a relaxation app, we expect that the terminal will instantly respond to, and even anticipate, our every desire. Whenever, wherever, and on whatever device we choose. As a recent study reports, adult users expect a webpage to load at—literally—the blink of an eye (Gilbertson, 2012), and random delays in their ability to connect or download that were routine a mere fifteen years ago have now become intolerable.

Thus, while users are attached to their terminals because they depend on them and because they inscribe their identity in them, this attachment is not only directed to the terminal-as-object but also to the terminal-as-experience. Roberts (2014, p. 9) sums this idea well by suggesting that much of what most purveyors of personal technology are really selling is "the ability to generate the highest level of momentary pleasure for the least effort." He further writes:

> moment to moment, we have the potential to make our leisure
> time . . . into a sequence of personal, personalizing experiences

---

[83] Current research on the loneliness epidemy also attests to this trend.

in which various smart technologies filter out the stressful and the mundane so we can get on with our real job, which, apparently, is self-expression. (Roberts, 2014, p. 121)

The consequences of these experiences (and expectations) must unavoidably shape users' face-to-face encounters and complicate their very relations to the world (Bauman, 2005). If "homo consumans becomes allergic to the slightest wait" (Lipovetsky, 2006, p. 102), Bugeja (2005, p. 24) reminds us, that "technology may function 'on demand' but people usually do not." However, such a lesson is difficult to absorb when users have been habituated to an interactional regime that typically delivers on its promise to satisfy literally every (virtual) desire "in the palm of your hand," with a "quick download," with "instant access," and "on demand" (Eriksen, 2001). For example, bots are reducing even the endless waits at customer service call lines so as to bring waiting time to near-zero (Balch, 2020; Ciechanowski et al., 2019; Daniel et al., 2018; Dredge, 2016).

The digital affordance of personalization complements and amplifies similar trends in contemporary society. Thus, Bauman (2007, p. 44) reminds us that "the society of consumers is perhaps the only society in human history to promise happiness in earthly life, and happiness here and now and in every successive 'now.'"[84] Feeling entitled to "the best and the most beautiful" contemporary 'turboconsumers' purchase commodities and services whose main function is to gratify hyper-individualistic sensuous, psychological, and affective desires (Lipovetsky, 2006, p. 44). Discussing the rapid proliferation of cell phones, Ebert (2011) also notes that

only in an age in which the private microsphere of the individual has become the basic elementary socio-cosmological unit, could cell phone technology exist. Indeed, the technology itself actually makes the hidden ontology visible. We have cell phones because each of us is now a world-island, a cosmos-in-miniature, unto himself and the cell phone, correspondingly, is a technological outgrowth made possible by this basic ontological fact of the status of the human individual who now exists "outside" of any protective macrosphere. (p. 139)

The dispositions prompted by personalized terminal interactions are interrelated, mutually reinforcing, and of course, pleasurable, because behind the high-tech language, these interactions reward infantile cravings. They induce self-centeredness, gratify the narcissistic need for validation, prompt impulsivity, nurture fantasies of omnipotence, endorse the sense of entitlement for immediate attention, and normalize the expectation of constant and instant gratification. Various social scientists are reasonably concerned that this 'technologically induced puerility' (Barber, 2008, p. 3) might prompt a profound 'global sociological mutation' (Lipovetsky, 1983, p. 11). Psychologist Tisseron (2008, pp. 224-225), for example, announces a "Society of Denial" where the new technological organization of society enables users to "ignore what one does not want to know . . . The role of the virtual sphere will be to normalize this refusal."

### Simplification

Interactions with terminals also prompt a simplification of cognitive functions, another key component of the infantilist ethos. We can perhaps better understand this idea by considering pre-terminal technologies that perform distinctive operations and function according to distinctive principles. Recording a conversation, for example, demands a different engagement, knowledge, gestures, and skills than taking pictures, calling someone on the phone, typing a note, playing the *Space Invaders* video game, consulting one's calendar, or locating oneself on a map. Today, we can perform all

[84] See also Dufour (2008).

these very different activities and an infinity more on the go, at the same terminal devices, many of which fit in our pockets, on our wrists, or under our arms. As the number and variety of functions we can/must now activate at the terminal grow exponentially, the expert manual skills one acquired by the increasingly dexterous and intelligent manipulation of concrete objects become simplified as artless gestures on the terminals' flat plastic surfaces. In some sense, the monotonous manual gestures we must perform on terminals already articulate—and invite—a simplified type of mental engagement we exercise there. The more we adjust to this simplified engagement and are rewarded for doing so well, the less likely we are to cultivate pre-terminal ways of knowing and skills. In turn, the less developed those are, the less confident we feel in their applications, and the more likely we are to turn to terminal shortcuts, in a rapidly escalating vicious cycle of dependence and ineptitude.

## Software Thinking

In 1964, sociologist of technology Jacques Ellul prophesized that
> knowledge will be accumulated in "electronic banks" and transmitted directly to the human nervous system by means of coded electronic messages. There will no longer be any need of reading or learning mountains of useless information; everything will be received and registered according to the needs of the moment. There will be no need of attention or effort. What is needed will pass directly from the machine to the brain without going through consciousness. (Ellul, 1964, p. 432)

I use the term "software thinking" to designate the simplified cognitive style we deploy when we 'sync' to terminal interactions.[85] For Hassan (2009, pp. 98, 120), this cognitive style prompts 'abbreviated thinking' where "the time needed to think critically and reflectively . . . is reduced through the combination of information overload and speed." For philosopher Lynch (2016), this cognitive mode is significantly different from—and undermines—the much more complex, experience-based, and creative 'understanding.' Unfortunately, he notes, 'Google-knowing' is rapidly displacing other types of knowledge and the very experience of knowing. For Ebert (2011) also,
> We are forced . . . to trade off a diversity of media sources— magazines, newspapers, etc.—for only one kind of media: digital. The disappearance of diversity, especially of media, is never a good thing, for in this case, it amounts to a massive cultural impoverishment. As a result of the elimination of choices, we are increasingly forced to rely more and more on the Internet in order to get access to our media, our news and our information, articles, essays, reviews, etc., which is only one means of purveying such media and arguably not even the best. (p. 12)

Turkle (2009) also detects other worrisome trends and quite a bit of anxiety among scientists who must increasingly rely on terminal simulations and immersion rather than on embodied and deep knowledge.

Paradoxically, therefore, while the sheer volume of information, speed, and analytic power enabled by the terminal should enhance knowledge workers' capacity to understand many topics at a most sophisticated level, the opposite obtains. We may have access to more information and faster than at any other time in the history of our species, but we are decreasingly capable of making sense of it, let

---

[85] It goes without saying that terminal interactions prompt physical and sensory adjustments as well. See for example, Vannini, Waskul and Gottschalk (2011), and Gottschalk (2018).

alone, evaluating, integrating, and using it. As cultural studies scholar Andrejevic (2013) finds, the analysis of gargantuan volumes of big data yields correlations and predictions, but rarely explanations. French sociologist Jauréguiberry (2014) reaches similar conclusions:

> our ability to connect in real time enabled by our informational prostheses coincides with a generalized disconnect in our capacities to understand, to put in perspective, to contextualize, and to interpret the information that reaches us. Information comes in, goes out, and circulates, but it does not stop. The proliferation of information blinds us. (p. 48)

This simplification of cognitive functions is especially worrisome for professionals whose work consists in producing and communicating information. At my university library, for example, an increasing number of books and articles are now only available as e-books. In addition to inducing a shallower engagement and less retention, many of these virtual texts that I download on my terminal are accessible for only two weeks, after which they magically become unavailable.[86] This curious management of intellectual resources not only betrays a poor understanding of how knowledge workers actually attend to information, it also invites (and even forces) them to simplify how they do so. As research suggests, more and more scholars cite fewer and fewer articles, and what they cite is predicated by self-fulfilling search engines that, as Carr (2016, p. 206) notes, "give precedence to popularity and recency over diversity of opinion, rigor of argument or quality of expression." Whether and how academics actually read the texts they cite also attests to simplification. As a study conducted by the British Library finds, users spend an average of four minutes on an e-book. Another research report that 60 percent of serious scholars do not read more than three pages of an e-journal, and 65 percent of them never come back for a second look.[87] With software thinking, knowledge workers simplify their engagement with texts by scanning it in order to locate and pluck out those bits of decontextualized information that seem immediately relevant for the task at hand.

Discussing the decline of what could once be considered 'scholarship,' Rosa (2013) also notes other trends:

> The speed and succession of conferences and articles are so high, and—even worse than the number of articles—the number of published books and journals is so excessive that those who write and express themselves in this era dominated by the 'publish or perish' motto have a hard time finding enough time to correctly develop their arguments, while those who read and listen are lost on a jungle of half-baked and repetitive publications and presentations. (p. 74)

As knowledge workers increasingly defer to the terminal to find information about pretty much any topic, as software thinking supplants other—and decreasingly valued—forms of knowing, their capacity to understand information is undermined (Lynch, 2016). Prophetically perhaps, Jacques Ellul (1964), decried a near future whereby

> The intelligentsia will no longer be a model, a conscience, or an animating intellectual spirit for the group, even in the sense of performing a critical function. They will be the servants, the most conformist imaginable, of the instruments of technique... And education will no longer be an unpredictable and exciting

---

[86] The most recent one I downloaded is available for only 24 hours.
[87] As described by Carr (2011, pp. 134-135), "F-reading" refers to an F-like eye movement when reading whereby the reader examines the top of the text, then scrolls down and reads a bit in the middle, and then slides down to the end.

adventure in human enlightenment, but an exercise in conformity and an apprenticeship to whatever gadgetry is useful in a technical world. (p. 348)

In sum, terminal interactions nurture a "new way not to think" (Turkle, 2011, p. 240). They "inhibit creative association, reduce randomness and serendipity, decontextualize, promote passive learning, yield incomplete knowledge, and favor hyper-focus rather than general knowledge and synthesis" (Carr, 2016). And beyond the simplification and stunting of specific cognitive competencies, software thinking also alters their integration and interdependencies, thereby re-designing our brain architecture.[88] We are unlikely to notice this degradation because—among other reasons—as long as we adjust to the rules of software thinking, the personalized terminals reward us. They validate us as skillful, efficient, productive, and powerful. In addition, as software thinking is increasingly supplanting other forms of knowing, we have diminishing alternative models with which to gauge our cognitive decline.

## Surveillance

"We know where you are. We know where you have been. We can more or less know what you're thinking about," Google CEO Eric Schmidt once famously claimed (in Rainie & Wellman, 2012, p. 18). "Google knows more about us than we can remember ourselves," writes Viktor Mayer-Schönberger (2009, p. 7). "It knows us so well that it finishes our sentences," remarks Lynch (2016, p. 155). In contrast to our relation to pre-terminal technologies, our activities at the terminal are constantly surveilled. As an example, up until quite recently, routine activities such as buying anything, reading a newspaper, listening to music, looking at pictures, watching a movie, consulting a website, locating an address on a map, or playing a video-game, were dispersed, anonymous, private, and unrecorded. In other words, the pre-digital era allowed individuals quite a wide latitude in what Goffman (1963) called 'information control'— the ability to control the information others have about oneself (Feaster, 2010). Today, as all those activities increasingly occur at the terminal, they can be precisely located, timed, attributed to a specific individual, stored, analyzed, shared, and used for manipulation purposes. More worrisome, it has now become cliché to remark that even when our terminal is turned off, it is constantly collecting and transmitting information about where we are, where we have been, for how long, what we say, what we do, etc. The most baffling aspect of this situation is not the terminal's surveillance capacities, as daunting as they are, but that it has become cliché. In other words, we have been forced to surrender to a condition of constant and remote surveillance that—except in spy movies or paranoid delusions—would have been considered preposterous a mere few decades ago (Andrejevic, 2007). In the hypermodern moment, however, "intense scrutiny—even in unexpected situations—is a realistic possibility" and "transparency is a new requirement" (Rainie & Wellman, 2012).

These coercive adjustments are unpleasant, to say the least. For example, research by Ball (2009, p. 650) finds that individuals who realize that their privacy has been exposed without their consent experience "emotional, psychoanalytic and corporeal responses which are sometimes stultifyingly profound." The terminal capacities for surveillance require our attention because they transfer an enormous amount of power to (not always benevolent) organizations, and in so doing, promote a more sinister kind of infantilization than the more "fun" ones discussed above. Calling this new form of surveillance power the 'Big Other,' social psychologist Shoshana Zuboff (2015, p. 75) explains that it "is constituted by unexpected and often illegible mechanisms of extraction, commodification, and control that effectively exile persons from their own behavior."

---

[88] Turkle (2011); see also Roberts (2014).

Perhaps one reason explaining our consent to such an outrageous situation is that this constant surveillance does not feel concrete, constraining, or coercive. On the contrary, hypermodern surveillance is "soft" (Marx, 2007), "remote and silent" (Ball, 2009, p. 647), "intrusive and invisible, more invasive but perceived as normal" (Ragnedda, 2011, p. 187) and "gains compliance by persuasion, rather than coercion" (Ball, 2009, p. 650). To wit, Ragnedda (2011, p. 47) finds that Italian students "completely underestimate the danger of privacy violation and the transfer of personal data." Turkle (2011) reports that American youth react to this erosion of privacy with despair, hopelessness, anxiety, or plain denial. And even those lucid enough to attempt to appraise the situation head-on have abdicated to the realization that there is simply no alternative. In France, Acquisiti (2011) discovers that when it comes to matters of privacy at the terminal, adult consumers defy traditional psychological models of rational behavior. Calling such models 'unrealistic,' he believes that they should be replaced by more complex ones that indicate psychological distortion. Those, he believes, will hopefully provide a more accurate understanding of adult consumers' decision-making.

This 'consent' to constant surveillance, however, is a myth. We no longer have a choice; we do not consent but submit. Although we increasingly find ourselves forced to interact with a terminal to access an exponentially growing array of resources, in many cases, we can only do so if we, first begrudgingly 'accept' or 'agree' with the terms of incomprehensible contracts that often contain the clause that its authors "reserve the right to change the rules of the game at any time," even retroactively (Pariser, 2011, pp. 239-240).

However, by denying individuals any meaningful choice in the matter, it "has decided for us" (Lynch, 2016, p. 107). This now normalized violation of privacy denies adult users the status of adults and demotes them to conditions of visibility typically enforced on incarcerated populations, social groups deemed dangerous or ineligible, and children (Foucault, 1977; Goffman, 1961). As Gary Marx (2016) notes, workers subjected to electronic surveillance

> may feel they are being treated like children . . . and interpret the workplace to be saying "We don't trust you. We expect you to behave irresponsibly, to take advantage, and to screw up unless we remove all temptation and prevent you from doing so or trick or force you to do otherwise." (p. 194)

The information necessary for the exercise of total surveillance and social control is enabled by the affordances of dependence-coercion and personalization. On the input side, adult users' interactions with their personalized terminals provide constant, instant, and non-judgmental gratification of all impulses and desires, and validate narcissistic fantasies. In so doing, these interactions invite adult users to spontaneously communicate the deepest recesses of their minds to a terminal that feels increasingly like an extension of their selves. On the output side, all this very personalized information that users produce when they interact with terminals (and even when they are not) provides all the 'data' necessary to implement the most sophisticated system of social control ever invented. Behind the personalized terminal screens hide the watchful eyes of those who/that operate them and collect information about users' behaviors. Behind the affordance for 'authenticity' and self-expression hide the algorithms of personalized manipulation. However, capitulation to surveillance invites a relationship to authority that blends "culpability, panic, a feeling of inferiority, and eventually, of submission" (Dubey, 2005, p. 284). In so doing, it reinforces the experience of infantilization in even more deleterious ways.

## Conclusion

The infantilizing subjectivity workers experience when they adjust to the four interrelated terminal affordances of necessity/coercion, personalization, simplification, and surveillance resonates with the infantilizing culture of the workplace and society at large. As the majority of occupations in contemporary society require employees to interact with terminals and with each other through terminals, one suspects that these devices will increasingly be used not just to communicate goal-oriented information and to organize tasks, but also to disseminate the corporate ideology, to impose an organization-sanctioned identity, to extract employee loyalty, to mobilize their emotional investments, and to enforce relationships and hierarchy. Their use will simultaneously enhance our performance as workers and disable us as adults.

It also bears remembering that, in contrast to a typewriter, a television, or a telephone, terminals evolve; they become smarter and respond faster. Today, we assume, humans are still in the control booth and program the terminal. But that too is rapidly changing. With the rise of the 'Internet of Things' and other technological leaps, the terminals that colonize our public and private environments will soon be able to autonomously analyze a near-infinite volume of information, to communicate between them, to compute desirable outcomes, to coordinate action, and to execute it.[89] Terminals are—to quote Dator et al.—'mutative technologies' that "are once again redefining what it means to be humans living on a planet mutating faster than ever" (Dator, Sweeney, & Yee, 2015, p. 109). As they warn, technologies "will be taking on a much more profound role in the shaping of society in the futures beyond the capacity of human agency, which has already been shaped by the tools that make and remake us as humans" (Dator, Sweeney & Yee, 2015, p. 109).

Mutually reinforcing, the socially-engineered infantilist regression enforced in everyday institutions and the technologically 'induced puerility' prompted by terminal interactions are rapidly deteriorating key adult capacities at the very moment when we need them most. Tragically, the infantilization of the adult population is almost symbiotically related to the rapid cognitive evolution of our terminal technologies. Once they reach the point of singularity, they will be able to autonomously program their own evolution, and hence, ours.[90] In this sense, perhaps, if the conditions of work and everyday life in the industrial regime alienate workers and citizens, the conditions of work in the digital one infantilizes them and renders them increasingly superfluous.

---

[89] 'The Internet of Things' refers to new and often miniaturized technological devices that will make our private and public environments increasingly "intelligent." They will, for example, be able to locate us, sense our moods, anticipate what we are about to do, and react accordingly.

[90] "Singularity" refers to the scenario where computers become self-aware, super-intelligent, and begin evolving at super-human speeds.

## References

Acquisiti, A. (2011). Les comportements de vie privée face au commerce éléctronique. *Réseaux, 167*(3), 107-130.

Andrejevic, M. (2007). *iSpy: Surveillance and power in the interactive era*. University of Kansas Press.

Andrejevic, M. (2013). *Infoglut: How too much information is changing the way we think and know*. Routledge.

Aubert N. (2008). Les nouvelles quêtes d'éternité. *Études, 408*(2), 197-207.

Barus-Michel, J. (2005). L'Hypermodernité, dépassement ou perversion de la modernité? In N. Aubert (Ed.), *L'individu hypermoderne* (pp. 246-247). Érès.

Balbus, I. D. (2005). *Mourning and identity: Essays in the psychoanalysis of contemporary society*. Otherness.

Barber, B. (2008). *Consumed: How markets corrupt children, infantilize adults, and swallow citizens whole*. W. W. Norton & Co.

Ball, K. (2009). Exposure: Exploring the subject of surveillance. *Information, Communication and Society, 12*(5), 639-57.

Bauerlin, M. (Ed.) (2011). *The Digital divide: Arguments for and against Facebook, Google, texting, and the age of social networking*. Tarcher Books.

Bauman, Z. (2000). *Liquid modernity*. Polity.

Bauman, Z. (2005). *Liquid life*. Polity.

Bauman, Z. (2007). *Consuming life*. Polity.

Bauman, Z., & Lyon, D. (2013). *Liquid surveillance*. Polity.

Baumbach, N. (Director). (2010). *Greenberg* [Film]. Scott Ruddin Production.

Baym, N. K. (2010). *Personal connection in the digital age*. Polity.

Baym, N. K., & Boyd, D. (2012). Socially mediated publicness: An introduction. *Journal of Broadcasting & Electronic Media, 56*(3), 320-329.

Belk, R. (2000). May the farce be with you: On Las Vegas and consumer infantilization. *Consumption Markets & Culture, 4*(2), 101-124.

Belk, R. W. (2013). Extended self in a digital world. *Journal of Consumer Research, 40*(3), 477-500.

Berman, M. (2000). *The twilight of American culture*. W.W. Norton.

Berman, M. (2006). *Dark ages America: The final phase of empire*. W. W. Norton.

Bernardini, J. (2014). The infantilization of the postmodern adult and the figure of kidult. *Postmodern Openings, 5*(2), 39-55.

Blatterer, H. (2007). Contemporary adulthood: Reconceptualizing an uncontested category. *Current Sociology, 55*(6), 771-792.

Bodford, J. E., Kwan, V. S, & Sobota, D. S. (2017). Fatal attractions: Attachment to smartphones predicts anthropomorphic beliefs and dangerous behaviors. *Cyberpsychology, Behavior, and Social Networking, 20*(5), 320-326.

Borges, I. (2018, February 26). Hiring adults? How about treating them as adults too? *Semco Style Institute*. https://semcostyle.org/articles/2018/02/hiring-adultseur-how-about-treating-them-as-adults-too-eur.

Brisman, A., & South, N. (2015). 'Life-stage dissolution,' infantilization, and antisocial consumption: Implications for de-responsibilization, denial, and environmental harm. *Young, 23*(3), 209-221.

Bugeja, M. (2005). *Interpersonal divide: The search for community in a technological age*. Oxford University Press.

Bunz, M. (2015). School will never end: On infantilization in digital environments—Amplifying empowerment or propagating stupidity? In D. M. Berry & M. Dieter (Eds.), *Postdigital aesthetics: Art, computation and design* (pp. 191-202). Palgrave-Macmillan.

Cabanas, E., & Illouz, E. (2019). *Manufacturing happy citizens: How the science and industry of happiness control our lives*. Polity.

Calcutt, A. (2000). *Arrested development: Pop culture and the erosion of adulthood*. Cassell.

Carr, N. (2011). *The shallows: What the internet is doing to our brains*. W. W. Norton.

Carr, N. (2016). *The glass gage: Who needs humans anyway?*. Vintage.

Castells, M. (2006). The network society: From knowledge to policy. In M. Castell & G. Cardoso (Eds.), *The network society: From knowledge to policy* (pp. 3-21). Center for Transnational Relations.

Ciechanowski, L. Przgalinska, A., Magnuski, M., & Gloor, P. (2019). In the shades of the uncanny valley: An Experimental study of human-chatbot interaction. *Future Generation Computer Systems, 92*, 539-548.

Daly, S., & Wice, N. (1995). *Alt.culture: An A-to-Z guide to the 90s—Underground, online, and over-the-counter.* Harper-Perennial.

Daniel, F., Matera, M., Zaccaria, V., & Dell'Orto, A. (2018). Toward truly personal chatbots. In H. R. Motahari Nezhad et al. (Eds.), *2018 ADCM/IEEE 1st International Workshop on Software Engineering for Cognitive Services* (pp. 31-36). Association for Computing Machinery.

Dator, J. A., Sweeney, J. A., & Yee, A. M. (2015). *Mutative media: Communication technologies and power relations in the past, present, and futures. Lecture Notes in Social Networks.* Springer.

Dery, M. (1999). *The pyrotechnic insanitarium: American culture on the brink.* Grove Press.

Dnes, A. W. (2017, March 17). We must reverse the infantilization of higher education. *The James G. Martin Center for Academic Renewal.* https://www.jamesgmartin.center/2017/03/must-reverse-infantilization-higher-education/

Dredge, S. (2016, September 18). Why Facebook and Microsoft say chatbots are the talk of the town. *The Guardian.* https://www.theguardian.com/technology/2016/sep/18/chatbots-talk-town-interact-humans-technology-silicon-valley

Dubey, G. (2005). Les systèmes d'information et de communication ou comment les sociétés se pensent. In P. Moati (Ed.), *Nouvelles technologies et modes de vie : Aliénation ou hypermodernité ?* (pp. 273-285). Éditions de l'Aube.

Dufour, R. D. (2008). *The Art of shrinking heads: On the new servitude of the liberated in the age of total capitalism.* Polity Press.

Ebert, J. D. (2011). *The new media invasion: Digital technologies and the world they unmake.* McFarlane.

Ehrenreich, B. (2011). *Nickel and dimed: On (not) getting by in America.* Picador.

Ellul, J. (1964). *The technological society.* Alfred A. Knopf.

Eriksen, T. H. (2001). *The tyranny of the moment: Fast and slow time in the information age.* Pluto Press.

Feaster, J. (2010). Expanding the impression management model of communication channels: An information control scale. *Journal of Computer-Mediated Communication, 16*, 115-138.

Foucault, M. (1977). *Discipline and punish: The birth of the prison.* Pantheon.

Furedi, F. (2004). *Therapy culture: Cultivating vulnerability in an uncertain age.* Routledge.

Furedi, F. (2017, January 2). Why millennials are so fragile. *Minding the Campus.* https://www.mindingthecampus.org/2017/01/02/why-millennials-are-so-fragile/

Gilbertson, S. (2012, March 2). Users expect websites to load in the blink of an eye. *Wired.* https://www.wired.com/2012/03/users-expect-websites-to-load-in-the-blink-of-an-eye/

Goffman, E. (1961). *Asylums: Essays on the social situation of mental patients and other inmates.* Anchor.

Goffman, E. (1963). *Stigma: Notes on the management of spoiled identity.* Simon & Schuster.

Gottschalk, S. (2018). *The terminal self: Everyday life in hypermodern times.* Routledge.

Greenfield, A. (2017). *Radical technologies: The design of everyday life.* Verso.

Gustavsson, B. (2005). The ethics of managing corporate identity. *Journal of Human Values, 11*, 9-29.

Guzman, J. (2015, July 10). 8 de cada 10 personas son incapaces de hacer discursos de un minuto. *El Pais.* http://elpais.com/elpais/2015/07/30/videos/1438279001_736056.htm.

Hassan, R. (2009). *Empires of speed: Time and the acceleration of politics in society.* Brill.

Hassan, R. (2012). *The age of distraction.* Transactions.

Hayward, K. (2012). Pantomime justice: A cultural criminological analysis of 'life stage dissolution.' *Crime Media Culture, 8*(2), 213-229.

Hayward, K. (2013). Life stage dissolution' in Anglo-American advertising and popular culture: Kidults, lil' Britneys and middle youths. *The Sociological Review, 61*(3), 525-548.

Hebdige, D. (2003) Dis-gnosis: Disney and the re-tooling of knowledge, art, culture, life, etc. *Cultural Studies, 17*(2), 150-167.

Herbert, P. (2019, May 6). The infantilization of the American workforce. *HR Examiner: The New Architecture of Work.* https://www.hrexaminer.com

Jappe, A. (1999). Sic transit gloria artis: 'The end of art' for Theodor Adorno and Guy Debord. *Substance, 28*(3), 102-128.

Jauréguiberry, F. (2003a). *Les branchés du portable.* Presses Universitaires de France.

Jauréguiberry, F. (2003b). Internet comme espace inédit de construction de soi. In F. Jauréguiberry and S. Proulx (Eds.), *L'internet, nouvel espace citoyen?* (pp. 223-244). l'Harmattan.

Jauréguiberry, F. (2004). Hypermobilité et télécommunication. In S. Allemand, F. Ascher, & J. Lévy (Eds.), *Les sens du mouvement : Modernité et mobilités dans les sociétés urbaines contemporaines* (pp. 130-138). Belin.

Jauréguiberry, F. (2005). L'immédiaté télécommunicationnelle. In P. Moati (Ed.), *Nouvelles technologies et modes de vie: Aliénation ou hypermodernité ?* (pp. 85-98). Éditions de l'Aube.

Jauréguiberry, F. (2014). La déconnexion aux technologies de communication. *Réseaux, 186*(4), 15-49.

Karakayali, N., Kostem, B., & Galip, I. (2018). Recommendation systems as technologies of the self: Algorithmic control and the formation of music taste. *Theory, Culture & Society, 35*(2), 3-24.

Keen, A. (2012). *Digital vertigo: How today's online social revolution is dividing, diminishing, and disorienting us.* St. Martin Griffin.

Kennedy, D. (2020, February 2). The Disneyfication of a university. *The Chronicle of Higher Education.* https://www.chronicle.com/article/The-Disneyfication-of-a/248015

Labasch, M. (2008, February 12). Are we having fun yet? The infantilization of corporate America. *The Weekly Standard.* https://www.utne.com/politics/are-we-having-fun-yet

Levy, M. (2011). A nation of faces, not laws: Facebook as ideological platform. *Fast Capitalism, 8*(1), http://www.uta.edu/huma/agger/fastcapitalism/8_1/levy8_1.html

Lipovetsky, G. (1983). *L'ère du vide : Essais sur l'individualisme contemporain.* Gallimard.

Lipovetsky, G. (2006). *Le bonheur paradoxal : Essai sur la société d'hyperconsommation.* Gallimard.

Lynch, M. P. (2016). *The internet of us: Knowing more and understanding less in the age of big data.* Liveright.

MacLellan, L. (2019, May 28). 'I deeply resent how we've infantilized the workplace': A manager's manifesto goes viral. *Quartz.* https://qz.com/work/1628017/a-viral-post-asked-for-workplaces-to-treat-employees-like-adults/

Martynnova, I.A., & Glukhov, G. V. (2015). Exploring the echoes of social changes: case study of language infantilism. *Mediterranean Journal of Social Sciences, 6*(6), 315-322.

Maslow, A. (1962). *Toward a psychology of being.* Van Nostrand.

Marx, G. T. (2016). *Windows into the soul: Surveillance and society in an age of high technology.* University of Chicago Press.

Mayer-Schönberger, V. (2009). *Delete: The virtue of forgetting in the digital age.* Princeton University Press.

Mühlhoff, R., & Slaby, J. (2018). Immersion at work: Affect and power in post- Fordist work cultures. In B. Röttger-Rössler & J. Slaby (Eds.), *Affect in relation—Families, places, technologies. Essays on affectivity and subject formation in the 21st century* (pp. 155-174). Routledge.

Muro, M., Liu, S., Whiton, J., & Kulkarni, S. (2017). Digitalization and the American workforce. The Brookings Institution. https://www.brookings.edu/research/digitalization-and-the-american-workforce/

Murphy, M. (2019, April 29). Cell phones now outnumber the world population. *Quartz.* https://qz.com/1608103/there-are-now-more-cellphones-than-people-in-the-world/

Nigam, S. (2018). The infantilization and degeneration of the politics in the recent times. *Social Science Research Network.* https://papers.ssrn.com/sol3/papers.cfm?abstract_id=3124861

Pagès, M. (2005). Massification, régression, violence dans la société contemporaine. In N. Aubert (Ed.), *L'individu hypermoderne* (pp. 229-238). Érès.

Pariser, E. (2012). *The filter bubble: How the new personalized web is changing what we read and how we think.* Penguin.

Perrin, A., & Kummar, M. (2019, July 25). About three-in-ten U.S. adults say they are 'almost constantly' online. Pew Research Center. https://www.pewresearch.org/fact-tank/2019/07/25/americans-going-online-almost- constantly/

Plass, U. (2009). The dialectics of regression: Theodor W. Adorno and Fritz Lang. *Telos, 149,* 127-150.

Ragnedda, M. (2011). Social control and surveillance in the society of consumers. *International Journal of Sociology and Anthropology, 3*(6), 180-188.

Rand Corporation. (2017). American working conditions survey. *Rand Education and Labor.* https://www.rand.org/education-and-labor/projects/american workingconditions.html

Ritzer, G., & Jurgenson, N. (2010). Production, consumption, presumption: The nature of capitalism in the age of the digital 'prosumer.' *Journal of Consumer Culture, 10*(1), 13-36.

Ritzer, G. 2015. Prosumer capitalism. *The Sociological Quarterly, 56*(3), 413-445.

Roberts, P. (2014). *The impulse society: America in the age of instant gratification.* Bloomsberry.

Rosa, H. (2013). *Social Acceleration: A New Theory of Modernity.* Columbia University Press.

Shank, D. B. (2014). Technology and emotions. In J. E. Stets & J. H. Turner (Eds.), *Handbook of the sociology of emotions, Vol. 2* (pp. 511-528). Springer.

Smith, A. (2017, January 12). Record shares of Americans now own smartphones, have home broadband. *Pew Research Center.* https://www.pewresearch.org/internet/fact-sheet/mobile/

Swartz, A. (2006, December 13) The Goog life: How Google keeps employees by treating them like kids. *Aaronsw.com.* http://www.aaronsw.com/weblog/googlife

Teodorescu, A. (2017). Contemporary imaginary of work: Symbolic immortality within the postmodern corporate discourse. In M. H. (Ed.), *Postmortal society: Towards a sociology of immortality* (pp. 114-137). Routledge.

Tisseron, S. (2008). *Virtuel, mon amour : Penser, aimer, souffrir à l'ère des nouvelles technologies.* Albin Michel.

Turkle, S. (2011). *Alone together: Why we demand more of technology and less of each other.* Basic Books.

Van Brakel, R., Moliner, L. A., & Clavell, G. G. (2015). Surveillance: Ambiguities and asymmetries. *Surveillance & Society, 13*(3/4), 324-326.

Van Maanen, J., & Kunda, G. (1989). Real feelings: Emotional expressions and organization culture. In B. Staw & L. L. Cummings (Eds.), *Research in Organization Behavior, Vol. 11* (pp. 43-103). JAI Press.

Van Maanen, J. (1991). The smile factory: Work at Disneyland. In P. J. Frost et al. (Eds.), *Reframing organizational culture* (pp. 58-76). Sage.

Vannini, P., Waskul, D., & Gottschalk, S. (2011). *The senses in self, society, and culture: A sociology of the senses.* Routledge.

Watzlawick, P. (1977). *How real is real? Confusion, disinformation, communication.* Vintage

Williams, R. (2014, July 7). The cult of ignorance in the United States: Anti-intellectualism and the 'dumbing down' of America. *Psychologytoday.com.* https://www.psychologytoday.com/intl/blog/wired-success/201407/anti-intellectualism-and-the-dumbing-down-america

Zuboff, S. (2015). Big other: Surveillance capitalism and the prospects of an information civilization. *Journal of Information Technology, 30*(1), 75-89.

# Chapter IX.
## "Childishness" as Social Control
### Yoad Eliaz

Our postmodern, post-industrial society is said to be generally characterized by de-differentiation, driven mainly by popular culture, of various statuses such as gender, class and age (Rojek, 1993; Tiryakian, 1985). In terms of the de-differentiation of age, it is often argued that children today seem less "childlike," and adults can be "childish" and continue to speak, dress, and act much like overgrown children. Scholars such as Meyerowitz (1984, p. 19) argue that "what seems to be happening in our culture is an overall merging of childhood and adulthood . . . related in part to our shift from a 'book culture' to a 'television culture.'" In contrast, this chapter explores the difference that "childishness" continues to make alongside processes of uni-aging. My point of departure is that "childishness" as a social construction is still used to control and discipline individuals of various ages. I return for this purpose to my study of the construction and labeling of "childishness" in the legal system (Eliaz, 2017). In addition, I look at old age, as well as cognitive disability, as comparative arenas of vulnerability illustrating the social construction of "childishness" as a mechanism of social control. These sites serve to draw a comparative model of "childishness" not as an objective age category but rather as a constructed label that reproduces and reaffirms relations of control, dominance and power within postmodern society.

Unlike Alemany Oliver and Belk's decision (2021) not to differentiate childlikeness from childishness in this book, my use of the term "childishness" remains distinct from "childlikeness." Often, the word "childishness" has a negative connotation, denoting behavior that is deemed "out of place"—immature, impulsive, irresponsible, selfish, indeed infantile. Adults who are said to display childish tendencies are labeled as having difficulty with self-regulation. This modern social construction of "childishness" has arguably developed together with the advent of industrialization as well as the positivistic worldview of psychology and sociology, whose proponents of progress constructed "childhood" and "childishness" as a diminished, irrational and even "primitive" condition (Neustadter, 1992, 1993), that is merely a stepping stone on the way to responsible and productive adulthood. Ironically, these defenders of the idea of progress were recycling traditional religious ideas. As Paul the Apostle said, "When I was a child, I used to speak as a child, think as a child, reason like a child; when I became a man, I did away with childish things" (1 Cor. 13: 11). However, it appears that we are living in a society where "becoming a man" (or a woman) does not entail doing away with childish things. In a recent post in "Psychology Today,"[91] an American psycho-therapist listed the following adverse traits under the title "Can You Spot 10 Signs of a Childish Adult?": Emotional escalations, blaming, lies, name-calling, impulsivity, need to be the center of attention, bullying, narcissism, immature defenses, and no observing ego—that is, no ability to see, acknowledge, and learn from mistakes."

"Childlikeness," in contrast to "childishness," sometimes (but not always) continues to preserve a positive connotation of innocence, with religious undertones of trust in God and others. In the *New Testament*, Jesus compares "childlikeness" to faithfulness and meekness: "Truly I say to you, unless you are converted and become like children, you will not enter the kingdom of heaven. Whoever then humbles himself as this child, he is the greatest in the kingdom of heaven" (Matthew

[91] https://www.psychologytoday.com/us/blog/resolution-not-conflict/201603/can-you-spot-10-signs-childish-adult

18: 1-4). Moreover, childlike people are sometimes labeled as playful and creative. To "become like children" thus has a long tradition of being contrasted with "doing away with childish things." Notwithstanding this lingering duality of childhood, my emphasis in this chapter is on its dark side, namely the social construction and use of "childishness" as a mechanism of control, most blatantly in contexts of social vulnerability and excluded social groups.

My continuous bracketing of "childishness" should serve as a reminder that I focus on its social construction which is arguably disconnected from biological age (as adults can be labeled "childish" too), or any other essential characteristics. Even though childhood, adulthood, and "childishness" may be based on biological and/or chronological facts, the ways in which these concepts are used in the three settings I examine are determined by culture. Furthermore, "childishness," because of its negative connotations, has become a social mechanism of control in various parts of our life, especially in vulnerable social contexts where processes of social discipline, surveillance and normalization take place more intensively.

### Childhood as a Social Construction

If Denzin is correct that "children . . . are political products—they are created, defined and acted on in political terms" (in Rogers & Rogers, 2002, p. 12), then "childhood" and "childishness" are also political labels that signal power relations. Jenks (1996, p. 68) develops this idea by arguing that: "Childhood is the most intensively governed sector of personal existence . . . The way we control our children reflects . . . the strategies through which we exercise power and constraint in the wider society." "Childishness" as a label is on the one hand a resource of protest, but also a sphere of multiple governmental measures and legislation. There is a long and well-accepted western tradition regarding childhood as an essential trait in need of protection, for example in the UN's 1989 Convention on the Rights of the Child. This assumption has, however, long been questioned by the understanding of childhood as a social construct. The construction of "childhood innocence" is inter-connected with the expansion of the child pornography law, where the emphasis on imagery sometimes replaces the concern for child abuse (Fischel, 2016). Legal understandings of "childhood" thus presuppose its construction as a political idiom for the promotion of social welfare.

Jenks (1996) discusses two dominant cultural tropes of childhood in the west: The Platonic image depicting angelic innocence and purity, and the Dionysian image depicting sensuality, hedonism and selfishness. "Childishness," in the Dionysian sense, is a deviation from normalcy whose result is shame; in contrast, childish or childlike behavior in the Platonic sense is the unique self-fulfillment of each individual. Parents and other adults invest age-specific rights and expectations with moral significance by (often) disapproving "childish" behavior and by using privileges to reward behavior they label "mature." On the other hand, we are often prepared to show some tolerance for "childish mischief." This dualism is captured in news stories of youth violence casting violent youth as simultaneously evil victimizers and innocent victims, arguably resulting from the appropriation of these two broader cultural discourses—that of the evil, violent "minor" and that of the innocent, vulnerable "minor" (Jenks, 1996). Postmodern theory has further deconstructed these dichotomies, replacing them by performances of age hybridity. Those encompass the adult-like child (the case of giftedness, for example) and the child-like adult (gaming and pop culture, for example). Investigating "childishness"—rather than children or childhood—takes this postmodern premise of anti-essentialism one step further. "Childishness," when applied to chronological adults, is a social construct in which adulthood and childhood exist simultaneously in a single individual.

Ariès's (1960) seminal work on childhood, despite the criticism it received, was one of the first influential scholarly works that de-naturalized childhood. Irrespective of the historical precision of Ariès's claims regarding the "social inexistence" of the child prior to age five due to frequent child mortality, his work was path-breaking in terms of exposing the culture-specific construction of childhood. According to Ariès, the schools of 16th-century Europe were much more disciplined in relation to the chaotic freedom of children in the schools of the Middle Ages. Only in the 16th century were dormitories built as part of school life to better supervise the pupils, alongside with military-like discipline including an hourly plan of activities. In Ariès's analysis, this was part of the new construction of children as innocent, savage-like and vulnerable, and thus in need not only of education but of social control and protection.

Fourteen years after the publication of Ariès's (1960) work, Foucault (1974) published his work on *Discipline and Punishment*, describing a shift from direct bodily punishment in the Middle Ages (including public torture) to indirect modern punishment techniques conducted through surveillance. The modern gaze, according to Foucault (1974), has been extended *into* the body, surveilling and controlling a host of inner defects such as deviance, heresy, mental illness, and so on. The discourse of "childhood studies" emerged against the background of these two complementary views: de-naturalization and control of childhood. The bodily and psychic control over the child came to be regarded, in the language of the modern court, as maintaining "external" and "internal" boundaries.

Towards the end of the 19th century, Durkheim (1979) illustrated how children have already become objects of surveillance and control. He argued that childhood is characterized by fragile weakness and ceaseless movement. Educators are instructed to allow movement, but in a manner that "allows the children to self-discipline their behavior in a controlled manner" (cited in Jenks, 1992, p. 149). Durkheim describes the child as a kind of anarchist who does not follow the rules and can overcome their inner chaos only through proper habits. Foucault (1967) further identifies the modern conception of madness with childhood: "madness is childhood . . . the mad are considered as children with immense power that is dangerously used. They must be immediately rewarded or punished" (cited in Jenks, 1992, p. 170). The educational view can thus be described as moving between self-control (internalization of control) and direct/external control, making the child, above all, into an object of control. Indeed, the foundational paradigms of modern development in industrial society—Freud's psychanalysis, Piaget's cognitive development, Kohlberg's moral development—all regard childhood as a pretext and a stepping stone to adulthood, a stage to be overcome and then repressed. "Childishness" in modernity has not only become a matter of control but also a matter of devaluation and repression—something that one needs to "grow up" from (Neustadter, 1993). In the modern-industrialist perspective, childhood and "childishness" are perceived as subversive to the development of rationality and the establishment of order. Even the pure innocence of childhood can thus be cast as a weakness and denigrated as an incomplete and dangerous state of being.

The modern era has ushered in unprecedented sophistication and growth of social institutions. Schools, prisons, and courts existed in non-modern societies, but new functions have supplemented their age-old functions of education, imprisonment, and judgment. These functions were critically highlighted by neo-Marxist scholars such as Gramsci (Gramsci & Hoare, 1971) and Althusser (2006). They and their fellow scholars from the Frankfort School challenged the Marxist belief that revolution is an historical inevitability and questioned why the proletariat did not revolt. Marx's explanation that the oppressed classes are imprisoned within a false consciousness was insufficient. People who had been exposed to ideas of justice, equality, and solidarity were in no hurry to join the revolution. What was stopping them? How did the hegemonic group succeed in retaining control? How did it exert its power over its subjects so successfully?

Gramsci described how hegemony controls its subjects through the intellectuals who serve it and through the educational system. Althusser emphasized how hegemonic ideology shapes the "self" and controls it. Foucault and Bourdieu placed an emphasis on the practices by which modern social institutions control their subjects. Bourdieu and Passeron (1990) used sociological concepts to describe how institutions of higher education in France reproduce the hierarchy of social classes. Foucault's (1969) archeological methodology contributed leading concepts and ideas (i.e., bio-power and power/knowledge) to this critical discourse of social control. Foucault's important insights regarding modernism are linked to his ideas about the controlling role of psychiatric hospitals, schools, prisons, and other institutions. Foucault claimed that social control constitutes the modern supplement to the pre-modern functions of institutions.

As mentioned above, the question of non-resistance or power's naturalization underlies Foucault's investigations. His point of departure was that social institutions act explicitly in the service of subordinating the subject (Foucault, 2012). Foucault (2012) identified the institutional practices that engender subjugation. Subjugation and control are attained, first and foremost, by gathering and producing knowledge about the subjects who are under such control. Knowledge about the subjects creates social order, and this social order is preserved, controlled, and supervised by experts and supervisors who serve the hegemonic powers. The basic action of obtaining knowledge and creating order within that knowledge about the subject involves the creation of categories and then classifying the subjects according to those criteria.

Hence, social institutions create the familiar categories of age, gender, marital status, occupation, etc. and attribute great importance to them. The aim of the "personal information" we are required to submit abundantly and repeatedly when filling out forms for institutions is to control us by means of their knowledge about us. This knowledge subjugates the individual (who are liable to revolt) and transforms them into subjects who can be placed within a social order founded upon categorization.

It is on the basis of this critical discourse of normalization that we can start to understand the inherent devaluation of childhood in the positivistic, progress-driven canons of psychology and sociology. This devaluation, in turn, has become an important basis for the ensuing negative and controlling application of "childishness" in the context of such categorization, subjecting individuals in general but particularly vulnerable and excluded groups. Modern psychologists have often used childhood as an

> example of primitivism, a stage in life that is undesirable and must be escaped from if civilization is to persist, or rationality prosper. The intellectual structure of adult cognitive functions, they hold, does not contain categories within which the childhood world can be experienced. Adulthood is held to be incompatible with the previous age. Several important psychologists, each a celebrant of progress and rationality, have measured childhood against the standard of adulthood, and in so doing have passed judgment on childhood as ontologically inferior. (Neustadter, 1993, p. 303)

A few illustrative examples include Freud (1964), who argued that for civilization to persist and to advance it was necessary to repress childish instincts and urges. Piaget (1971) similarly argued that for mature rational thinking to take place, child-like thinking must be eliminated. The child advances from a stage of infantile egocentrism pejoratively described as "a type of ignorance of the life and a deformation of the self, coupled to a misconception of objective relationships" (Piaget 1971, pp. 216-

217). The father of structural functionalism in sociology, Talcott Parsons (1964, p. 203) similarly contended that "the process of transcending childhood" is at the same time the process of internalizing "higher levels of value." Like Freud, Parsons views the repression of childhood as a precondition for the advancement of civilization. In Parson's schema, socialization was in effect a cure for the aberrant condition of childhood.

### "Childishness" in Court

These critical concepts of power-knowledge, the creation and maintenance of social order using knowledge and meticulous categorization, enable us to understand the interest on the part of courts regarding the chronological age of the defendants vs. the age that can be assigned to them and to their criminal (or innocent) behavior. Chronological age is the criterion for categorizing defendants into the two court systems: that of minors and that of adults, whereas the assigned age constitutes a tool for producing knowledge about defendants who may be entitled to having their sentence mitigated or aggravated.

My point of departure is that constructing the defendant as childish or childlike can either lead to the aggravation of punishment, or conversely, its mitigation. This dialectic provides an intriguing yet little explored arena for negotiation involving judges, lawyers, psychiatrists, probation service professionals, plaintiffs and defendants. Courts can provide a rich empirical field for discussing the discourse of "childishness" as a polysemic hybridization of childhood and adulthood, denoting and reinforcing the arbitrary nature of the court's power.

Recent studies have begun to explore the ascribed "ages" of defendants in Israeli courts as a means of control and hegemony. One such study (Viterbo, 2012) deals with verdicts given by Israeli military courts to Palestinian children of varied ages. These cases demonstrate that constructions of "age," and particularly of "childishness" as an ascribed psychological and emotional age, serve as means of judicial control. My focus is on trials of adults in civil courts, thus allowing to further explore the role of "childishness" and age-construction in the civil system and in the context of non-minor defendants. Labeling theory originally asserted that contact with the criminal justice system is predominantly stigmatizing (Braithwaite & Mugford, 1994; Lemert, 1972); however, the point of departure for the ensuing analysis is that much more is going on in courts in terms of labeling as well as identity construction, including labeling that may have a de-stigmatizing effect for the defendant.

The association between "childishness" and criminal deviance is blatantly reflected in the modern institutionalization of a separate juvenile court system. The child constitutes a unique character in the judicial drama; this character has even earned the special legal category of "minor." Previous studies of children in the judicial context have focused primarily on children's participation in custody hearings and divorce trials (Cradock, 2007; Murray & Hallett, 2000; Smith, Taylor, & Tapp, 2003), and in the juvenile justice system (Shook, 2005). Buckley (2014) conducted a qualitative analysis of 81 legal opinions in which children are mentioned, examining the correlations between the legal perceptions of childhood and the right to free expression of high school students in the United States. Based on this analysis he identifies three main perceptions of childhood: as a period separate from and unlike adulthood; as a transitional period of becoming an adult; or as a period fundamentally like adulthood, according to the principle of children's rights. The incompatibility between these three perceptions reflects the societal ambivalence with respect to the nature of children and childhood.

Such ambivalence may serve, and be accentuated by, political situations in which the court prescribes (often arbitrarily) what is "childhood" and what "childishness" is. Viterbo (2012) shows how in the occupied Palestinian territories, Israeli "domestic" courts consider childhood to end at the age of 18, while military law considers the threshold of "childhood" to be 16 years of age. Viterbo claims that this arbitrariness is also reflected by the difference between the domestic court where young "age" often leads to mitigation and the military court—where it does not.

How does "childishness" work in court as a mechanism of judicial control? Thematic analysis (Strauss & Corbin, 1998) of legal texts in which the defendant is described as childish led me to delineate four categories of the "childish defendant": innocent, influenced, unable to control him/herself, and lacking in boundaries. These will be illustrated here in brief to substantiate my analysis of "childishness."

In many cases, attributing "innocent childishness" to a defendant serves the purpose of mitigating the defendant's punishment. "Childishness" is used in these circumstances to mark the distinction between an unforgivable delinquent behavior and a forgivable offense which is "the consequence of foolish and childish behavior." In other cases, "childishness" is not attributed to the defendant's character or personality but rather to the offense itself. In one of the trials,[92] even though the defendant was found guilty as charged, the result of his labeling as innocently childish was a mitigated punishment. The defendant allegedly kidnapped his ex-girlfriend after she had broken up with him (their whole relationship lasted two months), pushed her violently into the trunk of his car, handcuffed her and drove to a remote and lonely place "in order to talk." After about five hours, she managed to persuade him to untie her and take her back to her apartment, where they spent the night together. The defendant, a single young adult aged 21, was described by his parents as "introverted, lacking self-confidence and childish." The psychiatrist assessed the defendant's personality as "childish and immature . . . he did not really plan what to do after kidnapping her but did it in a *childish whim to be 'a hero.'*"

Another trope of "childishness" that is associated with mitigation portrays the defendant as a secondary character in the execution of an offense. In some cases, two defendants are involved, one of whom appears dominant, and the other appears submissive, malleable, dependent, and childish. "Childishness" is in this case associated with diminished responsibility, diminished guilt, and a resulting mitigated punishment. The following two categories illustrate how "childishness" can also serve to legitimate liability and an aggravated punishment. Some defendants are described as impulsive and unpredictable persons who cannot control themselves. Childish impulsiveness is related by the court to the potential for recidivism. In the trial[93] of a man who assaulted a policeman, the prosecution quoted the probation service's review: "The fact that the defendant has a tendency to act in a *childish and impulsive* way in conflict situations is *worrisome.*" The court in these cases reasons that since the subject is unable to control him/herself, restrictions must be imposed upon him/her from the outside.

Finally, a defendant who is characterized as childish by the probation service is often described as having difficulty in setting internal or external boundaries for him/herself. In cases such as these, the probation service recommends aggravating the defendant's punishment to firmly set the boundaries that the defendant him/herself is unable or unwilling to set. In most cases, the exact "boundaries" that the defendant lacks are left vague and undefined. For instance, they may be described very generally as "boundaries of behavior" or "sexual boundaries." In other cases, it is stated that the boundaries being discussed are between "good and bad" or between "permissible and prohibited."

[92] Tel-Aviv District Court CF 29956-04-11.
[93] Petach Tikva Justice of the Peace Court CF 14889-09-10.

The four tropes of "childishness" that are expressed in court: the innocent, influenced, unable to control him/herself, and lacking in boundaries, all demonstrate the subjugation of an individual through his/her construction as childish. This practice entails a complex application of knowledge/power by criminologists, probation service officers, judges and counselors. Yet importantly, within this very bureaucratic, modern, professional, rational and knowledge-intensive system, there is an inherent ambiguity which is maintained precisely for its arbitrariness. There is no reliable or valid scale or test for "childishness" (or "adultness"). The defendant who is labeled as "innocent" has not been tested for innocence. In addition, *the use* of the label is inherently ambiguous. It can be used both positively or negatively, in different cases. The only logic is the logic of social control.

Labeling a defendant as "childish" may pave the way to the mitigation of their punishment, as someone who can be under surveillance yet without incarceration. If there was no intention to harm someone or engage in wrongdoing, it may follow that this defendant should not be jailed. Innocence is closer to normalcy in the sense that innocence is already disciplined. In the alleged kidnapping case discussed before, "childishness" was used to mark the distinction between an unforgivable delinquent behavior and a forgivable offense which is "the consequence of foolish and childish behavior." The Judges also compare, in similar cases, the "childishness" of the (adult) defendant to the behavior of a minor, thus connecting between young age and innocence.

In the case of the attribution of "childishness" as being "easily influenced," the mechanism of social control is highly visible. The probation service officers claim under such circumstances that the defendant is not dangerous but was "under the influence." Being influenced means that the defendant is already a disciplined subject. There is no need to invest in discipline in that case since the subject is already obedient. In contrast, when "childishness" is linked to dangerousness and lack of self-control, it leads to requesting the court for more discipline. Longer incarceration is usually justified as a remedy for the defendant's lack of self-control. Being labeled as impulsive and spontaneous, the defendant is constructed as an individual rather than a subject. Such individuals need to be disciplined in body and soul through incarceration that will educate them to be obedient.

The boundaryless childish individual is an "ideal type" of pure disobedience. The lack of boundaries (whatever that means) justifies discipline and normalization. The very ambiguity of the concept of boundaries is maintained for its justification of arbitrary control. These boundaries are defined by the system only through their lack. There is no positive attempt to delineate and define the areas on either side of that boundary.

It is important to note that because I based my analysis on legal documents depicting court discussions, the inevitable emphasis has been on "childishness" as social control. "Childishness," seen as predominantly attributed by those in power, can be regarded as part of the legal/professional gaze of the court. However, "childishness" may also become a matter of agency and manipulation. It may be actively taken by defendants to reinforce dominant perceptions and in so doing, to subvert those perceptions and make them work for the defendants. In a similar manner to "street children," such "status" is empowering precisely because there is a fear of the unknown—these "children" may take advantage of the myth, or threat, of an ability to act beyond the controls of normal society and, as such, they are ceded a certain degree of freedom of action (Davis, 2008; Ennew & Swart-Kruger, 2003). Such an extended analysis, however, requires a bottom-up ethnography that may hopefully be explored in the future by other scholars.

The use of "childishness" in court demonstrates that the very action of attributing "childishness" to the defendant, the very determination that his/her chronological age is not the age that defines his/her degree of danger to the public or his/her responsibility for his/her actions, is an act that reflects the arbitrary power of the court. This observation is repeated and extended by the next example regarding the application of "childishness" as a label of old age.

## The Childish Elderly

The growing characterization of old age as a "second childhood" and a period of childish behavior is a recent historical phenomenon in Western history (Covey, 1992), that can be linked to growing life expectancy accompanied by physical and mental deterioration, as well as to the relative rolelessness of the elderly and their cultural devaluation or even deculturation (Anderson, 1972). Once revered for their experience and wisdom, the elderly in post-industrial, secular, technological society are often seen as anachronistic, unproductive and even dysfunctional. Hence, the perceived and actual dependency of older people for asymmetrical care, much like children, has shaped the "second childhood" as a stage of life where the lifecycle returns to its beginning, and not in a good way (Covey, 1992). As Hazan and Raz (1997) argue:

> Age groups are constituted through cultural anticipations, echoed in the various metaphors related in each and every society to the "seasons of man's life." Such a social span of control demands different discursive frames of reference for "hearing," "discussing," "explaining," and ultimately "understanding" the various age groups defined. These discourses, in turn, often become part of their subjects' repertoire, internalized into forms of articulation which characterize the symbolic exchange practiced among members of the age group and between that group and others. (p. 259)

Seen and controlled from a middle age perspective, the "childishness" of children and elderly—the first and second childhoods—are part of a symmetrical, bell-like curve designating the primacy of middle age and the social marginalization of the beginning and end of life. A parallel conception of the life-cycle is found in Turner (1987), who discusses childhood and old age as homologous in terms of social liminality and disengagement, or what he calls lack of reciprocity, which is (he contends) the basis for social prestige, and the antithesis to being "childish." "Because the child and the elderly share a number of common social characteristics (such as the absence of work and social responsibilities, or 'roles') they are often described in the same pejorative and stigmatizing fashion," Turner (1987, p. 123) sums it up.

The labeling of the elderly as childish can influence caretakers' communication, notably in the use of so-called "elderspeak," similar to "baby talk." Elderspeak often demonstrates the following features: speaking slowly, speaking loudly, using a sing-song voice, inflecting statements to sound like a question, using the pronouns "we," "us," and "our" in place of "you:" "How are we doing today?;" using pet names such as "sweetheart," "dearie," or "honey;" shortening sentences; simplifying syntax and vocabulary; talking for the older adult. Elderspeak assumes that the older adult is dependent, frail, weak, incompetent, and childish. In turn, it reaffirms a social reality in which presumably all older adults equally suffer from memory problems, hearing problems, energy problems, etc. When older adults are exposed to the patronizing language of elderspeak, it would be reasonable to expect that their performance on tasks decrease and their rates of depression increase.

Elderspeak, as a mirror image of baby talk, illustrates how old age and childhood are prescribed and controlled with structurally similar social positions using literal language (Hazan, 1998; Hazan & Raz, 1997). In childhood, baby talk only gradually develops into nonliteral forms such as irony and metaphor. Additional literal forms of communication prescribed to children include storytelling, nursery rhymes and folktales. All these communicative tropes, seen as "childish" when addressed by adults, reappear and sometimes dominate communication in old age, where they take the form of "plotted prose with an explicit moral" (Mergler & Goldstein, 1983, p. 86), based on common idioms and proverbial vocabularies (Myerhoff, 1978). Some psycholinguists have suggested that such "literal talk" amongst the elderly is a result of deficiencies in working memory and linguistic competence (Kemper, 1988).

The childish, literal language of old age and the elderspeak used to address the elderly are an indication of what Hockey and James (1993) called the discourse of infantilization:

> The cultural pervasiveness of metaphors of childhood within the discourses surrounding aging and dependency . . . has become "naturalized." It is seen as somehow inevitable, as the way things are. Through this culturally constructed model of dependency, many of those in old age and others who are infantilized—the chronically sick or disabled, for example—may be made to take a conceptual position alongside children on the margins of society. (p. 13)

Such a discourse of infantilization, or "childishness," is a powerful mechanism of social control. It becomes so taken-for-granted that although prescribed from the outside, it can turn into a lived-in reality. The social mask can turn into a persona (Featherstone & Hepworth, 1989, 1991). This is a powerful mechanism of normative control, shaping a looking-glass self, that I will elaborate on later using labeling theory. Such a discourse of "childishness" can mask, mute and dub its target audience and legitimize the relegation of the elderly to old-age homes, housing projects and sun cities.

Goffman (1963) assumed that disorders with a highly unknown and arbitrary etiology or with symptoms that are believed to be beyond the individual's control are more likely to trigger public stigmatization. This prediction can be illustrated in cases like ADHD, intellectual disability or mental illness. Experimental studies examining healthy participants' reactions toward individuals displaying ADHD symptoms showed that participants highly discredited their diagnosed counterparts' behavior. Nearly all of the healthy participants quoted ADHD symptoms to be childish and socially inappropriate (Canu & Carlson, 2003; Stroes, Alberts, & van der Meere 2003). In other studies, however, ADHD was seen by educators and parents to relieve the individual (child or adult) of the stigma of "hyperactivity" by medicalizing the problem so that responsibility no longer falls on the individual (or on their family and/ or educational framework, see Conrad 1972).

A study of how the mentally ill are depicted in prime-time television dramas (Wilson et al., 1999) found that mentally ill characters are depicted as lacking comprehension and performance of everyday adult roles, appearing lost and confused. Typical actions include speaking in grammatically simple sentences, in a childish voice, and breaking into children's songs such as: "Incy, wincy spider." As with children, their actions show a lack of awareness of social conventions. Other characters are relatively more important as their talk about or interactions with the person with mental illness can mark the latter as childlike; making decisions for them, talking down to them, and explaining concepts in exaggeratedly simple terms. Personal characteristics include unkept appearance, such as disorganized or poorly matching clothes, which is given particular meaning for the character through the broader program context. Studies have also documented how, particularly in undeveloped countries, mentally ill persons are being told by those around them to "Man up" and "Stop acting childish" (Alloh et al., 2018). Such stereotypical expressions are frequent forms of coercion contributing to the burden of mental illness.

It is perhaps even more gripping to find characterizations of children and adolescents by psychiatrists linking between mental illness and "childishness." In a study of the perspective of the diagnosing psychiatrist in relation to symptoms described by young patients, LeFrançois and Diamond (2014) show how psychiatrists used judgmental descriptors such as

> being a 'drama queen,' 'not in touch with reality,' 'making stories up—fantasy and not reality stuff,' 'disturbed behaviour,' 'disturbing thought patterns,' 'very strange young lady,' 'very bizarre' or framing their 'mental illness' in relation to the practitioners' abilities to control them, for example: 'pushing boundaries,' 'boss in groups about following the rules,' 'difficult little boy to cope with,' 'belligerent,' 'pushing the limits,' 'very resistant—wouldn't engage' . . . In some respects, the psychiatrist appeared to be discrediting the children's thoughts and behaviour by dismissing them as 'childish' or outside the social norm in some colloquial way rather than adhering to criteria and symptomatology noted within the diagnostic texts. (pp. 48-49)

Here the children are given attributes that exist outside of the normative notion of the "ideal child" whilst being exposed by psychiatric authority as odd. Although the characterization of these experiences was clearly outside of the official diagnostic criteria, the psychiatrist named them as symptoms. The arbitrariness of such descriptions, coupled with their labeling power, is quite similar to the use of "childishness" in courts that I described earlier, where psychiatrists sometimes also participate in diagnosing/labeling defendants. Given the power of the psychiatric profession and the power of language, the mere utterance of these characterizations from a psychiatrist lends them immediate authority, thus underscoring the power of citationality from an authority, whether keeping loyal to the "party line" as set out in the DSM or not. As feelings, actions and judgments were continuously reified as "symptoms of childishness," they became part of the performance of mental illness that in turn proved their mentally ill status.

The point I wish to stress is that even though the psychiatrists in LeFrançois and Diamond's (2014) study did not maintain a strict usage of biomedical discourse in their description of psychiatric symptoms, their alignment with the institution of psychiatry rendered their words as powerful tools in proclaiming abnormality and medicalizing the behavior as problematic. Such "diagnosis"/labeling is irrefutable: If the children and/or their parents had resisted the mental illness construct, the psychiatrist would have likely named this as a symptom of their illness, turning resistance into part of the performance, as was done whenever the children resisted certain treatments, such as psychiatric drugs or group work. Compliance, on the other hand, was viewed positively, moving the children one step closer to meeting the imaginary ideal of adult normality, and one step closer to living a "normal" life, outside of the institution.

Another blatant example in this category of a socially excluded group that encounters stigma and prejudice are people with an intellectual disability (ID). They are often described as being "childish," younger than they are, and even sometimes assumed to be "eternal children" (Priestly, 2003). Through this "ableist" language, individuals with ID can never leave the phase of childhood (Priestly, 2000). Being identified as an eternal child means that they are denied benefits that are attached to adulthood; nor are they permitted the same needs as adults have, including access to adult practices such as sex. According to Starke, Bertilsdotter Rosqvist, and Kuosmanen (2016):

> The constructions of individuals with ID are, to great degree, based on ideas about age. In the participants' socially shared

knowledge about, and construction of individuals with ID, lies a distinction between chronological age and perceived age. Through comparing an adult (i.e. chronological age) with a child (perceived age) the professionals construct the person with ID as a desexualized "eternal child," an incompetent adult, and as an individual not equally deserving of civil and human rights, including sexual rights. (p. 325)

Once again, as in the other examples discussed here, we can see how "childishness," as a mechanism of social control, lurks in the difference that experts and institutions construct between chronological and perceived age. "Childishness," as something which appears to transgress the lines of the biological (chronological) and the social (normative), is thus constructed, like other forms of "matter out of place," as a danger, a pollution, ambiguous and anomalous, causing anxiety by disrupting classification systems and the "normal" ordered relations through which one understands the world (Douglas, 1966).

### "Childishness" Through Labeling Theory

The category of adulthood is connected to possibilities and rights, as well as assumptions of obligations and responsibilities that, on attaining a particular age, frame individuals' membership in society as full and equal citizens. Not all individuals, however, are admitted into this category. Age categories regulate the placement of the individual in the social structure and thus regulate access to social identities, prestige and reciprocity. Nevertheless, age is often referred to as an objective measure or statement of fact. Meaning attaching to age differs depending on context and, while such meanings are commonly used in different professional settings, they are seldom critically examined. The discursive framing of social problems, especially the moral and affective dimensions of the construction of *person categories* in social problems discourse, has been examined from a social constructionist perspective since the groundbreaking work by Blumer (1971) and Spector and Kitsuse (1987), more specifically for example in the construction of abused women (Loseke, 1992, 1993), threatened or abused children (Best, 1990; Johnson, 1995), and the homeless.

Borrowing from Gubrium and Holstein's (1999) analysis of interpretive practice, I see the framing of "childishness" as comprising both an alleged condition and an alleged person. Through interactions individual defendants, elderly or people with cognitive/intellectual disabilities purposefully project themselves into the roles assigned for them by others in a manner that combines external assessments and self-appraisals (Cooley, 1902; Bem, 1972). The self thus becomes an object (Mead, 1934) for which the individual and others attach labels, both positive and negative. This takes special importance in the psychology of punitive justice, as Mead (1964) already noted, but also in the construction of the mask of aging and mental illness.

Labeling theory is thus an appropriate theoretical lens to examine the construction of the "childish person" in courts, old age homes and psychiatric clinics as an alleged condition and an alleged person. Labeling theory focuses primarily on how institutions and social control agents define social objects, principally individuals and their acts. As a sociological theory, it is largely concerned with the role that authority, status, and power play in the assignment of social identities to individuals, especially in the context of deviance (Tannenbaum, 1938). The fundamental postulate of labelling theory is the assumption that the reaction of the "societal other" has a reinforcing effect on subject's behavior. Lemert's development of the "secondary deviance" concept is perhaps the classic statement of this hypothesis:

> The sequence of interaction leading to secondary deviance is roughly as follows: (1) primary deviation; (2) social penalties; (3) further primary deviation; (4) stronger penalties and rejection; (5) further deviation, perhaps with hostilities and resentment beginning to focus upon those doing the penalizing; (6) crisis reached in the tolerance quotient, expressed in formal action by the community stigmatizing of the deviant; (7) strengthening of deviant conduct as a reaction to the stigmatizing and penalties; (8) ultimate acceptance of deviant social status and efforts at adjustment on the basis of the associated role. (Lemert, 1972, p. 77)

Labeling theory originally asserted that contact with the criminal justice system has the counterproductive effect of increasing future offending, because of the stigmatizing effects of justice ceremonies (Braithwaite & Mugford, 1994). This has been termed the "deviance amplification effect" (Smith & Paternoster, 1990). More generally, criminologists have also studied the inter-relationships between reflected appraisals, parental labeling, and delinquency (Matsueda, 1992). The labeling of "childishness" illustrates the complex and polysemic practice of labeling. In line with Lemert's (1972) model of deviance, the primary deviation can be, as exemplified in the cases discussed, being trialed, being old, or having cognitive disabilities. These deviancies attract social penalties, being labeled as childish; this leads to a vicious circle of further deviance and labeling. Those labeled as childish retort by accentuating their "childishness," now also as a form of resentment and/or internalized self-image, focusing upon those doing the penalizing—the court system, the caretakers, the psychiatrists. Being labeled as childish has a role in the process of how an individual comes to believe in herself/himself, including how one learns to attribute fault and responsibility. Labeling can be part of service provision that does not take account of how people may react to the negative interpretations placed upon them and the alienating effect this is likely to have (Roets et al., 2007). Such a "helping" approach (ironically) stresses and may even increase incapacity.

As a result, people who are labeled as "childish" and told it is "their fault" might become even more childish, quite like performance anxiety or incontrollable eating. The increasing social rejection of fat people can be traced (much like "childishness") to processes of normalization: moralizing discourses on "excessive" food consumption, midlife commodification of slenderness and health, and the recent medicalization/definition of obesity as a disease (Gracia-Arnaiz, 2013). As a result, people labeled as "fat" (much like being labeled as "childish") may lose faith in themselves and blame themselves for their situation and their inability to prevent it:

> The transformation of obesity into a disease has not made life easier because health professionals consider it a self-inflicted problem rather than one to which they are predisposed by the nature of consumer society. The insistence that successful treatment depends on patients' ability to regulate their eating habits and exercise is the most common argument used by the young people I interviewed to blame themselves for being fat . . . A 35-year-old woman framed the problem in behavioral terms: "You start letting yourself go, getting fatter and fatter. Yes, it's our fault. I put on 22 kilos when I was pregnant, and when we split up I got really depressed and gained a lot more weight. I didn't feel like doing anything. What did I do? I just ate! Of course it's our fault." (Gracia-Arnaiz, 2013, p. 1985)

This is secondary deviance in action. As people act out their labeling, this may lead to further escalation in the response of those in social positions of power, expressed in formal action—legal sanctions, institutionalization, psychotherapies and medication—further stigmatizing the deviant. Such actions are likely to increase marginalization in, and exclusion from, middle-age society and the labor market. In some cases, as Lemert's predicted, this is indeed a vicious circle accentuating deviance through futile attempts of normalization that emphasize stigmatization without inclusion.

In the ideological hierarchies that constitute our social institutions, "childishness" can be applied to subjectify patients in hospitals, inmates in total institutions, the poor in their ghettos, people with intellectual disabilities who are seeking jobs, prisoners in jail, and elderly in nursing homes. In this manner, "childishness" promotes social control and justifies the existence of these social institutions and their control over their subjects.

My exploration of "childishness" as a means of social control led me, not surprisingly, to focus on subordinate groups, such as the elderly, defendants in court, and people with cognitive/mental disabilities. There are of course many other subordinate groups that have been denigrated for their similarity to children. For example, social scientists in the 1960s often noted the dysfunctional "child-like" qualities of the poor. Experts on poverty such as Michael Harrington (1964) and Oscar Lewis (1959) characterized the poor as victims of shared character defects transmitted through a "culture of poverty" which was present-day oriented, helpless, and dependent. These "traits of the poor" were the very opposites of the adult traits of long-term planning, discipline, and independence. In this caricature of "poorness," adult subjects exhibited childish behavior, unwilling and unmotivated to grow up, moving from one gratification to the next.

Not just minority subordinate groups were targeted as childish. The subordinate and dependent status of women has often been legitimated on the grounds of their "childishness" in both popular culture and sociological literature. Hollywood heroines and Disney princesses have been often traditionally treated like helpless, submissive creatures, rather than assertive, capable grown-ups (Johnson, 2015). Only recently have Disney princesses become more "self-rescuing." The early Disney princesses demonstrate some ability to be assertive; however, it is usually with animals and children, and their limited emotional range often focuses on crying (England, Descartes & Collier-Meek, 2011; Do Rozario, 2004). In line with this patronizing malestream stereotype, pop culture has played out the hidden "childishness" of all women that reveals itself when even adult women break "just like a little girl" (Bob Dylan, "Just Like a Woman"). Indeed, "feminine" behavior is often portrayed as child-like if not childish (Millett, 1969, pp. 220-233) with male dominancy often reassured as standing for self-reliance, adulthood and maturity, while females are described as subservient, obedient, nurturant, and childish.

Following the construction of the child as an object of control, "childishness" has also become an apparatus of control. Attributing "childishness" to the elderly, women, the poor, people with disabilities and court defendants also serves as a way of controlling them. In the context of psychiatry, using "childish" characterizations as a basis for diagnosis reaffirms Jutel's (2009) recent call for the establishment of a critical sociology of diagnosis. She suggests to examine the role that diagnosis plays both within medicine and within the social sphere, the authority linked to diagnosis as well as the ways in which that authority may be critically analyzed and challenged. Diagnosis can be analyzed as "both a process and a label" (Jutel, 2009, p. 279) in that it serves to evaluate functioning as well as to name or categorize deviance from "normal" functioning. Such theorizing in the context of "childishness" compels us to focus on the linguistic aspects of diagnosis, linking it with the way language is intimately connected to power and control, which expands on labelling theory (Becker, 1963; Goffman, 1963).

If the "enlightened adult" (in the Kantian sense) pre-requires rationality and autonomy, then the childish adult who lacks them is the opposite of that Western, middle-age, masculine ideal. "Childishness" thus becomes an educational manipulation, an attempt to discipline one's behavior by labeling them. However, as labeling theory implies such an attempt of discipline through stigma can potentially have adverse effect and lead to further deviance. This is, as we saw, the crux of how "childishness" is being used in court by legal professionals. Cases in which "childishness" is interpreted in conflicting ways demonstrate the arbitrary expression of the legitimate power of the court to apply "childishness" as a label and use it as a controlling device.

Most of us live up (or down) to the beliefs and expectations held by others. Understanding this premise of symbolic interaction and the "looking glass self" (Cooley, 1902) holds a possible way out of the vicious circle of labeling. "Childishness" is not just a derogatory label. It is also worthy of care and protection. It is also cute and funny, but at the same time can be savage and boundaryless. Messages of hope, trust and potential, need to complement (if not replace) negative messages of "hopeless childishness."

In his lecture on "The Adult's View of the Child," Merleau-Ponty (1949-1950/2010) argues that:

> the child's consciousness is different from the adult's both in content and organization. Children are not, as was previously thought, 'miniature adults.' Thus, contrary to the negative account, the child's consciousness is not identical to the adult's in everything except for its incompleteness and imperfection. The child possesses another kind of equilibrium than the adult kind; therefore, we must treat the child's consciousness as a positive phenomenon. (p.131)

Merleau-Ponty points at a positive alternative of viewing childhood not from the point-of-view of adulthood, as a "miniature adult." Under such myopic circumstances, "childishness" is doomed to be perceived as diminutive. Instead, we can view "childishness" and childhood as a different modality of sensing the world. As Bahler (2015) sums it,

> Merleau-Ponty is adamant that the child is not a derivation or deviation of adulthood, just as perception is not a deviation or lesser form of understanding than knowledge. There are different ways of knowing, different ways of being, that are not simply a negation of my own existing or the negative pole of some transcendental norm. The child, as a "positive phenomenon," has something to teach us about ourselves. (p. 215)

My point is that the child is neither "innocent" nor "primitive," while potentially embodying elements of both categories. The way out of this dilemma, it seems, is transcending it by reconceptualizing childhood from its own point of view, its own alternative modality.

In addition, rather than placing the weakness or deficit in the individual, who is perceived to be at fault for his/her own "childishness," we should try to understand the social circumstances that labeled him/her as "childish." Judges, psychiatrists, caretakers and the public in general should realize the circular self-fulfilling prophecy that is also known as "victim blaming" (Ryan, 1971). This might be a way out of the vicious circle of labeling and (at least secondary) deviance.

### Epilogue: The Ubiquity of Childishness

> *"The child and the adult are in a relationship of solidarity."*
>
> Maurice Merleau-Ponty

Discussing "childishness," or "childlikeness," can be regarded as esoteric, seemingly focusing on an insignificant area or even a "no man's land" in-between two large and stable social territories, namely childhood and adulthood (fig. 1).

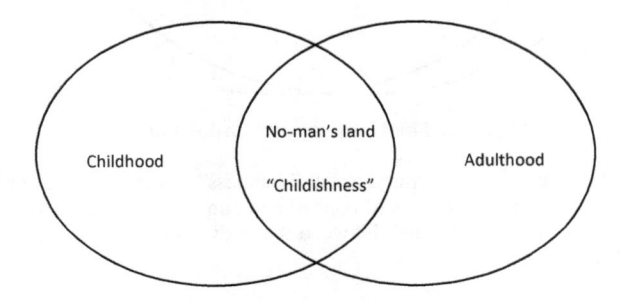

**Figure 1. "Childishness" as "no-man's land"**

   Against this well-established social construction of reality, I would like to argue, in conclusion, that "childishness" is not an insignificant overlapping between childhood and adulthood. As a result, it should not be "matter out of place," polluting and ambiguous. In contrast, while "childishness" is (perhaps too) well-established, childhood and adulthood may be ambiguous. Expressions of "childishness" have many examples, as this chapter has shown, while "pure" childhood and adulthood are hard to find. For example, work is supposed to be an adult domain. However, a significant number of children around the world are also doing work. War is also considered an adult domain, while in reality a significant number of children take part in wars either as combatants or as victims. Children consume and traffic tobacco, alcohol and drugs. Children have sexuality. Popular culture, the global channel of de-differentiation, is not surprisingly a major medium of childlikeness. "Girlishness" is popularly displayed not only by young girls, but also by women in general, with childlikeness and childlike behaviors as the chief constituents (Maynard & Taylor, 1999). Baby talk has been an intrinsic part of Pop-Rock music, from Little Richard's *Tutti Frutti* (1955) to Lady Gaga, and was described as the becoming-child of the adult musician (Appel, 2014). Parenthood supposedly turns one into an adult, even in cases of teenage pregnancies. On the other hand, adults engage in many activities that are conventionally considered part of childhood, such a play, games, school, animation, comics and entertainment.

   Post-modern social reality is to a large extent uni-age and de-differentiated. Wherever there are children we can find adults too, and vice versa. It is perhaps those areas that are specifically kept separated for "adults" and "children" that have become "no man's lands" in the sense of being extra-ordinary, polluting, dangerous and even taboo (see Fig. 2).

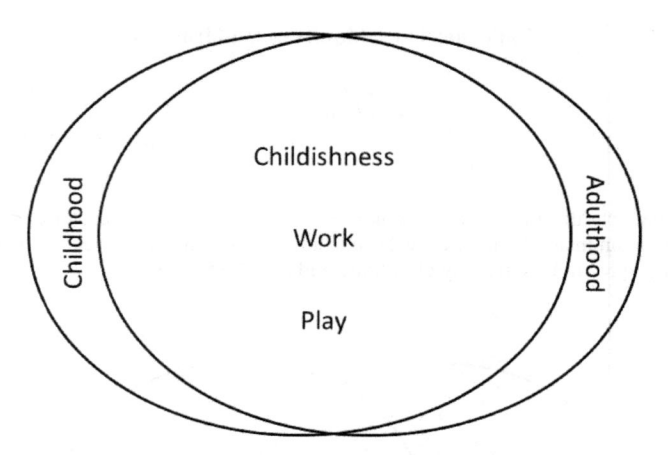

**Figure 2. The Ubiquity of "Childishness"**

Perhaps the broader lesson of studying "childishness" is that age and generational categorization must involve efforts to control and supervise trespassers. There is no "pure" childhood, nor a total match between the body's size, chronological age, and other aspects of life.

# References

Alemany Oliver, M., & Belk, R. W. (2021). Childlikeness in adults. In M. Alemany Oliver & R. W. Belk (Eds.), *Like a child would do: An interdisciplinary approach to childlikeness in past and current societies*. Universitas Press.

Alloh, F., Regmi, P., Onche, I., Teijlingen, E., & Trenoweth, S. (2018). Mental Health in low- and middle income countries (LMICs): Going beyond the need for funding. *Health Prospect, 17*(1), 12-17.

Althusser, L. (2006). Ideology and ideological state apparatuses (notes towards an investigation). *The anthropology of the state: A reader, 9*(1), 86-98.

Anderson, B. (1972). The process of deculturation: Its dynamics among United States aged. *Anthropological Quarterly, 45*(4), 209-216.

Appel, N. (2014). 'Ga, ga, ooh-la-la': the childlike use of language in pop-rock music. *Popular Music, 33*(1), 91-108.

Bahler, B. (2015). Merleau-Ponty on children and childhood. *Childhood & Philosophy, 11*(22), 203-221.

Becker, H. (1963). *Outsiders: Studies in the sociology of deviance*. The Free Press.

Bem, D. J. (1972). Self-perception theory. In L. Berkowitz (Ed.), *Advances in experimental social psychology* (pp. 2-62). Academic Press.

Best, J. (1990). *Threatened Children: Rhetoric and Concern about Child Victims*. University of Chicago Press.

Blumer, H. (1971). Social Problems as Collective Behavior. *Social Problems, 18*, 298-306.

Bourdieu, P., & Passeron, J. C. (1990). *Reproduction in education, society and culture, Vol. 4*. Sage.

Braithwaite, J., & Mugford, S. (1994). Conditions of successful reintegration ceremonies: Dealing with juvenile offenders. *British Journal of Criminology, 34*(2), 139-171.

Buckley P. (2014). Subjects, citizens, or civic learners? Judicial conceptions of childhood and the speech rights of American public school students. *Childhood, 21*(2), 226-241.

Canu, W. H., & Carlson, C. L. (2003). Differences in heterosocial behavior and outcomes of ADHD-symptomatic subtypes in a college sample. *Journal of Attention Disorders, 6*(3), 123-133.

Cooley, C. H. (1902). *Human nature and the social order*. Scribners and Sons.

Conrad, P. (1975). The discovery of hyperkinesis: Notes on the medicalization of deviant behavior. *Social Problems, 23*(1), 12-21.

Covey H. C. (1992). A return to infancy: old age and the second childhood in history. *International Journal of Aging & Human Development, 36*(2), 81-90.

Cradock G. (2007). The responsibility dance: Creating neoliberal children. *Childhood, 14*(2), 153-17.

Davis, M. (2008). A childish culture? Shared understandings, agency and intervention: an anthropological study of street children in northwest Kenya. *Childhood, 15*(3), 309-330.

Do Rozario, R.-A. C. (2004). The princess and the magic kingdom: Beyond nostalgia, the Function of the Disney princess. *Women's Studies in Communication, 27*(1), 34-59.

Douglas, M. (1966). *Purity and danger: An analysis of the concepts of pollution and taboo*. Routledge.

Durkheim, E (1979). *Essays on morals and education*. Routledge.

Eliaz, Y. (2017). Labeling "childishness" in court. *Law, Culture and the Humanities*. https://doi.org/10.1177/1743872117713656

England, D. E., Descartes, L., & Collier-Meek, M. A. (2011). Gender role portrayal and the Disney princesses. *Sex Roles, 64*(1), 555-567.

Ennew, J., & Swart-Kruger, J. (2003). Introduction: Homes, places and spaces in the construction of street children and street youth. *Children, Youth and Environments, 13*(1), 81-104.

Featherstone, M., & Hepworth, M. (1990). Images of aging. In J. Bond & P. G. Coleman (Eds.), *Aging in society: An introduction to social gerontology*. Sage.

Featherstone, M., & Hepworth, M. (1991). The mask of aging and the post-modern life course. In M. Featherstone, M. Hepworth, & B. Turner (Eds.). *The body: Social process and cultural theory* (pp. 370-389). Sage.

Fischel, J. (2016). Pornographic protections? Itineraries of childhood innocence. *Law, Culture and the Humanities, 12*(2), 206-220.

Foucault, M. (1967). *Madness and Civilization*. Tavistock.

Foucault, M. (1969/2002). The archeology of knowledge. Routledge.

Foucault, M. (2012). *Discipline and punish: The birth of the prison*. Vintage.

Freud, Sigmund. (1964) *The Future of illusion*. Anchor.

Goffman E. (1963). *Stigma: notes on the management of spoiled identity*. Prentice-Hall.

Gracia-Arnaiz, M. (2013). Thou shalt not get fat: Medical representations and self-images of obesity in a Mediterranean society. *Health, 5*(7), 1180-1189.

Gramsci, A., & Hoare, Q. (1971). Selections from the prison notebooks. Lawrence and Wishart.

Gubrium, J., & Holstein, J. A. (1999). Phenomenology, ethnomethodology, and interpretive practice. In N. Denzin and Y. S. Lincoln (Eds.), *Handbook of Qualitative Research* (pp. 262-72). Sage.

Hazan, H. (1998). The double voice of the third age: Splitting the speaking self as an adaptive strategy in later life. In Lomranz J. (Ed.), *Handbook of aging and mental health* (pp. 183-196). Springer.

Hazan, H. (1994). *Old age: Construction and deconstructions*. Cambridge University Press.

Hazan, H., & Raz, A. E. (1997). The authorized self: How middle age defines old age in the postmodern. *Semiotica, 113*(3/4), 257-276.

Hockey, J., & James, A. (1993). *Growing up and growing old: Ageing and dependency in the life course*. Sage.

Jenks, C. (1996). *Childhood*. Routledge.

Johnson, J. M. (1995). Horror stories and the construction of child abuse. In J. Best. (Ed.), *Images of issues: Typifying social problems* (pp. 17-32). De Gruyter.

Johnson, R. M., (2015). The evolution of Disney princesses and their effect on body image, gender roles, and the portrayal of love. *Educational Specialist, 6*, https://commons.lib.jmu.edu/edspec201019/6.

Jutel, A. (2009). Sociology of diagnosis: A preliminary review. *Sociology of Health & Illness, 31*(2), 278-299.

Kemper, S. (1988). Geriatric psycholinguistics: Syntactic limitations of oral and written language. In L. Light & D. Burke (Eds.), *Language, memory and aging* (pp. 58-76). Cambridge University Press.

LeFrançois, B., & Diamond, S. (2014). Queering the sociology of diagnosis: Children and the constituting of 'mentally ill' subjects. *CAOS: The Journal of Critical Anti-Oppressive, 1*, 39-62.

Lemert, E. M. (1972). *Human deviance, social problems, and social control*. Prentice-Hall.

Lewis, O. (1959). *Five families*. Basic Books.

Liebow, E. (1967). *Talley's corner: A study of negro street corner Men*. Little, Brown and Company.

Loseke, D. (1992). *The battered woman and shelters: The social construction of wife abuse*. SUNY Press.

Loseke, D. (1993). Constructing conditions, people, morality and emotion. In G. Miller and J. A. Holstein (Eds.), *Constructionist controversies: Issues in social problems theory* (pp. 207-16). De Gruyter.

Millett, K. (1969). *Sexual politics*. Doubleday.

Matsueda, R. L. (1992). Reflected appraisals, parental labeling, and delinquency: Specifying a symbolic interaction theory. *American Journal of Sociology, 97*(6), 1577-1611.

Maynard, M.L. & Taylor, C.R. 1999. Girlish images across cultures: analyzing Japanese versus US Seventeen magazine ads. *Journal of Advertising, 28*(1), 39-45.

Mead, G. H. (1934). *Mind, self and society*. University of Chicago Press.

Mead, G. H. (1964). The psychology of punitive justice. In A. J. Reck (Ed.), *Selected writings: George Herbert Mead* (pp. 212-239). University of Chicago Press.

Mergler, N., & Goldstein, M. (1983). Why are there old people? Senescence as biological and cultural preparedness for the transmission of information. *Human Information, 26*(2), 72-90.

Mergler, N., & Schleifer, R. (1985). The plain sense of things: Violence and the discourse of the aged. *Semiotica, 54*(1/2), 177-199.

Merleau-Ponty, M. (2010). *Child psychology and pedagogy: The Sorbonne lectures, 1949-1952*. Northwestern University Press.

Meyerowitz, J. (1984). The adult child and the childlike adult. *Daedalus, 113*(3), 19-48.

Murray, C., & Hallett, C. (2002). Young people's participation in decisions affecting their welfare. *Childhood, 7*(1), 11-25.

Myerhoff, B. (1978). *Number our days*. Dutton.

Myerhoff, B. (1982). Life history among the elderly: Performance visibility and re-membering. In J. Ruby (Ed.), *A crack in the mirror: Reflexive perspectives in anthropology*. University of Pennsylvania Press.

Neustadter, R. (1993). 'Grow Up!'—The devaluation and stigmatization of childhood as a threat to progress in contemporary thought. *Sociological Focus, 26*(4), 301-314.

Neustadter, R. (1992). An end to 'childhood amnesia': The utopian ideal of childhood in critical theory. *Mid-American Review of Sociology, 16*(2), 71-80.

Parsons, T. (1959). The social structure of the family. In R. N. Anshen (Ed.), *The Family, Its Functions and Destiny* (pp. 258-283). Harper.

Parson, T. (1964). *The social system*. Free Press.

Parsons, T. (1965). *Social structure and personality*. Free Press.

Piaget, J. (1970). *Genetic epistemology*. Viking Press.

Piaget, J. (1971). *The child's perception of time*. Ballantine Books.

Piaget, J. (1975). *Psychology and epistemology*. Viking Press.

Priestley, M. (2000). Adults only: Disability, social policy and the life course. *Journal of Social Policy, 29*(3), 421-439.

Priestley, M. (2003). *Disability: A life course approach*. Polity.

Roets, G., Kristiansen, K., van Hove, G., & Vanderplasschen, W. (2007). Living through exposure to toxic psychiatric orthodoxies: Exploring narratives of people with 'mental health problems' who are looking for employment on the open labour market. *Disability & Society, 22*(3), 267-281.

Rogers, R. S., & Rogers, W. S. (2002). *Stories of childhood: Shifting agendas of child concern*. University of Toronto Press.

Rojek, C. (1993). De-differentiation and leisure. *Society and Leisure, 16*(1), 15-29.

Ryan, W. (1971). *Blaming the victim*. Vintage.

Shook, J. J. (2005). Contesting childhood in the US justice system: The transfer of juveniles to adult criminal court. *Childhood, 12*(4), 461-478.

Smith, A. B, Taylor, N. J., & Tapp, P. (2003). Rethinking children's involvement in decision-making after parental separation. *Childhood, 10*(2), 201-216.

Spector, M., & Kitsuse, J. J. (1987). *Constructing social problems*. De Gruyter.

Starke, M., Bertilsdotter Rosqvist, H. & Kuosmanen, J. (2016). Eternal children? Professionals' constructions of women with an intellectual disability who are victims of sexual crime. *Sexuality and Disability, 34*, 315-328.

Strauss, A., & Corbin, J. (1998). *Basics of qualitative research*. Sage.

Stroes A, Alberts, E, & van der Meere, J. (2003). Boys with ADHD in social interaction with a nonfamiliar adult: An observational study. *Journal of the American Academy of Child and Adolescent Psychiatry, 42*(3), 295-302.

Tannenbaum. F. (1938). *Crime and the community*. Ginn.

Tiryakian, E.A. (1985). On the significance of de-differentiation. In S.N. Eisenstadt & H.J. Helle (Eds.), *Macro sociological theory: Perspectives on sociology theory* (pp. 118-34). Sage.

Turner, B. S. (1987). Aging, dying and death. In B. S. Turner (Ed.), *Medical power and social knowledge* (pp. 11-31). Sage.

Wilson, C., Nairn, R., Coverdale, J., & Panapa, A. (1999). Mental illness depictions in prime-time drama: Identifying the discursive resources. *Australian and New Zealand Journal of Psychiatry, 33*, 232-239.

Viterbo, H. (2012). The age of conflict: Rethinking childhood, law, and age through the Israeli-Palestinian case. In M. Freeman (Ed.), *Law and childhood studies. Current legal issues* (pp. 133-155). Oxford University Press.

## About the editors

**Mathieu ALEMANY OLIVER**, PhD, is Associate Professor of Marketing at TBS Education in Toulouse, France, and Academic Director of a graduate program dedicated to the management of cultural and creative activities. His core research interests focus on consumption-mediated interpretations and constructions of reality, with ongoing and published work on childlikeness and adulthood, conspiracy theories, new materialism, eco-anxiety, or local marketplace mythologies.

**Russell W. BELK**, PhD, is York University Distinguished Research Professor, Royal Society of Canada Fellow, and Kraft Foods Canada Chair in Marketing at the Schulich School of Business at York University, Canada. His research involves the extended self, meanings of possessions, collecting, gift-giving, sharing, digital consumption, and materialism. He is past president of the International Society of Marketing and Development, and is a fellow, past president, and Film Festival co-founder in the Association for Consumer Research. He also co-initiated the Consumer Behavior Odyssey and the Consumer Culture Theory Conference. He has received the Paul D. Converse Award, two Fulbright Fellowships, the Sheth Foundation/Journal of Consumer Research Award for Long Term Contribution to Consumer Research, and has over 700 publications. His work is primarily qualitative and is often conceptual, visual, and cultural.

## About the contributors

**David F. BJORKLUND**, PhD, is a Professor of Psychology at Florida Atlantic University in the USA, where he teaches graduate and undergraduate courses in developmental and evolutionary psychology. He served as Associate Editor of *Child Development* (1997-2001) and is currently serving as Editor of the *Journal of Experimental Child Psychology* (since 2007). His books include *The Origins of Human Nature: Evolutionary Developmental Psychology* (with Anthony Pellegrini); *Origins of the Social Mind: Evolutionary Psychology and Child Development* (edited with Bruce Ellis); *Why Youth is Not Wasted on the Young*; *How Children Invented Humanity: The Role of Development in Human Evolution*; *Child Development in Evolutionary Perspective*; and *Children's Thinking: Cognitive Development and Individual Differences*, now in its sixth edition. His current research interests include children's cognitive development and evolutionary developmental psychology.

**Edwige COMOY FUSARO**, PhD, is a Professor of 19th- and 20th-century Italian literature at the University of Rennes 2 in France, and a member of CELLAM. In parallel to her work on Italian culture from the Italian Unity to Fascism, she conducts and animates research on contemporary art and street art.

**Yoad ELIAZ**, PhD, is a Lecturer in the department of Education at Yezreel Valley College, in the Jezreel Valley, Israel. He has published *Land/Text: The Christian roots of Zionism* (Hebrew), and is engaged in research and theory of childhoods and schooling. His latest projects include Palestinian children working on Israeli roads, how childhood of gifted children is constructed through their parents' discourse, or schools and poverty in Israel.

**Simon GOTTSCHALK**, PhD, is Professor of Sociology at the University of Nevada, Las Vegas, USA. As a critical social psychologist, he has published on topics as diverse as terrorism, the mass media, countercultural youth, environmental identity, acceleration, the senses, Las Vegas, the transmission of trauma, ethnography in virtual spaces, and qualitative research methods, among others. His latest book *The Terminal Self* explores how our interactions with digital technologies shape our everyday lives and experiences. He is currently researching emotions and interactions on white supremacist websites.

**Katriina HELJAKKA**, PhD, is a toy and play researcher who studies toys and the visual, material, digital, and social cultures of play at the University of Turku in Finland, and leads the Pori Laboratory of Play research group. Heljakka's main areas of expertise are adult play and contemporary toy cultures. Her current research interests include the emerging toyification of culture, playful environments, and the technology-oriented and intergenerational dimensions of the current paidic (r) evolution with related play practices.

**Juliet ROHDE-BROWN**, PhD, CHT, is a licensed clinical psychologist in Santa Barbara and Carpinteria, California, USA. She is Chair of the Depth Psychology: Integrative Therapy and Healing Practices doctoral specialization at Pacifica Graduate Institute. She has taught psychology in higher education for over 23 years and has practiced in both private clinical practice and inpatient settings. She has presented internationally at professional conferences and other venues and has co-led retreats and workshops. Her book and journal articles are on topics such as forgiveness, trauma, imagery, families and disability, and spiritual practice, among others. She is also a mentor with the Spiritual Paths Institute.

**Frances WEIGHTMAN**, PhD, is Associate Professor of Chinese Studies at the University of Leeds, UK, and is Director of The Leeds Centre for New Chinese Writing. She has published widely on Chinese fiction of all time periods and has particular research interests in authorial identity, paratexts and children's literature. Main publications include *The Quest for the Childlike in Seventeenth Century Chinese Fiction: Fantasy, Naivety and Folly*, and her most recent articles have appeared in journals such as *East Asian Publishing and Society, JOMEC Journal and Prism: Theory and Modern Chinese Literature*. She is co-editor of the open access e-journal *Writing Chinese: A Journal of Contemporary Sinophone Literature*.

**Lorna WILKINSON**, PhD, is a graduate in English from the University of Exeter, England. Her thesis looks at trickster figures in mid-twentieth-century British women's fiction, and her research interests include allusion, deception and artifice in women's writing, although she is currently focusing on her own creative writing. She now lives in Oxfordshire, UK, and works in publishing.

S

safe, 12, 49, 54, 167

savagery, 150, 152, 157-158, 163, 167

self, 7-8, 11, 15-16, 22-28, 34-36, 45-52, 56-64,
72, 78-85, 97-99, 106-119, 127-128, 132-
140, 146-167, 178-182, 189-191, 200-201,
208-214, 219-232, 239

serious, 9, 13, 23, 33, 58, 103, 107, 109, 179,
191, 201, 211

sex, 15, 75, 82, 101-105, 110, 113, 159, 164,
187, 228; sexual, 10, 21, 25, 27, 54, 61, 82,
84, 101-114, 159-160, 187, 224, 229; sexuality, 7, 101, 105, 108, 110, 153, 159-160, 233

shame, 48-49, 52, 160, 163, 182, 184, 192, 220

soul, 12, 54, 59, 157, 225

space, 11, 13, 60-61, 77, 79, 81, 86, 87, 130,
133-134, 137, 139, 164-165, 178, 204-205

spontaneity, 12, 15, 34-35, 93-99, 104, 109,
127-129, 152, 162, 165, 179, 180, 184

stupidity, 71, 75, 103-104

supernatural, 71, 94-95, 114, 155

surveillance, 16, 112, 199, 203, 205, 212-214,
220-221, 225


T

tales, 72-77, 81, 94-95, 100-112, 116

technology, 8, 16, 31, 161, 166, 178, 182-183,
187, 193, 202-214, 240

thoughts, 13, 32, 97, 124, 204, 206, 228

transcendence, 50, 52-56, 94, 150, 232

transgression, 72, 86, 95, 121, 130, 136-137;
transgressive, 123, 138

transition, 56, 132, 155, 166, 189, 192; transitional, 53, 58, 223


U

unconscious, 45-65; collective unconscious,
14-15, 47-51, 60


V

values, 10-11, 97, 106, 114, 124-125, 128-129,
136-138, 157, 165, 191, 192

vulnerable, 11, 46, 201, 220-222


W

wisdom, 49, 52, 79, 95, 102, 105, 124, 127, 226


Y

youth, 11-14, 27, 33-37, 71, 87, 115, 125, 139,
150-156, 161, 165, 180, 184, 192-193, 208,
213, 220, 239; youthfulness, 21-22, 29, 33,
35, 153-154


Z

zombie, 84, 166